BEST OF CFW ——— VOL. 1
GRAPPLING

EDITED & COMPILED
JOSE M. FRAGUAS

EMPIRE BOOK/AWP LLC
Los Angeles, CA.

Disclaimer

Please note that the author and publisher of this book are NOT RESPONSIBLE in any manner whatsoever for any injury that may result from practicing the techniques and/or following the instructions given within. Since the physical activities described herein may be too strenuous in nature for some readers to engage in safely, it is essential that a physician be consulted prior to training.

Revised Edition published in 2024 by AWP LLC/Empire Books. Copyright (c) 2024 by Jose M. Fraguas.

All rights reserved. No part of this publication may be reproduced or utilized in any form or by any means, electronic or mechanical, including photo- copying, recording, or by any information storage and retrieval system, without prior written permission from Jose M. Fraguas.

ISBN-13: 978-1-949753-76-9

24 23 22 21 20 19 18 17 16 15 14 13 12

Library of Congress Cataloging-in-Publication Data

Best of CFW Grappling. Edited and Compiled by Fraguas, Jose M. -- ed. p. cm.

ISBN 978-1-949753-76-9 (pbk. : alk. paper) 1. Martial arts-- philosophy. 3. Large type books. I. Title. GV1114.3.F715 20021261.815'3--dc22

20043562492

Printed in the United States of America.

BEST OF CFW ——————— VOL. 1
GRAPPLING

Dedication

To all of you—those who deserve the most of the credit, the writers who supply us with an enormous amount of material every year to fill the pages of our magazines.

Acknowledgements

Our special thanks go out to the usual suspects, our staff editors, for taking time and effort to make every article better and comprehensive for the reader.

Contents

Foreword 10
   Jose M. Fraguas

Cleber Luciano: The Volcano of Jiu-Jitsu 13
   Todd Hester

Nathan Marquardt: A Vision of the Future 23
   Loren Franck

Mark Tripp: The Judo Jinx 31
   Anthony Perticaro

5 Shooto Transitional Leg Locks 39
   Erik Paulson

Pedro Sauer: A Man On A Mission 47
   Kid Peligro

My Top Ten Tips for Winning Fights 53
   Charlie Kohler with Loren Franck

The Magnificent Seven 61
   Matt Furey, photos by Zhannie Furey

The Ultimate Training Camp 69
   Tami Goldsmith

Chris Brennan: The Robin Hood of Mixed Martial Arts 79
   Loren Franck

A Talk with Luca Atalla, Editor of Gracie Magazine 87
   Eddie Goldman

Takedown Throws That Really Work 93
   Sheldon Marr

Carlao "Cao" Valente: The Storyteller of Brazilian Jiu-Jitsu ... 99
   Kid Peligro

Muay Thai Strikes on the Ground 105
   Jermaine Andre, photos by Clarke Kincaid

Hurricane Diniz Hits South Florida 111
   Todd Fischer

Garth Taylor: A Modern Day Mountain Man 117
   Scott Nelson

Fight Strategy for the Big Boys! 125
   Tedd Williams

Fabio Santos: Attack and Conquer 133
   Kid Peligro

Megaton Diaz: Jiu-Jitsu's Son of Thunder 139
   Loren Franck

GRAPPLING

BEST OF CFW — VOL. 1

Mastering the Kimura *147*
   Marcus Soares and Stephan Kesting

Catch Wrestling: America's Martial Art *151*
   Matt Furey

John Donehue: On Top Down Under *163*
   Todd Hester

The World Sambo Federation Hybrid Grappling System *175*
   Joe Schmidt

The Essence of Brazilian Jiu-Jitsu *181*
   Rigan Machado

Secrets of the De La Riva Guard *191*
   Kid Peligro

John Will: Where There's a Will, There's a Way *197*
   Jeremy Ta'kody

Leka Vieira: A Fist in a Velvet Glove *207*
   Jose Fraguas

Advanced Spider-Guard Sweeps *215*
   Kid Peligro

Sheldon Marr: Life on the Edge *221*
   Beau Clark

Marvin Eastman: No Justice, No Peace *229*
   Marvin Eastman with Loren Franck

Gerson Sanginitto: Generation X-cellent *235*
   Jose Fraguas

Leozinho Vieira's Extreme Jiu-Jitsu: The Star Guard Pass *243*
   Kid Peligro

Bart Vale: Behind the Vale *247*
   Martin Bartlett

2002 Brazilian Jiu-Jitsu Pan American Tournament *257*
   Kid Peligro, photos by Paul Thatcher

Bob Schirmer: Chicago's Trainer Of Champions *263*
   Loren Franck

The Big Four: Basic Sweeps From the Guard *273*
   Jerry Laurita

Leozinho Viera's Extreme Jiu-Jitsu: Taking The Back *277*
   Kid Peligro

The 7 Methods of Low-Kick Defense *283*
   Erik Paulson

Foreword

To say we get a lot of mail at CFW Enterprises would be quite an understatement. Every year we receive literally hundreds and hundreds of story submissions for all of our various magazines. These manila envelopes contain works ranging from fascinating to—well, to put it diplomatically, "fanciful." Yet we open nearly each and every piece of mail to separate contents from the envelope while doing our best not to commit an eco-crime.

Kidding aside, what we look for in the mail is the best martial arts writing in existence. To be considered "the best" there are some basic criteria which must be met. The editors at CFW Enterprises carefully evaluate the articles they receive to finally decide those which will be published. It is not an easy task since many variables are involved in the process.

Needless to say, while we receive a lot of good submissions we also, as an occupational hazard, have to read a lot of "really bad stuff." Fortunately, after years of working as an editor you develop an instinct and can quickly identify an unusable submission.

That's what this series is all about: bringing you the "Best of Grappling" for each year, without prejudice in terms of the writer, the source, or the subject. Our aim is to provide the readers with a wide selection of styles and systems. The collection includes many different authors who offer their own perspectives of the arts and the influences of their respective arts in the field. All of them have expressed their ideas in a very different way. But whether expressed in the language of the teachers, the language of the students, or the language of the thinker, there is truth in concepts, philosophies and techniques that so many martial artists have believed and lived by for decades.

Here at CFW, we have made every effort to present each article and work as accurately as possible within the limitations of the book format. In addition to being a resource for researches, writers, students and teachers, we hope this collection of works will provide comfort and inspiration for all those who love the martial arts. There are many excellent books about the martial arts with more on the way. My hope is that this book of collective works and articles will prove a worthy companion to them in two main ways: first, in its size and scope; second in its practicality and ease of use.

There have been many changes in the martial arts but some things are still the same. A well-written article is one of them. Our job and responsibility at CFW as the world leaders in the publication of martial arts magazines, videos, and books is to inform and educate the reader, promoting all the styles and approaches without being limited by any of them.

BEST OF CFW ——— VOL. 1
GRAPPLING

As early as I can remember. My house was filled with martial arts magazines from around the world. For many years, I gathered publications and became curious about many of the authors who wrote for them. The more I researched, the more I realized that those "great people" were a lot more like you and me than they were different. Today I have written hundreds of articles in magazines around the world, more than a dozen of books under my own name and a couple under some else's. At CFW, our editors have read, written, edited and re-written more articles and books than one could possibly imagine. Although it is unlikely any of us will ever be awarded the Nobel Prize, the writing that we like is the writing that we like. Nothing can change that.

I bring all this up because I believe all the writers who have submitted material to be published in the different magazines owned by CFW Enterprises have followed similar paths.

Walk on!

—**Jose M. Fraguas**
General Manager
CFW Enterprises

BEST OF CFW — VOL.1
GRAPPLING

GRAPPLING

Cleber Luciano
The Volcano of Jiu-Jitsu

Todd Hester

Cleber Luciano is one of the most well-known and respected jiu-jitsu fighters and teachers in the United States. A champion in Brazil, where he begin training at age 5, Luciano trained and competed against the biggest names in the sport. His expertise was rewarded by a black belt before he reached age 20. With countless matches in jiu-jitsu tournaments with the gi, and recent experience in Abu Dhabi no-gi submission grappling, Luciano is very familiar with what techniques work with the gi and without. But more than that, he is familiar with how life works with jiu-jitsu and without it. A "hyper" kid who liked to fight on the street and who was headed down the wrong path, jiu-jitsu gave Luciano an outlet for his aggression and a structure that gave his life new meaning. Now settled in Huntington Beach, California, and running two schools, Luciano's passion for jiu-jitsu has led him to attract nearly 300 students—60 of which are kids between the ages of 5 and 15. "Kids need jiu-jitsu and jiu-jitsu needs kids," Luciano says. With a commitment to grow jiu-jitsu in the U.S. and to use it to help kids better themselves, Cleber Luciano is at the forefront of the modern jiu-jitsu and grappling revolution.

Q: How did you get started in jiu-jitsu?
A: I started because I was very hyper as a kid in the Rio area. So my mom wanted to put me in sports to calm me down. So I had two friends who did jiu-jitsu and the mother of one of them took me to watch the class one day. So I went and checked it out and liked what I saw and so I started training. This was with one of Helio Gracie's students who was a very high black belt. I was just a kid, only six years old, but I knew that it was fun. I loved to train, I loved jiu-jitsu, and I loved grappling. So I just kept going. So I also took a lot of judo classes, because judo is also very popular in Brazil. So I eventually got my black belt in judo also.

Q: Did you start taking judo after you started jiu-jitsu?
A: I started both at about the same time. Because I figured that judo would help me in my jiu-jitsu. But I always liked jiu-jitsu the best between the two. It was just more fun for me. Now, even though I have a black

"It is very important to be patient. Once I get an idea of what he is doing, I can play my strategy and decide which attacks to use. I don't want to get crazy early, try to hard, and then get points scored on me or, even worse, get submitted."

belt in judo, I've forgotten most of my moves. I probably still do some of them without thinking, but I don't compete in that or teach it formally or anything. Part of it was just that I got a little bored with judo. When you do a match you just start to get going and they end the match after only a minute or two. I didn't like how fast it was. One takedown or throw and the fight was over—even when you were not hurt or in any real danger. So it was too far removed from a real situation for me. So I figured out that jiu-jitsu was more complete. You can do everything—takedowns, throws, pass the guard, get points, get submissions—everything.

Q: When did you become closely associated with the Gracie family?

A: When I was 15 I was a blue belt and I went to the Gracie Academy and started

GRAPPLING

Takedown Counter to Reverse Shoulder-Lock

Facing an opponent with a gi (1), Cleber Luciano is caught with a single-leg takedown (2). Luciano responds by pressuring the opponent's head (3), and then trapping his arm (4). Lifting his leg to trap the elbow (5), Luciano the executes a forward roll (6), and then comes to an upright position and applies the finishing shoulder lock (7).

Cross-Mount Opposite-Side Submission

Cleber Luciano controls his opponent from the side mount (1). Swinging his outside leg over his opponent's, Luciano traps his head in a single-leg scissors (2). From this position he can either finish his opponent with a front choke (3), or trap the wrist and apply a straight arm-bar (4).

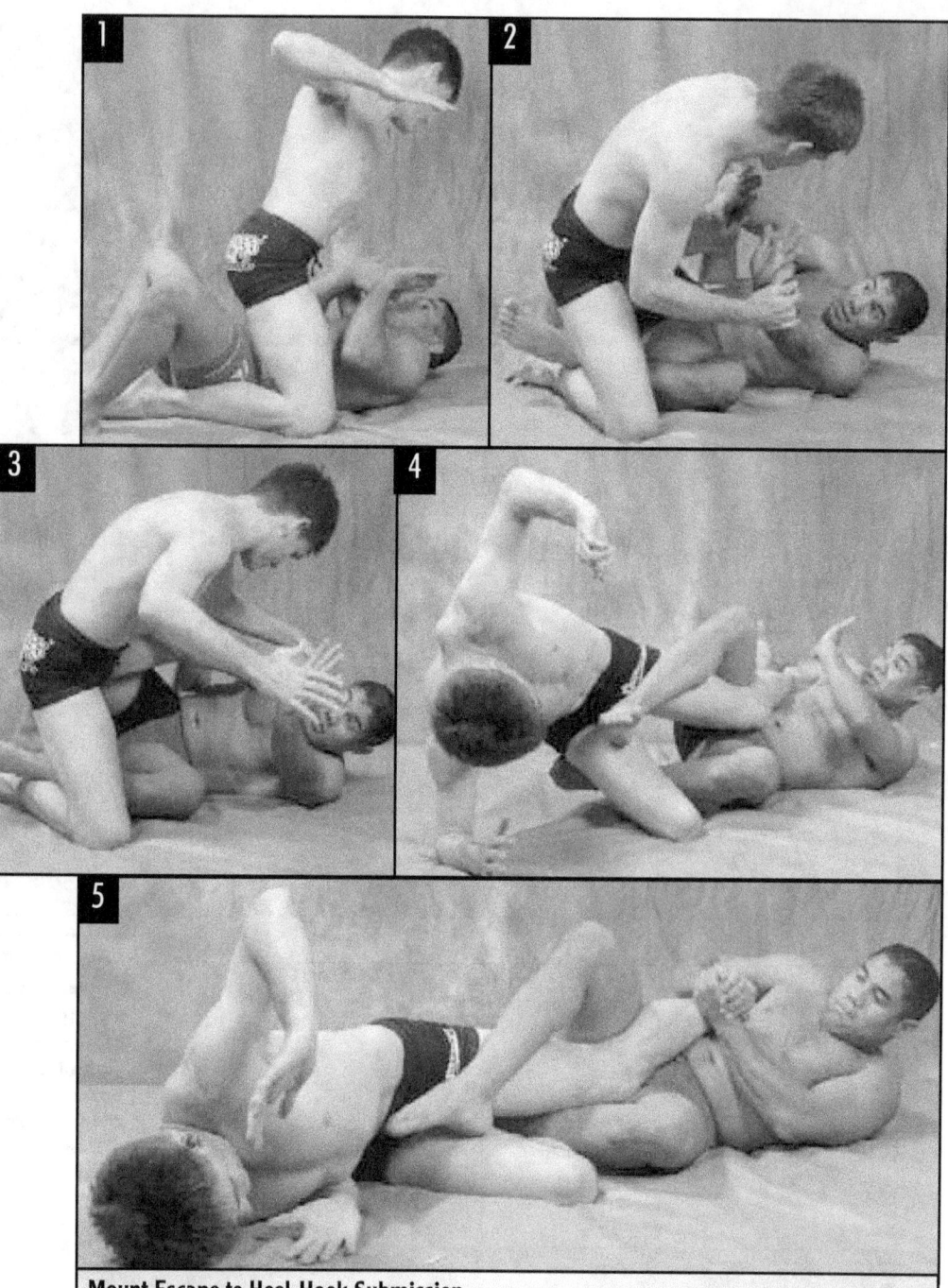

Mount Escape to Heel-Hook Submission
Cleber Luciano is caught in his opponent's mount (1). Turning to his side, his traps the opponent's outside leg with his foot (2), then puts his other leg in his opponent's stomach to create distance (3). Scissoring his legs, Luciano then throws his opponent to the side while maintaining control of his ankle (4). Stretching his legs to defeat any possible counters, Luciano then applies the finishing heel-hook (5).

training with Carley Gracie and got to know Royler, Rokker, and all the rest. Everyone really accepted me and made me feel like I belonged and was part of the family. So I continued to train there with some of the top guys in the world like Royler Gracie, Saulo Ribeiro, Carlos Barreto, and all the top guys. I got my black belt together with Saulo and Carlos and several other guys. I guess that I was at the Gracie Academy for nearly 5 years before I got my black belt. I felt like I really got a great jiu-jitsu education and got my black belt just before I turned 20. I was very proud of that because it is very young in jiu-jitsu to get it then.

Q: When did you decide to come to the United States and teach?
A: I did some tournaments in Brazil—some really big ones—and in one of them I beat Leo Viera, who is really good. We were both at the same level and the two top guys, so everyone really wanted to see us compete to see who would win. I won that—and don't know how—but I beat him. After that I started getting a lot of calls from people wanting me to go to different places to open a school. A few of the calls came from this area, and I knew that there was already a lot of Brazilians teaching in Southern California, and I decided to come here. I wanted to come to a place where my students would have a chance to compete against other schools. Los Angeles probably has the most jiu-jitsu schools in the United States of any city. So that was a big part of it for me.

Q: What it hard when you first came?
A: Yeah, it was. But I knew I wanted to be in Huntington Beach the moment I got off that plane and came here. It is a great area with the water very close and a lot of nice people and also a lot of people who want to train jiu-jitsu. So I just immediately loved it here. I want to be here forever. When I first came I started the school with two American guys and that didn't work all that well because I was working for them at a school called Brazilian Martial Arts. But I was the one who knew jiu-jitsu and knew how to teach. So after a year I left to open my own school—Cleber Luciano Jiu-Jitsu. With my own school I can teach the way I want to on my own schedule—so for me it is better. I have more freedom. So I've been here at my own school for five years now and I have over 150 students just at this school. I opened another school in Costa Mesa recently, and I have around 100 students there. So for me to have 250 students in two schools is wonderful. I'm very grateful to my loyal students and I'm committed to teaching them the best jiu-jitsu in the world to show them my appreciation.

Q: You're known as one of the world's top tournament fighters. What is your philosophy of competition?
A: My strategy is to be very relaxed. In all my fights I relax and make sure in the first two or three minutes that I don't make a mistake and get behind on points. So I'm very careful early in a match. I don't want to get taken down, let someone get to my back, let someone get cross-side on me—things like that. I just try to figure out my opponent's game and get a feel for what he likes to do and what he is trying on me. It is very important to be patient. Once I get an idea of what he is doing, I can play my strategy and decide which attacks to use. I don't want to get crazy early, try to hard, and then get points scored on me or, even worse, get submitted. Relaxation and breathing is my game.

Q: What do you do once you've figured out your opponent's game plan?
A: Then I start to attack. But I always attack with good balance and good grip. Those two factors are the most important things to establish when you start your attack. As soon as you have a good grip and good balance then you can go for the takedown. If you're grappling with a good wrestler, for example, you can really feel his balance and so you need to be rock solid in your base.

Q: In a tournament situation do you like to fight from the guard or do you like to operate from on top?
A: You need to go for a superior position from the top. I don't believe in falling back into the guard and pulling your opponent on top of you. I teach my students to try to establish a strong top position during the first two minutes. In your first minute, if you put somebody in the guard, they are very fresh and will be alert and able to defend any submissions you might try. So if you work for two or three minutes, then you can get your opponent a little tired and also confuse him a little so when you get the position you want, you have a much better chance of your attacks working.

Q: What is your favorite position to work your attacks from?
A: I like the cross-side position a lot. There are more opportunities for submission from this position. I'm very comfortable from this position. The good thing about the cross-side is that you can apply it with equal success whether you are fighting no-gi Abu Dhabi rules or fighting with jiu-jitsu rules with the gi. This is because you are able to use the weight of your chest to pressure your opponent, but yet your hips and legs are free to move with him when he tries to escape. I work a lot of neck cranks and a lot of arm-neck combination chokes so it doesn't matter to me if I compete with a gi or without one. Of course there are a lot more moves that you can do with the gi— I can make a thousand moves with it. My whole life I trained with the gi for tournaments in Brazil. Plus you have material to grab at the lapel and the elbow and the back of the neck, et cetera that you don't have without the gi. So you have a lot more options. Without the gi I can do my basic positions, but I can't do all the advanced moves that I can do with the gi. With the gi it is really more fun because there are a lot more options.

Q: Is it difficult to transfer submission sport techniques into no-holds-barred?
A: My techniques are very effective in vale tudo fighting. So I don't have a lot of problems transferring them over. But kicking and punching do add a lot more dimensions to the grappling game, so while the sport techniques do work when you get into position, you have to be much more careful coming in, so you don't get caught during the entry. Plus, when you get on the ground you can use strikes to set-up your submissions. If you're cross-side, for example, and going for a choke, and your opponent is tightly guarding his neck, then you can drop a few elbows on him to make him block, which will then expose his neck for the choke. The same thing can done in different situations with the knees. The old technique of circling and then shooting in on him just doesn't work as well as it used to. People practice against it. Three of four years ago it was much easier to take strikers down. Now with everyone practicing kickboxing and Thai boxing there is a lot more danger coming in. So timing is the more important aspect for grapplers now. Saulo Ribeiro got caught with a knee by Yuki Kondo in an NHB match when he was shooting in and lost by a cut. Renzo had the same problem a couple of times. You have to come in behind a kick and you have to time your entry very carefully.

Q: Do you think the guard still works for no-holds-barred?
A: If you lock somebody in the closed guard, but then only defend from it, you are going to have problems. You can defend for two or three minutes but after that you will get tired and the punches will start to get though. So you can't stay in a defensive guard for a long time like a sitting duck. However, if you work from the open guard, where you move your hips, use the inside hooks, and use sweeps and half-guard moves to keep your opponent off-balance, then you can survive and potentially even submit your opponent. The key is to be active from the guard—you have to have mobile hips, legs, and feet.

Fighting Tips

Using the Guard
If you lock somebody in the closed guard, but then only defend from it, you are going to have problems. You can defend for two or three minutes but after that you will get tired and the punches will start to get though. So you can't stay in a defensive guard for a long time like a sitting duck. However, if you work from the open guard, where you move your hips, use the inside hooks, and use sweeps and half-guard moves to keep your opponent off-balance, then you can survive and potentially even submit your opponent. The key is to be active from the guard—you have to have mobile hips, legs, and feet.

Best Submission Position
I like the cross-side position a lot. There are more opportunities for submission from this position. I'm very comfortable from this position. The good thing about the cross-side is that you can apply it with equal success whether you are fighting no gi Abu Dhabi rules or fighting with jiu-jitsu rules with the gi. This is because you are able to use the weight of your chest to pressure your opponent.

Strategy
I don't believe in falling back into the guard and pulling your opponent on top of you. I teach my students to try to establish a strong top position during the first two minutes. In your first minute, if you put somebody in the guard, they are very fresh and will be alert and able to defend any submissions you might try. So if you work for two or three minutes, then you can get your opponent a little tired and also confuse him a little so when you get the position you want, you have a much better chance of your attacks working.

Mental Preparation
The more you compete, the more relaxed you will be. When I was younger I made a big mistake of going into a fight as if my opponent was my enemy—I took the competition personally. I was like a volcano waiting to erupt and when I did I just forgot everything and I would not do well. I don't want anyone to make this same mistake and I don't want to make this mistake again, either. Every time you go into a fight you should worry about yourself, and not worry about your opponent. Your goal is to fight the fight, not fight the opponent. If you do your job the outcome of the fight will take care of itself. What happens is that you get so intense that you forget all your techniques and your entire game plan and you just brawl mindlessly.

Q: What is best way to mentally prepare for a tournament?

A: In any tournament I do now I am very relaxed beforehand because I have done so many. Ten years ago I was really tense before a competition but I did so much that I don't worry about it so much anymore. Mental relaxation is as important as physical relaxation. The more you compete, the more relaxed you will be. When I was younger I made a big mistake of going into a fight as if my opponent was my enemy—I took the competition personally. I was like a volcano waiting to erupt and when I did I just forgot everything and I would not do well. I don't want anyone to make this same mistake and I don't want to make this mistake again, either. Every time you go into a fight you should worry about yourself, and not worry about your opponent. Your goal is to fight the fight, not fight the opponent. If you do your job the outcome of the fight will take care of itself. What happens is that you get so intense that you forget all your techniques and your entire game plan and you just brawl mindlessly. It happened to me. Everything went out the window—all I could think was "Kill! Kill! Kill!" When I fought it was as if I had never taken a single jiu-jitsu lesson. But I learned from that mistake big time. Now when I fight I don't care if my opponent is screaming and cursing at me—it doesn't matter. Let's just do the fight in a professional manner and then forget about it when the fight is done.

> *"It happened to me. Everything went out the window—all I could think was "Kill! Kill! Kill!" When I fought it was as if I had never taken a single jiu-jitsu lesson. But I learned from that mistake big time."*

Q: Do you see a big potential for jiu-jitsu in the U.S.?

A: Of course! The key to the future of jiu-jitsu is the kids. Jiu-jitsu is great for kids because it teaches

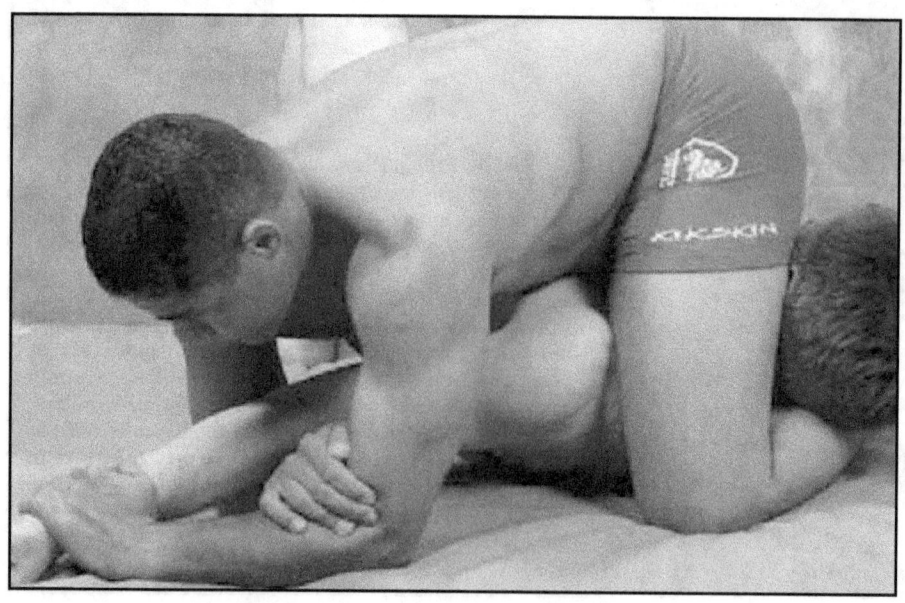

them respect and discipline and gives them something positive to do. I have about 60 kids who train in jiu-jitsu now, and as those kids grow up they are going to compete in tournaments. They will tell their friends about it and they will want to compete. I see so many kids who are as young as 5 years old and they already know how to move on the mat really well! These kids are going to be very hard to beat as they get older and move into the higher divisions. But more than that, it will help kids to become better much better persons. When I was a kid, for example, I was really hyper and I loved to fight on the street. So jiu-jitsu took me off of the streets and gave me an outlet for my aggression. Jiu-jitsu calmed me down mentally and gave me a much more cooperative attitude towards my family and people in general. Jiu-jitsu teaches fighting techniques to kids but it also teaches kids not to fight. It will change your attitude for the better. Without jiu-jitsu I don't think I would be here today.

For information on classes or seminars with Cleber Luciano call (714) 842-4554.

BEST OF CFW — VOL. 1
GRAPPLING

Nathan Marquardt
A Vision of the Future

Little known in America, this two-time King of Pancrase is working to make the future of mixed martial arts in America a reality today.

Loren Franck

On December 4, 2000, when Nathan Marquardt entered the ring to fight Kunioko Kiuma in Japan, the swift and savvy Kiuma appeared shocked. The two battled each other 10 weeks earlier, Marquardt eclipsing the Japanese fighter by decision, but the youthful American was in better shape the second time around. He was more self-confident too, and that especially worried Kiuma.

Standing 6'1" and weighing 175 lbs, Marquardt captured the middleweight King of Pancrase crown the previous September and Kiuma wanted nothing more than to possess it himself. But fate was with Marquardt that December night in Japan. Only 21 years old, he narrowly slid past his motivated opponent, and for the second time in his 17-1 fighting career was awarded a King of Pancrase title.

Since committing himself to mixed martial arts three years ago, the versatile, soft-spoken grappler from Bloomfield, Colorado, has caught a vision of the sport. It was an epiphany of sorts. Although Marquardt yearns for worldwide acclaim as an athlete, his most important mission may be to help raise mixed martial arts from its current raw adolescence to mature adulthood at the Olympic Games.

But before he can help the sport mature, he must reach athletic adulthood himself. Fortunately, he's enjoying the ride.

Humble Beginnings

At first glance, Marquardt's martial arts history resembles that of other fighters: A teenager who started martial arts by joining a karate school, he discovered shootfighting, developed a passion for it, and eventually turned pro. However, what distinguishes Marquardt is how completely he immersed himself mentally as well as physically in the sport. And he cares just as much for the future of grappling as for his present role in it.

"People say I have a lot of heart for the sport," admits Marquardt. "Submission fighting is a passion for me, not merely a pastime. My training became serious when I learned a few basic submission holds as a teenager. Around that time, I also saw one of the Ultimate Fighting Championships. That inspired me to study Brazilian jiu-jitsu."

He located a school that taught the fast-growing grappling art, and after attending several training sessions, felt right at home. "In particular, I liked Brazilian jiu-jitsu without the gi," he explains. "It

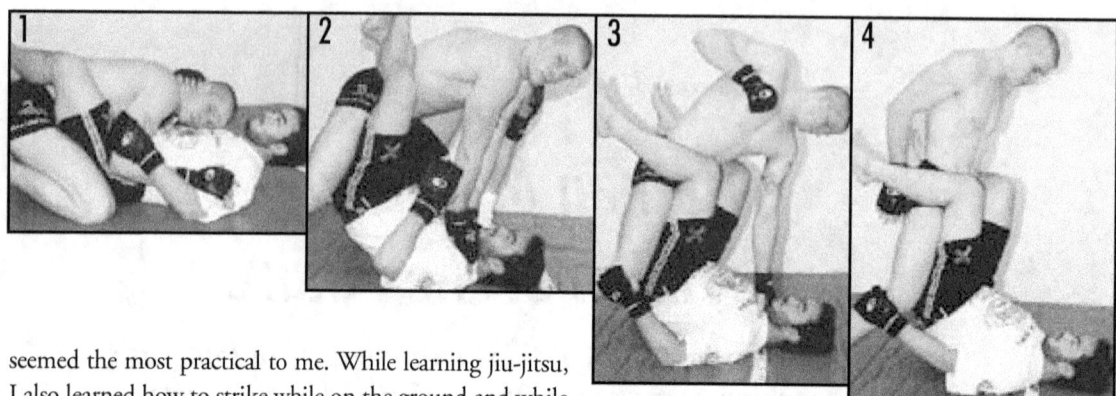

seemed the most practical to me. While learning jiu-jitsu, I also learned how to strike while on the ground and while standing, both of which appealed to me because of how it complimented ground work."

Pancrase Training

For Marquardt, traveling from the American Midwest to Japan, a nation steeped in Samurai warrior tradition, was like squeezing a square peg into a round hole. In fact, many Westerners visiting Japan for the first time are shocked by the cultural differences. Marquardt was no exception in December 1999 when he stepped onto Japanese soil for the first time to face Genki Sudo, who submitted him with an arm bar 13 minutes into the bout. That first trip taught Marquardt many valuable lessons about the Land of the Rising Sun.

"That first trip taught me a lot about Japanese culture," says Marquardt, now a veteran of seven Pancrase fights. "Going to Japan definitely changed my career. Pancrase training differs significantly from the training of American grapplers. For example, many Pancrase fighters live and train in Tokyo and other large centralized cities of Japan. They're not sprinkled throughout the country as most grapplers in the United States are. And while Pancrase fighters tend to move frequently in the ring, U.S. fighters often tie-up opponents and remain in one position throughout a match. Most grapplers in Japan are good at foot locks too, even if they don't specialize in them," Marquardt adds. "Unfortunately, these techniques aren't a strong point for many jiu-jitsu specialists in America. Pancrase fights really flow. They look like college wrestling matches."

Just One Of The Guys

Marquardt trained in Japan for only seven days before battling Sudo in 1999. But he returned to Japan the following June, living and training in a Pancrase dojo through September, and then knocking out his next opponent, Takase Daiju, with a knee strike. On September 24, he won two of the most important fights of his career. After defeating Kiuma for the first time, he bested the dangerous Shonie Carter, capturing the first-ever Middleweight King of Pancrase title.

"Except for the week before the fight, I lived at the dojo," Marquardt recalls. "A ring, mat, weights, bags and other training equipment were downstairs. A kitchen, showers, a bathroom and a bedroom were upstairs."

At the dojo, Marquardt was treated like a pro, which was unusual because fighters awaiting their Pancrase debut are usually relegated to menial tasks such as cooking, cleaning and caring for the gym.

"If those 'young boys,' as they are called, do anything wrong, they are punished severely," Marquardt points out. "And even after a young boy's first pro bout, he remains at the bottom of the totem pole for a while. Essentially, you obey others who have trained at the dojo longer, even if

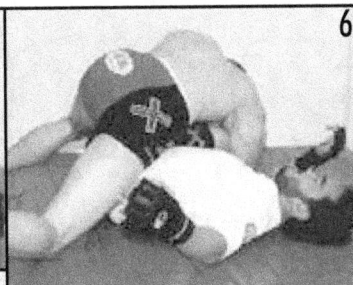

Guard Pass To Side Control
Caught in his opponent's guard (1), Nathan Marquardt pushes on the shoulders and stands up in base (2), where he prepares to punch (3). When his opponent counters by grabbing the ankles and threatening to topple him backwards (4), Marquardt collapses his weight on his opponent's legs (5), throws them to the side (6), and then goes chest-to-chest for side control (7).

you're a better fighter than they are. But I was well-treated there and spared the household duties. Even my laundry was done for me."

Top Secrets

While he trained in Japan, Marquardt found that most Pancrase fighters are dedicated, hardworking, and have an insatiable desire to learn. Most don't quit the sport or blame size differences after losing a fight. Instead, a defeat was an invitation to increase their training and learning.

"The Pancrase fighters I trained with really impressed me," Marquardt reflects. "They consistently try to learn new techniques and refine old ones. In addition, most of my Pancrase workouts were tightly structured. For instance, everyone in the dojo sparred for five-minute rounds. After each one, we switched partners and sparred again, one five-minute round after another."

Marquardt was amazed at how intense the workouts were. While training, he and other fighters donned headgear, gloves, shin pads and sparred at 90-percent intensity. Strikes, takedowns and locks were all fair game. Periodically, Marquardt and other students sparred while wearing gloves but no head protection. Full-power strikes were forbidden during workouts, but while on the ground, fighters pushed their grappling intensity to the limit.

Back In The USA

Last May was the most recent bout in Japan for Marquardt, who arm-barred Masaya Kojima into submission. The fight couldn't have gone better for the eager American grappler, who applies the vital lessons learned in Japan to his fight training at home. If training overseas taught Marquardt anything, it was to continuously learn top-notch fighting skills, to train his hardest, and to go all-out in the ring.

"I began wrestling intensively only about a year ago," he says, reflecting on his rapid progress in mixed-martial-arts competition. "I'm good on the ground with submissions, a capable fighter on my feet, and I can strike with the best of them."

Of course, some of Marquardt's opponents have taken him to the canvas. But when they do, he usually slaps a submission hold on them. "Takedowns are probably my biggest weakness in the ring," he concedes. "So I try to improve those skills every day."

Nathan Marquardt Titles

First Middleweight
King of Pancrase

Two-time
King of Pancrase

Pancrase Trans
Tournament Champion

Bas Rutten Invitational
Middleweight Champion

Ring of Fire
Middleweight Champion

IMA Rumble in the
Rockies Champion

Nathan Marquardt Fight Record

Date	Event	Opponent	Outcome
13 May 2001	Pancrase/Japan	Masaya Kojima	Submission Win
31 Mar 2001	Pancrase/Japan	Hikaru Sato	Submission Win
04 Dec 2000	Pancrase/Japan	Kunioko Kiuma	Draw Win, KOP
24 Sep 2000	Pancrase/Japan	Shonie Carter	Decision Win, KOP
24 Sep 2000	Pancrase/Japan	Kunioko Kiuma	Decision Win
26 Jun 2000	Pancrase/Japan	Takase Daij	KO Win
18 Apr 2000	Ring of Fire/USA	A. Washington	TKO Win
18 Dec 1999	Pancrase/Japan	Genki Sudo	Submission Loss
14 Aug 1999	Bas Rutten/USA	David Harris	Submission Win
14 Aug 1999	Bas Rutten/USA	Josh Rodes	Submission Win
14 Aug 1999	Bas Rutten/USA	Yves Edwards	Submission Win
06 Jul 1999	IMA/USA	Josh Madina	Submission Win
06 Jul 1999	IMA/USA	Jose Garcia	Submission Win
04 Jun 1999	WVF/USA	Mike Lee	Submission Win
18 Apr 1999	SFC/USA	Jeremy Stone	Submission Win
18 Apr 1999	SFC/USA	Dan Stiner	Submission Win

Pancrase Takedown to Knee Bar
Nathan Marquardt clinches with his opponent (1). Controlling the head (2), he slips his thigh between his opponent's legs (3), hooks his ankle with his other leg while supporting himself with one arm (4), and then falls back into the knee-bar submission (5).

Staying In Shape

Many pro athletes dream about a better tomorrow, but Marquardt is working hard to make his vision for the future come true today. His goal? To elevate mixed martial arts to a level where every fighter trains 100 percent. In short, Marquardt envisions submission grappling as an Olympic sport.

"Sure, it's a lofty goal," Marquardt admits, "but it's achievable. And if enough people in the sport are willing to work hard and work together, we can make it happen."

A decade from now, when fighters and fans reflect on Marquardt's career, he wants them to remember a pioneer who was light-years ahead of his time. Before that can happen, though, Marquardt must first perfect his fighting skills and whip his body into top shape. Like all effective leaders, he knows he must first change himself before he can change others, and that's why he has plunged headfirst into a comprehensive conditioning and fight-training program.

Marquardt lifts weights for one-hour, three-times a week, each session beginning at 3 p.m. Yet he doesn't pump too much iron because he wants lean muscle mass for fighting. He feels that excessive bulk could bump him to a higher weight class, or even worse, slow him down in the ring. Employing a moderate number of sets and reps, Marquardt performs barbell, dumbbell, and machine movements for his major muscle groups. He sees himself as a professional grappler, not a

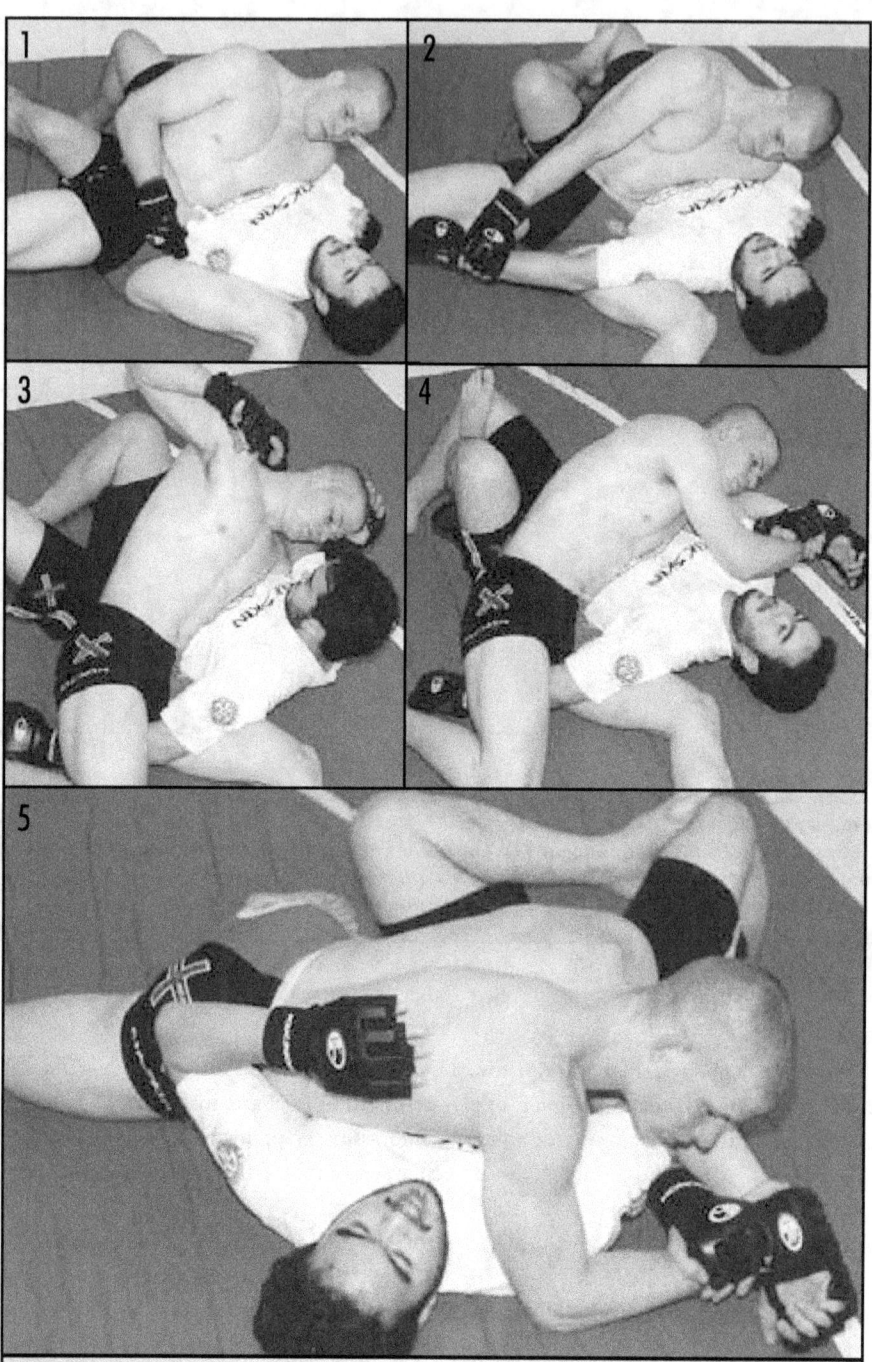

Side Control to Opposite-Side Elbow Lock
Controlling his opponent from the side (1), Nathan Marquardt pushes his opponent's arm down (2), and locks it between his legs and prepares to punch (4). When his opponent raises his arm to block, Marquardt grabs the wrist (5), the passes his arm under his opponent's elbow and secures the submission (6).

bodybuilder, and he maintains this perspective to make his conditioning program succeed. Each weight-training workout lasts an hour. After a high-protein snack, Marquardt starts practicing wrestling moves at 5 p.m. "Two great guys help me," he explains. "One wrestled in college, the other for the Marines. We go against each other hard, and they've taught me a lot."

At least three times a week, Marquardt teaches a one-hour class in martial arts techniques. At the beginning of each session, which starts at 6 p.m., students use pads and gloves to develop striking techniques. "We often focus on muay Thai or Western boxing moves," explains Marquardt, who enjoys nurturing the future generation of grapplers. Before he dismisses class at 7 p.m., Marquardt teaches takedowns, positioning or submissions.

From 7 p.m. to 8:30 p.m., he grapples on the ground or practices takedowns. When preparing for a fight, Marquardt also performs rope climbs, abdominal crunches, sit-ups, pull-ups, and other exercises that build strength and stamina. By 9:15 p.m., after nearly six hours of training, he's finished for the night.

Nutrition is also crucial to conditioning, and Marquardt knows that an excellent food plan can make or break a fighter. So, whether training for a fight or not, he follows a healthy, well-balanced diet. To help build and maintain muscle, he ingests protein throughout the day, especially after weight training. Tuna, chicken and high-quality protein drinks are his favorite sources.

A Shining Light

Setting an example for upcoming fighters appeals to Marquardt, perhaps because of the indelible impression left by his own role model, Frank Shamrock. "I've patterned myself more after him than I have after any other fighter," Marquardt confides. "He trains hard, is well-rounded, and is extremely successful."

To gain an edge Marquardt studies numerous grapplers, capitalizing on their fight-winning techniques and cutting-edge training strategies whenever possible. "I want to be fully developed as a fighter," Marquardt emphasizes. "I don't want to be labeled as a ground fighter or a striker. However, when training with ground fighters, I want to be the best ground fighter; and while working out with strikers or wrestlers, I want to be the best striker or wrestler."

Early in his career, Marquardt realized that great athletes in all sports excel mentally before they reach their pinnacle physically. "To succeed in mixed-martial-arts competition requires exceptional inner drive. You need a lion's share of heart and intelligence. Those who merely act and react while fighting usually don't become champions," Marquardt maintains. "And if they do, they don't stay champions very long."

It's harder to remain a champion than to become one," contends Marquardt, concerned that too many fighters surrender their mental edge to complacency. "Stay hungry," he admonishes. "Don't lose the drive that makes you number one. If all grapplers maintained that fierce drive, we will be hailed as the greatest athletes in the world, and mixed martial arts will be an Olympic sport."

It's quite a vision. And Nathan Marquardt is making it a reality.

Los Angeles-based writer, researcher, and martial artist Loren Franck is a frequent contributor to Grappling.

BEST OF CFW —— VOL. 1
GRAPPLING

GRAPPLING

Mark Tripp
The Judo Jinx

Anthony Perticaro

Since the end of the Second World War, Judo has become far removed from Jigoro Kano's original concept. While this departure from its roots has led to judo becoming an Olympic sport, it has also resulted in many of judo's *ne-waza* (ground) techniques becoming lost and forgotten. If you ask most martial artists what the differences are between judo mat work and other grappling arts, the usual reply is, "Judo has a lot of the same moves, but doesn't spend as much time on the ground as Brazilian jiu-jitsu does." Actually, there is a great deal more to judo *ne-waza* (ground work) than most people realize. Coach Mark Tripp has been studying and teaching judo for 40-plus years. He trained Dan Severn in judo for Severn's UFC 5 victory during NHB's early glory days and has trained countless judo competitors over the years. In this fascinating interview, Coach Tripp offers some razor-sharp insights into judo groundwork history, its development, and the sports' ups and downs.

Q: When did you begin training in judo?
A: I began at age 5 at a local YMCA program with my uncle, Tom Tripp, and people like Ernie Cates, Charlie King, and John Osako. In those days, the Detroit Judo Club ran almost all of judo in metro Detroit. I also attended the DJC on Saturdays when my grandfather would take me there. Eventually Frank Hubbard opened a school in Dearborn and that is where I trained until I went into the Army.

Q: When you first started judo, was the ground-game stressed very much? Was the level of the judo players' grappling the same level that exists in MMA today?
A: I really can't answer that due to the rules of judo at that time. In those days you had to be a black belt to apply *kansetsu-waza* (arm bars) and I think an adult (perhaps 16) to choke. I am not sure about the choking as it really was a very long time ago. I do know I pinned a lot of people in those days so *ne-waza* (ground work) was taught; but the throw was the major point of training.

Q: Where did the ground fighting in judo originally develop?
A: To answer that we need to get into the core philosophy of Kodokan Judo and how the early matches were fought. The old *bu-jutsu* concept of the samurai where you "prepared for death daily" was something Jigoro Kano wanted to preserve. The problem was he didn't want any *judoka* injured in training, let alone killed! The solution was to create a "token death," one to the ego rather than the body. In early judo the only way to win was to quit or get knocked out by a throw. Some *judoka*

felt the throwing aspect was the way to train for this, while others felt the submission aspects, which included not only chokes and arm locks but neck cranks, leg locks, wrist locks, and all submissions really, were the way to go. Kano felt a balanced training program was the best.

Q: Was ground fighting frowned upon during the early Kodokan days?
A: Not really. Like I said, Kano wanted balance. However as people got injured he did remove things that he felt were too dangerous to practice, such as full power against a resisting opponent. Now, and its true even to this day, some people felt mastering throwing was the way to go, and others felt the submission game was the one to master. I, as did Kano, feel the key to judo is balance, and think one needs to master aspects of both.

Q: Was becoming an Olympic Sport Jigoro Kano's original goal for judo? Is Olympic judo something Kano would approve?
A: Why don't we read his thoughts on the subject? In 1936, Dr. Jigoro Kano, the founder of Kodokan Judo, revealed his attitude towards the possible inclusion of judo in the Olympic games in conversation with Gunji Koizumi, the father of European judo, printed in the *Budokwai Bulletin*, April 1947, made the following statements:

"I have been asked by people of various sections as to the wisdom and possibility of judo being introduced with other games and sports at the Olympic Games. My view on the matter, at present, is rather passive. If it were the desire of other member countries, I have no objection. But I do not feel inclined to take

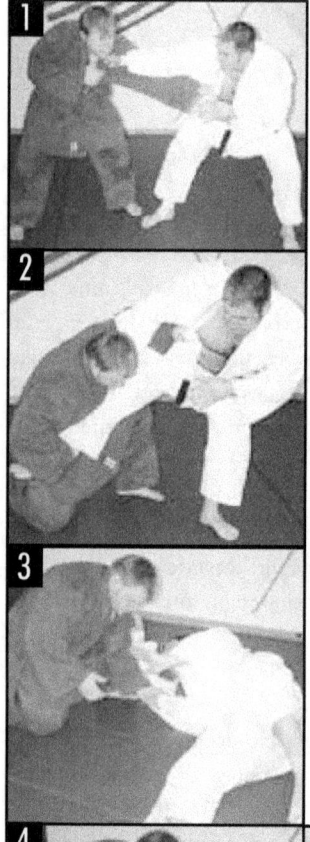

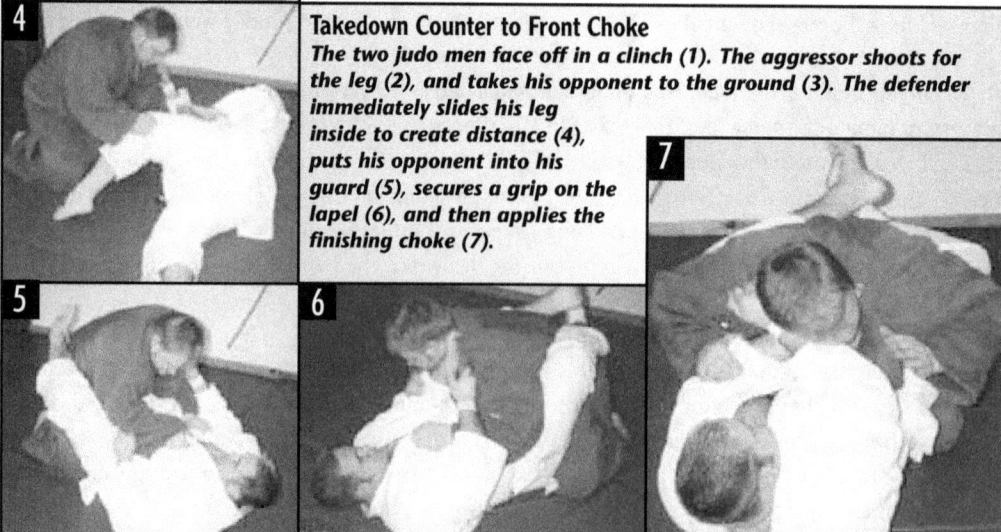

Takedown Counter to Front Choke
The two judo men face off in a clinch (1). The aggressor shoots for the leg (2), and takes his opponent to the ground (3). The defender immediately slides his leg inside to create distance (4), puts his opponent into his guard (5), secures a grip on the lapel (6), and then applies the finishing choke (7).

any initiative. For one thing, Judo in reality is not a mere sport or game. I regard it as a principle of life, art and science. In fact, it is a means for personal cultural attainment. Only one of the forms of Judo training, so-called Randori or free practice can be classified as a form of sport.

"The Olympic Games are so strongly flavored with nationalism that it is possible to be influenced by it and to develop 'Contest Judo,' a retrograde form, as jujutsu was before the Kodokan was founded."

"Judo should be free as art and science from any external influences, political, national, racial, financial, or any other organized interest. All things connected with it should be directed to its ultimate object, the benefit of humanity. Human sacrifice is a matter of ancient history.

"Success, or a satisfactory result of joining the Olympic Games would depend on the degree of understanding of judo by the other countries."

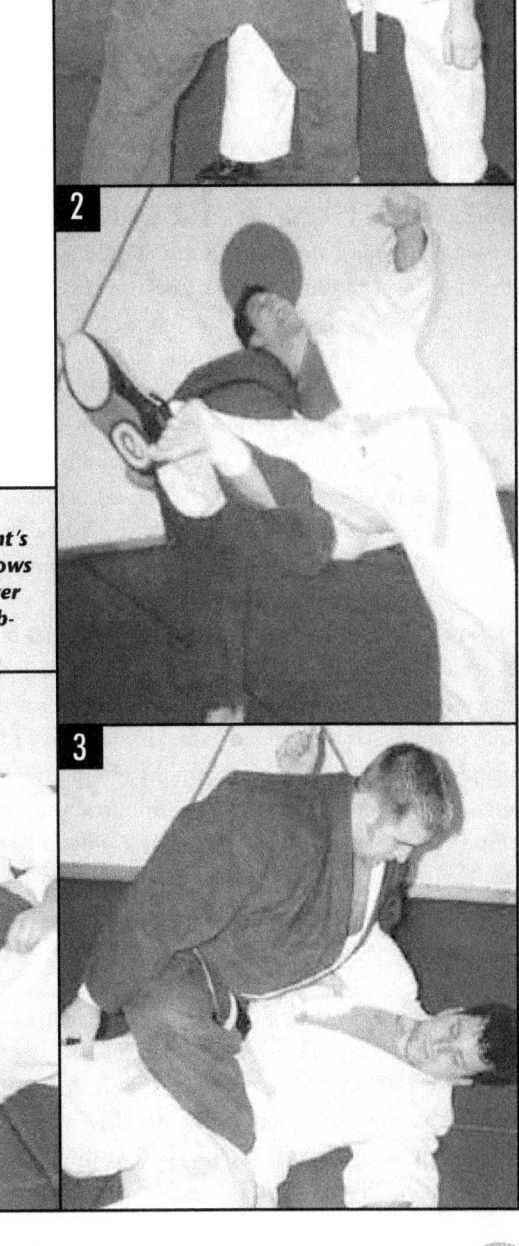

Leg Throw Takedown to Leg-Bar Submission
The aggressor secures a firm grip on his opponent's belt (1), then steps behind his opponent and throws him to the ground (2), where he hooks his leg over the waist (3), the leans back for the knee-bar submission (4).

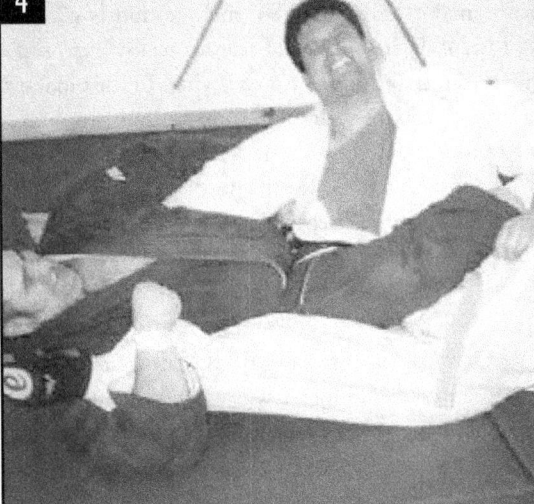

> "Prior to the US occupation Kodokan Judo was trained as, and meant to be, a total system of Bujutsu and Budo. Kano wanted judo to be about effective fighting techniques as well as the sporting and philosophical aspects of his work."

Q: Did judo change further in post-WWII Japan?
A: There is no doubt that Kano wanted something more for Kodokan Judo than sport, even the spectacular Olympic sport it is today. The difference is that before the war Kodokan Judo stressed training in combat effective techniques, as well as exercise, kata, and sporting training. After the war the movement began to teach it only as a sport.

Q: Was it the U.S. occupation that caused the changes?
A: To be sure the occupation caused major changes in judo; but I think they created more groundwork, not less. Prior to the US occupation Kodokan Judo was trained as, and meant to be, a total system of *Bujutsu* and *Budo*. Kano wanted judo to be about effective fighting techniques as well as the sporting and philosophical aspects of his work. Those effective techniques included the chokes and arm locks, as well as numerous leg locks, spine locks, neck cranks, strikes, and VERY hard throwing techniques. We have only to look at the old rules and understand that people died in the judo vs jujutsu matches in 1886 from being thrown by *judoka* to see the throwing was very different then than now. In fact, there are VERY few people who know the difference in the throwing aspects between then and now. In the case of certain throws we have only a guess as to how they were performed. But, when Japan lost the war ALL martial programs were banned. Eventually Resei Kano got the Kodokan re-opened but only if the Kodokan taught Judo as a sport. When you do that all you have left is the throws and some of the submissions.

Q: How did the current bias against ne-waza rules of judo come about?
A: First, people need to understand there is a big difference between the art of Kodokan Judo, and the Olympic sport known as judo. There are some major differences. So, the question is why the lack of emphasis the ground game in the sport of judo? There are lots of reasons really. First, some people feel that too much time on the ground slows things up for Olympic viewing. In the old days, matches had time limits from 30 minutes to an hour. Today's championship matches run 4 to 5 minutes. The time just isn't there for a protracted ground match. Others feel that huge throws are the key to the appeal of the game and want to see more of that. I assure you that there have been more rules changes to the standing game than the ground game lately. All of the changes have been to make the sport of judo into a game of throwing rather than submission.

Q: Overall, has the Olympics helped or hurt judo?
A: Who is to say what is good or bad? Clearly the Olympic sport of judo is HUGE in many places all over the world. However, in the U.S. the drive to create a gold medal winner and the instruction of judo as only an Olympic sport has driven away people who could benefit from judo practice as exercise or as self-defense. Think about it this way—how many people would play tennis if you had to play at an Olympic level?

GRAPPLING

Q: Do you ever see a return to "old" Kodokan Judo?
A: I really don't think so. There will be pockets of people teaching judo in the manner Kano wished it; but more and more of the "old guard" are passing on, and I think sooner or later we will be left with sport judo and kata judo.

Q: Despite the fact that self-defense is more attractive than competition to the average person, why do so few people try to preserve the "old" judo?
A: The reason is that the emphasis is placed primarily on winning tournaments. That is really not the way it is in other places. Although it is worth noting that the Kodokan in Japan is now pretty much a sport-only training center.

Q: How much time do Olympic *judokas* spend honing their *ne-waza* skills?
A: As I said, the modern concept of judo is as a sporting event. The rules will dictate how you practice and how you play the game. You seen that now in the differences between NHB matches, where people would pit one style of fighting against another, and MMA, which is clearly a martial arts style unto itself. NHB is dying out and being replaced by MMA, which is based on rules and playing the game.

Q: With the strong background in throwing, is ground skill truly needed for competition?
A: I think it *is* needed for competition. Kano wanted it that way; I think he was correct. The idea of "balance" is central to Kodokan Judo. While you can win matches with a strong leg and a good throw; that is not building a balanced *judoka*. Moreover, learning how to apply a choke or lock on the ground is MUCH easier than learning how to get it standing up. You will never master submissions on your feet if you don't master them on the ground first.

Q: How much of a difference is there between traditional Kodokan Judo and Brazilian jiu-jitsu (BJJ)?
A: The two are FAR more alike than most people want to believe. BJJ came from Kodokan Judo. There is NO evidence of ANY battlefield jujutsu *ryu-ha* being taken to Brazil and taught there. There is a very clear paper trail from the Kodokan in Japan to the National Governing Body for Judo in Brazil that plainly shows that Maeda was a Kodokan Judo master, who was sent to the Americas to teach and promote Kodokan Judo. Maeda's own letters home say as much and Kimura was the greatest Kodokan Judo expert who ever lived. So there is NO doubt that BJJ is based on Kodokan Judo not a jujutsu *ryu-ha* from Japan.

> **There is a more ground work in judo that most grapplers realize, and a closer relation to BJJ than most MMA fighters want to admit.**

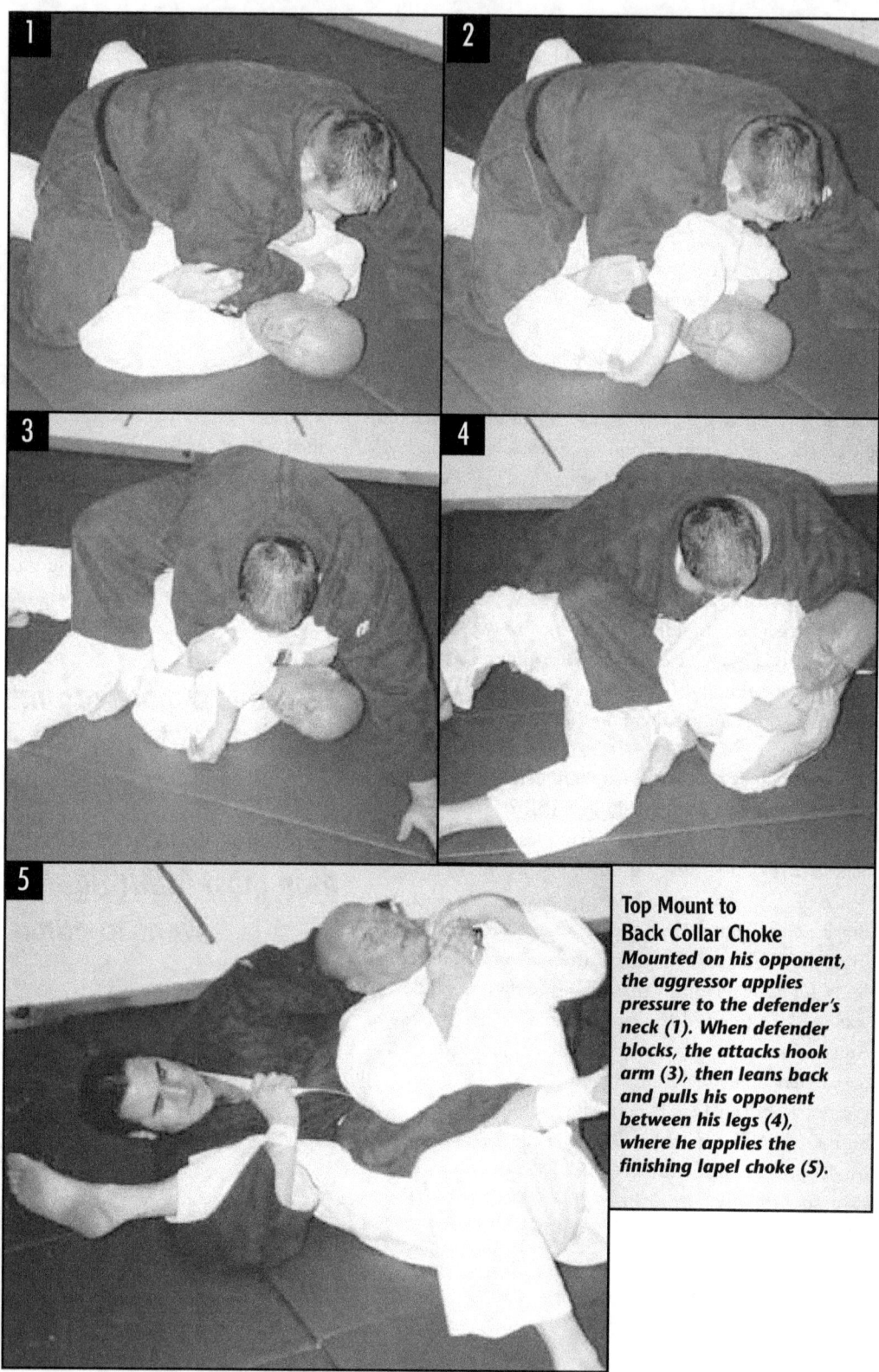

Top Mount to Back Collar Choke
Mounted on his opponent, the aggressor applies pressure to the defender's neck (1). When defender blocks, the attacks hook arm (3), then leans back and pulls his opponent between his legs (4), where he applies the finishing lapel choke (5).

Q: Are there any other ground-grappling sports that have derived from Kodokan Judo?
A: Yes, Kosen Judo. Like BJJ, Kosen Judo played with a different set of rules. We need to be clear on that, or we really can't understand much. Football in the XFL is very different from the football in the NFL; because the rules mean you play the game differently, but BOTH are still football. It's like saying Michigan Football or Iowa Football; it refers to a philosophy how they play the sport, but it doesn't change the sport. Kosen Judo is played by either winning by submission or, in the case of a draw, BOTH people are eliminated from the contest. Obviously this is a team sport, and one that I would dearly love to get going in this country as we could have one of the most exciting sports around for those who WANT to see the groundwork and protracted battles.

It would take a lot of space to show you how much Kosen and BJJ are alike; but, in short, the positions, the techniques, the core ideas, and the way they fight are very similar.

Q: Have your attempts to clarify the relationship between BJJ and Judo made you unpopular?
A: Only if you call being insulted, unpopular! In many interviews and articles, Judo is presented as a 'weak sister" to BJJ. So I show BJJ's history comes from Judo, not some obscure battlefield *ryu-ha*, and some people do not believe it is true and get angry with me. I don't see how understanding the true nature and history of your system invalidates what you are doing or the game you want to play. That's not the right attitude for either a good judoka or Brazilian jiu-jitsu man; and it has no place in legitimate sport or serious martial art training.

Those wishing to contact Mark Tripp can visit the Judo Q&A folder at www.mixedmartialarts.com *where he offers excellent training advice at no charge.*

BEST OF CFW — VOL.1
GRAPPLING

GRAPPLING

5 Shooto Transitional Leg Locks

One of the best ways to apply a leg lock is while countering a standing kick, punch, knee, or takedown.

Erik Paulson, *Grappling Magazine* Technical Advisor

Fighters often train muay Thai and Brazilian jiu-jitsu for mixed-martial-arts competition. While muay Thai is a devastating standing art and Brazilian jiu-jitsu is an extremely effective ground-fighting system, there is a gray area of transition that neither really addresses effectively. This gray zone is where the stand-up fighting ends and the ground game begins. Gray-zone transitions are where cuts, black eyes, broken noses and cracked cheekbones occur. One of the best ways to control the gray zone and turn it to your advantage is through using transitional takedown leg-locks.

Contrary to popular belief, there is no one single position that legs locks are limited to. The legs can be successfully attacked from virtually every ground and standing position. My theory is that any grappler, to be complete, must be able to use his legs every bit as well as his hands. Therefore, the legs are consistently coming into play when you are in the process of transitioning from a standing position to ground grappling. You are only limited in your use of leg locks by your imagination.

The legs can be attacked from the following opposing fighting postures: ground vs. ground; ground vs. standing; standing vs. ground; and standing vs. standing. The common leg attacks are the knee bar, Achilles or foot lock, the figure-four foot-lock, the shin lock, the knee key-lock, the heel hook, and the hip lock. These all fall into the category of "leg locks" and are known by many other names as well. Don't fuss over terminology—just learn them and learn their counters.

In Shooto, because standing, punching, kicking and kneeing are allowed, fighters are taught how to catch a kick from many different positions and take the opponent down and finish the fight with a leg lock. There are basically three attack zones that you must be ready to counter with a transitional leg lock: the upper attack zone (head), the middle attack zone (the body), and the lower attack zone (the legs).

Typical kicks that must be caught in order to initiate a leg-lock sequence include the shin kick, the roundhouse kick, the straight kick, the push front-kick, and the side kick. The thing that I like about Shooto is that its anti-grappling techniques are geared towards keeping a grappler away and preventing him from taking you down. From the other perspective, Shooto grappling techniques are geared towards taking a kickboxer down and controlling him on the ground. So the two methods synthesize to form a very complete fighting art.

I refer to the quick catches of punches and kicks, and the subsequent takedowns to leg-lock finishes, as "quick kills." The following "quick kills" are seek-and-destroy attack counters that are effective in the ring, on the mat, or on the street. These catch-and-finish transitions are ways to bridge the gap between striking and grappling and control the gray zone. The key is to synthesize elements of stand-up and grappling in order to create smooth transitions.

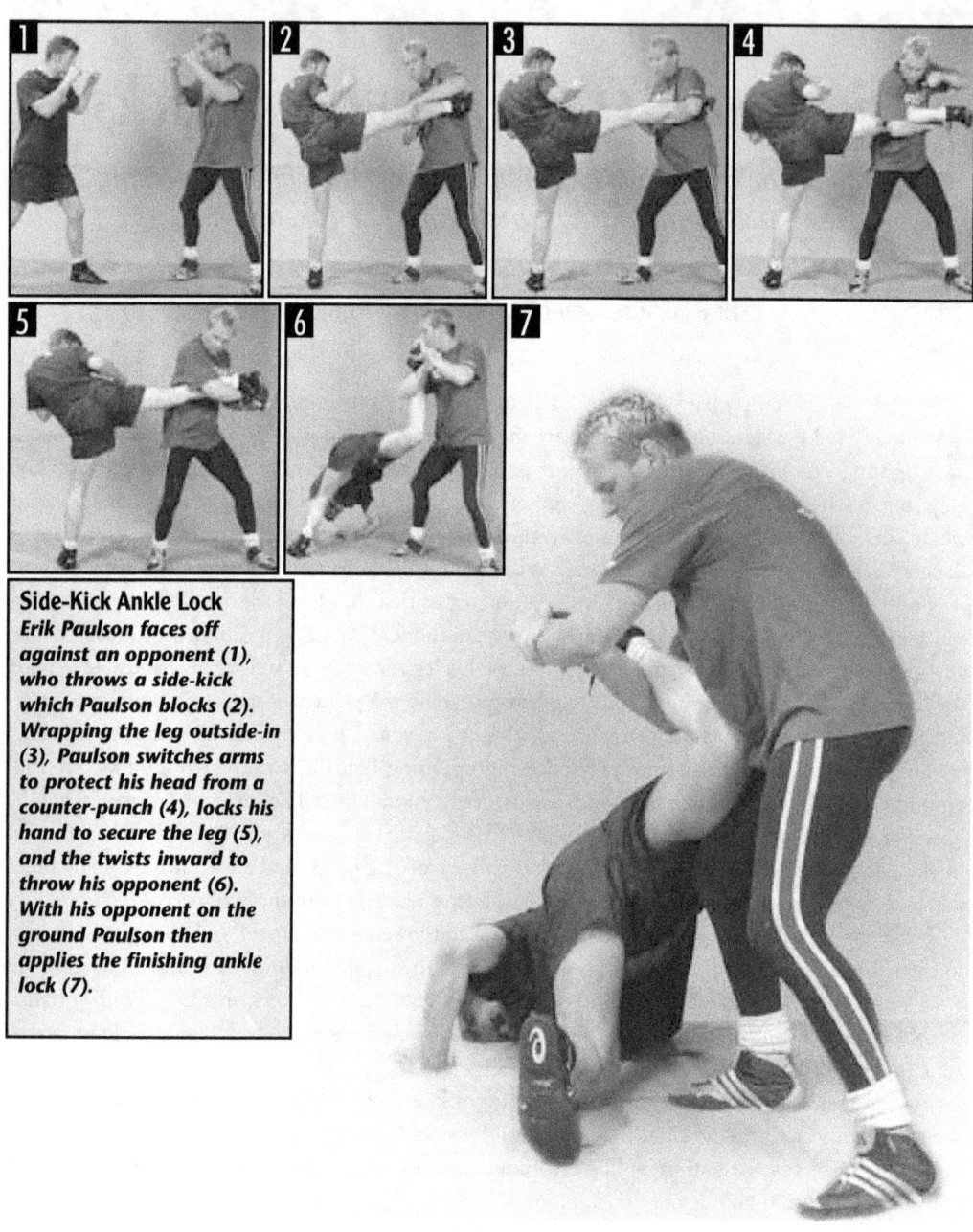

Side-Kick Ankle Lock
Erik Paulson faces off against an opponent (1), who throws a side-kick which Paulson blocks (2). Wrapping the leg outside-in (3), Paulson switches arms to protect his head from a counter-punch (4), locks his hand to secure the leg (5), and the twists inward to throw his opponent (6). With his opponent on the ground Paulson then applies the finishing ankle lock (7).

GRAPPLING

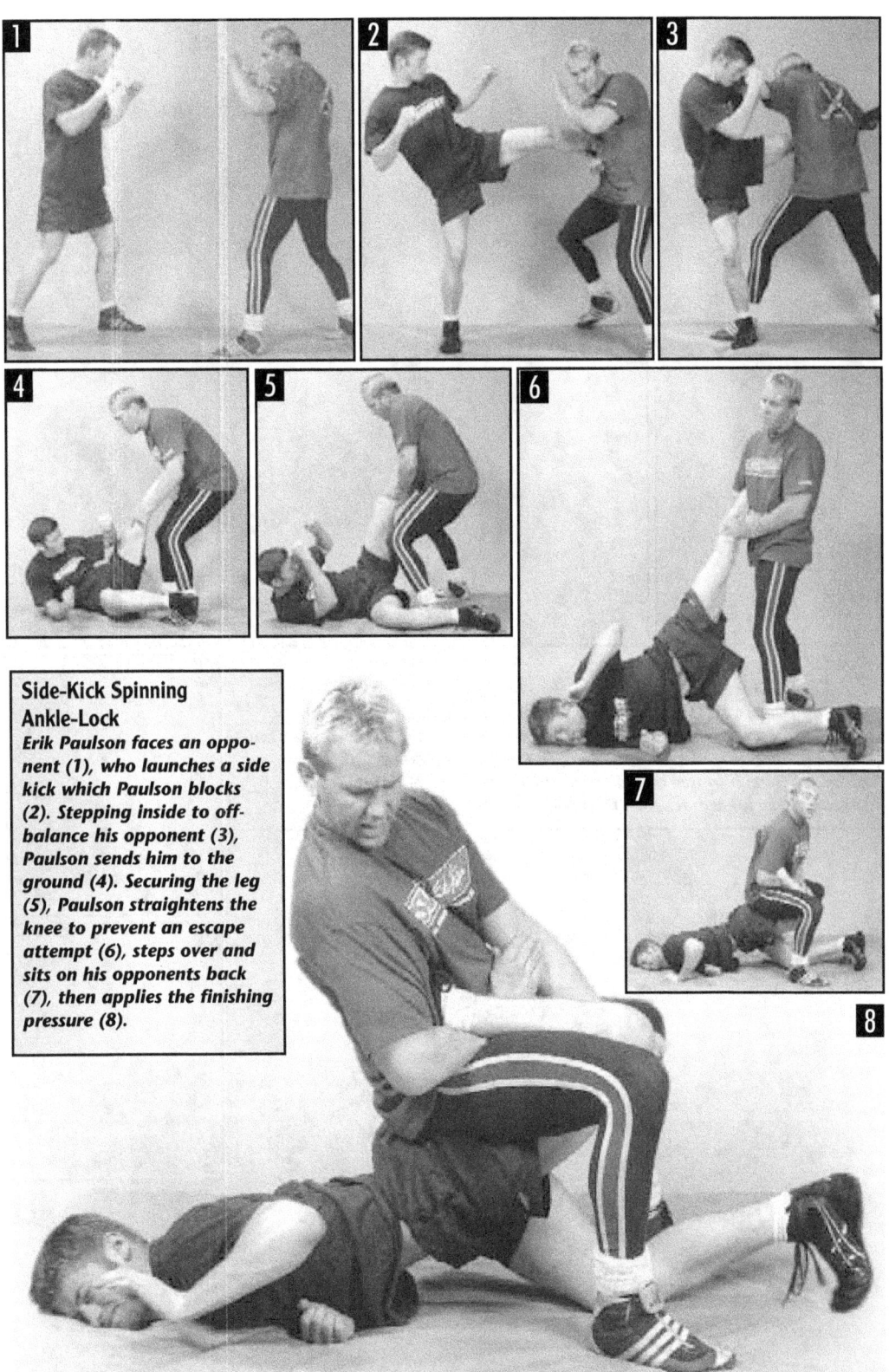

Side-Kick Spinning Ankle-Lock

Erik Paulson faces an opponent (1), who launches a side kick which Paulson blocks (2). Stepping inside to off-balance his opponent (3), Paulson sends him to the ground (4). Securing the leg (5), Paulson straightens the knee to prevent an escape attempt (6), steps over and sits on his opponents back (7), then applies the finishing pressure (8).

Front-Kick Knee Bar
Erik Paulson faces an opponent (1), who snaps out a front kick which Paulson blocks (2). Stepping inside to close the distance (3), Paulson hooks the neck (4), steps between his opponent's legs (5), and throws him to the ground (6). Trapping the leg (7), Paulson then locks the ankle (8), puts his knee on his opponent's stomach to immobilize him (9), and then leans back into the knee bar (10).

GRAPPLING

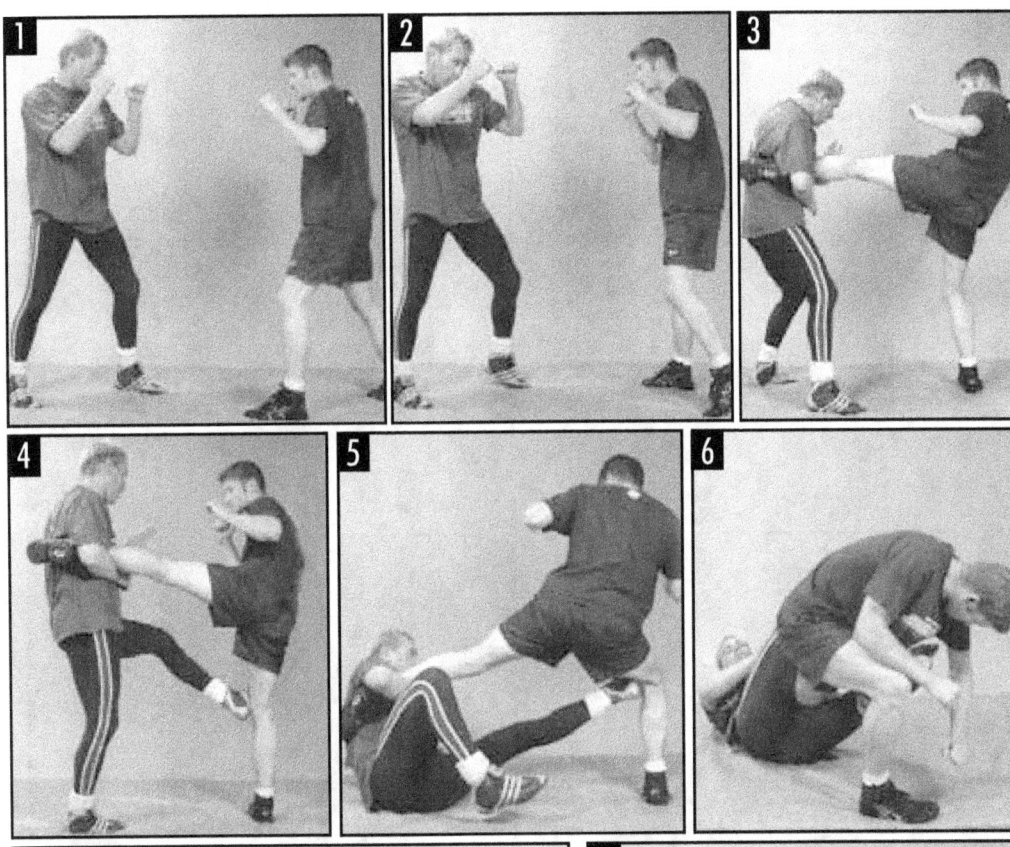

Side-Kick Knee Bar
Erik Paulson faces an opponent (1), who feints a punch (2), then launches a side-kick which Paulson blocks (3). Paulson then attacks the knee with his foot (4), then falls down and off-balances his opponent (5), throwing him to the ground (6). Putting a figure-four leg lock onto his opponent's thigh (7), Paulson then applies the finishing knee-bar (8).

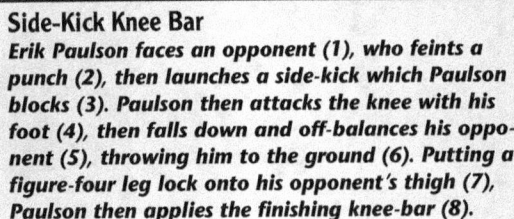

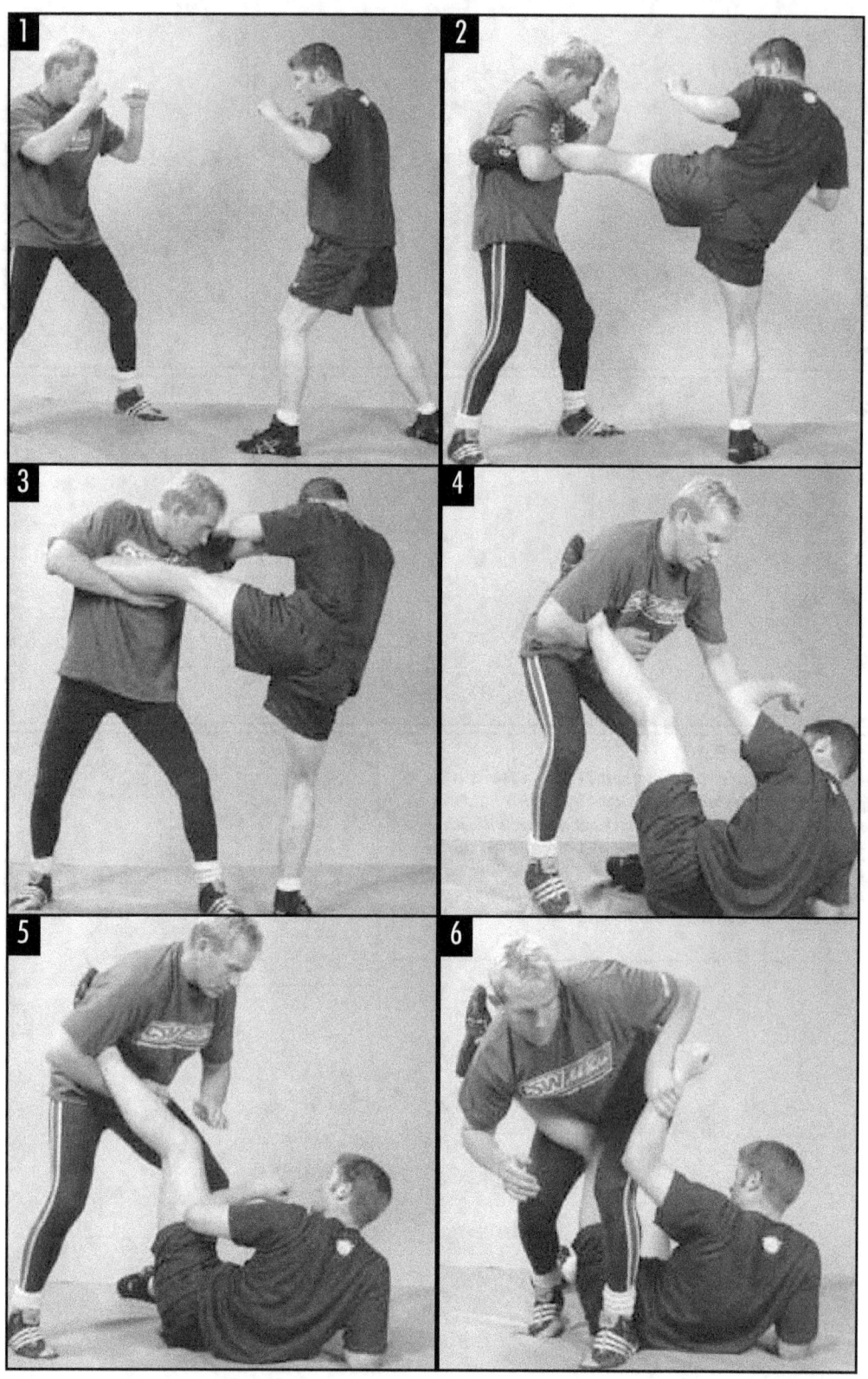

Side-Kick Spinning Knee-Bar
Erik Paulson faces an opponent (1), and then block an attempted side kick (2). Wrapping the leg he off-balances his opponent (3), throwing him to the ground (4). Spinning over the leg (5), he leans back (6), and applies the finishing knee bar (7).

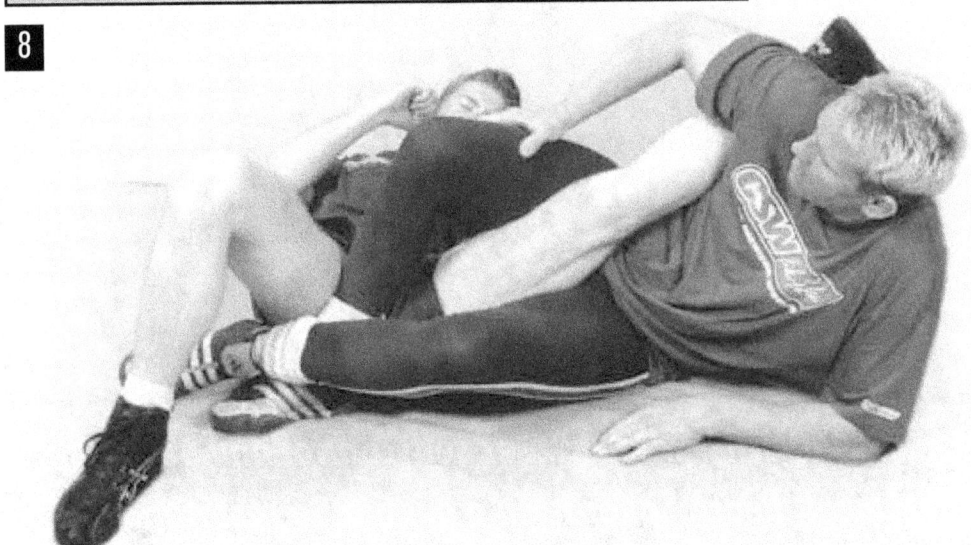

Erik Paulson is available for classes or seminars by calling 310-785-5805. His "Killer Leg Lock" video series and "Quick Kills" tape is available at www.erikpaulson.com

GRAPPLING

A true martial artist who stresses self-control and personal advancement, Pedro Sauer is on a mission to restore honor to Brazilian jiu-jitsu and elevate the art to a higher level.

Pedro Sauer

A Man On A Mission

Kid Peligro

Brazilian jiu-jitsu black belt Pedro Sauer has been around the mat a few times. The 43-year-old native of Rio de Janeiro started training at the tender age of 12, at the Gracie Academy in Rio de Janeiro, by invitation of his friend Rickson Gracie. At the time, Sauer had been already training boxing for several years. "I remember going to the academy with Rickson. Professor Helio was there and said, 'You're the boxer, huh? Put on some gloves and let's check you out.' So I went to the mat and they had Royler on the other side warming up. Royler must have been 7 or something and he proceeded to take me down and choke me time after time until I begged for mercy."

Helio and Rickson

From that day on, a fire started to burn inside the young Sauer and he signed up for lessons and proceeded to study under Professor Helio and Rickson both. "I must be the person that got the greatest number of private lessons from those two over the years. My parents would pay for an entire year of classes until I started to work, and then I paid for them myself. It was the early days and the school was fantastic; they would give you a gi and it would be yours for the entire time you trained there. They would clean it and have it ready for you the next time you came to train. All the gi's were clean in hangers, ready to be used."

Sweet and Sauer

At the time, Sauer was working at the Rio de Janeiro Stock Market; times were good then and money was no problem. "I was making a lot of money at the time, but I felt the need to give something back, not just take!" Pedro states. "So when Rickson called me and asked me to move the United States and teach, I was ready to go. I figured, he did me good once, he would for sure do me good the second time."

But things weren't as easy as Sauer thought. "I got over here and couldn't speak any English, but I was able to hook up with Rorion (Rickson's brother) and train at the Torrance School. Soon after that I decided to open my own school in Salt Lake City, still associated with Gracie Academy, of course. Those were hard times, I had very few students and BJJ wasn't as popular as it is today. I had to work during the day and then teach at night. After a while, though, the school became more well-known and grew quickly."

Pedro's school grew so much that eventually he had students going everywhere and spreading his word. Eventually, he had to open an association as his grass-roots fame spread across the country. Currently the Pedro Sauer Brazilian Jiu-Jitsu Association has over 25 representatives throughout the U.S. and is adding more each year.

A Man With A Plan

Sauer supports the association and maintains quality control by visiting his associates at least once or more a year. Additionally, Sauer has several four-day workshops per year in his modern 8,000 square foot academy in Sandy, Utah. This event gathers all the Pedro Sauer representatives together to clarify and unify the association's teaching and training methods, and to standardize the way every instructor should conduct themselves as a professor and as a businessman. The result of all this support is that Sauer is respected and admired by all of his representatives. and every one of them mirrors his success.

When asked what led him to start an association, Sauer states that he quickly realized that jiu-jitsu teachings needed to evolve from the fighting-only mind-set that was developed in Brazil. Pedro's approach is different because he has an interest in developing the student as a whole. "We work a lot on the improvement of personal skills," Sauer says. "I want to make you a better person in addition to making you a better fighter, because one is nothing without the other. In my mind, the academy is a place for a person to grow in fighting knowledge and in the development of themselves as a human being."

The Frank Cucci Connection

When asked how he achieved his tremendous success so quickly, Sauer is quick to give credit where credit is due. "To be honest, I had a lot of help from Frank Cucci. Frank is a fantastic individual and he taught me a lot. He taught me about being a better businessman and about being a better teacher and person. He is a great fighter, an animal in training, and he knows everything about Brazilian jiu-jitsu. Frank taught me a lot about what an instructor is supposed to be like and act like. An instructor teaches by example, and Frank Cucci is the ultimate example."

According to Sauer, the initial jiu-jitsu association was comprised of mature individuals who were already accomplished martial artists in their own field and who had large followings. "Many of them," Sauer explains, "came from Cucci's large and well-organized association. These people then took an interest in helping me become a better instructor; so there was a tremendous exchange of ideas—it wasn't just me being the master and them following blindly; it was definitely a two-way street." Sauer's open-mindedness and natural humility allowed him to combine his BJJ knowledge with the teaching, training, and business methods of Frank Cucci's group.

Hard But Safe

One of the major differences between Sauer's program and conventional BJJ programs is its organization and presentation. As Sauer points out, "We start by presenting the student with a curriculum they can follow. The student knows exactly what is expected of them and what steps they have to take to achieve their goals. We also emphasize staying injury free. One of the steps we take is that every time someone gets injured, we write the name of the person they were training with on the blackboard. If several people get injured training with a certain partner, we can easily see that. So we

GRAPPLING

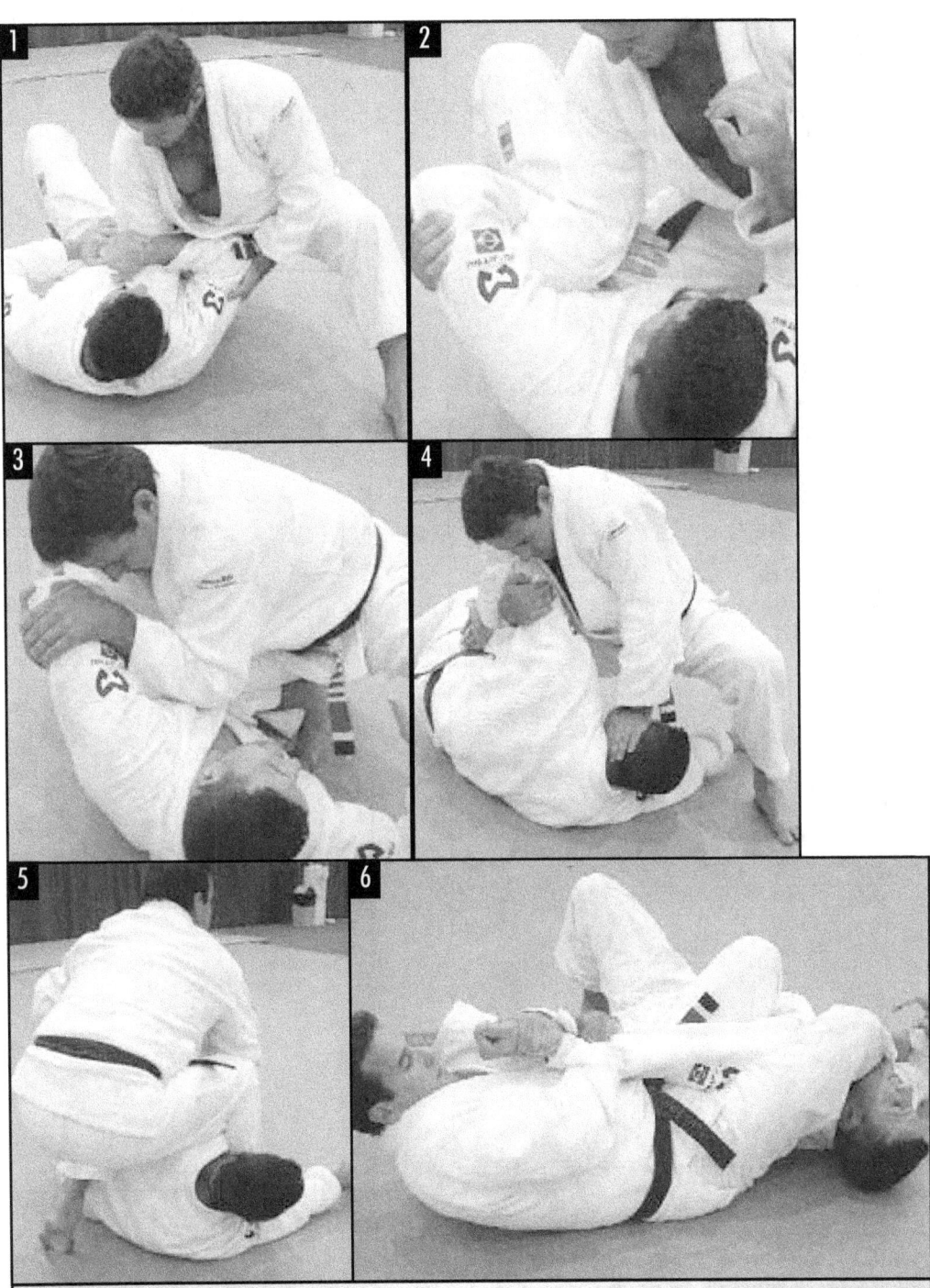

Knee-On-Stomach Spinning Arm-Bar
Pedro Sauer controls his opponent with the classic knee-on-stomach position (1). When his opponent pushes Sauer's knee to break the position, Sauer under-hooks the elbow to control the arm (2), then uses his other hand to turn his opponent towards him (3). Pressuring the head to create distance (4), Sauer then spins his back leg over the head, trapping the body (5), then lays back and executes the finishing arm-bar (6).

Open-Guard Reversal

Pedro Sauer traps his opponent's arm while putting his feet inside the thighs (1). Rolling in the direction of the trapped arm, Sauer lifts his opposite foot to elevate his opponent (2). He then completes the roll and ends up in the top mount position (3).

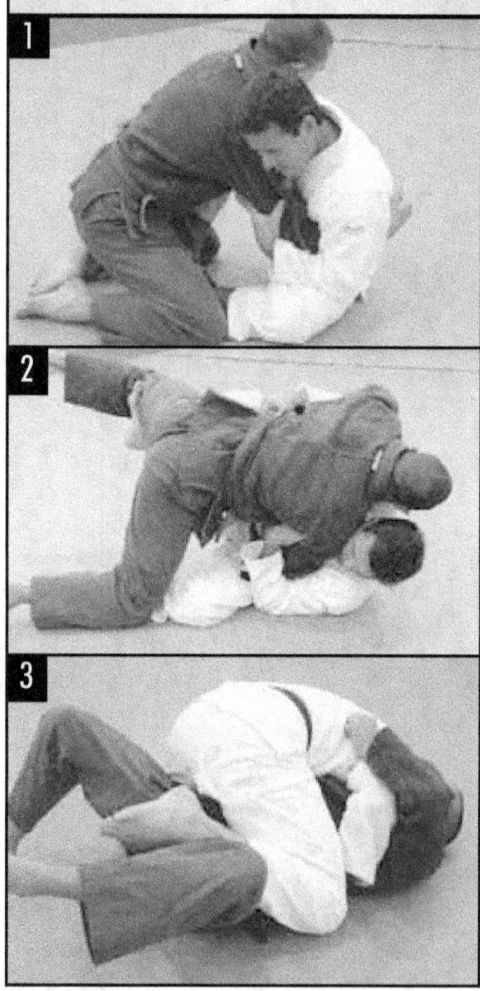

Inside-Hook Throw to Side Control

Pedro Sauer controls an aggressive opponent by trapping the arm and putting his legs inside his thighs (1). Rolling in the direction of the trapped arm (2), he keeps his foot inside his opponent's thigh (3), elevates his opponent by lifting his foot (4), and rolls on top into side control (5).

implemented the following rule: The first time you injure someone, your name goes on the board; the next time you injure someone, you are suspended from training until that person is ready to return to training. If you injure a third person, you are expelled from the school. In our schools people just don't get hurt; I think it has a lot to do with this rule. The object is to train and have fun, not to hurt people. So you learn to train hard but to also have control."

Cleaning Up The Sport
One of Sauer's main objectives is to spread his system to other associations and other schools: "I'm concerned about what might happen in America if we don't take some serious steps to avoid the pitfalls that have occurred in Brazil. In Brazil, right now, the sport of jiu-jitsu is in disarray. There are press reports nearly everyday about criminal incidents involving BJJ practitioners. Whether all of those criminals are really practitioners or not is irrelevant, because the perception of violence has caused huge damage to the image of the sport. So in America, I want to unite all of the black belt instructors and get everyone to agree on certain positive standards. That way, we can control the quality of the students and the quality of instruction so we don't end up with the same problems here."

"As instructors," Sauer points out, "it should *not* be our objective to just accept any person that walks in the door, and teach him to fight so that he can be a tough guy and beat up everyone on the street. We should teach him that he is here to learn how to defend himself and to protect himself and his family from assault and to preserve the name of the sport. The student needs to know that picking fights outside the school will not be tolerated. If he wants to fight, he can enter tournaments, do NHB, or whatever. We will support him in this 100 percent. But if all he wants is to become a bully, then there is no place for him here."

Success Breeds Success
The success of Sauer's program can easily be seen by the fact that his students are constantly winning tournaments and NHB fights. His students include Jeff Curren, a purple belt from Chicago who has made a name for himself as a successful NHB fighter at the young age of 22. Another is Gregg Nelson of Minnesota, the current Pan-American BJJ Champion who coached international-level NHB fighters Dave Menne and Sean Sherk.

When asked what it takes to become a certified representative Sauer is very firm: "The first step is for me to get to know you. I won't accept anyone without getting to know them. After I certify that you are a person of good character and a solid individual, then we can talk about getting you into the program." This meticulous, thoughtful, and personal approach is the way Sauer does everything. He is always searching to perfect his technique, and to perfect himself and others around him. In recognition of his outstanding contributions to the sport, Sauer was voted "The Best of the Best BJJ Instructor" by ADCC News in a Year 2000 survey, and was recently invited to Abu Dhabi to showcase his teaching methods and to train Sheik Tahnoon's numerous adopted orphans.

Sauer is very focused on his professional goals in life: "My main objective is to spread the jiu-jitsu that I learned from Professor Helio Gracie and his son Rickson Gracie, while following the principles of being a decent human being that I learned from my mother."

For more information on classes, seminars, or the instructor's program, Pedro Sauer can be contacted at 801-561-2535, by email at pedro@pedrosauer.com, *or through his Web site at* www.pedrosauer.com

BEST OF CFW — VOL.1
GRAPPLING

My Top Ten Tips for Winning Fights

Mixed martial arts is just a way for some fighters to earn a living. But for die-hard grapplers like me, the sport is in our blood. More than a way of life, it's life itself.

Charlie Kohler with Loren Franck

In 1979, when I was 5 and living in Hong Kong, my parents enrolled me in taekwondo. I needed more physical activity, and like most kids that age, I lacked discipline. Little did my parents know that the martial arts—especially grappling—would become the focus of my adult life.

When my family and I moved back to the United States in 1984, I was 10 and had earned my black belt in taekwondo. However, I quickly discovered that many American martial arts schools were inferior to those in Hong Kong—you could hit each other there. And though I trained in various fighting arts throughout high school and college, I grew disenchanted with them, so I played baseball and football instead.

I had watched videos of the Gracies' early fights, so I had heard about them before they became famous. But I didn't realize how good the Gracies were. Soon after graduating high school, I met Nelson Monteiro, who taught under the Gracies. While visiting him, I tried Brazilian jiu-jitsu and grappling and was amazed at what he taught.

My career has flourished since then. Proud of my 8-1-1 record, I've discovered ten terrific tools to winning fights. They're deep dimensions of grappling that extend far beyond strikes, submission holds and other hands-on techniques. Why am I sharing them? Because I want you to succeed in the sport like I have.

1. Get Serious

I'm extremely serious in everything I do, especially when training and battling it out in the ring. You have to be. Taking the sport seriously is the first step in winning fights. I learned this important lesson early in my grappling career. As a football player at Grossmont College in San Diego, I repeatedly suffered small injuries. They often sidelined me but didn't prevent me from fighting. "If I'm going to grapple," I reflected, "I'll do it right and go all the way." Fights came up and I decided to compete. "Train hard," I told myself. "Get serious and be the best."

2. Toughen Up

Grappling is tougher than any other sport. To win fights and become a champion, you must be tough too. Admittedly, most of today's submission fighters are tough, some more so than others. Joe Hurley was my toughest opponent. Awarded a split decision in our bout, he kept coming at me and

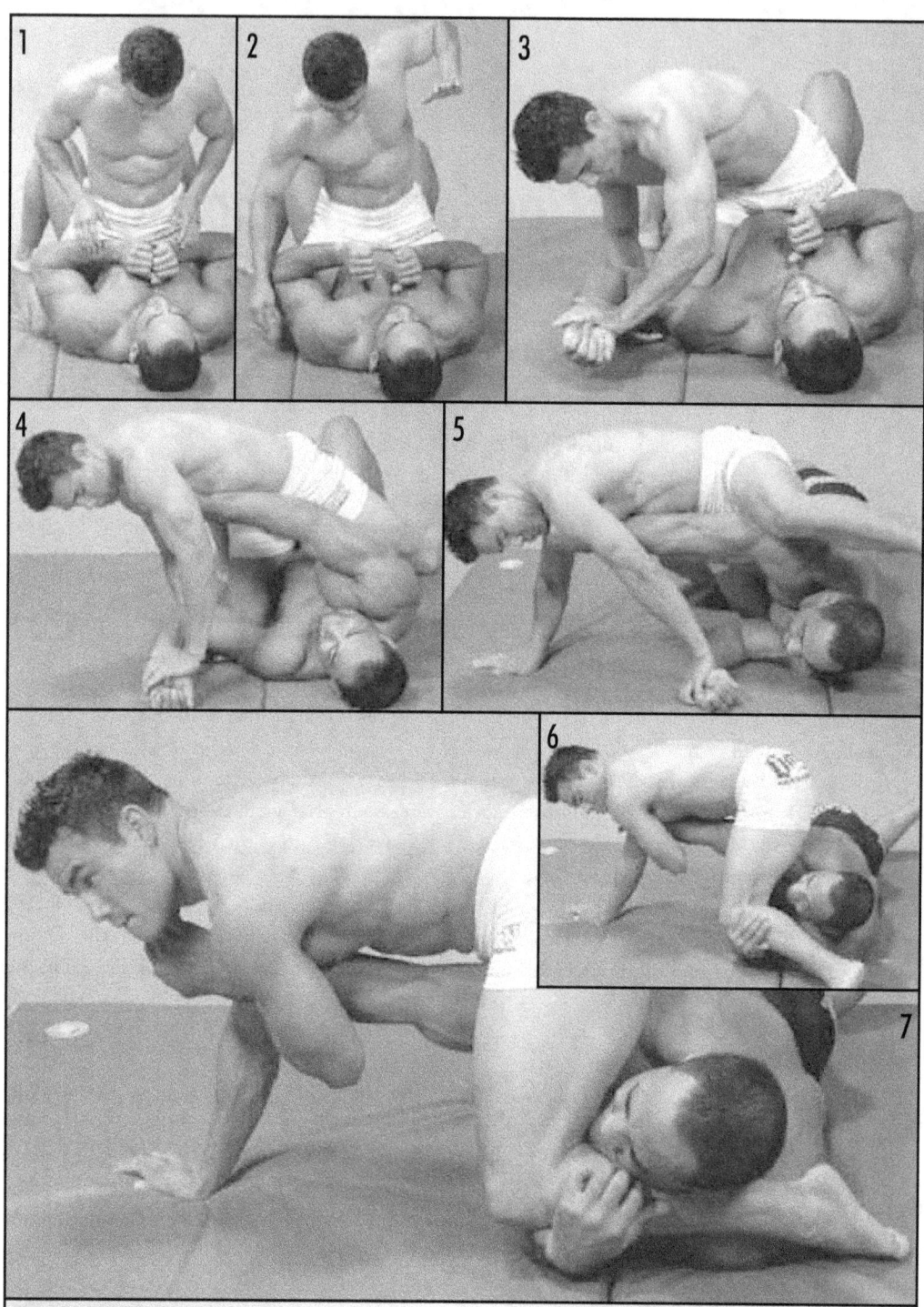

Ground-and-Pound Arm Bar
Mounted on his opponent (1), Charlie Kohler uses strikes to break down his foes defense (2). When he opponent reaches up to block, Kohler pins his arm and goes for the shoulder lock (3). When his opponent counters by pushing with his right arm (4), Kohler swings his leg over the head (5), traps the arm (6), and then applies a finishing arm lock (7).

GRAPPLING

refused to lose. Joe taught me two important lessons. First, I learned to prepare for the toughest possible opponents and to never underestimate anyone. Second, I realized that a fight environment can be a formidable adversary. It was raining when Joe and I battled, and the slippery mat completely took me out of my game. The more aggressive I was, the more my hands slid while trying to take him down. I had no footing, either, so I couldn't apply pressure effectively and pass his guard. In fact, the rain prevented me from using many of my fighting techniques. It affected Joe too, but it hurt me more. The environment gave him an advantage, which cost me the fight.

3. Turn On And Tune Up

Like many grapplers, I have an extensive martial arts background. Before getting hooked on mixed martial arts, I trained in muay Thai, Western boxing, kali, escrima and, of course, taekwondo. But grappling turned me on because it's so devastating. You feel hopeless when locked in its submission holds. When Nelson started training me, he put me in arm locks, chokes and other holds. At his mercy, I felt I was drowning, but he'd laugh and have fun as I strained to escape. Nelson's knowledge of grappling—especially Brazilian jiu-jitsu—blew me away. It really turned me on to the sport. And that's crucial if you hope to win consistently.

4. Become A Predator, Not Prey

Most grapplers offer to fight anyone, anytime, anywhere. And that's good. If you can't display such aggressive-

> *"From the beginning of each match, I move toward my opponents, grounding and pounding them. Then I try to submit them. I always take the fight to my opponents, whatever their size, strength or skill level."*

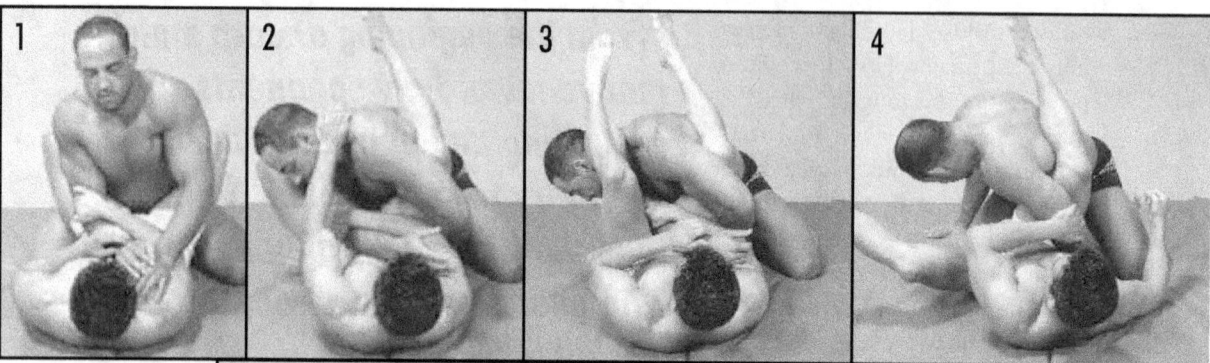

Rollover Reverse Elbow Lock
Charlie Kohler, trapped beneath his opponent (1), slides his hips out (2), and attempts an opposite side arm-bar (3). When his opponent counters by pressuring his weight forward (4), Kohler hooks his leg over the near arm (5), rolls over and traps the arm (6), and then comes to a knee and applies pressure for the finishing lock (7).

ness, perhaps you shouldn't be in the sport. But if you want to win fights, trade the tough talk for aggressive behavior. *Aggressive* is the word that best describes me as a fighter. From the beginning of each match, I move toward my opponents, grounding and pounding them. Then I try to submit them. I always take the fight to my opponents, whatever their size, strength or skill level. My powerful martial arts abilities, especially the devastating Brazilian jiu-jitsu techniques I've learned, help me dominate. Aggressiveness helps you control your fights and persevere until your hand is raised in victory.

5. Switch Strategies

Strategy is vital to every combat sport. Most successful fighters chart their own paths to victory. Some grapplers depend on striking power, while others rely on speed, endurance or timing. I've incorporated all of these into my fighting arsenal, but Brazilian jiu-jitsu techniques usually work best for me. Adaptability is often more important than prearranged techniques. That's why I don't limit myself to one fighting strategy. Instead, to gain the best advantage in the ring, my strategy changes with every opponent.

Although I mix it up with some opponents, I take others straight to the ground. Because of my extensive grappling experience, opponents rarely surprise me once we're on the ground. Sure, they try, but they rarely succeed.

Boxing skills are overrated in mixed martial arts. Grapplers wear small gloves, or no gloves at all, so even a mediocre punch could knock you out. If opponents use strikes to defeat me, they'll have to hit me while I'm standing. By quickly going to the ground, however, I prevent them from doing that. And they probably won't submit me or knock me out while I'm on top. So my game plan is predominantly jiu-jitsu. But if my opponents want to stand and box, I'll do it. I'm probably a better striker than most guys I fight.

6. Go For The Gold

You'll achieve much more in grappling if you vie for titles. That's what I've done. In my first title fight, my opponent outweighed me by 20 pounds. But I didn't care. I've always needed motivation

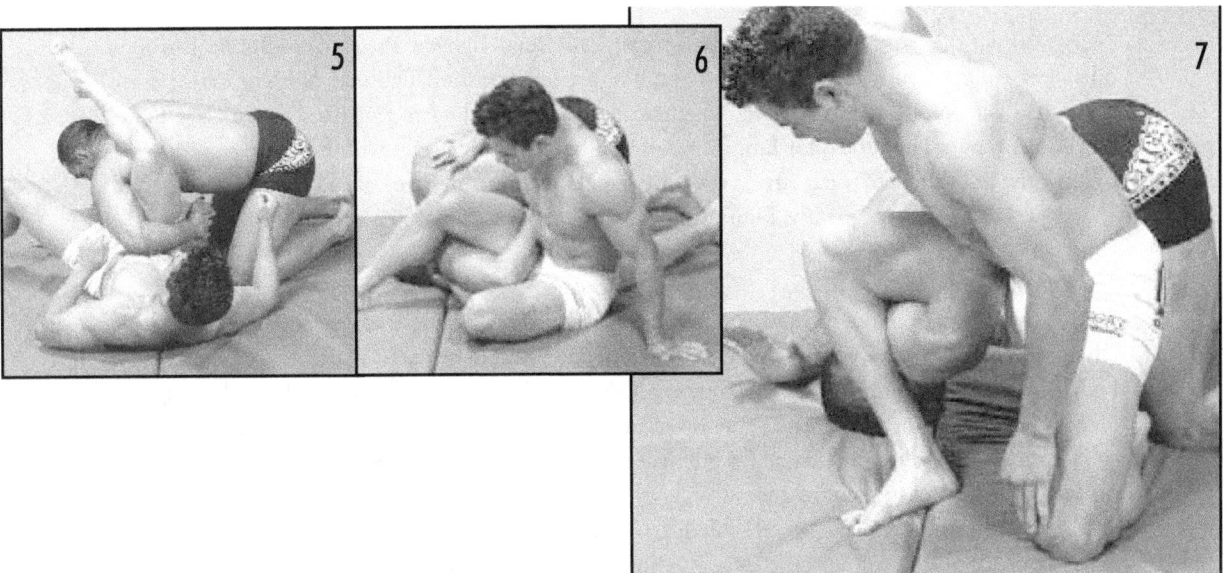

to extend my abilities and accomplishments to the next level, and competing for titles helps. I've sought a different title during each of my King of the Cage battles. My recent bout with Joe Hurley was for the 175-pound championship. And though I didn't win, the experience made me a better grappler. Whatever your level of expertise in mixed martial arts, don't remain there. Constantly strive for titles, better fighting skills, and higher-level experience in the ring. Push your grappling career forward and never dwell on the past. Don't look back unless you want to go there.

7. Go Global

The broader your perspective of mixed martial arts, the more likely you are to win fights and become a champion. I was one of the first modern grapplers to train in Abu Dhabi in the United Arab Emirates. What an experience! Thanks to Prince Tahnoon, it was the turning point in my career. He supports me and other fighters in every way. My Abu Dhabi experiences transformed me from a local grappler to an athlete with a global perspective. I lived in Abu Dhabi for three months my first time there, training hard and polishing my fighting techniques. Predictably, I've returned several times over the years. If not for Prince Tahnoon, I probably would have quit the sport long ago.

It's expensive to train in mixed martial arts, especially at the top level. Fighters easily spend thousands of dollars on airfare, food, hotels and other related expenses. Prince Tahnoon has picked up the tab for me several times. One of the sport's greatest ambassadors, he's flown me and other grapplers all over the world to train and compete. Other athletes I've known have traveled to Brazil to train, or even to Japan. The experience has helped them all. So don't limit yourself to local, state or national events. Set your sights higher. Expand your horizons and you'll win fights.

8. Learn By Teaching

Many tools can help you win fights. Hard work is one. Having a superb trainer like Nelson Monteiro is another. Teaching is a third. Teaching mixed martial arts helps students learn, but more important, it also makes *you* a better fighter. That's one reason I opened my own school in El Cajon, California, several miles east of San Diego, where I teach hard-core grappling. About half my students work for the San Diego Police Department, California Highway Patrol, U.S. Border Patrol or other law enforcement agencies. The rest want to learn submission fighting. Nothing satisfies me more than when my students succeed, whether they're cops on the street or King of the Cage fighters. I don't train many people for fun, fitness or as a hobby. People train with me because they want to learn the real thing. To teach effectively, I must remain at least one step ahead of my students, and always razor sharp. Consequently, I improve my own grappling skills when I teach them to others.

9. Focus On Fighting

There are plenty of politics in most professional sports, and grappling is no exception. Politics usually raise their ugly head when grapplers from different schools compete against each other. Sadly, because politics interfere with judging and event organization, the athletes suffer. I avoid the sport's politics like the plague. They're the one aspect of mixed martial arts I don't like. Sometimes they're so intense that grapplers can't train at more than one school. If they train elsewhere, their curiosity is deemed disrespectful to their instructors.

These same teachers may also feel inferior, threatened, and might forbid students to share techniques with competitors from other schools. But grappling is so popular that most serious students need to train with multiple instructors. How do you avoid politics in the sport? Focus on your training. If you always try to improve your mat game, you won't have time for mind games outside the ring.

GRAPPLING

Yoga for Grapplers

Unfortunately, your grappling training can plummet from exciting to boring in a heartbeat, so don't be afraid to spice it up. My Abu Dhabi experiences put an unusual twist on my fighting career, and my movie and TV work continue to do so. While conditioning my body, however, I tried something unconventional. To get in top shape, fighters usually run, cycle, and lift weights. But what if I said yoga is vital to my physical conditioning? Would you believe me? Well, it's true

I took up yoga by accident. After a run during a rainy Southern California morning, I ducked into an exercise room at a gym where I had planned to train. I didn't know that a senior citizen's yoga class was about to start in that room. Well, because everyone was so friendly and nice, I participated in the class anyway, not wanting them to think I didn't want to hang out with them. Well, I had fun, made friends, and decided to go again. As the weeks passed, wanting to stay in touch, I just kept attending.

The surprising result? My joints and tendons improved immensely and I felt better. Yoga is physical therapy for me. Holding the positions strengthens my muscles while improving their flexibility. My newfound yoga training works parts of my muscles unaffected by weight training and other standard exercises. So try new approaches to training, even if they're unusual, and even if you don't initially believe they'll work. Much of your success in grappling depends on your willingness to reach out, experiment, and go beyond the norm into the unknown.

10. Have Fun

Mixed martial arts is the toughest sport on earth. It demands consummate mental and physical prowess. Because the sport is so rigorous, however, it also offers exceptional intrinsic rewards. And when you make decent money grappling, that's even better.

If you need more help to win fights, you can use your grappling skills in less conventional ways. One of my favorites is movie and TV work. My involvement in the sport has opened doors for work as an extra and also stunt opportunities. Look closely and you'll see me in the movie *Bring It On*. I've also appeared in *Silk Stalkings, Pensacola* and other television shows. It's very rewarding to appear on-screen with James Brolin, Kristen Dunst, Penny Margolis (Miss America) and other stars.

How do acting and stunt work help me win fights? They give me a break from fight training. By helping me relax, they prevent me from getting stale and bored. After completing an acting job, I resume training, refreshed and more enthusiastic than ever.

Make It Happen

Now you have my top ten tips for winning fights. But if you're searching for secret submission holds or my favorite ways to beat opponents into oblivion, that's a topic for a future article. Instead, I've presented my most effective mind-set tools. These are ways to improve your self-discipline, perspective and motivation. For my tips to be effective, though, you must use them. What do you have to lose? Try them and you'll quickly improve your fighting. They'll make you a winner. And in grappling, it doesn't get any better than that.

Charlie Kohler is available for private or group classes and seminars. Phone: 619-206-3589. School Address: 941 Broadway, Suite N, El Cajon, CA 92021. Website: www.kccombat.com. Email: cjkohler25@home.com

BEST OF CFW — VOL. 1
GRAPPLING

GRAPPLING

The Magnificent Seven
The 7 Best Conditioning Exercises For Combat Athletes

Matt Furey, Photos by Zhannie Furey

Over the course of many years, I have learned hundreds of different body-weight conditioning exercises. Most require no equipment. Some, like pull-ups and rope climbing, do. These exercises are great for martial artists because they simultaneously increase strength, speed, endurance and flexibility while improving mental focus. When I began learning these exercises, I didn't simply observe and make notes. Not at all. I got into the thick of it and worked on doing each exercise to the best of my ability. And it was through this method that I formulated my list of the seven best conditioning exercises for combat sports.

Close Misses

As you read about the seven body-weight exercises I have selected, bear in mind that there are many exercises that missed the list by slight margins. Three missed by a fraction of a hair. At least a dozen more were only a point or two away. Also, there are many body-weight exercises that I believe increase strength even more than the selected seven. But because so many martial artists are not ready to start with them, they didn't make the list.

For example, in terms of developing powerful upper body strength, there isn't much that can compete with the muscle-ups and iron cross of gymnastics. Although rings are required to do these exercises (and most people don't have them), they are still incredible body-weight exercises. Make no mistake about it, when you're on the rings, it is YOU fighting against your own weight.

How many athletes can learn to do an iron cross muscle-up in one session? Or in a week? Or a month? It's not easy. And I, for one, began to seriously re-injure and aggravate a hibernating shoulder while trying. If the exercise injured me, and I train constantly, you can bet that it would cause others many problems as well. This not to say you shouldn't try or do it. Not at all. Just make sure you take into account any previous orthopedic injuries before beginning and pay close attention to the signals your body receives while trying.

Another example of an exercise that almost made the list is the gymnastic bridge, which I teach along with 50 other exercises in my book, *Combat Abs*. The gymnastic bridge is a fantastic total-body exercise that is even harder to master than the wrestler's bridge—and may have more benefits. Why isn't it on my list then? Because most people can't do it on day one. Most people have enough trouble doing reverse push-ups—and the gymnastic bridge goes a few steps beyond that. First of all, you fall into it from a standing start. Then you land on your palms with locked arms. Most people have a pronounced fear of falling—and falling backwards toward your head is even scarier.

Then there is an ingenious exercise that I invented a couple years ago called the *Furey One-Arm Hindu Push-up*. I created it because I had an injury to my right shoulder, and the pain was so severe I couldn't do a regular push-up without making things worse. So I began doing one-arm push-ups with my left arm. Then I wondered what I could do for variety—and that's when heaven cracked open her gates and the knowledge came to me like a bolt lighting. It was "voila" and "eureka" all at once.

Formulating the List
Making this list was not easy, and for the following reasons: a) I had to learn each exercise by actually doing it; b) I had to consider the injury potential of each exercise; c) I had to figure out which exercises were beyond the ability level of most athletes: d) I had to figure out which exercises were within the ability level of most athletes; e) I had to determine which exercises gave multiple benefits as I was especially interested in those that gave simultaneous improvement in strength, endurance and flexibility; f) I had to decide, based upon the above reasons, and based upon my own experience and the experiences of those who have learned from me, which exercises helped the athletes improve the most.

> **These exercises are great for martial artists because they simultaneously increase strength, speed, endurance and flexibility while improving mental focus.**

The 7 Best Bodyweight Exercises for Combat Athletes

1) WRESTLERS' BRIDGE: This is a tough one for many people who are uncoordinated and inflexible, but the benefits are enormous. I receive testimonial letters every day from someone who has greatly benefited from it. Even those who can't do the bridge the way it is explained in my book, *Combat Conditioning*, still benefit from doing the best they can. When you practice the wrestler's bridge, you will improve your posture, eliminate lower back and neck pain, improve digestion, and greatly increase your current level of stamina. That's saying a lot, especially when these benefits begin taking place before you've reached perfection. The mere act of giving the wrestlers' bridge your best effort works wonders.
Instructions: Lie on your back and arch until your forehead and nose touch the mat. Breathe deeply and hold for time. Use your hands for support as you learn if required.

2) HINDU SQUATS: When people do Hindu squats, their legs get bigger and stronger and lung capacity increases because of the deep breathing involved. The athlete will become more explosive. He'll have more energy while running and more spring in his step when simply walking around. Additionally, despite the criticism of this exercise by those who think it is bad for the knees, Hindu squats actually rehabilitate and strengthen the tendons of your knees and ankles. Many who have had nagging pain or previous injuries to these areas greatly improve and become pain free. This does NOT mean that Hindu squats are for everyone. There are always exceptions. But most people can

GRAPPLING

and should do this. Those who knock this exercise would be surprised to find out how wrong their assessment of them is.

Instructions: When doing the Hindu squat, begin with your arms straight out and parallel to the floor. Pull them into your chest like you're rowing a boat. Then bring them behind your buttocks and lower yourself to the ground. Touch your finger tips to the floor while keeping your back straight. Exhale, then swing your arms up, returning to the original position.

3) HINDU PUSH-UPS: Because Hindu push-ups build the upper body while simultaneously increasing flexibility in the spine, hips and shoulders, they have more benefits than regular push-ups. If someone has a chronic shoulder injury, I recommend that you train with a rubber cable power chest expander and the video I made to go, *The European Strand Pulling Challenge*. In many cases, after 2-4 weeks of training with the power chest expander, you'll probably be able to do Hindu push-ups without pain.

Instructions: Start with legs wider than your shoulders and your back straight. Push backward and look at your feet. Lower in a circular arc then curve your body and look to the ceiling. Finish by pushing back to the original position, but without bending your arms a second time.

4) ROPE CLIMB OR PULL-UPS: Climbing a rope improves strength throughout the entire body: It hits the hands, forearms, upper arms, back, shoulders, abs, legs and everything in-between. It isn't easy for those who can't do it, but persistence is well worth it. Once you can climb with hands and feet, switch to hands alone. Keeping in mind that most people don't have ropes, I recommend pull-ups as an alternative that is not as good, but important nonetheless. You

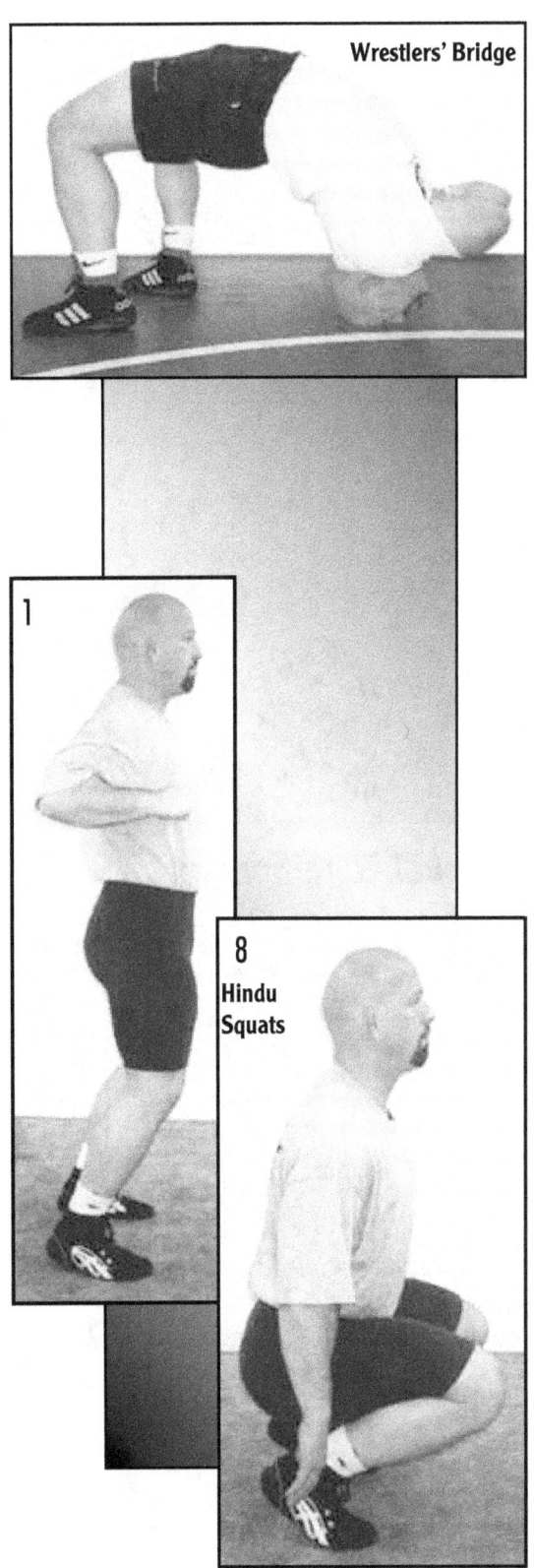

GRAPPLING

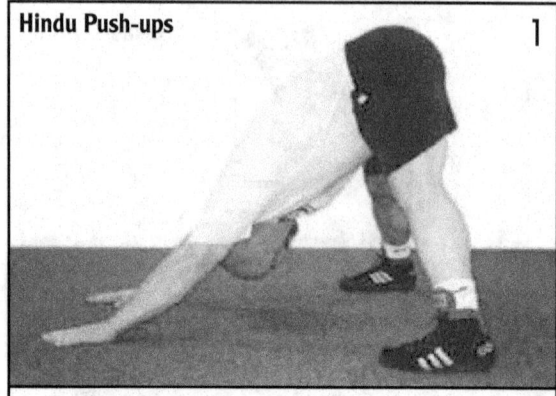

Hindu Push-ups

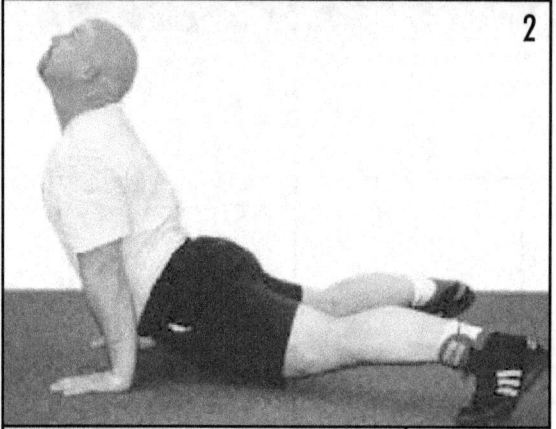

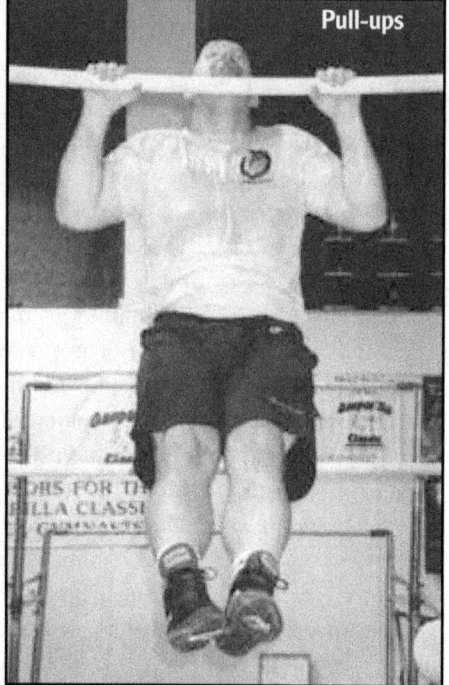

Pull-ups

Jackknife Sit-Ups

Combat Conditioning Fitness Test

If you're not used to doing the seven exercises in this article, and are not convinced that they are the stuff of legend, then take the following test. See if you can finish it, without cheating and without stopping, in 12 minutes.

1-minute back bridge

100 Hindu squats

50 Hindu push-ups;

3 climbs up a 20-foot rope (or three sets of 10 pull-ups)

25 jack-knife sit-ups

10 Reverse Pushups

1/4-Mile Bear Crawl

GRAPPLING

can do pull-ups on a variety of apparatus and in many different ways. For most people, this means a straight bar. I like to use gymnastic rings because, with my hands separated, all weaknesses are revealed. When doing pull-ups, be sure to use your thumbs. God gave them to you for a reason. You wouldn't try to climb a rope without thumbs, so ignore the advice of other "experts" who say to do pull-ups with a thumbless grip. **Instructions:** Grab the bar with an overhand or underhand grip. From a dead-hang position, pull upward until you chin is over the bar. Then lower yourself to the starting position and repeat until failure.

5) JACKKNIFE SIT-UPS: When you do a jackknife sit-up you are simultaneously working the entire abdominal region as well as strengthening the lower back and hip flexors. This exercise also helps improve digestion as the internal organs receive a well-needed massage from the muscle compression.
Instructions: Lie on your back with your arms stretched overhead. Simultaneously raise your upper and lower body off the floor. Touch your toes with your fingers when both your legs and arms are directly over your navel center. Lower and repeat.

6) REVERSE PUSH-UPS: Once this exercise is mastered, you're able to do the gymnastic bridge with ease. The key is being able to lock your elbows while arching your chest forward. When doing this exercise, begin with your upper back flat on the ground, then press up. Reverse push-ups work

Reverse Push-Ups

the arms, shoulders, lower back, hips, buttocks and legs.

Instructions: The ending position on the reverse pushups, when performed properly, is the same as the gymnastic bridge. However, you don't have to fall into it. Just lie on your back with your palms resting on the floor. Now arch and press your body upward and forward.

Bear Crawl

7) BEAR CRAWL: Whenever you think that bear crawling is simply another cardiovascular exercise, then try it for one-tenth of the distance you would normally run. If you normally run 2.5 miles, this means a good beginning-level bear crawl workout would be 1/4 mile. It won't be easy, that's for sure. Bear crawling works your heart and lungs in a big way, but it also strengthens your arms, shoulders, chest, back and legs. Consider that a half-ton grizzly can run down a rabbit, and do so while making cuts that surpass those of any NFL receiver. A grizzly also has remarkable endurance, allowing him to run down the quick and nimble deer. Once you've given this exercise a whirl, you'll know why it's so great.

Instructions: From a tripod position, begin running forward, moving your hands and feet just like a grizzly bear running in the wild. Be sure to breathe deeply. You'll need all the oxygen you can get.

Get Cracking

Sometimes it takes a 2x4 over the head to help pry open the mind contained within the human skull. These exercises are that 2x4. Get cracking and good luck.

Matt Furey is a world shuai-chiao kung-fu champion, NCAA wrestling champion and the author of "Combat Conditioning" and "Combat Abs". Each book is available for $29.95 plus $5 S&H. To order call 1.813.994.8267 or visit www.mattfurey.com.

GRAPPLING

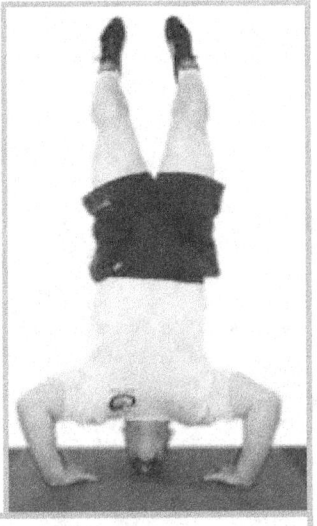

3 Exercises That Almost Made The List

These exercises may be perfect for you right now, but because they are too hard for many fighters just starting body-weight conditioning, it is better to start with a more basic routine—which believe me, is as hard as hell anyway.

1) Handstand Pushups:
In this exercise, kick into a hand-stand with your feet braced against a wall. Now lower yourself until your head touches the floor, then press back to the starting position.

2) The Furey One-Arm Hindu Push-up:
Put one hand on the ground and the other behind your back. Now with both legs wider than your shoulder-width, lower yourself in a circular manner, then press up and arch your back while looking to the ceiling. Then simply push back to the original position.

3) Gymnastic Bridge:
This exercise begins from a standing position. Place your hand over your head and lean backwards until your palms touch the floor. Keep your arms locked. Now bridge upward and forward, removing tension from your back and shoulders.

GRAPPLING

T.R. Goodman spots Damian Rhodes of the Atlanta Thrashers.

GRAPPLING

The Ultimate Training Camp

Wallid Ismail, Mark Kerr, and Bruce Buffer are just a few of the athletes, actors, and celebrities who swear by T.R. Goodman's intense regimen of hybrid training and conditioning.

Tami Goldsmith, Story & Photos

It's 6:45 a.m. on Monday morning and NHL star Chris Chelios, actor D.B. Sweeney, architect Frank Gehry and artist Peter Alexander arrive at T.R. Goodman's office. Later in the morning 20 more professional hockey players will arrive. Around lunch, Keanu Reeves stops by to say hello. In the early afternoon, James Caan will finish his session and walk with Goodman to Koo Koo Roo to grab some lunch. A few hours later MMA star Mark Kerr arrives around the same time as ring super-announcer Bruce Buffer. Somewhere in-between, Wallid Ismail joins in as well.

Is T.R. Goodman a Hollywood director, entertainment lawyer, or super-agent? Nope, he's the founder and brains behind Pro Camp, a revolutionary strength and conditioning training program geared towards professional athletes based out of the Venice Beach Gold's Gym in Southern California.

Pro Camp was initially formed in the early 1990s as a training program for professional athletes. T.R. Goodman's first client was Gabrielle Reece, the statuesque volleyball player and model. Word of mouth and promises of better athletic performance enticed players from the National Hockey League to enlist Goodman's services. His clientele now includes some of the best athletes in the world representing hockey, football, basketball, baseball, volleyball, and surfing.

Most recently, Goodman started a program for mixed martial arts competitors Mark Kerr and Wallid Ismail. Ring announcer Bruce Buffer trains with Goodman and recommended the workout regimen to Kerr, citing the positive results that Pro Camp offers. Goodman's affordable program, which takes between 60 and 90 minutes daily, is an elite and effective way to train for mixed martial arts competitions.

The effects of T.R. Goodman and Pro Camp's training can ultimately have a positive influence in the world of mixed martial arts by prolonging the careers of the athletes as well as increasing their fitness, flexibility, agility, and strength. Pro Camp is not only for professional athletes, but for any professional who takes their training seriously.

Q: When did you start Pro Camp?
A: In 1993. Volleyball star Gabrielle Reece was one of my first clients along with Alan May, who has since retired from hockey, and Chris Chelios, who is still playing in the NHL. I just asked them to give me an opportunity to show them what I could do for them. This was way before Gabby was famous.

T.R. Goodman

"Goodman's affordable program, which takes between 60 and 90 minutes daily, is an elite and effective way to train for mixed martial arts competitions."

Q: What is your background?
A: My college minor at Trinity College in Connecticut was related to athletics but my major was economics. My first job after graduation was with the school, and I found that I wasn't cut out for sitting behind a desk all day. I started to work part-time in a gym, and the way my mind works, I wanted to know everything. I wanted to learn how to do the maintenance on the equipment, I cleaned the bathrooms, and I helped out at the front desk.

I basically worked my way up from there. I graduated from Trinity College in 1983 and by 1984, I was working full-time in a gym. I learned as much as I could and started to put my own gym together. By the end of 1986 I had my own gym which was about 15,000 square feet, as well as another that was around 6,000 square feet, which was then merged with a bigger company. In October of 1990, I moved to Los Angeles. The concept of fitness in Connecticut and fitness in California was like night and day. When I first got into the fitness industry, people didn't know if it was going to be a fad, or if it would last. Fortunately, the fitness movement has spread all over the world.

GRAPPLING

Q: Why did you move to California?
A: All the fitness information we got back East came from California. A lot of my ideas were ahead of their time. So I thought, "Why do I want to keep banging my head against the wall out here? I'll come out where all the entertainment people and athletes are and start again." We now have players from hockey, football, basketball, baseball, and most recently mixed martial artists such as Wallid Ismail and Mark Kerr. When I was in Connecticut, I trained a few taekwondo practitioners who were trying out for the Olympic team—one of the kids became a first alternate. I understand martial arts so that helps me to relate to the specific physical needs of combat athletes. When I was a kid I took judo. I have a black belt in a combination of gojo-ryu karate and wing chun kung-fu from my teacher, Duke Grise and my other other instructor, Calsanz Hernandez, who is still in Connecticut

Q: How did the MMA athletes hear about you?
A: Wallid was the first guy who approached me. He was in and out of the gym a lot, back and forth to Brazil. He watched our approach to training and one day we started talking. I was excited because I like watching the various competitions, such as the UFC. So that's how we started a relationship. Mark Kerr came to us by way of a referral from Bruce Buffer. Bruce started his training early in 2000.

Q: Does your program also include diet?
A: We have a brilliant nutritionist on staff, Alfred Krautgartner. What makes him so exceptional is that he possesses an unbelievable ability to interpret blood work—which is an objective biochemical measure of how you are eating and how your body processes the food you consume. This is an invaluable tool, because when you are evaluating which supplements to take or the effect of your eating habits, it is a true indicator of what's going on.

Q: Do you measure flexibility as well?
A: Yes, always. It's important to know if the client's hips are even, do his or her shoulders line up the way they are supposed to? Is the spine straight, are the hips too tight, do they have the right range of motion? There are two ways we measure flexibility—passive and active. Active is when you do it yourself. Passive is when we take you through a range of motion when you are more relaxed.

Q: What is the structure of the training program?
A: There are four basic phases which are modified for the needs of each individual client. In phase one, we increase the range of motion as much as possible. Not necessarily just stretching, but getting the body to move in an uninhibited way by building endurance and stability. In phase two we work on increasing strength. In phase three, we put everything together in circuit or explosive-type training. Phase four is an in-season maintenance program.

Q: How long does each phase last?
A: It depends on the individual as well as the cycle we have to work with. For example, when Mark Kerr came to us before the Abu Dhabi competition, we had less than 8 weeks from the time he stepped through the door before the fight occurred. The way we organize the workout is to go from the day of the fight and work backwards. Depending on the fighter's recoverability, 5 to 10 days before the competition they should back off and just do things to maintain, so the body can be healed up before the fight. So originally what looked like 8 was reduced to 6 weeks.

Josh Dempsey and Lou Ferrigno

Bruce Buffer

Goodman and Caan share a laugh.

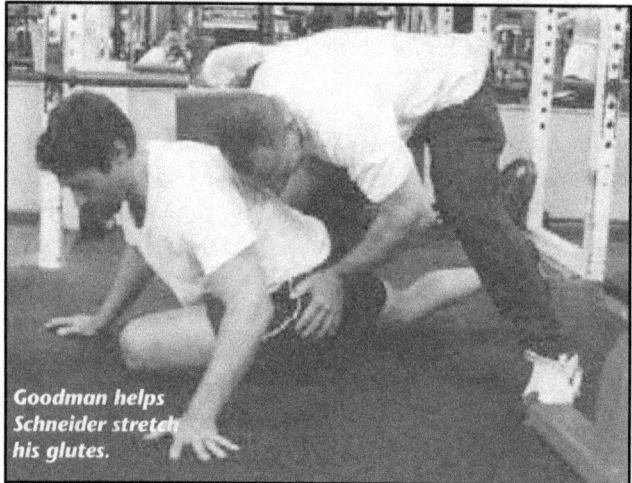

Goodman helps Schneider stretch his glutes.

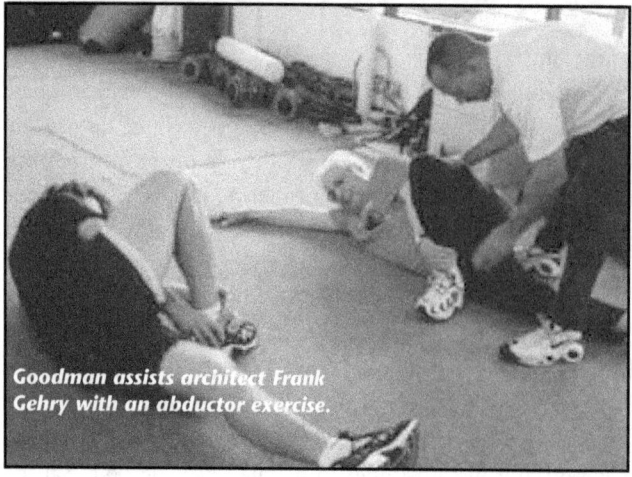

Goodman assists architect Frank Gehry with an abductor exercise.

Then, you have a fighter like Wallid, who likes to reduce his strength and conditioning routine about 6 weeks prior to his event, and increase more of the sports-specific workouts such as boxing, wrestling, and jiu-jitsu. The ratio of what we do from a weight and strength-training side has to back off due to the prioritization. So it is better if we know in advance when they will be competing.

Q: Do you customize each fighter's training routine?
A: There are a few different factors that figure into the workouts. Some techniques will be similar. Even though they have different body types and fighting styles, they all have shoulder joints, knee joints, hip joints, et cetera. These guys are beat up—there's a lot of trauma in their bodies whether they are a martial artist or a hockey player. When they come to us, most athletes aren't even at zero—they're at negative because they have so much trauma in their systems from participating in their sport. Over the years they have injuries, and most of them never do the things that they need to do to completely get rid of the injury, so they find ways to compensate.

GRAPPLING

T.R. Goodman poses with some satisfied clients.

One of our first objectives is to try to help get the trauma out of their system. We educate them about their injuries and how to train properly. A lot of times they don't even know that a problem exists because they've compensated for so long.

What can happen when there is trauma is that certain muscles that are supposed to do one function might be lessened, or other ones might be enhanced because they are compensating for something that can't be done. What we want to accomplish is to try to get them to move the way they should move in an uninhibited way. That's one of our objectives. Then you have to look at the athlete's personality and his style. I like to watch tapes of them fighting. I want to see a great fight they had, as well as a fight that they didn't think was good.

Q: Why?
A: To see what happened and what ingredients were there. Aside from winning or losing, why did they think they had a great fight in this situation and why a bad fight in another? In the fight game anyone can get caught by accident and lose while they're on the top of their game. And just because you win, it doesn't necessarily mean you were at your best. There are certain things you can pick up in a tape, watching the fights. I'm not looking at their fighting technique. I'm looking to see how their body moves. What's their conditioning like? What's their breathing rhythm like? All these different components are visible when you watch the tape. Why is a fighter more susceptible to getting hit more on one side of his head than the other? If he has a hip flexor strain or an abdominal tear on one side he might not be able to move the same way. You look at all those different factors and come up with a training plan for a particular athlete. You have to take a look at their style and personality. Wallid likes to feel certain things going into a fight. Mark likes to feel other things going into a fight. As an athlete, you find certain sensations that let you know you're ready. So the general formula we use is similar, but how we manipulate the specific variables for each fighter are different.

Q: So fight tapes help?
A: They can be useful tools for the fighters to refer to. The last time the Trinidad fight was on, Mark and Wallid came over to watch. From the television, I could visually show them things that I was

T.R. Goodman watching Mathieu Schneider of the L.A. Kings perform squats on the balance board.

Goodman performing medicine ball twists with Mark Kerr.

All of Goodman's clients have enjoyed positive results. The growing number of professional athletes he trains is a testament to his success.

"I swear by T.R. and the methods he uses. It's no picnic, but it's all worth it in the end."

—Chris Chelios, Detroit Red Wings, recently selected as Captain of the 2002 U.S. Olympic Men's Ice Hockey Team.

"T.R. Goodman is the most intelligent trainer that I've ever had the experience of knowing. He watches the mechanics of my sport and really applies that to my training."

—Gabrielle Reece, volleyball star and top model.

"The guidance and mental push I receive to stay in peak athletic condition from them is invaluable to me, especially with my travel schedule. Guru T.R. Goodman and trainer Kurt Elder design my training to keep me fine-tuned from the inside out, with emphasis on the internal structural strength and endurance that allows me to train with the pro athletes in their off-season time, such as doing conditioning training with members of the Los Angeles Kings and other major athletes."

—Bruce Buffer, ring super-announcer.

GRAPPLING

T.R. Goodman and Wallid Ismael

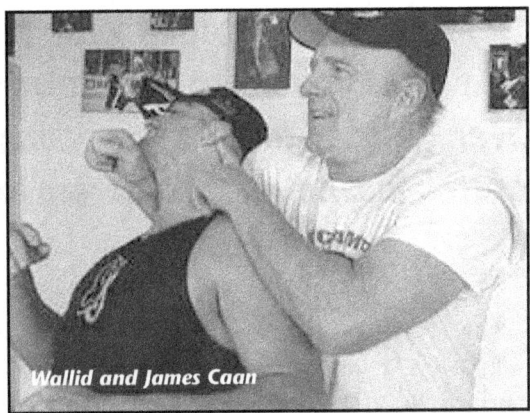

Wallid and James Caan

trying to get them to understand the first time they went through the circuit training. When they saw the fight, they could see the openings, and their awareness increased. Now when they go to practice, they start to feel it themselves.

When you watch a fight you'll see what these guys do when they start to compensate—especially when they start to fatigue. In boxing, for example, Felix Trinidad never overexerts himself. I'm not sure he's completely conscious of it, but he stays within a heart rate range, and he's trained himself to do that. In his early days, George Foreman did not pace himself in his fights, and that's how Ali knocked him out. He overexerted, and got uptight.

If you're an athlete in a combat sport, and you're in trouble, you're automatically going to burn twice as much energy. A competitor who has his opponent in trouble does not have to overexert, he has to stay within a certain heart range. If a competitor is able to withstand a barrage, then his opponent is done. You see this a lot in the UFC when a fighter is overly aggressive when he comes out—such as Kevin Randleman. If you can withstand his initial attack, he will run out of gas, because he exerts too much energy so early on. This happens in all sports from horse racing to boxing. The important thing is to pace yourself, and know the proper heart range to stay in during competition.

We teach athletes to pace themselves through the circuit training during our third phase. For regular athletes, we give them a maintenance program to follow during the season. Mixed martial artists are not the same because they have a one-day, one-event competition and need to relax for awhile before they come back to train.

Q: Do you feel that there is enough recovery time between fights for MMA athletes?
A: Not really. The fights happen so quickly that there is a short period of time to improve yourself. Right now, it looks to me like the cycle between fights is 8-10 weeks, which is not enough time for the body to recuperate. This is problematic and a fighter's career will be shortened. If the body does not have enough time to recover after a fight, it will wear down. I was listening to Tito Ortiz describe his training routine after one of his UFC victories. He might be able to get away with training 6-8 hours a day now because he's in his mid-20s. It is doubtful, however, that he will be able to keep up that type of training for an extended period of time, for too many more years, because it's way too hard on the body. His training routine will shorten his career.

Look what's going on in pro-wrestling right now—the number of guys who are getting injured. That's due to the type of schedule they keep. It's too rigorous, even if the moves are choreographed. We

GRAPPLING

"A lot of athletes wrongly use fight training and sparring as a way to condition themselves because they haven't been exposed to the more advanced and modern methods of training, nutrition, and recovery."

are trying to make our athletes understand that aspect of conditioning. A boxing coach, for example, will spend a lot of time working on physical conditioning. That will reduce the time he can spend teaching the actual techniques of boxing. So if you train properly with a conditioning coach, then that doesn't have to happen and you can use your boxing coach to teach you the techniques of boxing.

Martial or fight training should be used to improve technique—not to condition. If you look at someone at the skill level of Wallid in jiu-jitsu, or Mark in wrestling, there is no reason for these guys to go into the gym and start traumatizing their bodies by over-training. They should only practice certain skills and techniques in order to improve themselves overall, not for conditioning. A lot of athletes wrongly use fight training and sparring as a way to condition themselves because they haven't been exposed to the more advanced and modern methods of training, nutrition, and recovery. That's the biggest thing that we teach—how to get that balance.

Actor D.B. Sweeney training with the balnce board at Pro Camp.

Q: Does your training add to fighting skills?

A: Our goal is get a guy into a position where he can do what he wants for as long as he wants. After that, it's just a matter of skill on the part of the athlete. We're not trying to teach someone how to throw a punch or how to wrestle—but we can expose him to certain stretches, or range of motion exercises, that will enable him to perform movements better when he's on the mat or in the ring. We are basically getting the body so it can do what the athlete wants it to do without breaking down. The mixed martial artists need their boxing, wrestling, or jiu-jitsu coaches for the specific skill sets that they want to focus on. Even if you look at martial arts on a beginning level, it's not that the beginner doesn't understand the concept of what the teacher wants them to do.

Everyone can look at a kick and can see the height they want to reach. The biggest inhibiting factor is having the strength and flexibility to lift your leg the way you want to. For most people, the sheer physical weight of their leg is too much for the support muscles to actually be able to lift it. It takes years of repetition of lifting and lowering the leg which allows a person to advance from the lower belt levels. Unfortunately, in some situations, you find ways to compensate, which can lead to other problems such as muscle tears, lower back pain, uneven hips, and sore hip flexors. This all comes from not building the right strength base.

That's why, in Phase I, we work on strengthening the internal body and building endurance before we work on increasing strength. It is very important to lay down the proper foundation. If you go through the movement of throwing a punch, there's a certain symbiotic relationship that occurs between the muscles. At a certain point, one set of muscles is dominant, at another point, they start to fade. If that synergy isn't right then compensation will occur. When we see mixed martial artists, most of their fighting style is a result of compensations for injuries they have sustained previously. It's not the way they ideally want to move. Do you want to get rid of one problem or create two?

The difference that I see between athletes who succeed and the athletes who don't succeed has very little to do with talent as much as it has to do with the work ethic and what's going on inside their heads.

For more information about Pro Camp write to Pro Camp Athletics, 356 Hampton Drive, Venice, CA 90291, or call 310.664.9908.

BEST OF CFW ———— VOL.1
GRAPPLING

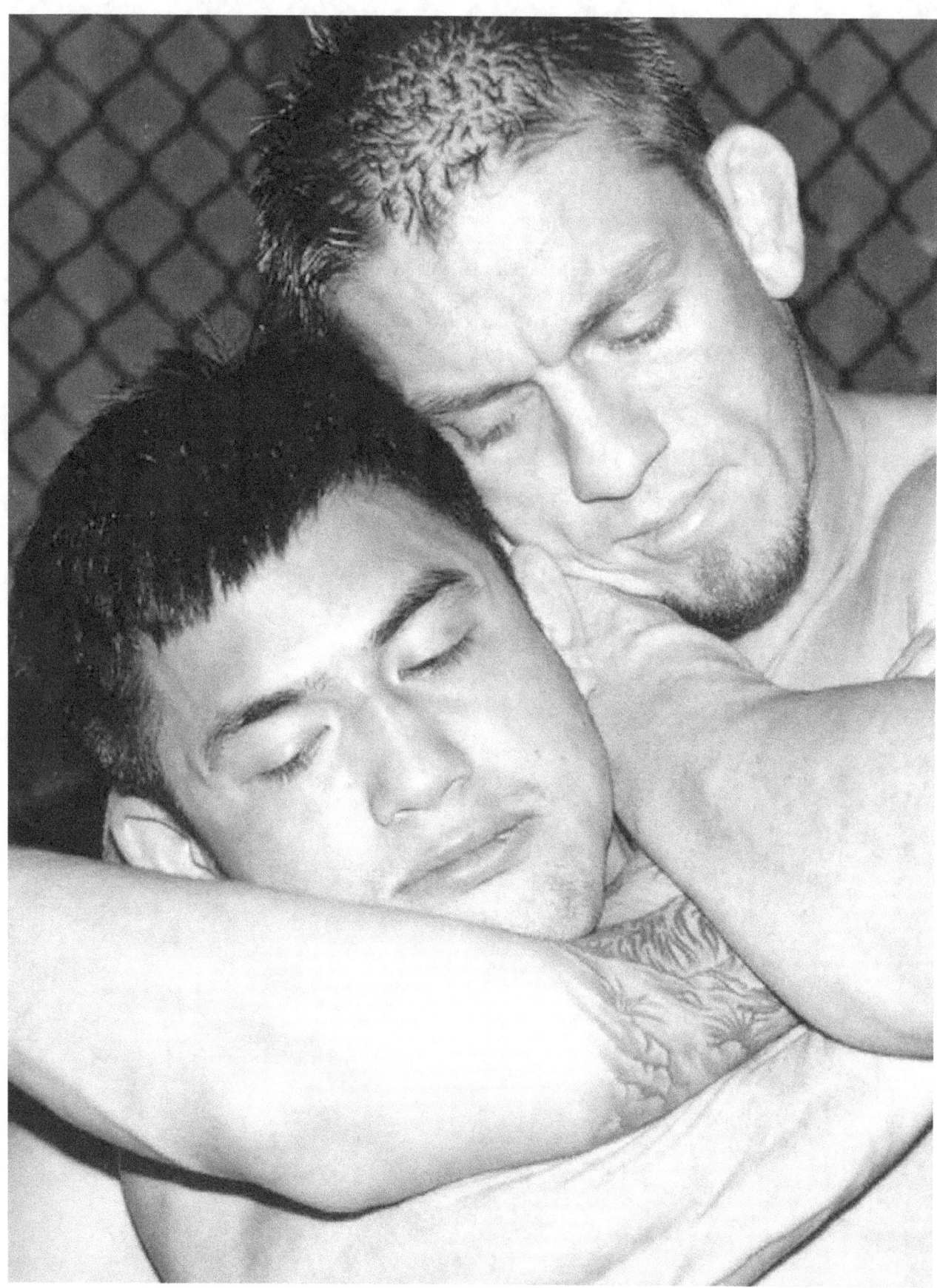

Chris Brennan
The Robin Hood of Mixed Martial Arts

Taking knowledge from those "rich" in technique and giving it to those with a "poor" understanding of Brazilian jiu-jitsu, Chris Brennan has gained a reputation as one of mixed martial arts most successful fighters and teachers.

Loren Franck

Chris Brennan thought long and hard about the gift he had just received. The date was October 12, his 30th birthday, a perfect time to reflect. The current King of the Cage middleweight champ didn't receive a custom Rolex or a bright red Ferrari, though he could buy both. He couldn't unwrap his gift, either, because it arrived without ribbon and festive paper. That morning, as Brennan sat quietly in his Irvine, California, fighting school, he reflected on everything he has gained from mixed martial arts. And then it hit. He had reaped the most from grappling, not by amassing his impressive 11-4-1 fight record and three King of the Cage titles, but by giving the sport away.

For slightly more than four years, Brennan has been taking valuable grappling knowledge from the rich (himself) and giving it to the poor (his students). "That's my real satisfaction in mixed martial arts," insists the 5'8" 170-pound Brennan, who recently dropped five pounds because of weight-class restrictions. "Since my first day of mixed-martial-arts training, my main goal has been to be a great teacher." But *Grappling* had its own birthday surprise for the ambitious fighter: an in-depth interview. Always eager to share his treasure chest of knowledge about the sport he loves, he discussed his career, his unusual training methods and his September 29, 2001 upset win over Steve Burger.

Q: What got you started in mixed martial arts?
A: I had boxed a little, and one day my coach told me about some Brazilians who could take you down and submit you at will, which sounded a little unusual. Well, those Brazilians turned out to be the Gracies. So in 1993 I went to the Gracie Academy in Torrance, California. Sure enough, they could submit anyone at any time, and that really shocked me. They even let me wear boxing gloves and swing away. I was a decent boxer, but I didn't land one punch before I was on my butt with my arms locked out and my neck choked. I was a scrappy fighter in high school, but I never knew how to fight. I wanted to learn, though, and after seeing the Gracies in action, I was hooked. My first fight came two years later.

Q: How long did you train with the Gracies?

A: I trained four years with Royce Gracie, then lived in Brazil for a year while training with Jacare. Upon returning to the United States, I trained at Rickson Gracie's school for a year. But I never met him, not even once, so I quit going there because I was paying for Rickson but never seeing him. Shortly afterward, I flew my friend Roger Brookings from Brazil to Southern California, and we trained in my garage every day for a year. Then I opened my own school, met Marco Ruas, and trained with him for two years, although he won't admit it. I've run my own school, the Next Generation Fighting Academy, for a little over four years, and it's doing very well.

Q: Have you trained in any traditional martial arts?

A: No, just boxing and Brazilian jiu-jitsu.

Q: Have any special coaches or personal trainers especially helped your career?

A: Chuck Williams. He's my strength-and-conditioning coach. A two-time Mr. Universe, he's also a sports psychologist and has helped build my self-confidence. I'm a much better fighter because of it. During most of my fighting career, I've lacked self-confidence right before my fights. Too often I tell myself, "This is my last time. I can't do it anymore."

Rollover Shoulder Lock
Chris Brennan fights off his opponent who has shot in for a single-leg takedown (1). Going to a tripod position to off-balance his opponent (2), Brennan rolls forward while keeping control of the arm (3). Coming to an upright position (4), Brennan applies pressure to the arm with his stomach for the shoulder lock (5).

Q: You're in great shape. What's your conditioning program?
A: I was a bodybuilder at age 19 and was a lot bigger than I am now—muscular but not very agile. I don't weight train much anymore, but when I do, I lift light weights and keep my repetitions high. I prefer isometrics, plyometrics, pull-ups, push-ups and sit-ups. I also do explosive cardio work that pushes me to the limit. I recently began training before fights in Big Bear, a popular Southern California mountain resort. My last time there, I ran from the bottom to the top of the Snow Summit ski run. It begins at 7,000 feet and climbs to 8,400 feet. What a workout!

Q: What about your everyday cardio training?
A: There's a hill of soft beach sand in Dana Point. It's 100 feet high at a 45-degree angle. The record is 70 times in one day; mine is 50. It's a grueling hill. And twice a week I run the nearly vertical stairs at "1,000 Steps" in Laguna Beach. Talk about challenging. I also do treadmill work, straight live boxing, and train in my school's King of the Cage octagon. That's the best cardio workout because it's the same cardio used for fighting.

> "I was a scrappy fighter in high school, but I never knew how to fight. I wanted to learn, though, and after seeing the Gracies in action, I was hooked. My first fight came two years later."

Q: Let's switch to your fighting experience. Who was your toughest opponent?
A: Pat Militech, because we've had three wars. The first was a 20-minute draw in September '97. The second, two months later, was a 30-minute split decision. Everybody said I won, but we fought in Davenport, Iowa, his hometown. You know how that goes. Our third fight was a March '98 UFC battle in New Orleans, which I lost in about 10 minutes.

Q: Why were those three fights so difficult?
A: They were my third, fourth and sixth fights, but they were his 18th, 19th and 21st, so he had experience on me. I wasn't worried during the first two, though, because I had nothing to lose. But I was very nervous at the UFC because, until then, my goal had been just to compete in the UFC. I was too content being there and didn't have the killer instinct I have now. Militech is an exciting fighter now, but back then he was a stale, baiting fighter who tried to hold opponents down. If I could relive that fight, I'd be more aggressive and more active. He makes everybody fight his fight, so I'd make him play my game.

Q: Would you say you have an aggressive fighting style?
A: I'm an extremely aggressive fighter. Out of 11 wins, nine are submissions, one's a knockout and one's a decision. All of my victories were in the first round except two, which came one minute into the second round. Aggressive is the way I am, the way I train and the way I fight. I put pressure on my opponents every second. Sometimes that works against me, though, because my losses came within the first five minutes. But I'll either kill you or be killed quickly. People tell me I'm also relentless. When I go for something, I attack until it's mine. That doesn't work for everybody, but it works for me.

"If I have the cardio conditioning to go 100 percent throughout a fight, I don't think anyone can beat me. Remember, I'm aggressive and relentless."

GRAPPLING

Q: When you fought Steve Burger last September 29 in San Jacinto, California, at KOTC, your victory surprised a lot of people. Were you surprised?

A: No, I wasn't. It was the first time we fought each other, but I thought I'd win because I was so well prepared. If I have the cardio conditioning to go 100 percent throughout a fight, I don't think anyone can beat me. Such conditioning enables me to pressure my opponents nonstop. Remember, I'm aggressive and relentless. I trained cardio extra hard in Big Bear two weeks before our fight, so I was ready to go the maximum three five-minute rounds. Big Bear cleared my mind, too, and prepared me to push the fight to the limit without getting tired. And it did go the distance.

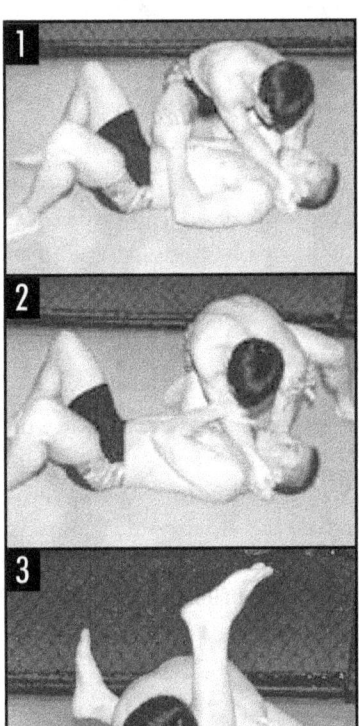

Q: Why was Burger was favored to win?

A: He had recently fought in the UFC, and three weeks before our fight he submitted the seventh-ranked Shooto competitor. Also, I was inactive for seven months, so Burger fought more often than I did. He fought top-name guys and handled them well. Plus, some people judge me harshly by my loses. Take my fight with Joe Hurley, for example. I had to lose 13 pounds before we fought, but I wasn't told until the night before. It was my first time cutting weight. People thought I lacked ability, but I was sick the day of the fight. They saw me and thought, "If Brennan lost to Hurley like that, Burger will kill him."

Q: Were you in top shape when you fought Burger?

A: Yes, I was very healthy. I shocked the hell out of him. He probably expected a quick and easy victory, but instead suffered a long and painful beating. I pursued him nonstop for 15 minutes, stood up at the end of the fight and wasn't even breathing hard. I was the aggressor throughout the match,

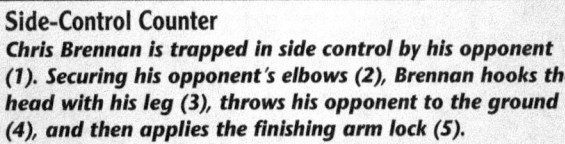

Side-Control Counter
Chris Brennan is trapped in side control by his opponent (1). Securing his opponent's elbows (2), Brennan hooks the head with his leg (3), throws his opponent to the ground (4), and then applies the finishing arm lock (5).

83

punching and moving the whole time, but I wasn't tired. Sure, my mouth was dry, but I could have easily gone another two rounds. If it were a UFC five-round championship, I would have easily dominated the next two rounds.

Q: What were you thinking when the fight began?
A: I was confident but a little nervous. When I compete at King of the Cage, most of my 180 students are there cheering for me, so I feel pressured to win. Before a match, I never worry about getting hurt. I worry about disappointing others, which should be the last thing on my mind. But I don't earn my living by fighting. My school provides most of my income, so I feel pressure when my students watch me fight. When my bout with Burger started, though, that pressure was behind me, and I felt very confident.

Q: Were you ahead from the start?
A: I dominated Burger all three rounds. He never put up an offense. In the third round, he tried to guillotine me, and though the announcers panicked, I was never in danger. In fact, I guillotined him in the third round too, but he escaped. I knew I'd win the fight, but I didn't think I'd dominate him so much.

Q: What was your strategy?
A: We started standing. After Burger struck twice, I kicked his leg; and when he approached aggressively on foot, I took him down. Passing his guard and planning to take an arm, I moved to his side and circled, but he defended himself. Rather than submit him immediately, I wanted to maintain my position, beat him up a little and then submit him. All of my opponents have been good wrestlers, so I usually wind up on the bottom. But I was on top of Burger the entire fight.

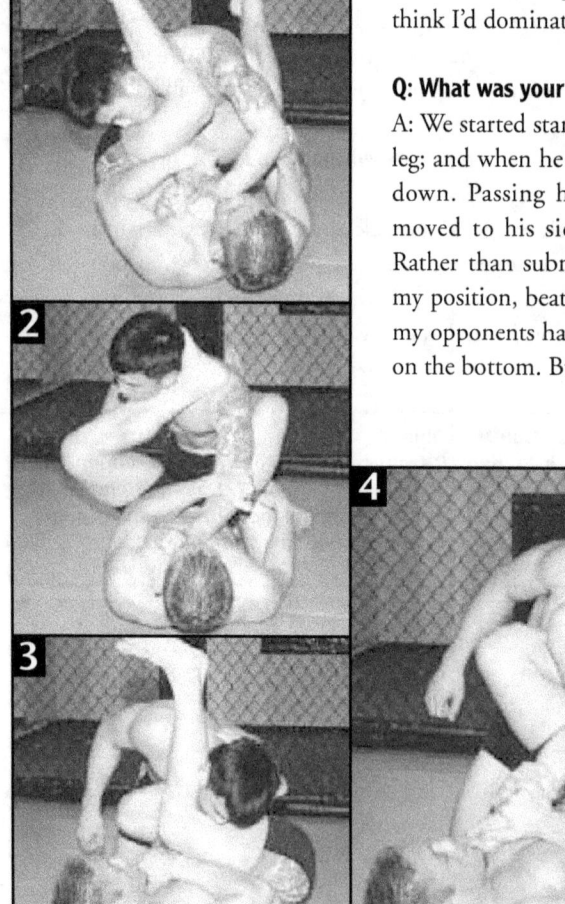

Reverse Guard Arm-Lock
Chris Brennan fights off an attempted guard pass (1). His shifts his knee to the outside and pressures his opponent's face to create space (2). He then release his far leg from his opponent's and passes it to the reverse side of his guard (3). Extending his body, he applies the finishing arm lock for the submission (4).

GRAPPLING

Q: When you realized you could remain on top, what did you do?
A: I punched and elbowed his head. At various times, I was halfway or completely past his guard. I was even in it twice. He tried a few arm locks and was very crafty. As the fight evolved, he was a bloody mess, but he never stopped trying to arm lock or triangle me. His heart was gigantic. In the third round, he and I stood in our corners to start over. As he turned to face me, I could see how bloody he was. Yet his mouth was closed, and he looked ready to fight. Breathing easily through his nose, he seemed relaxed and ready for more punishment. I could tell he was a very experienced and capable fighter. After the first round, though, he lost heart because the bout didn't go as planned.

Q: What do you think did him in?
A: A Golden Gloves boxer and traditional martial artist, Burger was good on his feet and on the ground. But he was susceptible to takedowns, and this worked against him. I took him down six times in three rounds, and I'm not a wrestler.

Q: Is there anything you would have done differently? Was there anything you did right but would have pursued further?
A: I would have stood up with him more. He's a good boxer but so am I, and I know when a guy's good on his feet. Nobody wants to take a punch. I'd rather fight on the ground where I'm more comfortable. But if my opponent wants to ground fight, that's when I test my standing skills.

Q: OK, imagine it's the year 2111. You're 40 years old, not 30, and you're looking back on your career. Any regrets? Will you still be fighting at 40?
A: I definitely don't want to fight when I'm 40. If I compete throughout my 30s, that would be long enough. I have a thriving school and a terrific grappling team. Of the nine guys fighting under me, several are destined to become big names. As time progresses, I plan to spend more time on their fighting careers and less on mine. We all train together now, but it's hard for me to push them and myself simultaneously. Before I retire, however, I want to win more fights and cop another UFC title.

Q: To do that, what if you had to sacrifice some teaching time?
A: Believe me, I won't. The more experienced I become, the more important my students are to me. I've always loved to teach, even if it was showing my little brother how to tie his shoes, and I've always been a good teacher. From my earliest days at the Gracie Academy, I've wanted to be an excellent teacher more than everything else. I love to watch my students succeed. That's the mark of a great teacher. The way to succeed in mixed martial arts isn't to grab all the fame and fortune possible. It's to teach. Watching my students succeed in grappling and in life is a priceless gift, and I wouldn't trade it for anything.

Chris Brennan may be contacted for classes, seminars, or fight bookings at the Next Generation Fighting Academy, *15791 Rockfield Blvd., Suite D, Irvine, CA 92618;* (949) 768-3580.

GRAPPLING

Luca Atalla winning the 1998 Pan Am Lightweight title.

Luca Atalla with Rickson Gracie.

Taking it on the chin from Renzo Gracie at the Pride video game shoot.

Luca Atalla laughing with Helio Gracie.

A Talk with Luca Atalla, Editor of Gracie Magazine

Luca Atalla is a black belt in Brazilian jiu-jitsu and one of the pioneers in mixed martial arts journalism. Since the beginning of the sport, he has covered countless events in numerous countries.

Eddie Goldman

It's not every day that you can sit down and talk with a wise man. In mixed martial arts, this is even more difficult, as there is a shortage of wise men and women, and what often tries to pass as wisdom is about as profound as a late-night infomercial. Yet I did have that chance recently at the Grapplers Quest tournament in New York.

Little did I know as I was watching the advanced 170-pound division that one of the participants, who was busy choking someone out, is an old friend, Luca Atalla, editor of the Rio de Janeiro-based *Gracie Magazine*. Luca is not only a black belt in Brazilian jiu-jitsu, but also one of the pioneers in mixed martial arts journalism. He has been there from the beginning, and we have talked and consulted each other in countless events in numerous countries. So after he got done applying a nice rear naked choke, I flagged him down to get his views on a wide number of topics.

For those who have not seen *Gracie Magazine*, although it is mainly a Portuguese-language publication, its Web site does have news and features in both English and Portuguese. "My dream is to put the magazine in the United States," Luca said. "But for a while the only thing I can do is let the Americans read the web site. So I'm trying to make all efforts to put all news in English as well." The Gracie Magazine web site address is http://www.gracie-magazine.com/.

Much of that news in recent years has involved an unexpected topic: a string of losses by members of the Gracie family in mixed martial arts to Kazushi Sakuraba in Pride. Luca had a lot to say about this, and each of the fights that Sakuraba had defeated a Gracie.

"Everybody is learning the sport right now," Luca explained. "With the television, with the tapes, it's very hard to show something new. So now it's not a matter of style of the fight. It's just a matter of the conditioning, of heart, and of course technique. But you have to mix technique with conditioning, very good conditioning, and very good heart. So about Sakuraba's fights against the Gracies, each fight he won for a different reason."

The first was the loss by Royler Gracie at Pride 8 on Nov. 21, 1999, by a referee stoppage because of an armlock at 28:16 of a scheduled 30-minute fight. "In the first fight against Royler," Luca said,

(L-R) Claudio Coelho, Nelson Monteiro, Ricardo Moraes, Adilson Bita, Luca Atalla, and Sean Alverez at Rings.

Luca Atalla training hard with Shiek Tahnoon.

"he was much heavier than Royler. And Royler's technique couldn't go beyond the weight difference." Sakuraba outweighed Royler by about 40 pounds, and that fight was supposed to be declared a draw if it went the full 30 minutes. Royler protested the stoppage, saying he was unhurt, and many agreed, but the decision stood. In any case, Sakuraba did dominate that fight.

Next was the fight against Royce Gracie in the Pride Grand Prix tournament on May 1, 2000, in which Rorion Gracie threw in the towel after a total of 90 minutes and six grueling rounds. "The second fight against Royce," Luca said, "Sak showed he had more endurance than Royce. They fought a pretty close fight the whole time. But he showed he had more conditioning to go more and more. And Royce had to give up."

Then there was the classic battle between Renzo Gracie and Sakuraba at Pride 10 on August 27, 2000. In that fight, Sakuraba defeated Renzo by referee stoppage at 9:43 of the second round, meaning with just 17 seconds remaining, after Sakuraba got an inverted Kimura armlock on Renzo and Renzo dislocated arm.

"Against Renzo," Luca philosophized, "I think he got his only real opportunity in the fight, so he was very, very opportunist. But the fight was very close as well and it was just a matter of one move that decided the fight. So I think that if they fight again, it could be a different result."

On Ryan's fight, Luca took a different tack. In that 10-minute bout at Pride 12 on Dec. 23, 2000, Sakuraba won a unanimous decision. "And against Ryan," Luca said, "I think Ryan was totally unprepared—it wasn't the time for Ryan to fight against Sakuraba. It was just his second professional fight, and Sakuraba has like 20 fights, so it made the difference."

Luca concluded, "You got to be professional, especially in the conditioning training, and the technical study." He pointed out how UFC and Pride fighter Ricardo Almeida, who is Renzo's student and one of the instruc-

Hang loose, brudda!

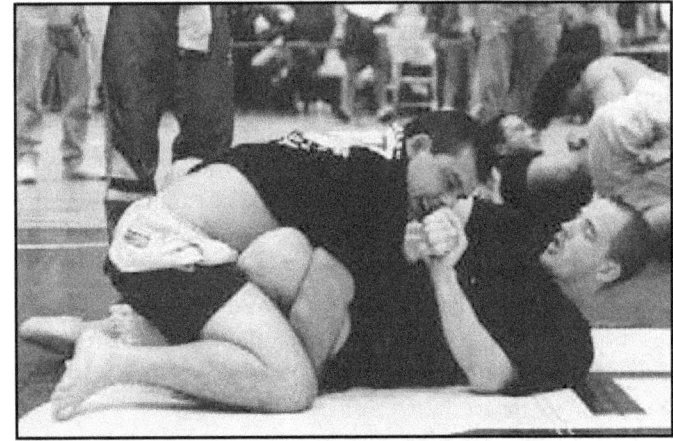

Luca Atalla winning a November 1998 NAGA tournament.

Luca Atalla receiving the 1996 Pan Am Light Heavyweight gold medal.

tors at his academies, has been training at a facility in New Jersey that caters to professional athletes from many sports.

That facility is located in Fair Lawn, New Jersey, and is run by Martin Rooney. It focuses on athletic performance training, and currently trains athletes from the New York Giants football team as well as other NFL players, the NJ/NY Metrostars soccer team, several major league baseball players, thousands of high school athletes in New Jersey, and a list of fighters including Renzo and Rodrigo Gracie, Ricardo and Flavio Almeida, Sean Alvarez, John Rallo, and boxer David Telesco.

"I've never seen such professional work in mixed martial arts before," Luca commented on the training there. "So he had several kinds of ways to push the athletes to make the fighter an athlete. So we will see the result."

Luca also saw the need to tailor one's training and techniques to the specific rules of the fight promotion. "In the tactical area," he said, "you have to study because it's very different to fight in UFC and Pride." And here he made one of his strongest comments.

"I'm totally against the cage," Luca argued. "I think the cage holds the fights. When you fight in the ring, you get much more movement. In the cage you have a problem when somebody takes the other guy down. He just pulls to the cage and stays there. And it's bad for technique. It's bad for the guy in the guard to try some moves like arm bars, sweeps, and anything, because they are always held by the cage."

He went on, "And I'm against the cage also because it's kind of hard for the people, the audience, to watch in the stadium. I know the tradition of the UFC is the cage. But I think they have to think about it because the cage is really against the sport. But if you are going to fight in the cage, you must be prepared for this kind of fight. It's a really different fight from fighting in a ring."

We also discussed the training injury to Vitor Belfort, who had been scheduled to fight Tito Ortiz at UFC 33, but gashed his arm in a freak accident as it went through a window as, ironically, he was training for techniques used in a cage. Vitor was training with long-time boxing coach Al Stankie and former U.S. Greco-Roman wrestling national champion and UFC fighter Darrell Gholar for this fight.

"Vitor, in the last fights in Pride, didn't show much of his boxing," Luca observed. "But now against Tito, he thought he had to improve, to use those skills again. So he got Al Stankie to train him. He was close to him a long time before the fight. And he was smart in getting a good wrestler to train him, because Tito is a good wrestler. But I think with good training, good orientation, Vitor could avoid Tito's takedowns. So it was very smart on Vitor's part putting those guys to train him." There is talk that Vitor might finally get his chance to fight Tito in early 2002, although nothing has been signed yet.

We also talked about the photo of Vitor's injury that appeared on the ADCC News Page and the accompanying article I wrote about it. "It was a good surprise that you are working for ADCC News as well as *Grappling Magazine*," Luca said. "We are missing you in Brazil, and eYada was the only live talk show we had. But unfortunately the thing got down, and now we have one of the first mixed martial arts journalists again in the business."

It's good to know that I still have some friends in such influential places. Whether you agree or disagree with his perspective, Luca Atalla is not only one of the good guys in mixed martial arts, but also one of the most perceptive analysts of this business.

And to tie up loose ends, no, Luca didn't win that division in which he was competing at the Grapplers Quest. "I just came here to watch Flavio's fight," Luca said. "And then I just decided to fight. And I had this opportunity, and I took that [laughs]." But after just one match, Luca stepped aside. "I just did one fight because Renzo's student was in the same final against me, and I wasn't here to fight against my friends of the same academy. And then I decided to give up my place to him, to let him fight in the finals." The grappler Luca was referring to was Joe Scarola of Renzo Gracie's academy. Joe went on to capture this division, while Luca took third after another fellow Renzo student, Stan Beck, also decided not to compete against a team member.

See, we told you he was a good guy. Hopefully Luca's observations will stir up some healthy discussion about issues like the Gracies, training and conditioning, and the use of a ring or a cage. I know he has already gotten my juices flowing on these issues.

BEST OF CFW —— VOL. 1
GRAPPLING

Takedown Throws That Really Work

Sheldon Marr

The Whizzer

"Whizzer" is another term for the wrestling "overhook." It is a lock-up or tie-up position commonly used in Collegiate, Freestyle and Greco-Roman wrestling, where the gripping of a gi, kimono, or uniform is not an option. However, the whizzer also works just as well when your opponent is wearing a uniform such as in judo, sombo and Brazilian jiu-jitsu competitions, and it often catches your opponent by surprise as it is a somewhat unorthodox grip to these systems of grappling.

To apply the right-side whizzer grip when facing your opponent, simply reach over your opponent's left shoulder with your right arm, then back under their left upper-arm (or armpit) with your right forearm. Now you have a whizzer (or right overhook), and your opponent subsequently has a left underhook.

Another advantage to the whizzer grip (besides not needing a gi) is that when you throw with a whizzer, you land with a very tight grip. This places a tremendous amount of pressure on the shoulder joint, and the outer blade of your forearm presses directly on the sensitive rib, serratus and/or intercostal area of your opponent, which can be quite painful and perhaps lead to a quick submission.

Sweeping Hip Throw

To execute a right-side *harai goshi* or sweeping hip throw with a whizzer, apply the whizzer with your right arm, and grasp the opponent's right triceps area with your left hand. Grasping above the elbow, as opposed to grabbing the wrist or forearm, is much more effective as it makes the throw much tighter and therefore more effective.

From here, backstop-in with your left foot then sweep with your right leg. The sweeping action knocks both of your opponent's legs out from under them. Continue to pull with your left hand, and

> *U.S. Pankration Team Coach Sheldon Marr is an eight-time Martial Arts Hall of Fame Instructor of the Year inductee. His students have won national and international titles in jujitsu, judo, wrestling and pankration, as well as competed successfully in the no-holds-barred arena. His Grappler's Edge team has also won six U.S. national team titles in jujitsu and submission grappling to date. In this series, Marr introduces takedown techniques he and his students have used successfully in competition. While Marr does not claim to have invented any of the techniques he teaches, through decades of training and teaching, Marr feels he may have perfected a few.*
>
> —Editor

The Whizzer
Apply a whizzer with your right arm and grasp the triceps with your left hand (1). Back step with your left leg, and sweep with your right leg (2). Maintain control on the ground (3). Choke with the outer blade of your forearm (4).

push with your right (whizzer). This action will rotate your opponent over onto their back, and send you crashing down onto their ribs.

Lateral Drop

The lateral drop is another throw initiated with a whizzer grip (or the over/under grip), and can be used in combination with the sweeping hip throw. The over/under grip is when you have an overhook with one arm and an underhook with the other, and your opponent has the same thing on you. An example of this is when you have an overhook with your right arm and an underhook with your left arm, and your opponent has an overbook with their right arm and an underhook with their left arm. This tie-up is commonly seen in Greco-Roman wrestling. To execute a right lateral drop, apply the whizzer with your right hand and fake the right sweeping hip entry.

GRAPPLING

The Lateral Drop
From the whizzer grip, fake a right hip throw entry. Your opponent will react by squaring into you (1). Keep your lock on the whizzer and hit the lateral drop (2). Maintain control to the ground (3). Mount and follow up with an arm bar (4).

In order to get the desired response from your opponent to set up the lateral drop, you're going to have to sell the fake. To get your opponent to bite on the fake, it's best to first hit your opponent with one or two actual hard sweeping hip-throw attacks. Now, when you're ready to fake the hip throw, you should be able to get away with merely twitching your hips to get the desired response.

With the threat of the right hip throw coming, your opponent will give you the reaction or response you need to initiate the lateral drop. A judo player's reaction will be to block with and/or extend their left hip forward. A wrestler's reaction will be to square up with you and/or step forward with their right foot to face you.

From here (with the right-side whizzer), pop or punch your hips into your opponent, pull with the whizzer and push with your left arm (or underhook). Then twist and rotate to your right, and throw your opponent over your right shoulder with an arching (or suplay) type action.

The Pancake
From the quarter-nelson position, press the head downward (1). Allow your opponent to slip their head up (2). Clothesline the face or neck, and pancake your opponent to the ground (3). Follow-up with an arm bar (4).

The Pancake

The pancake is very similar to the lateral drop, but is usually done from a kneeling position on the ground instead of from the standing position. To execute a right pancake from a kneeling position, apply the whizzer with your right hand and grasp the right triceps with your left hand. Fake a right throwing (or rolling) entry. This will give you the same desired response from your opponent that sets up the lateral drop. From here (with the right-side whizzer), pull with the whizzer. But instead of pushing with your left arm (or underhook) clothesline your opponent across the face with your left arm. Continue to twist and rotate to your right, and throw your opponent to the ground. Another effective way to execute the pancake is to apply a right-side whizzer from the kneeling position along with a quarter-nelson (push down on the head/neck with your left hand, and grasp your own left wrist with your right hand). From here, allow your opponent to slip or pop their head up (to escape the quarter nelson), then clothesline with your left arm and pancake.

Practice Tips

Some of the throws described and demonstrated in this article are advanced-level throws and are not intended for beginners. These throws can be dangerous and could cause serious injury if not executed correctly, and if your training partner is not experienced in *ukemi waza* (falling techniques).

In practice and competition, the *uke* (or throwee) needs to remember to keep their chin tucked, their arms in, and just take the fall. If the chin isn't tucked, head and/or spinal injuries may occur. If the arms aren't kept in, shoulder and/or elbow dislocations can be a common occurrence. Crash pad usage is also recommended when experimenting with all new takedowns and throws. In the included sequences I demonstrate the moves on student Eric Koble, the 2001 U.S. National Middleweight Grappling Champion. Good luck with these techniques. Train hard and win easy!

To contact Mr. Marr for seminars or to order Sheldon Marr's Grappling Seminar *video series, call* (303) 433-EDGE *or visit* www.grapplers-edge.com.

GRAPPLING

Carlao "Cao" Valente is a legendary Brazilian jiu-jitsu personality who is as well-known for his off-the-mat antics as he is for his on-the-mat success.

Carlao "Cao" Valente
The Storyteller of Brazilian Jiu-Jitsu

Kid Peligro

Brazilian jiu-jitsu (BJJ) is an art rich in folklore, legend, and tradition. With its history of challenge fights and other unconventional ways of disseminating the art, BJJ has attracted many colorful and free-thinking characters of the world. Carlao "Cao" Valente is one of these—a legendary Brazilian jiu-jitsu personality who is as well-known for his off-the-mat antics as he is for his on-the-mat accomplishments. Valente started his BJJ training with the legendary Rolls Gracie and obtained the rank of purple belt prior to Rolls' death in a hang gliding accident. After that tragic event, Carlao continued training with the Gracie family and became involved in a personal crusade to expand the art he loved beyond the confines of Rio de Janeiro. Shortly after receiving his black belt, Valente moved to the state of Bahia, Brazil and with Master Reyson Gracie, founded the Bahia Federation of Jiu-Jitsu. When the organization became established and self-sufficient, Valente then moved to Hawaii and was able to lure Relson Gracie to the Aloha State and thereby establish the first foothold of BJJ in the Pacific islands.

A few years later, Valente was approached by friend Rorion Gracie with the opportunity to become one of the original investors in a new fight show concept that would come to be known as the Ultimate Fighting Championship. After being involved in the first few UFC shows, the nomadic and restless Valente was ready to tackle another challenge and so moved to California and became an assistant instructor at the famed Rickson Gracie Academy in Santa Monica. It was there that Valente was convinced by friends to embark on yet another adventure—to teach Brazilian jitsu-jitsu to Sheik Diab (brother of famed ADCC patron Sheik Tahnoon), and a member of the United Arab Emirates royal family, Once again Carlao picked up his gi and off he went—this time to the Middle East—to continue his mission in life of spreading BJJ around the globe. After teaching in Abu Dhabi for a while, Valente was ready to move again. This time he chose San Diego, his current home base.

True to his passion, Valente immediately established "The Training Center" in Pacific Beach. The Training Center has one of the largest mats areas in San Diego and offers, in addition to Brazilian jiu-jitsu, classes in muay Thai kickboxing, traditional Japanese karate, and the athletic and beautiful Brazilian art of capoeira. The Training Center is a mandatory stop for traveling Brazilian jiu-jitsu masters in California and has received visits from Rickson Gracie, Royler Gracie, Renzo Gracie, Saulo Ribeiro, Roberto Traven, Romero "Jacare" Cavalcante, Rodrigo "Comprido" Medeiros, "Leozinho" Vieira and Fernando "Margarida" Pontes—a world champion who trained under Valente for several months.

Calf-Cutter Leg Lock
Carlao Valente controls his opponent (1). Slipping to the side he traps his opponent's calf (2), positions his rear leg under his opponent's ankle (3), then raises his rear leg up for the painful submission (4).

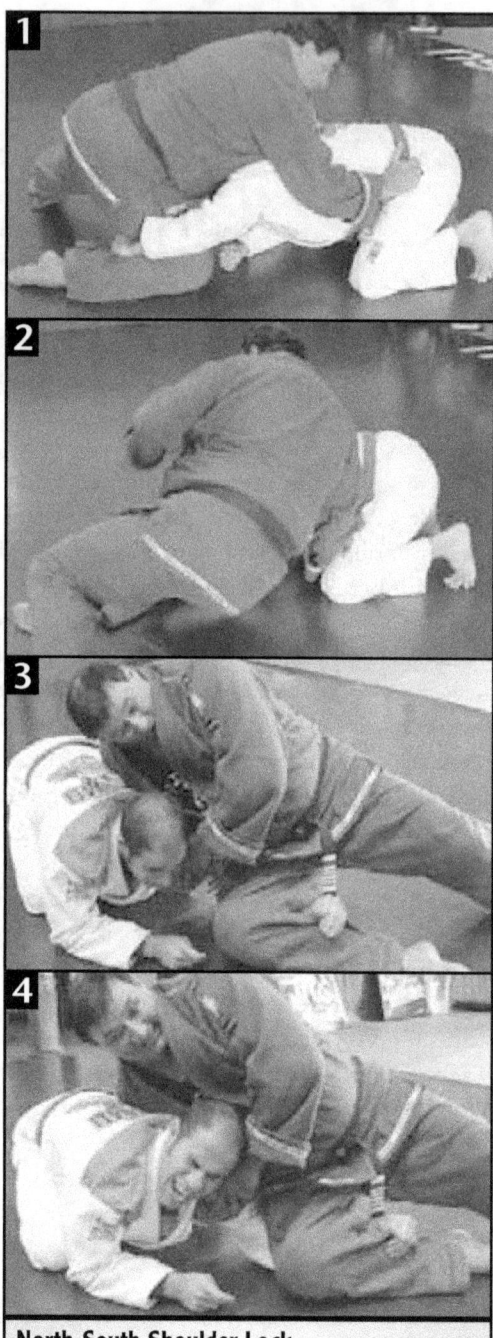

North-South Shoulder Lock
Carlao Valente in the dominant north-south position (1). He spins to the side while keeping his weight on his opponent (2), underhooks the shoulder and traps the arm (3), the leverages upward for the shoulder-lock submission (4).

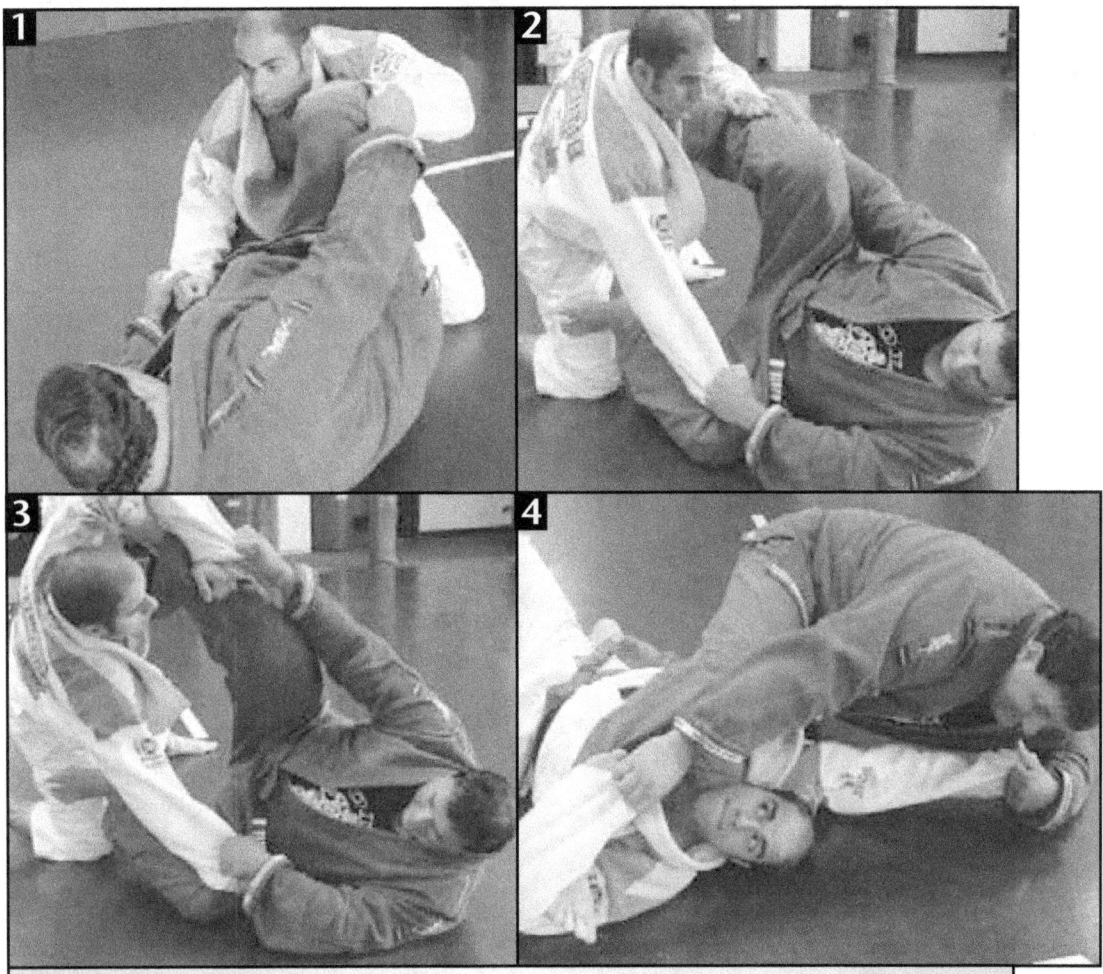

Open-Guard Sweep to Elbow Lock
Operating on the bottom with the open guard (1), Carlao Valente puts his foot on his opponent's thigh (2), kicks out and sweeps him to the ground (3), then traps the wrist and pressures elbow with his foot for the submission (4).

Big Man Techniques

Although Valente knows grappling from the inside out and can teach jiu-jitsu to anyone of any size, he is a big man and likes to do personal techniques that are suitable for someone of large physical size and strength. He prefers attack series that set his opponents up to be submitted when they least expect it. "I try to demonstrate a variety of attacks that are effective when you have passed the guard and the person turns to all fours," says Valente. "That is usually a position where not many attacks occur—one option that I really like is the clock choke, but most people are aware of that and protect it very well. Because of this, I prefer to hold the collar kind of loose, this way they don't feel the danger. Then I will hold their sleeve which again presents a feeling of no danger. Now the choke is set, I will move to the north-

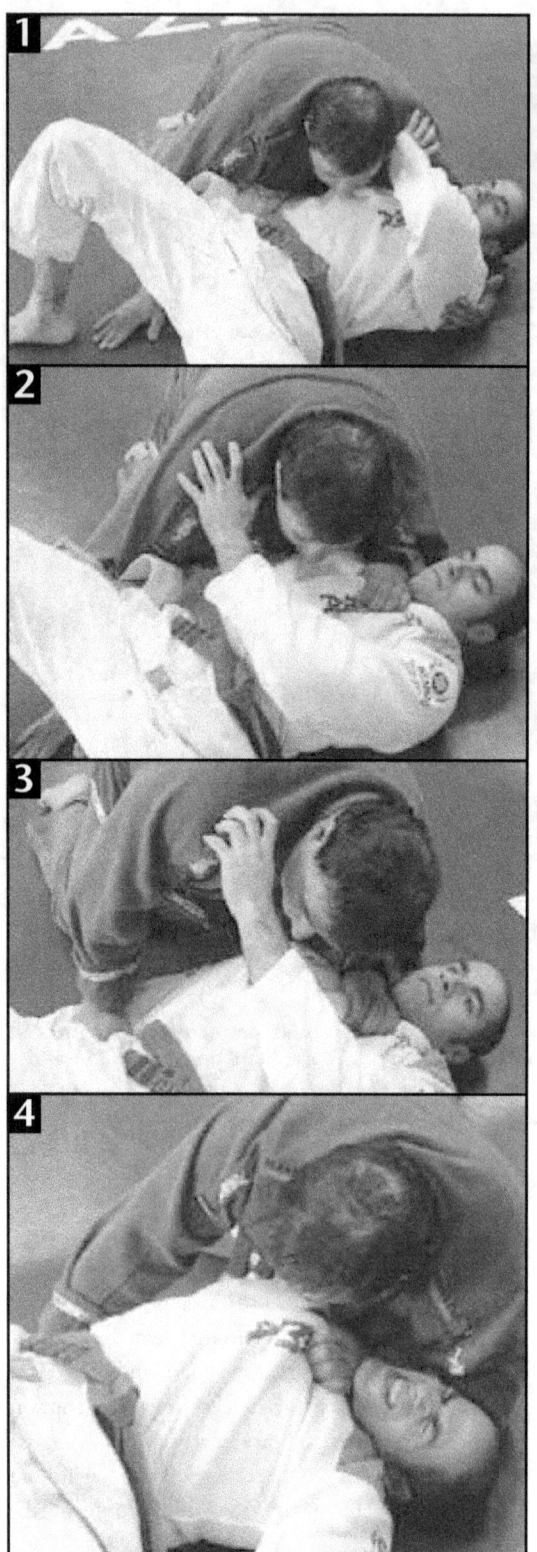

Side-Control Collar Axe-Choke
Controlling his opponent from the side mount (1), Carlao Valente grabs the collar from the inside (2), puts his weight forward (3), and then leverages his forearm downward for the submission choke (4).

south position and apply the pressure to the neck and they tap. You can surprise many people with this one."

Another movement that Valente favors for big men is the arm-bar attack from the back. "I like this submission because of the surprise factor. The opponent is expecting me to try to put the hooks in or to turn him over for side control, but I just sneak in and take the arm." Another variation that is a big favorite of his is to start from the same position on the back and then attack the leg with a calf cutter. "In this variation," Valente says, "I attack the calf. It is a good option, especially when combined with the arm attack. It keeps the opponent off-balance and not knowing what is coming next."

But in jiu-jitsu, Valente says, there are no certainties and you must expect the unexpected. "There are so many positions in jiu-jitsu because there are so many attacks and counters that you must be ready for. For example, when you're attacking from the back, your opponent will sometimes turn and get your leg and you will end up facing them. This causes a stalemate and it becomes a fight for the leg. In this case, they are worried about the collar and the clock choke and forget that their arm is vulnerable. I have developed this quick submission that takes advantage of that. The tighter the opponent holds the leg, the easier it is to apply."

As Valente often points out, big guys sometimes aren't used to being on the bottom, but will sometimes end up there. "My favorite big-guy sweep is from the spider guard," says Valente. "Big guys can use their weight and strength to their advantage from the bottom too. Once I have this position, it is very easy to sweep, and then I am either across the side and can use the choke, or they turn quickly onto all fours and I can either take the arm or the leg."

The Storyteller of Brazilian Jiu-Jitsu

But Valente is far more than just a master BJJ instructor, he is also a master storyteller who keeps the traditions of Brazilian jiu-jitsu alive by sharing its oral history. It

is not unusual for Valente to break into a classic insider BJJ story during a class. If you are interested in learning Brazilian jiu-jitsu from someone who has "seen it all" or simply want to hear great historical tales, then stop by The Training Center and meet Carlao "Cao" Valente.

GRAPPLING

BEST OF CFW — VOL.1

Muay Thai Strikes on the Ground

Muay Thai is one of the world's most feared martial arts and is known for it's crushing blows. These devastating standing strikes can be easily adapted for use on the ground.

Jermaine Andre, Photos by Clarke Kincaid

The birth of muay Thai was well over 1000 years ago. Many techniques that no-holds-barred (NHB) fighters take for granted are actually muay Thai techniques. The infamous low leg-kick, for example, that everyone fears so much, stems directly from muay Thai. Elbow and knee combinations also found their birth among muay Thai fighters. Thai fighters are well-known for the toughness of their shins and the rest of their body. It is a fighting art that combines beauty, discipline, pure courage and brutality. There are no punks or phonies allowed in the muay Thai ring. If you don't know what you're doing, one may come out badly hurt or crippled—if one makes it out at all.

Muay Thai Popularity
The popularity of Muay Thai has grown since its introduction to the world of mixed martial arts. It has proven itself to be one of the only (if not *the* only) stand up martial art capable of surviving and even prevailing in the NHB cage. It's front stance, speed and indisputable power has helped lots of great mixed martial arts (MMA) strikers in the NHB world defeat some of the best wrestlers and jiu-jitsu players without question. The stance and style of muay Thai is also easily adjusted to battle against ground fighters, by using footwork and sprawling. Its flexibility allows it to borrow techniques from other arts—making it even more dangerous.

Muay Thai has helped to bring much more excitement to the cages and rings of NHB. Thanks to this fighting form, fans of the mixed martial arts are getting more and more interested in seeing "strikers" rather than "grapplers." You go to a mixed-martial-arts battle and you'll see most of the fans looking for a knockout rather than a tapout—especially if the knockout comes while both fighters are still on their feet.

Looking For Leverage
Back near the beginning of my grappling career, I had to figure-out some sort of leverage to use while battling it out on the ground with experienced grapplers. Of course I didn't want to limit my learning by trying to find a quick way out of a grappling situation—that is not the best way to think in order to improve. I love grappling and I know that it is one of the most beautiful arts. Still, I didn't want to try and catch-up to all the fighters who had been grappling for five or more years—that would take too long. So, I decided to add something to my grappling—muay Thai strikes while on

the ground. Not surprisingly, it worked great! Bringing the power and technique of muay Thai to the ground helped to confuse experienced grapplers and gave them something to fear while in their favorite position. It also helped to bring an advantage to me that they didn't have. When applied correctly, the same amount of striking damage can be done on the ground that can be delivered standing up. Knees, elbows, and punches can be easily executed. Even the muay Thai front push-kick can be delivered while on the ground. It didn't matter whether I am holding someone in my guard or am inside someone elses guard—there is always a muay Thai strike looking to be born.

Battle Tested

I proved the effectiveness of muay Thai strikes on the ground during a recent Rings USA battle in 2001. My match was against a tough Japanese opponent named Kojima. Kojima decided from the beginning of the fight that he had no plans to stand with me, and immediately started shooting. I sprawled on some of his shots and dodged others. When he did get me down a couple of times I made it right back to my feet, one time executing a back flip from the ground. (If you don't believe me, contact Monty Cox and get one of the tapes—he'll be happy to sell you one.) As time went on, I got tired of this game and so I decided to go ahead and introduce him to my muay Thai ground strikes.

From a half-guard side-mount I delivered a few hooks to my opponent's ribs, then I rolled to my back and pulled him into my guard. From there, I sat-up as he sat back and delivered a right cross to his sternum. That was it. I rolled him off of me and the fight was over. He received some damage to his rib cage but left proudly, as a warrior should. Many were amazed at how I'd won but to me it was simply some stuff I had trained to use in a situation where I needed to beat someone up before I got beat up. It's all good.

Ground Strikes That Work

Here are some examples on how to put your muay Thai to use while on the ground. These may seem a little awkward at first. If so, I suggest contacting a qualified muay Thai instructor and taking private classes. You'll be amazed at how much your NHB game improves.

Muay Thai Knee Strikes

This particular technique works great from the side mount. First lay chest-to-chest and be sure that your opponent isn't going to shrimp on you. Now extend the leg that you are gong to strike with by sliding it across the mat. Do not lift your knee off the mat. Drive your knee into your opponent's rib cage or head while keeping your leg on the mat. You can deliver this strike as many times as you would like but watch out for the shrimp.

GRAPPLING

Muay Thai Mounted Elbow Strike
Jermaine Andre controls the mount (1), lands a punch (2); then is grabbed at the waist by his opponent (3). Positioning himself (4), he creates striking space (5); and lands a muay Thai elbow on the ground (6)

Downward Elbow Strikes

This move is also a perfect weapon from the side mount. Again, while laying chest-to-chest, raise your hand as if reaching for the stars. Bring your elbow down into your opponent's sternum or rib cage by acting as if you're blowing a train whistle. This elbow strike also works while sprawling. Make the same movements but bring your elbow down into your opponent's spine or back (rules permitting) while defending against the shoot.

Muay Thai Front Elbow-Strikes

This blow can be delivered from the guard, from inside the guard, and from the mount. First, be sure to keep your head protected so that you don't get hit. Close your guard tightly around your opponent and pull him to you with your legs. Sit-up slightly and then deliver an elbow to your opponent's head. Be sure to strike with the bone of your elbow and not your forearm. Try to keep your hand open and relaxed when delivering any kind of elbow strike. You can strike with your left or right elbow.

Hitting your opponent with an elbow from inside the guard can also be an effective weapon. Always remember that you need distance and balance while throwing an elbow strike. Sit back in your opponent's guard. Keep your head and chest covered so that you don't become a victim of *his* muay Thai ground strikes. Use your hands to work your opponent's hands away from his chest. When you see an opening bring your downward elbow strike onto his rib cage. You can also use a front elbow strike while in this position. Just lean towards your opponent and deliver an elbow to his temple or face.

Ground Front-Kick

Using the front kick on the ground can cause serious damage and quickly end a fight. It can be used effectively when your opponent is going for an ankle lock. Just chamber your free leg (while defending your trapped ankle) and deliver a front push kick to your opponent's face. The push kick also comes in handy when your opponent is going for a knee bar. Again, chamber that free leg and deliver a push kick right to the buttocks of your opponent. This will launch him like a rocket and free your knee. If your opponent is standing over you during your match, immediately go to your

GRAPPLING

"Bringing the power and technique of muay Thai to the ground helped to confuse experienced grapplers and gave them something to fear while in their favorite position."

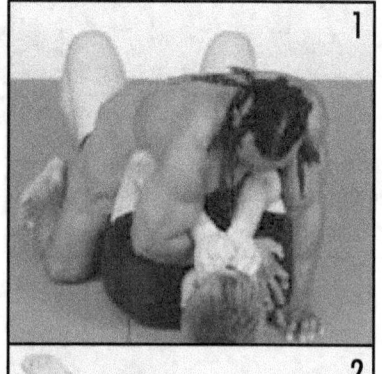

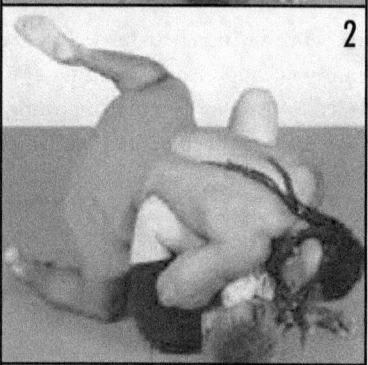

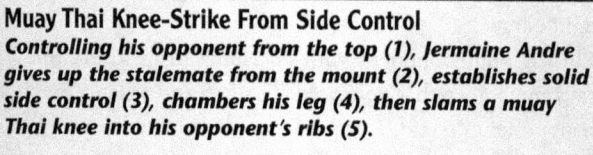

back. Lift your head off the ground and wait for him to get close to you. As soon as he gets in range, deliver a front push kick to his knee, chest or face.

Improving Your Game

Muay Thai strikes on the ground will increase your arsenal of weapons for mixed martial arts and no-holds-barred matches. Just as with anything in life, if you want to get good at it, you must practice consistently and hard. Striking on the ground has helped me to become a better and more dangerous fighter. It has also helped all of the fighters of NHB (strikers, grapplers and wrestlers) to become better martial artists. The more we create, the more we all learn and the better we will all become. Our world is one of discipline, courage, growth and most-definitely reality. Ain't no punks in this game!

Muay Thai Knee-Strike From Side Control
Controlling his opponent from the top (1), Jermaine Andre gives up the stalemate from the mount (2), establishes solid side control (3), chambers his leg (4), then slams a muay Thai knee into his opponent's ribs (5).

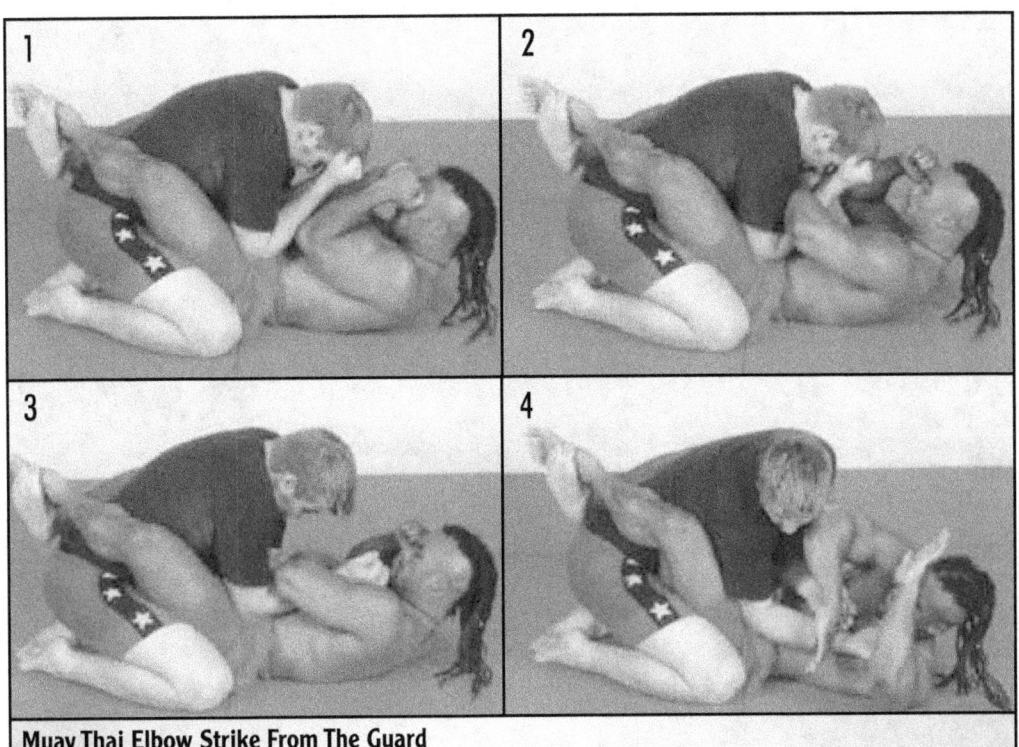

Muay Thai Elbow Strike From The Guard
Caught on the bottom (1), Jermaine Andre traps his opponent's forearm (2), creates striking space (3), then lands a muay Thai elbow from the guard (4).

"From there, I sat-up as he sat back and delivered a right cross to his sternum. That was it. I rolled him off of me and the fight was over."

For more information on Jermaine Andre's training and fighting methods visit www.jermaineandre.com or www.streetdefense.net.

GRAPPLING

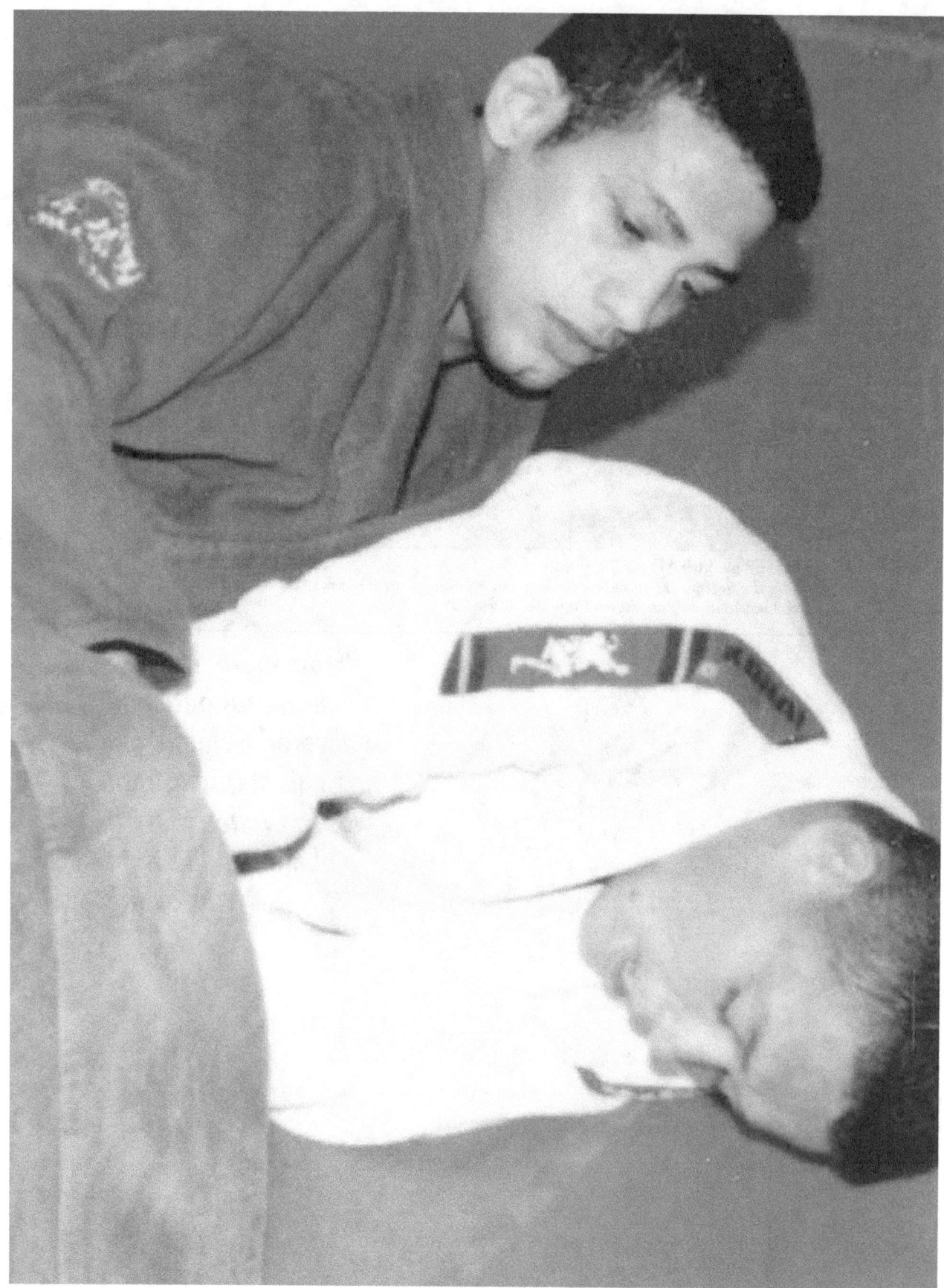

Hurricane Diniz Hits South Florida

Brazil's new whirlwind entry into the world fighting scene is carving a name for himself in the Southern landscape.

Todd Fischer

Beyond any advantage one may acquire through martial arts, weight training, boxing, or any other form of physical discipline, natural talent is inarguably the base element of a true champion's arsenal. Edson Diniz, an up-and-coming new fighter, is a perfect example of what someone blessed with both the inherent ability to be a champ and the discipline to make it stick can achieve.

Born Edson Diniz Fidelis in Rio De Janeiro, Brazil, in 1978, he decided recently to make the move to the United States in order to advance the progression of Brazilian jiu-jitsu in this country. When asked, Edson says that his mission here in South Florida is to create instructors, citing California as the current national center of BJJ activity. "There are very few Brazilian black-belts on the East Coast," he states. "I wanted to bring the art to a new place." Given South Florida's ethnic diversity and large population, success is sure to come.

A Competitor From the Start

A proud smile spreads across his youthful face when asked about his competition experience. He unzips an over-stuffed green bag and dumps sixty or so medals on the table—some gold, some silver, and some over four inches across! This seems remarkable, considering the fact that he has only been a black belt since October 1999. In 1993 he began training under several great Brazilian champions, including his idol, Royler Gracie. His natural talent earned him a yellow belt that very same year. Also that same year came Edson's first experience with competition at the Rio De Janeiro Vice Championships, where he took home a second place medal.

Since then he has done well in countless Brazilian competitions, including the world championships—which he has competed in since 1997. He placed first in 1999, the same year that his belt turned from brown to black. The year 2000 competition, in which he placed second, pitted him against the current president of Japan's Brazilian Jiu-Jitsu Foundation, Yuki Nakai. Edson scored an impressive 10-0 victory, but found his tenacious opponent, enlightened by the hands of the venerable Rickson Gracie five years previously, impossible to finish. Among other big name fights, he boasts a victory over Marcos Barbosa, a grappler who once defeated Relson Gracie.

When asked about his most difficult match, Edson recalls his defeat against B.J. Penn at Mundial 2000. "Usually you are either strong and stiff," he says, "or flexible and weak. B.J. Penn is very strong *and* very flexible—he is a truly great fighter." On the other side of that coin is his favorite

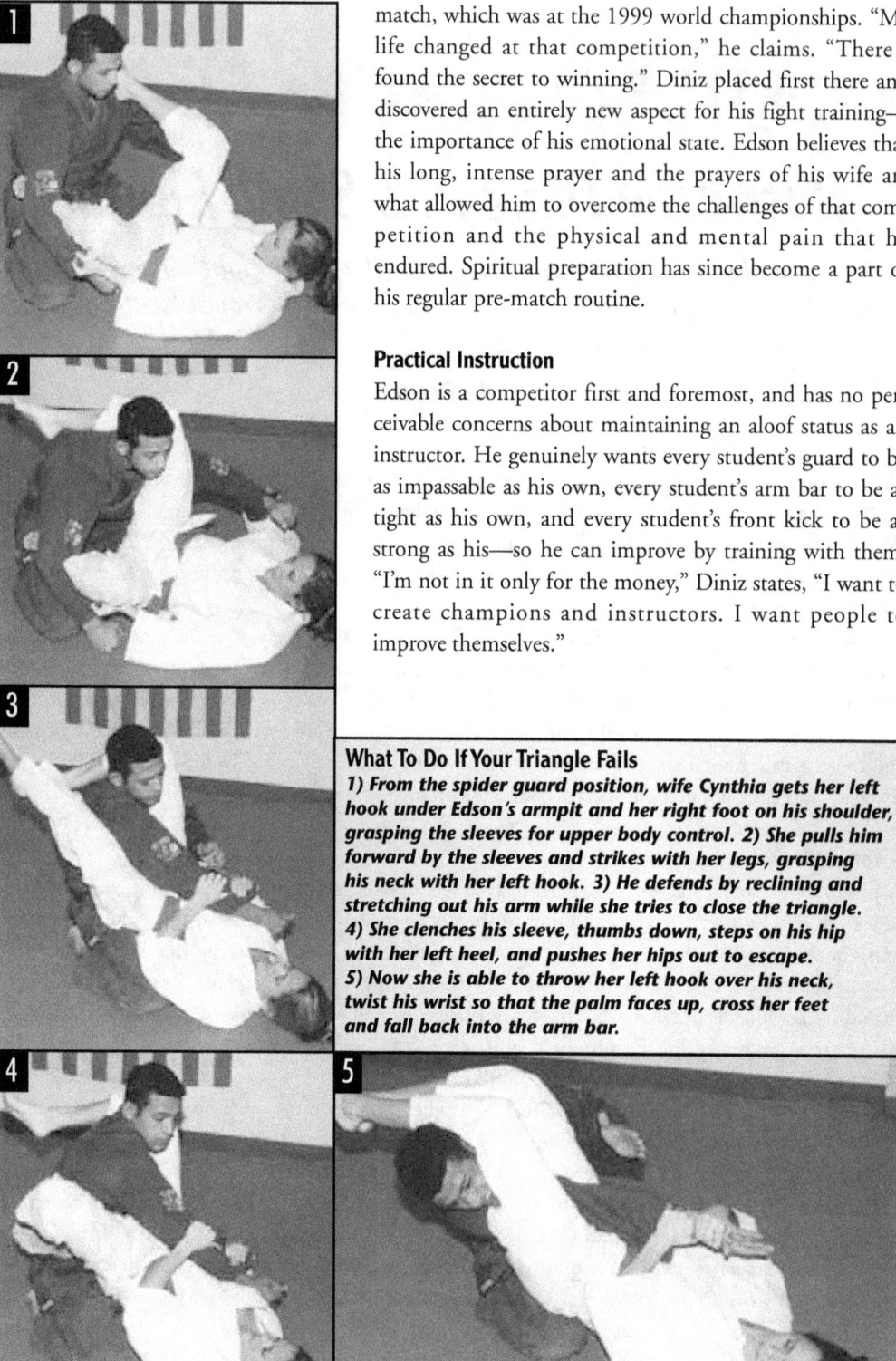

match, which was at the 1999 world championships. "My life changed at that competition," he claims. "There I found the secret to winning." Diniz placed first there and discovered an entirely new aspect for his fight training—the importance of his emotional state. Edson believes that his long, intense prayer and the prayers of his wife are what allowed him to overcome the challenges of that competition and the physical and mental pain that he endured. Spiritual preparation has since become a part of his regular pre-match routine.

Practical Instruction

Edson is a competitor first and foremost, and has no perceivable concerns about maintaining an aloof status as an instructor. He genuinely wants every student's guard to be as impassable as his own, every student's arm bar to be as tight as his own, and every student's front kick to be as strong as his—so he can improve by training with them. "I'm not in it only for the money," Diniz states, "I want to create champions and instructors. I want people to improve themselves."

What To Do If Your Triangle Fails
1) From the spider guard position, wife Cynthia gets her left hook under Edson's armpit and her right foot on his shoulder, grasping the sleeves for upper body control. 2) She pulls him forward by the sleeves and strikes with her legs, grasping his neck with her left hook. 3) He defends by reclining and stretching out his arm while she tries to close the triangle.
4) She clenches his sleeve, thumbs down, steps on his hip with her left heel, and pushes her hips out to escape.
5) Now she is able to throw her left hook over his neck, twist his wrist so that the palm faces up, cross her feet and fall back into the arm bar.

GRAPPLING

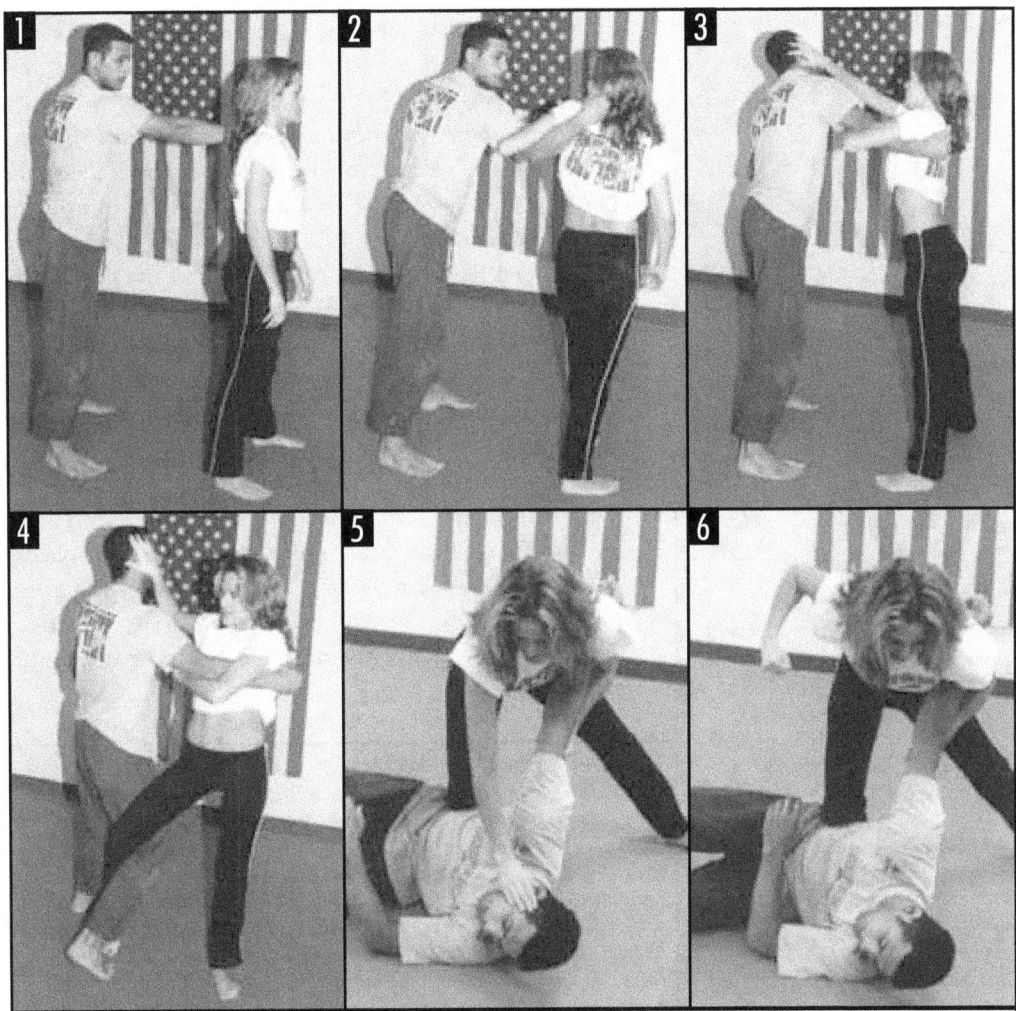

Women's Self-Defense
1) From behind, the aggressor seizes her left shoulder with his right hand, as if to turn her around.
2) She turns on her own, throwing her left arm over his right, leading with the elbow, hooking his right triceps for control. 3) With her free hand she pushes his face away while her right foot (4), moves behind his right knee for the takedown. 5) Keeping her knee in his ribs for control, she can either fall into the arm bar, or strike the face (6).

Having experienced his instruction firsthand, I feel quite sure that this is the truth. His approach to teaching epitomizes the phrase "hands on,"—in fact it is as "hands-on" as training can be without becoming injurious. His style is hard grappling, and while imparting to his students a basic knowledge of the rules for jiu-jitsu competition, he keeps the class largely devoid of academic overtones.

The best part of his classes, however, is that each student has the privilege of grappling with Diniz himself. In fact, this aspect of his teaching is actually vital to his training. He fights each of his students—fresh competitor after fresh competitor—to enhance his anaerobic endurance. This, com-

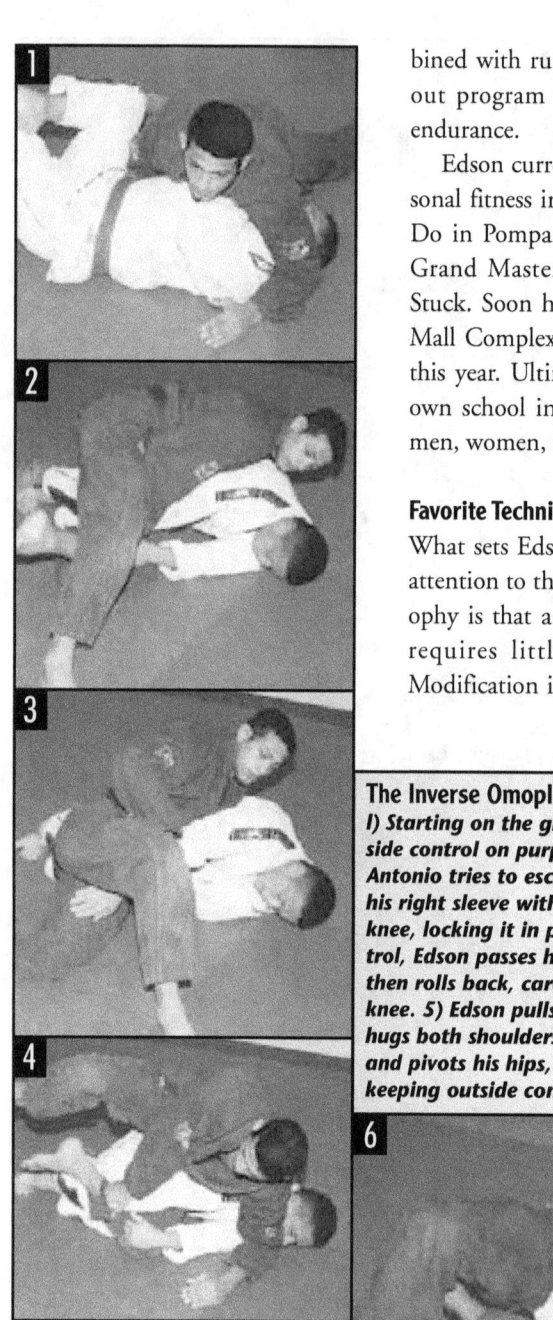

bined with running on sand, makes for a convenient workout program designed to enhance agility, flexibility, and endurance.

Edson currently teaches his students self-defense and personal fitness in addition to pure jiu-jitsu at Park's Tae Kwon Do in Pompano, Florida, with the consent and support of Grand Master Jung Soo Park and his sons, Cheong and Stuck. Soon he will also be teaching out of the new Sports Mall Complex opening up in Deerfield Beach, Florida later this year. Ultimately, Edson wishes to own and operate his own school in South Florida, where he intends to instruct men, women, and children—morning, noon, and night.

Favorite Techniques

What sets Edson's Team Infight apart from the crowd is his attention to the little details of form and posture. His philosophy is that a good technique, executed with perfect form, requires little or no force in order to be effective. Modification is another favorite tool—Edson customizes his

The Inverse Omoplata (Arm Lock)
1) Starting on the ground, Edson uses his left elbow to establish side control on purple belt Antonio Sousa, his top student. 2) Antonio tries to escape by shifting his hips, but Edson (3), grabs his right sleeve with his right hand and forces it under his left knee, locking it in place with his leg. 4) Maintaining sleeve control, Edson passes his face and makes a base with his left elbow, then rolls back, careful to hold control of the right leg at the knee. 5) Edson pulls back Antonio's right arm with his leg and hugs both shoulders. 6) He closes the triangle with his right leg and pivots his hips, allowing his left knee to drop to the floor, keeping outside control on the right knee.

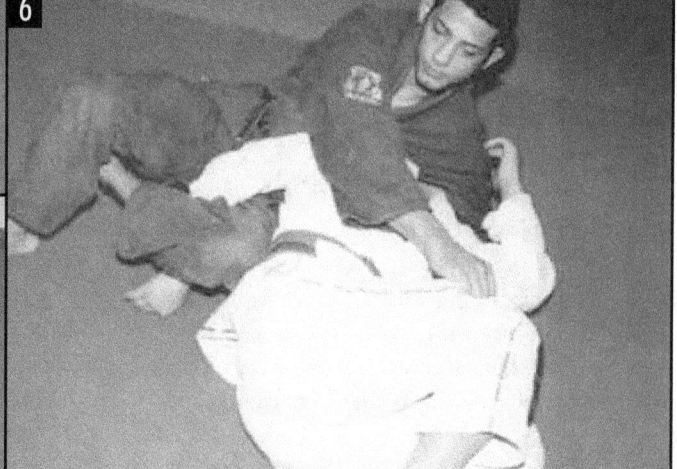

moves to cater to his body type and intrinsic abilities, and he helps his students do the same. This includes teaching women to be effective by using flexibility and leverage, rather than speed and strength.

Future Fights

Clearly, at age 23, Edson is just getting started on his way to grappling stardom. With several impressive major victories already under his belt, one cannot help but wonder where we will see his name next. When asked about mixed martial arts and NHB fighting, Diniz makes clear that his true passion is traditional Brazilian jiu-jitsu. However, he does express real interest in no-gi competitions, especially after winning top honors at the Reality Superfight Vale Tudo match in Ft. Pierce, Florida, July 2001. This was his first taste of NHB fighting, and he liked the flavor. "I like no-gi because you don't know your opponent," say Edson. "He could be a jiu-jitsu guy, a Sombo wrestler, or a Greco-Roman fighter—you don't know so it's more interesting."

This means that we will be seeing more of Edson in upcoming NHB events. In fact, he may soon close a contract with James Levine of Rival Team, whom he befriended at the Reality Superfight. This contract could open doors to higher profile venues such as UFC—one of Edson's top ambitions. So if you hear of a storm warning in South Florida watch yourself—Hurricane Diniz is on the loose and he's picking-up steam!

BEST OF CFW — VOL. 1
GRAPPLING

Garth Taylor
A Modern Day Mountain Man

Garth Taylor is a true local hero and a living example of how jiu-jitsu has inspired both fans and students alike and brought together an entire community.

Scott Nelson

About four years ago, I was watching the Purple Belt Open Division at Claudio Franca's U.S. Open in Santa Cruz, California. As the athletes in the finials were being announced, all of a sudden the entire crowd went berserk! Screams and chants of "Mountain! Mountain! Mountain!" left me wondering what in the world was going on? Who was this guy and why did he inspire this army of rowdy fans? I soon found out it was west side local, Garth "The Mountain" Taylor who they were cheering on to victory.

History

Garth moved to Santa Cruz at age 11 and became an avid surfer until his senior year in high school when his friends encouraged him to try out for the wresting team. He fell in love with wrestling and continued his career in college at the infamous West Valley College in San Jose, California. "I had a great coach at West Valley, Jim Root. I was a decent wrestler but never really did anything great, I went to State my last year but I didn't place. I was a little undersized at the time. I was wrestling heavy weights. I couldn't make the190's because we had the top ranked guy in the State at that weight on our team and I could never beat him. I was only about 200lbs at the time but I was fighting heavy weights so I could never really get over the hump and place at state. I learned a lot. It was valuable to have competed. Coach Root was a great coach. He runs a good room. It's hard training. He's opened up to a lot of jiu-jitsu guys, Bob Southworth, Cameron Earle, and BJ Penn have all trained at West Valley. He's been quite a resource for local jiu-jitsu guys."

Passion For Learning

Garth's passion for grappling didn't die after college; he began coaching wrestling locally at Santa Cruz high school. Like most of the American pioneers in jiu-jitsu, it was the original UFC that introduced him to the sport. "I had actually heard of Brazilian jiu-jitsu prior to the first UFC. I heard of this street-fighting judo that did some amazing stuff. So when I saw the first UFC, I thought this must be the stuff. And sure enough, Royce Gracie went in there and handled people

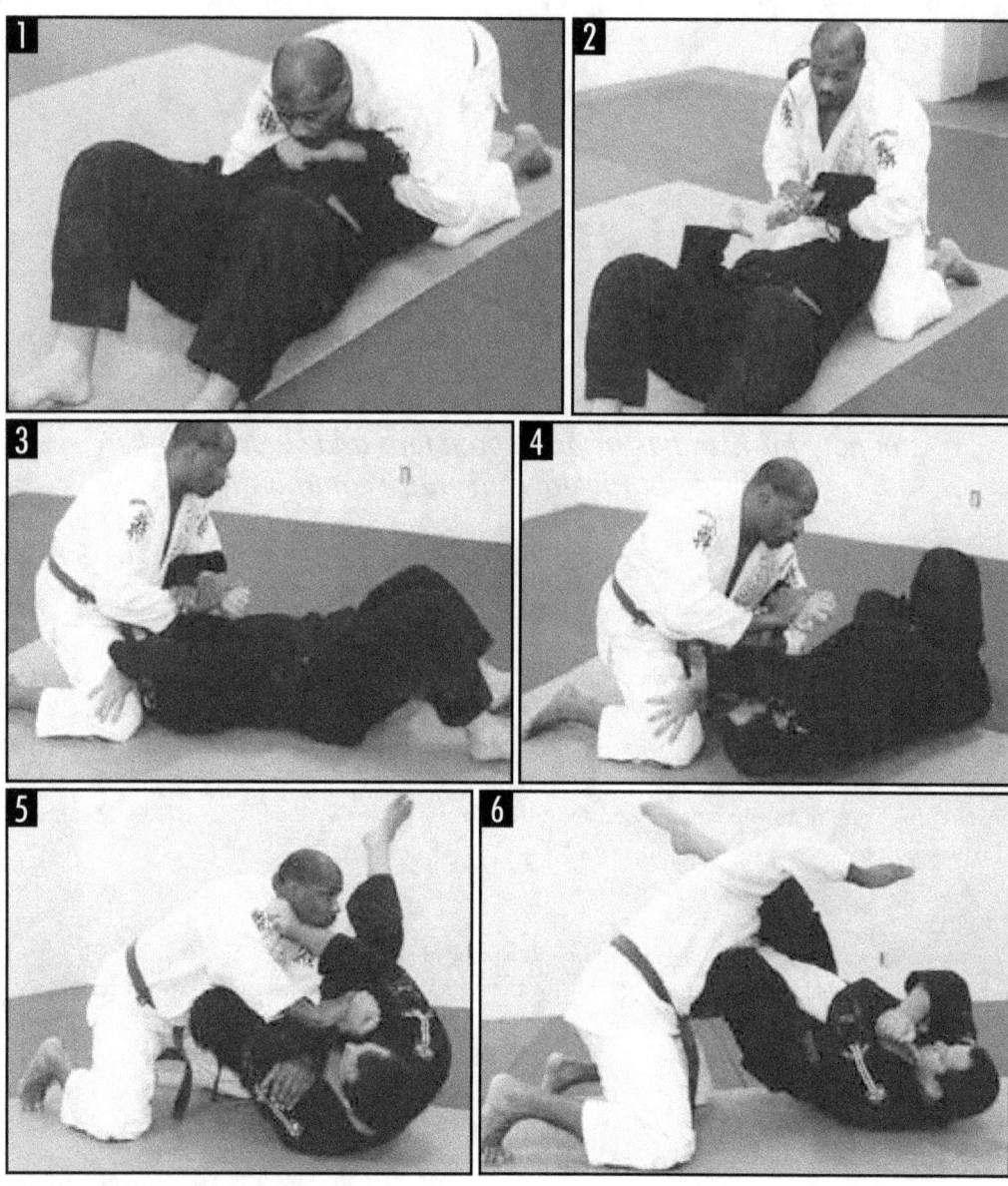

North-South Arm-Lock Counter
Garth Taylor is caught underneath his opponent in a north-south position (1). When his opponent secures the elbow to try for an arm bar (2), Taylor pushes on the knee to create space and reduce his opponent's leverage (3), spins sideways (4), traps the collar and lifts his leg over the head (5), and applies a finishing arm-bar (6).

with a style of wresting that was made to end fights. His style really appealed to me. About two months later, Rickson Gracie held a seminar in Watsonville, a small farm town about twenty minutes from Santa Cruz. I couldn't believe he was there. I'd had the chance to wrestle with many real

GRAPPLING

> "It's the way jiu-jitsu used to be and, for Claudio, how jiu-jitsu will always be. My style comes from his. It's simple. I really like to take guys down, pass their guard, and then smash them. That is my intention in every fight."

good guys, national-level guys, but I had never felt anything like that. I couldn't understand what he was doing. I would love the chance to train with him again. I'm sure the result will be the same. He'll finish me just as fast, but now I have a better grasp of what jiu-jitsu is. I'd just like to see if I have a better understanding of what he is doing to me. At the seminar, I was one of the last guys to train with him and I think people thought I was going to be able to put up some kind of a fight against him. I was a bigger guy and no one else there was a wrestler—I had the shoes on and stuff. I knew exactly what was going to happen but people thought I was actually going to be able to give him a wrestle. He played with me just as he had played with everyone else. I was there to take the seminar and I was already very impressed with his family's skills. After the seminar, I hooked up with Claudio (Franca) and the rest is history."

The Unknown Grappler

Surprisingly, Garth is relatively unknown in the jiu-jitsu world, considering his list of accomplishments in the last seven years of fighting. He has won a medal while wearing every belt, blue through black, at the most prestigious jiu-jitsu tournament in the world—the Mundials de Jiu-Jitsu, held yearly in Rio de Janeiro, Brazil. Most recently, Garth took second place as a black belt in the heavyweight division. He is the second American to ever medal as a black belt in the Mundials. Strong fundamentals and an open mind have driven him quickly to the top. "I was always open to jiu-jitsu. I see a lot of wrestlers struggle with jiu-jitsu because they can't let wrestling go. They need to understand that you will always have the wrestling to fall back on whenever you want, but if you open up and learn the principles of jiu-jitsu then your wrestling will improve too. They need to grasp jiu-jitsu not resist it. Let your wrestling blend with jiu-jitsu; don't try to blend jiu-jitsu with your wrestling—because jiu-jitsu is the stronger, more technical style."

Abu Dhabi Success

Another major accomplishment for Garth is a 4th place win in the Absolute Division of the Abu Dhabi Combat Club's annual submission grappling tournament. Abu Dhabi, without any argument, is where the best grapplers in the world test their skills. "The guys from Abu Dhabi called me a week before the event and invited me to come and fight. I would have liked to have been better prepared for the tournament. But I took my chances and went. I was just a purple belt at the time, but I beat some really good guys. I beat Josh Barnett, Barret Yoshida, and a few others before losing to Roberto Traven. All my fights were really close, so I felt good about the tournament. I wish I had done better. I definitely could have done better with a little more time for preparation. Given the circumstances, I think I did pretty well."

Have Black Belt, Will Travel

Garth's first time fighting as a black belt was at the Pan American games hosted by Carlos Gracie Jr. in Orlando, Florida—the largest Brazilian jiu-jitsu tournament held on U.S. soil. Garth was set to face some big-time opponents, but this new kid made sure there was room for him on the block. "I took second at the Pan Am's this year; I was nervous and I didn't know if my new belt was going to fit or how I was going to do out there. I was in real good shape so I just went for it. My first fight went real well. I felt comfortable in the match and I beat the guy convincingly. I had a bye in the fist round so that put me in the finals against Macaco. It was a good fight, I thought maybe I won. I had a couple of good throws I didn't get points for. One throw was out of bounds and one he didn't quite hit his back on the mat. The decision didn't go my way but I was real happy with my effort."

Garth never stops competing. Just after the Pan Am's he was back in California competing at Cleber Lucinao's Copa Pacifica in a black belt super fight against veteran Brazilian black belt Ricardo Pires. "It was a tough fight. Ricardo is a strong guy and a good competitor. The first five minutes of the fight we were on our feet and I wasn't really effectively working for a takedown. I was putting a lot of pressure on him and he made a mistake. I was able to catch him and get on his back. He was forced to go to his guard and in the last thirty seconds of the match I was able to pass his guard for the win."

The Challenge

Garth faced his biggest challenge yet going to the Mundials de Jiu-Jitsu in Brazil. Garth is no stranger to winning at the Mundials but this would be his first time fighting as a black belt there. "It was real exciting to fight there as a black belt and do well," says Garth. "On the first day, I fought in the Absolute Division. I fought Casio Wernick, maybe I felt too good. I almost passed Casio's guard but we went out of bounds. I was very confident that I would be able to pass right away again. I went to stand-up in Casio's guard and he swept me and took my back right away. He held on to win the match from there. I was really disappointed because I wanted to do well in the Absolute and to at least place. So the next day when I came back for my weight class, I fought a little more cautiously than I should have. I didn't want to make any mistakes this time and that strategy ended up costing me in the finals. I won my first two fights then my cautious strategy ended up costing me in the finals. I think, if I had played my regular game, I would have won that final match. I had an early lead and lost my aggressiveness, which made me not pay as much attention as I should have. It was a little scary going out there. I have a lot of respect for jiu-jitsu in Brazil. It's not like here where some people might not have a clue as to what's going on. There the whole crowd is into it and it can be a little intimidating."

Secrets of Success

Garth attributes his success in jiu-jitsu to his teacher Claudio Franca. "I like his teaching style because it is very basic. He doesn't do a lot of fancy moves. His techniques aren't real fancy. It's just very simple, good old school jiu-jitsu. When you come to Claudio's school you're not going to learn a ton of real pretty sweeps, but you will learn a lot of techniques that really work for everyone. His style is a good game, gi or no-gi, it doesn't really matter. It's the way jiu-jitsu used to be and, for Claudio, how jiu-jitsu will always be. My style comes from his. It's simple. I really like to take guys down, pass their guard, and then smash them. That is my intention in every fight. Well, not just to smash my opponents, but I'm going to keep working for positions all the time throughout the whole match. Most of my submissions don't come early in a match—I can't just run out and jump for a flying arm lock. My submissions come later and they come from keeping the pressure on. I like to

GRAPPLING

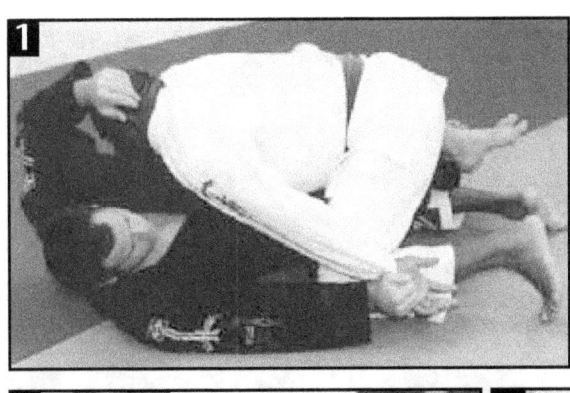

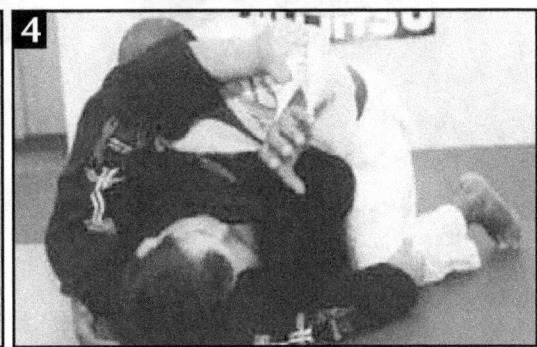
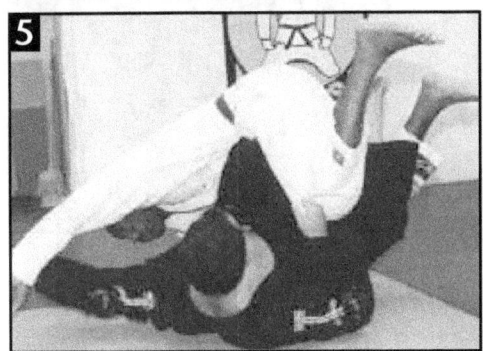

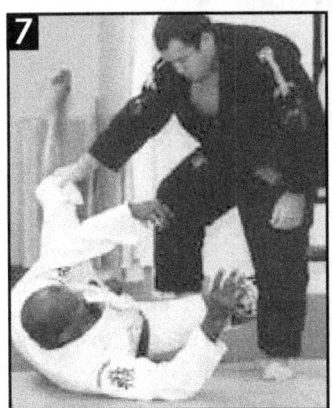
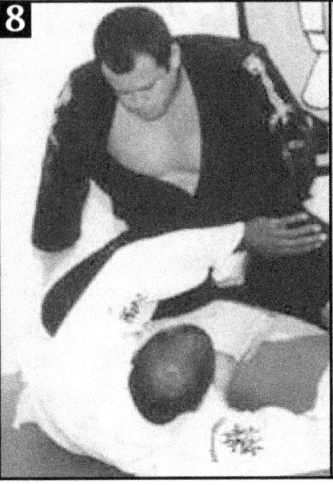

Half-Guard Escape to Top Control
Garth Taylor fights his opponent from the half-guard (1). Pushing on his neck to create space (2), Taylor then traps the knee (3), applies pressure to the neck (4), then rolls to the side, throwing his opponent (5) When Taylor's opponent comes out of the roll and establishes himself in strong base (6), Taylor pulls the near leg (7), and throws his opponent down (7). After stepping etween his legs to prevent and escape, Taylor then collapses his knee onto the ground and prepares to take the mount.

"Let your wrestling blend with jiu-jitsu; don't try to blend jiu-jitsu with your wrestling—because jiu-jitsu is the stronger, more technical style."

get a lead, then I keep the pressure on, forcing my opponent to make a mistake. I try to give the guy two choices: he can lay there and loose or he can try to win and I'll finish him."

Fitness Training

If you ever get the chance to see Garth fight, you will see he moves really lightly on his feet considering his size. He is also very strong and has great stamina for a large guy. "I always thought that if you just trained hard it was enough," Garth says. "But Claudio impressed on me that if I was going to fight at the highest level I was going to need more. Claudio met Greg Glassmen, the owner of Crossfit (www.crossfit.com), while working out at the gym. Greg is a phenomenal trainer who has worked with many Olympic athletes. I started working with Greg, applying his Crossfit system.

What Greg stressed to me was the ability to be able to maintain your strength while training at high heart rates. So that means as opposed to doing cardio and weights separately, he works them both together. Greg also really increases the intensity. He works intense sprint intervals, intense weightlifting, and combines them with functional gymnastic movements."

A Matter of Time
Right now, Garth doesn't have any plans to open his own school; however, he does teach in Claudio's Santa Cruz and San Jose schools. "I have a few more years where I want to compete at a high level. It is really difficult to both be an instructor and a fighter—it is too hard to balance both. But since the World Championships I have been focusing more on my teaching and my students."

If you think that a world championship isn't in the cards for Garth, then you'd better dust off the old Magic Eight Ball. With his work ethic and his dedication to learning it is only a matter of time before he breaks through.

To see footage of Garth Taylor's matches visit www.OntheMat.com.

BEST OF CFW — VOL. 1
GRAPPLING

GRAPPLING

Fight Strategy for the Big Boys!

When it comes to fighting, take a page out of Godzilla's playbook—size does matter. If you're big, take advantage of it. The big boys shouldn't try to train and fight like the little guys.

Tedd Williams

When I was in college, my wrestling team had several different coaches—one for the lightweights, one for the middleweights and one for heavyweights. Most professional and top-level college sports teams today have specific coaches for specific types of athletes—mixed martial arts should be no different.

There are a variety of ways that a full-contact fighter can train for a fight. I believe that one of the main issues a fighter should concentrate on is body type and body strength. A smaller fighter will most typically use speed and flexibility as the main base of their arsenal. A bigger athlete, however, is often better served by using position and strength as the basis for both their training and their fighting strategy.

Weight-Class Coaching

I have heard many a fight instructor scream at their athletes, "You're using too much strength!" Nothing drives me more crazy than this blanket attitude. While in some cases this can be very true, and the fighter *should* focus more on technique, it is not always the case. If what the athlete is doing

Standing Clinch Leg Throw
Tedd Williams ties-up Jason Lambert in a clinch (1) steps inside, making sure to not let Lambert had his back (2), then executes a judo leg throw (3).

Inside Position Counter-Throw
Operating from a clinch, Tedd Williams gives up the critical inside control to Jason Lambert (1). Williams counters by grasping Lambert in a body-lock (2), stepping behind his leg (3), and throwing Lambert to the ground (4).

stops a technique, or controls a fight situation by not allowing a technique to work, then why change something that isn't broken? There is no need to reinvent the wheel and try to change bigger men and make them fight like smaller men. Often, it is far more efficient and effective to just make an athletes better at what he does best! This is where the beauty of weight-class coaching becomes very evident.

The fact of the matter is that bigger and stronger fighters should not train like lightweights. Perhaps in cardiovascular training this is allowable, but certainly not in fighting technique and strategy! Even the rare fast and flexible heavyweight should make allowances for his body style. If you're a Mack Truck, why should you try to drive your body around like it was a Honda Accord?

While winning numerous judo titles, grappling in college and on the U.S. Army Wrestling Team, and fighting in the cage for many years against the world's biggest and baddest, I have found myself in many different training environments. Now that I'm the promoter and matchmaker for Gladiator

Knee-Up Side Leg-Trip
Tedd Williams faces Gladiator Challenge Champion Jason Lambert (1). Williams ducks under the straight right, making sure to keep his feet, and secures the leg (2). Pulling it off the ground (3), Williams stretches it out (4), uses his knee to assist raising it up, (5) underhooks the ankle (6), then switches legs and sweeps Lambert to the mat (6).

Challenge, I have been intimately exposed to virtually every type of grappling and striking art there is. This wide experience has given me a very unique perspective of how the different martial arts work with fighters of different sizes and weights—including the current flavor of the month, Brazilian jiu-jitsu.

The Limits of Brazilian Jiu-Jitsu

Don't get me wrong, Brazilian jiu-jitsu is a very dangerous and effective martial art and I am a big fan of it. However, you have to remember that Brazilian jiu-jitsu was developed for use by smaller men against much bigger men. So if you're a big guy, the art was actually made to work against you! Almost every Brazilian jiu-jitsu instructor I know weighs from 145 to 185 pounds. As they teach all of their marvelous spider-guard techniques with its spinning throws and flying arm bars I always have to bite my tongue. I want to tell them from personal experience that a 250-pound double-whopper like me will never be able to work the guard like that! There are physical limits to what a human body the size of Rhode Island can do. By definition, there will not be as much flexibility, mobility, or sensitivity that those welterweight whizzes have. That doesn't mean that jiu-jitsu or judo can't work for a big guy—far from it. As a Gene LeBell black belt I was schooled by one of the best big men fighters and trainers there ever was—Judo Gene himself. A master instructor like Gene LeBell can take your body style and body size into account and customize techniques that will work for each and every student—including big guys. But where do you start?

Big Guy Moves

For example, there are many ways to shoot a double leg. Do you shoot from the outside, or do you shoot from the clinch? For throws, do you go for the high, arching throws or from a bear hug or a body lock? For ground attacks do take the mount or operate from the side? For stand-up, do you stay outside and try to land long kicks and punches with the hands and feet or do you come in and fight with elbows and knees? There are many more variables to fight strategy than most big guys thing about. For almost every position you can imagine, a big guy must take everything into account.

The Clinch

The clinch is the domain of the big man. Once you get in close, you can control your opponent by establishing inside position by making sure that your arms stay inside of his elbows. Keep your knees bent and your butt down in order to keep your center of gravity low. From a solid clinch you can wait for your opponent to make a mistake, such as trying to shoot low, and then control his head and put your weight on him. Once in the clinch stay patient and make your opponent play your game.

Takedowns

More often than not, a bigger man will be more successful attempting a takedown from the clinch rather than trying to shoot low going for the single or double-leg takedown. If you try anything low at all, make sure that you keep your feet and do a move where you don't allow your opponent to get his weight on top of you. Remember that you're a big man, but your opponent is also. Let him try to make little man moves—when he does then strike with weight and power.

Throws

While lighter fighters tend to throw high arching throws that need speed and momentum, a heavier fighter should try for a body-lock throw that uses less speed and more position and strength. In a

"If you're a Mack Truck, why should you try to drive your body around like it was a Honda Accord?"

cage, I don't like the judo-type throws where you completely turn your back because you expose your head to elbows strikes. However, leg whips and trips work very well—especially if you've prepared your opponent by keeping inside control and tired him out by bodying up.

Ground Attacks

The handbook of Brazilian jiu-jitsu always teaches to go for the top mount before attempting a submission. This might work well for the quick, speedy guy—but for big guys I much prefer side con-

Upright Single-Leg Takedown
Tedd Williams faces Gladiator Challenge Champion Jason Lambert (1). Shooting underneath the left jab, but making sure to keep his feet and stay upright (2), Williams grabs Lambert's forward leg (3), and then takes him to the ground (4).

trol. It is an easier position to get and hold, and it allows you to go chest-to-chest with your opponent while looking for neck cranks or side arm-bars. In addition, once you have a solid side-control you have the option of softening up your opponent with elbows and knees prior to looking for the submission.

The Stand-Up Game
High kicks and long punches, or low kicks and inside elbows? For the big guy the choice is clear—use the low kicks and inside elbow strikes that take advantage of your natural body style and strength. If you start trading punches and kicks from the outside, it just becomes a contest of who is quicker—and that is not to the big guys' advantage. If your opponent tries to play the outside game then he is playing right into your hands. Use the opportunity to come in close and strike with knees and elbows from the inside—leave the flashy stuff to the guys in the Bruce Lee movies. Your goal is to win a fight.

Takedown Defenses
For me, one of the worst positions for a big guy to be in, is the guard. Sometimes, of course, you get caught and fall back and can't avoid it. In that case, you'd better know how to operate from there. However, the guard should never be your goal and it should only be used as a last resort. Far more effective than the guard for a big guy is the sprawl-and-brawl. When your opponent tries to shoot in simply sprawl back with your feet splayed to the sides, push his head and shoulders to the mat, and then knee and elbow him. He'll think twice before shooting low again. But if he does, let him.

Conclusion
In general, the most important training factor for big guys is to recognize, find, and then accept your strengths. Finding techniques that fit your body type is key! Many flashy ground moves that people see in the cage are predicated on extreme flexibility and quickness. Don't be upset if you're not as flexible and mobile as the little guys and therefore cannot execute some of the more spectacular moves. Remember that the little guys can't drop someone with one hammer smash to the top of the head, either! You can work on your flexibility—and it's a good thing practice—but if the position-and-strength game works for you, then go for it!

GRAPPLING

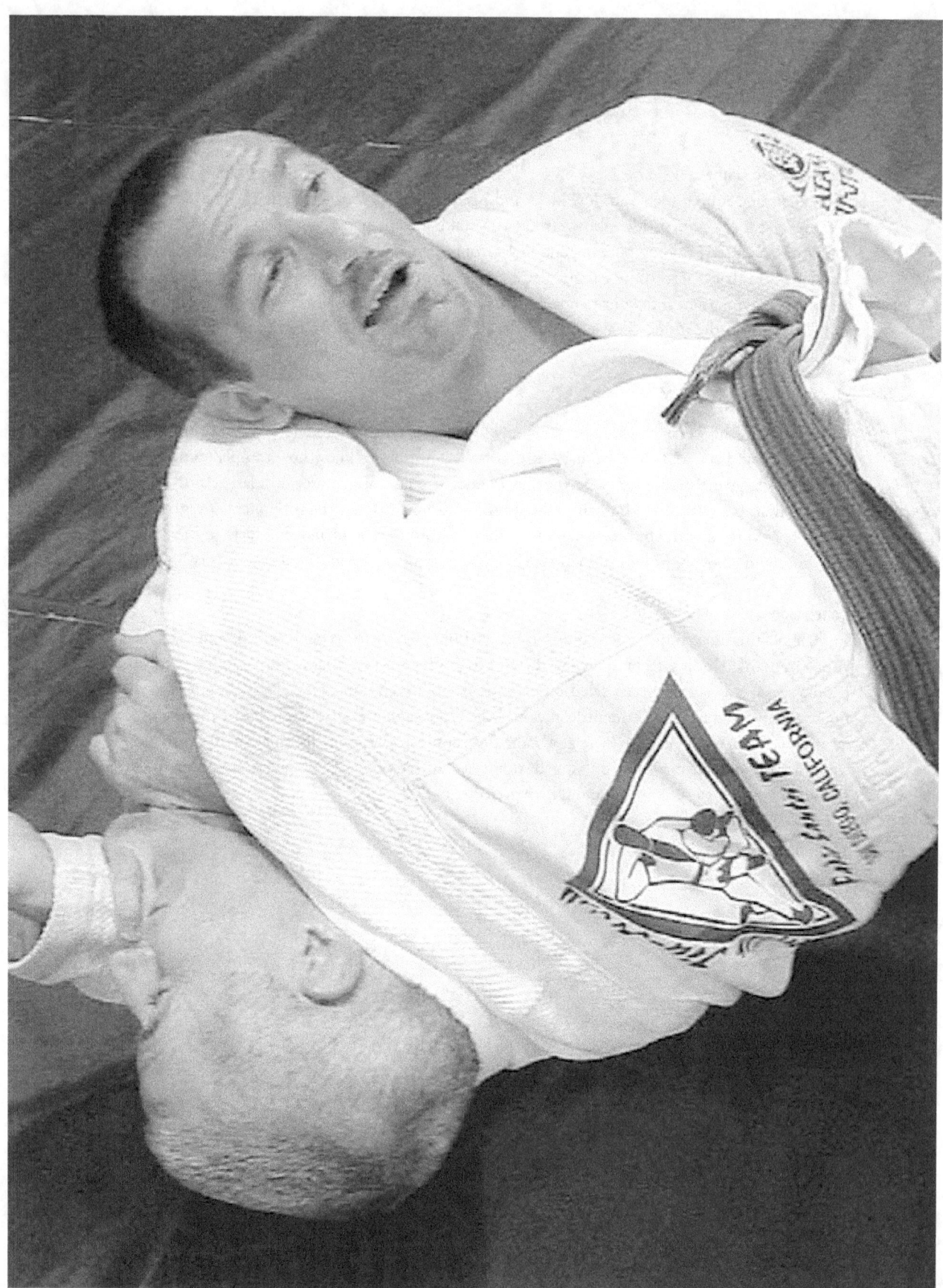

GRAPPLING

Fabio Santos
Attack and Conquer

Fabio Santos, a San Diego-based Rickson Gracie black belt, is not one to rest on his laurels. At 45 years of age, he is still going strong and competing against all comers.

Kid Peligro

Fabio Santos, a constant presence on the California tournament circuit, is a big fan favorite for his aggressive, attacking style. Since moving to the U.S. over 20 years ago, Santos has amassed quite a collection of trophies and medals. He is a two time Pan-American Champion, two time World Brazilian Jiu-Jitsu Masters Champion, and has won several superfights in various U.S. submission events. Santos encourages his students to compete as much as they can. "Competition is the quickest way to improve your game," Santos says. "I lead by example and enter as many tournaments as I can. If a teacher doesn't compete, how can he expect his students to?"

Having passed on his competition energy and commitment to his students, it is only natural that he is getting results. One of his best students and fiercest competitors is black belt Alexandre "Xande" Brandao. Brandao has been training BJJ for over 12 years and hates to miss any competitions. "The only reason I won't fight is if I am injured or there isn't anyone to fight against me—otherwise I am on the mat," says Brandao. "I mold my fighting attitude after Fabio. He is always putting himself on the line, win or lose, and I have always admired him for that. I want to compete in order to show Fabio what I have learned."

Stealth Moves

An extremely well-rounded grappler, Santos is an expert in judo and fights equally well from the bottom or top ground position, or from the feet. As anyone who has seen him fight can attest, Santos is particularly dangerous from the guard or when someone is cross-side on him. His deceptive moves mask his attacks from opponents until the last possible moment, leaving the countermoves too late to stop the submission.

"I believe submission should always be the goal of jiu-jitsu, and so I am always looking for it!" says Santos. "The third move I show in this article is one of my favorites. With a little slide of the hip to create space, I like to sneak my hand around the neck for a collar choke. I do this so much that one of my students once told me that he spent many sleepless nights just thinking about this choke!"

Inside Spinning Shoulder-Lock

Alexandre "Xande" Brandao faces teacher Fabio Santos from the open guard (1). Trapping Santos' elbow with his leg (2), he spins underneath the arm (3), secures the elbow with his knee (4) then rolls on top and applies the shoulder-lock submission (5).

GRAPPLING

Santos' deceptive attacking style is best utilized when he is in a supposedly inferior position. "Sometimes my opponent will get careless with their arm when they are across the side, because they think they are in control and don't have to worry about any counters. So I stay alert and keep looking for an opportunity to strike back. Usually, as they move their arm across my head to adjust their position, that is when I attack. I get them in an Americana or paintbrush type lock. Once I secure it I will either get the sweep, the submission or both."

Attack! Attack! Attack!
"The three main things that Fabio teaches," says top student Brandao, "is to attack, attack, and then attack some more." In keeping with Santos' theory of misdirection, Brandao also has developed a very offensive style. "From the open

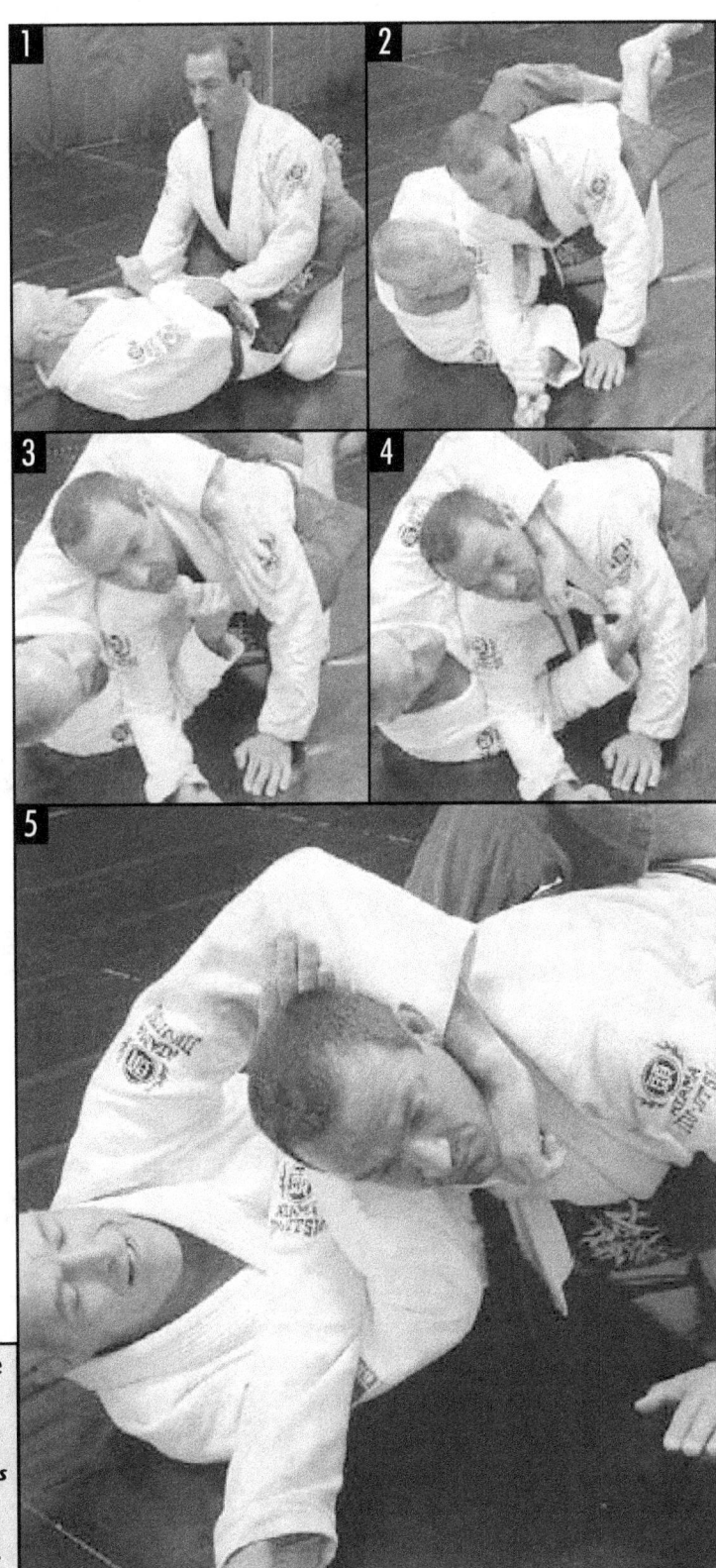

Closed-Guard Clock Choke
Fabio Santos holds Alexandre Brandao in his closed guard (1). Sliding to his side (2), Santos grabs the collar (3), passes it to his other hand (4), and applies the clock choke (5).

135

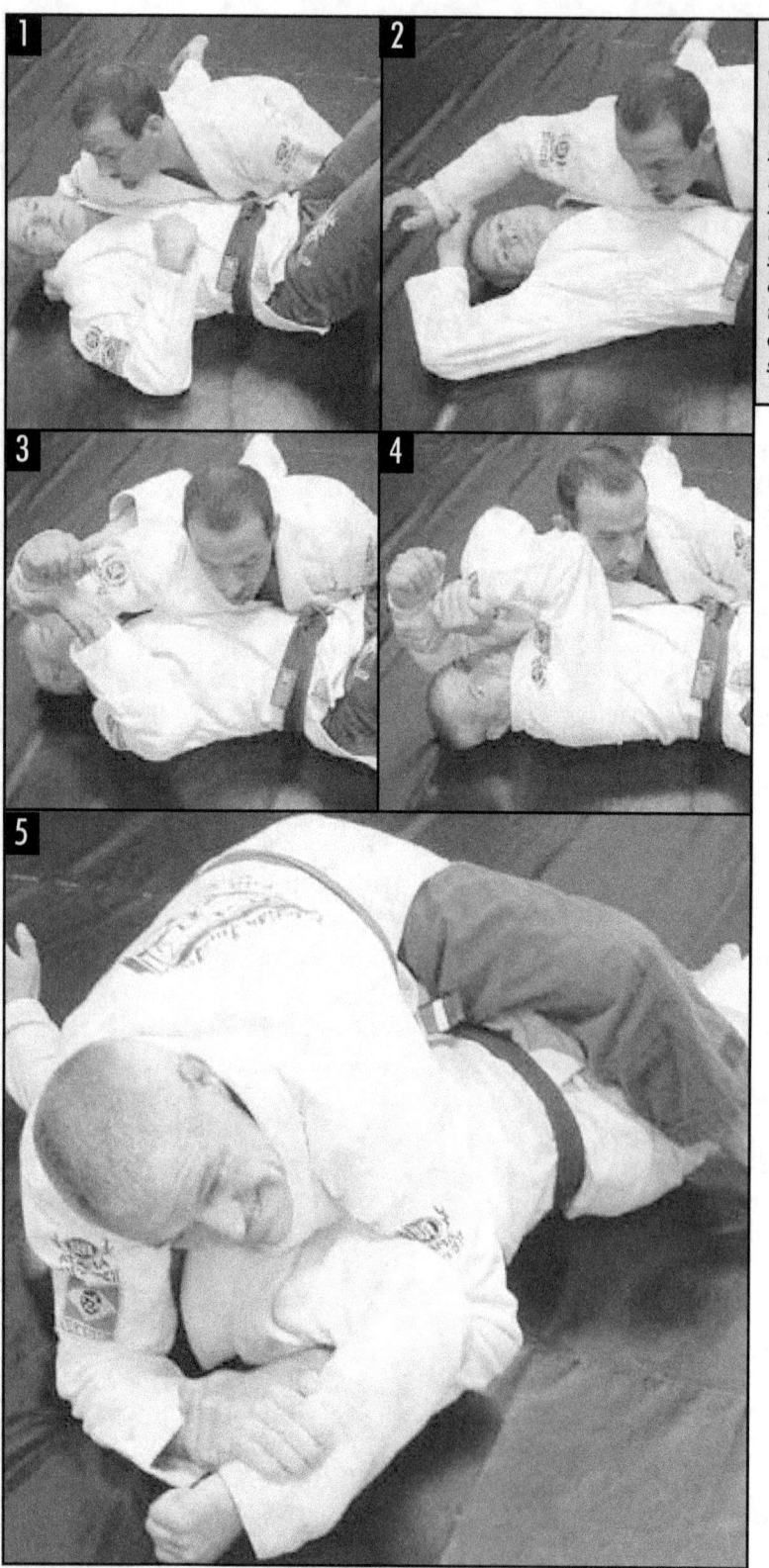

Side-Control Counter Arm-Lock
Fabio Santos is trapped underneath student Alexandre Brandao (1). Creating space by pressure the arm (2), Santos secures the wrist (3), clinches his hands (4), the rolls on top and applies the Americana submission lock (5).

guard," he says, "I love to go for a sneaky shoulder-lock. I make them think that I am going to sweep them but what I am really looking to do is to finish them with the shoulder lock. If your opponent does not know what to expect, then he will not be ready to defend your attack. That is really the essence of jiu-jitsu."

Passing The Guard

As Santos readily acknowledges, however, not everything can be accomplished from the bottom position and no one in their right mind will only fight from there. "Passing the guard is perhaps the most important thing you can do in competition," says Santos. "When you pass and score points, everything after that is in your favor. It puts pressure on your opponent to score points to catch you. Then when they start to hurry or rush, that will open up even more chances for submission." In the Santos theory of jiu-jitsu, the key to making a modern and effective guard pass is to maintain pressure on your opponent's shoulder, keep your arm under your opponent's armpit, and then slide your hips as close to the ground as possible. "This one is my favorite ways pass," says Santos. "If my opponent lets me get that position, I will pass their guard."

The Most Dangerous Weapon

"More than anything else," Santos says, "the most dangerous weapon in jiu-jitsu is the mind. You can't be frozen in one position or only be looking for one thing. You have to be adaptable to every situation and always be ready to change your position when your opponent shifts his. If you look at my teacher, Rickson Gracie, you'll see that he is a master of position. He always shifts positions with his opponent and he never gets caught in a place that he doesn't want to be. If there is one secret to Rickson's game, that is it. The ability to quickly change comes from being mentally flexible, and always being alert to what your opponent is doing."

Fabio Santos and Alex Brandao can be contacted for classes and seminars at (619) 229-0022 or fabiosantos@ix.netcom.com

GRAPPLING

BEST OF CFW — VOL. 1

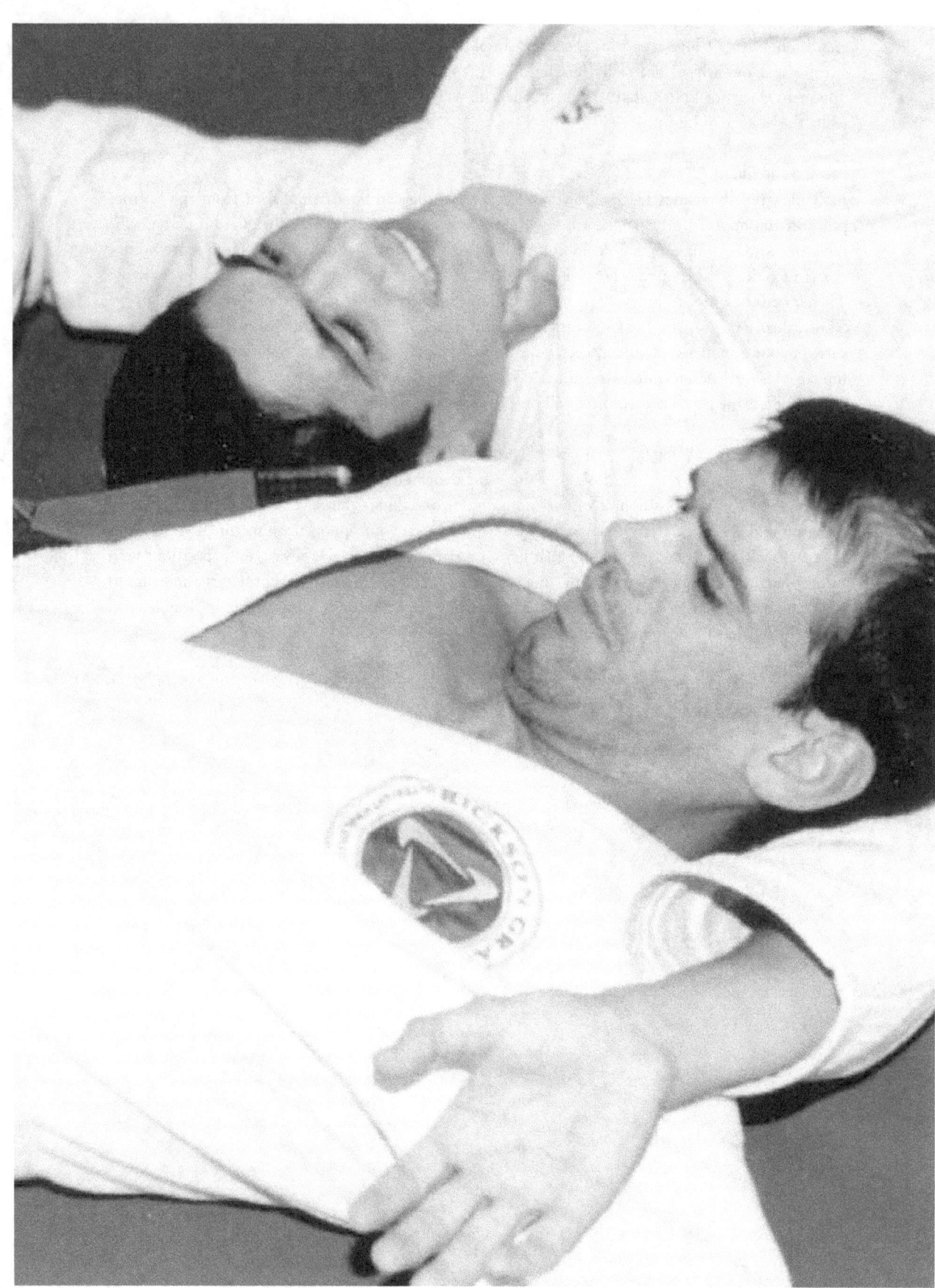

Megaton Diaz
Jiu-Jitsu's Son of Thunder

Leaving Brazil with only $400 in his pocket, Wellington Diaz, took a gamble and fulfilled his lifelong dream to live in the United States. The gamble paid off, though, and Diaz has been a legendary fixture on the American BJJ scene every since.

Loren Franck

In 1989, when 24-year-old "Megaton" Diaz landed at Denver International Airport, he planned a first-place victory the next day at a Brazilian jiu-jitsu tournament in the Mile High City. But the 5'7" 134-pounder also had something else in mind: fulfilling his dream to live in the United States. Hopelessly ambitious, he had updated his visiting-athlete visa, packed essential gear, and with $400 in his pocket had leaped into the future. Coming to America was worth the risk, Diaz reassured himself. Far from impulsive, the Denver move was a carefully calculated career decision—a turning point destined to unleash his hotbed of potential.

Like many others in Rio de Janeiro, where he was born and raised, Diaz became hooked on Brazilian jiu-jitsu as a youth. His "addiction" wasn't surprising, though. After all, what else would you expect from an action-packed sport vying to become Brazil's national pastime? Yet Diaz wanted more—much more. "I must extend my martial arts experience beyond Brazil," he vowed to himself. The solution? Move to America.

Rocky Mountain High
Colorado is beautiful. And though the weather is often cold, many residents of the Centennial State are warm and friendly, which adds to its appeal. Denver, the state capital, has a burgeoning population of some 550,000, yet retains many of its rural Midwestern roots. For Diaz, determined to jump-start his life and career, it was the consummate choice of cities. The Denver tournament went well for the young, eager Brazilian, who easily dominated the competition. But before the night ended, his heart was submitted, not by a bruising opponent, but by Luka Tavares, who was in town to topple the tourney's female competitors. Now a former Pan American champion and three-time bronze medal winner at the World Brazilian Jiu-Jitsu Championships, Luka displayed impressive fighting skills that night. Her competitive spirit floored Diaz. "Her best asset, though," he recalls, "was that she had everything I wanted in a woman, and she was very enthusiastic about Brazilian jiu-jitsu."

The Gracie Connection

Growing up in Rio is very different than being raised in the United States. In many ways, American and Brazilian cultures are opposites. For example, athletic opportunities American kids take for granted are often luxuries to the rising generation of Brazilians.

"Most kids in America participate in basketball, football and wrestling," explains Diaz, who despite disadvantages worked hard to become a professional athlete. "Some kids in Brazil don't have many athletic opportunities, but they do have judo. In fact, many Brazilian jiu-jitsu competitors there also know judo."

Diaz took up the Japanese grappling sport when he was five. But as months passed, his coach became a bodybuilder and put judo on the back burner. Although still new to the martial arts, Diaz realized that his judo training was about to be change drastically. Fortunately, his coach placed him in terrific hands. "I won't be able to teach you martial arts anymore," he told a sad-faced Diaz. "I could have helped you become good. But don't worry. I'm going to set you up with some people who can make you great." Those "people" were the Gracies.

While training with Rickson and Royler Gracie, Diaz soon fell in love with Brazilian jiu-jitsu. "They had taught my judo coach," Diaz recalls, "so he arranged for me to train with the Gracies too. I worked a lot with Rickson during my early years in Brazilian jiu-jitsu, and we became close friends." Yet Royler remains Diaz's primary instructor. During one of Royler's extended visits to Los Angeles several years ago, he and Diaz trained extensively with each other, soaking up sun together after workouts at Southern California beaches. And despite demanding schedules, they still practice together whenever possible. Their teacher-student relationship is stronger than ever. In fact, Diaz recently returned from East Africa, where he helped Royler conduct an innovative series of seminars. He also took a group of students to Los Angeles last December to train with the Gracies. "I am what I am because of Royler Gracie," declares Diaz, eager to give credit where it's due. "Upcoming Brazilian jiu-jitsu students need guidance so the true meaning of the art isn't lost."

Turtle-Defense Counter
Megaton Diaz fights to penetrate the tough defense of Luka Tavares (1). Wrapping her body with his arms (2), Megaton barrel rolls to the side (3), goes completely under (4), and ends up on bottom (5). Sliding out to the other side (6), Megaton throws his legs over his opponent's body from the far side (7), then settles into side control (8).

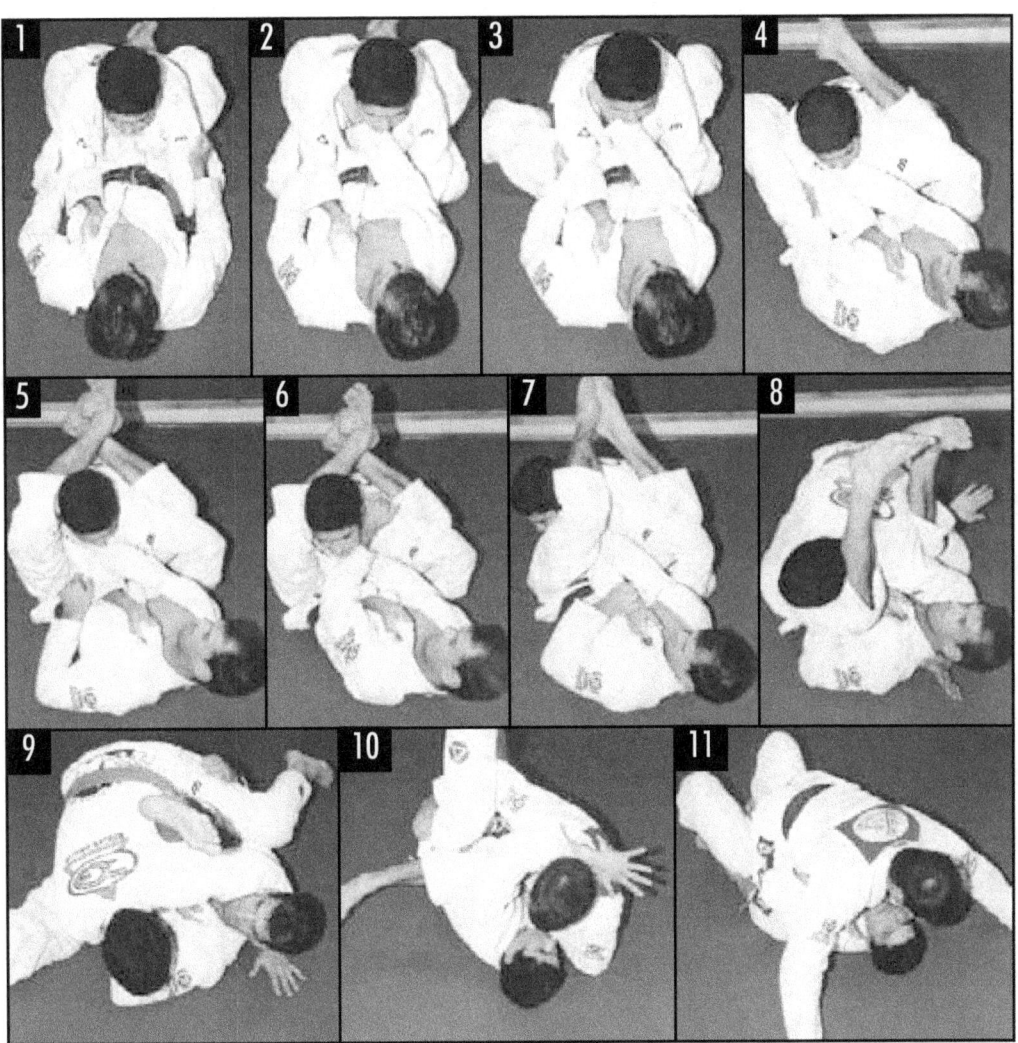

Mount Reversal
Megaton Diaz in trapped under the mount of Luka Tavares (1). Megaton grabs the collar (2), traps the elbow (3), and then swings his legs over the (4), and locks them together (4). Inserting his other hand into the collar, Megaton starts to apply the front choke (6). When his opponent pulls out and counters the choke, however (7), Megaton slides his hips to the side (8), thrusts his feet forward (9), and then throws his opponent's back leg, rolling her over (10), and allowing him to take the top mount (11).

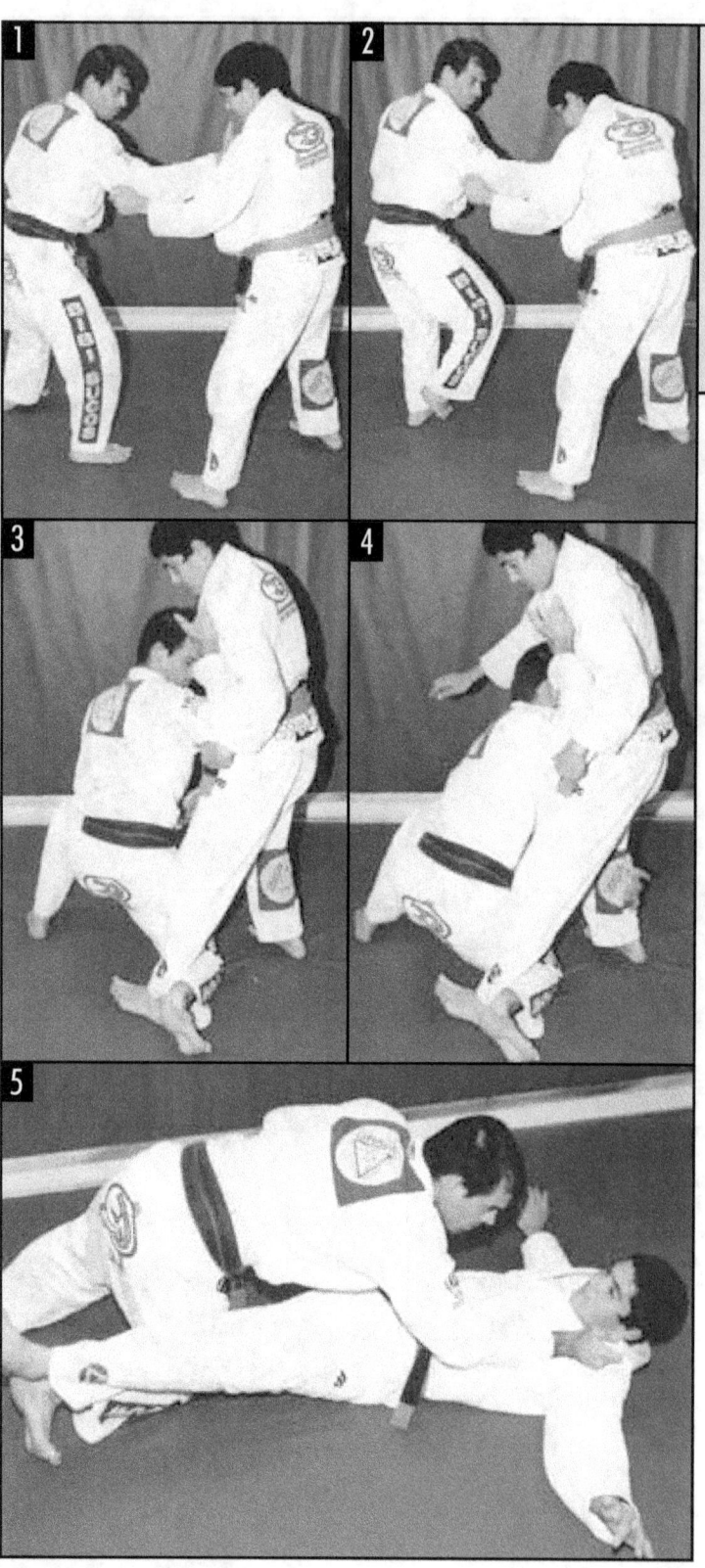

Leg-Sweep Takedown
Megaton Diaz locks up with Luka Tavares on the feet (1). Pulling her towards him (2), he steps in when she pulls back to avoid the pressure and hooks her leg (3). Hooking her other heel with his hand (4), he presses forward and throws her to the ground for the successful takedown (5).

GRAPPLING

From his earliest days in judo, Diaz wanted to run his own martial arts school. That opportunity arrived when he and Luka recently moved to Phoenix, where they run the Megaton Brazilian Jiu-Jitsu Academy. Diaz liked Denver, but he loves sun-drenched Phoenix. He's planted roots and intends to stay.

Gold Medalist
Always on the prowl for further challenges, Diaz has an impressive competition history. For instance, he captured Pan American gold medals in 1998, 2000 and 2001, and he fought nobly in Abu Dhabi two years ago. Diaz also took home gold from the 1998 Korea Black Belt Challenge. In addition, he placed second at the World Brazilian Jiu-Jitsu Championships in 1996, fought his way to third in 1999, and returned in 2001 to take third again. Yet he doesn't consider himself a submission fighter. While interested in mixed martial arts, he prefers straight Brazilian jiu-jitsu competition.

"I don't have much experience in the UFC or in other forms of no-rules fighting," admits Diaz, who, whatever the venue, relies on judo and Brazilian jiu-jitsu to defeat opponents. "I'd like to have more no-rules matches in the future, but I've never had much opportunity to become a full-on submission fighter."

But lack of opportunity isn't the only barrier to a mixed-martial-arts career for Diaz. He's also put off by the minuscule payment most grapplers receive, which is why he believes in a minimum wage for fighters. "Clearly, most fighters don't make enough money in mixed martial arts," Diaz observes. "If you're not a big name, it's hard to earn top dollar. Besides, why get hurt for $500 or $1,000? Show me the money—the big money—and I'll fight anywhere at any time."

Bombs Away
Though christened "Wellington" at birth, Diaz has been known as "Megaton" much of his life. People in and out of jiu-jitsu use the catchy moniker. It's a good thing too, because Diaz likes the name and will never forget how he earned it. "While growing up in Rio, I competed in dozens of judo tournaments," Diaz recalls. "In most of them, I threw my opponents to the mat extremely hard, and it made a thundering noise. Someone said my throws sounded like a megaton bomb. Well, the name stuck, and I've been known as Megaton ever since."

True to his good nature, Diaz has fun with the nickname, which better describes his judo matches than his bouts in Brazilian jiu-jitsu. The name does have its drawbacks, however. For example, most of Diaz's recent opponents were prepared to counter his judo moves. They feared his uncanny ability to throw them to the mat like a rag doll. Is Diaz flattered by his opponents' preparation? Not really. Most are ready for his stand-up style, so his reputation for thunderous throws can actually make winning difficult. In anticipation of being hurled through the air and slammed to the ground, many of Diaz's opponents try to pull him down as soon as the fight starts. "If an opponent stands up with me, he knows I'll probably throw him," says Diaz, a glimmer of satisfaction sparkling in his eyes. "He'll usually try to pull me to the mat right away. If we both fight while standing, though, I will throw him—and he knows it."

Well-Rounded Fighter
Whatever the fighting art—boxing, wrestling or mixed martial arts—success rarely hinges on one technique. Thanks to Royler Gracie, Diaz learned this valuable lesson early and became a versatile competitor who uses all fighting techniques. Throwing opponents to the ground with deafening force is but one part of his arsenal. Proudly, Diaz has lived up to his nickname throughout his

"Diaz has an impressive competition history. For instance, he captured Pan American gold medals in 1998, 2000 and 2001, and he fought nobly in Abu Dhabi two years ago. Diaz also took home gold from the 1998 Korea Black Belt Challenge."

Brazilian jiu-jitsu career. Yet countless hours of training have made him a superb all-around competitor. He hasn't used many booming judo throws in recent matches, but if Diaz can win with a judo throw, he'll apply it instinctively. He considers all options, so his fighting strategy is unlimited. "I choke as well as I throw," Diaz explains, "but if my opponents give me an arm, I take it; if they offer a leg, I take that too. It's the same with judo throws. There are all kinds of them, and of course, I have my favorites. However, I use every opening and every technique to my advantage."

Priority One

More than 30 years of training have given Diaz plenty of time to reap the benefits of the martial arts. His most important advice to upcoming fighters? Set priorities. Brazilian jiu-jitsu wasn't meant to be an avenue of fame and fortune, warns Diaz, who also believes there's more to the sport than being a tough guy.

"When I began my judo training, I did it for the love of the art," he reflects. "I felt the same when the Gracies started teaching me. Granted, I wanted to become a black belt someday, but I never planned to get rich off the martial arts. And though I make a living from Brazilian jiu-jitsu, I don't have a mansion, a Beamer or expensive jewelry. Instead, I love the art, and my training, competing and teaching stem from that love."

Remember your martial arts genealogy too, Diaz urges, because it provides a solid foundation for training and fighting. Jiu-jitsu organizations exist worldwide, and many claim to offer students the ultimate in fight training. Treat these claims skeptically, Diaz cautions. "There are various Brazilian jiu-jitsu clans," he concludes, "but trace the art back. Where do their instructors' roots lead? To the Gracies. Too many people forget that. The Gracies never claimed to be the greatest. They just wanted the best for Brazilian jiu-jitsu. People from various organizations might obtain the highest belt ranks, but they shouldn't forget where their art originated. In Brazilian jiu-jitsu, you need to know your origins because they help shape your destiny."

Megaton Diaz may be contacted at the Megaton Brazilian Jiu-Jitsu Academy, 2106 West Camelback Rd., Phoenix, AZ 85015; (602) 841-9779.

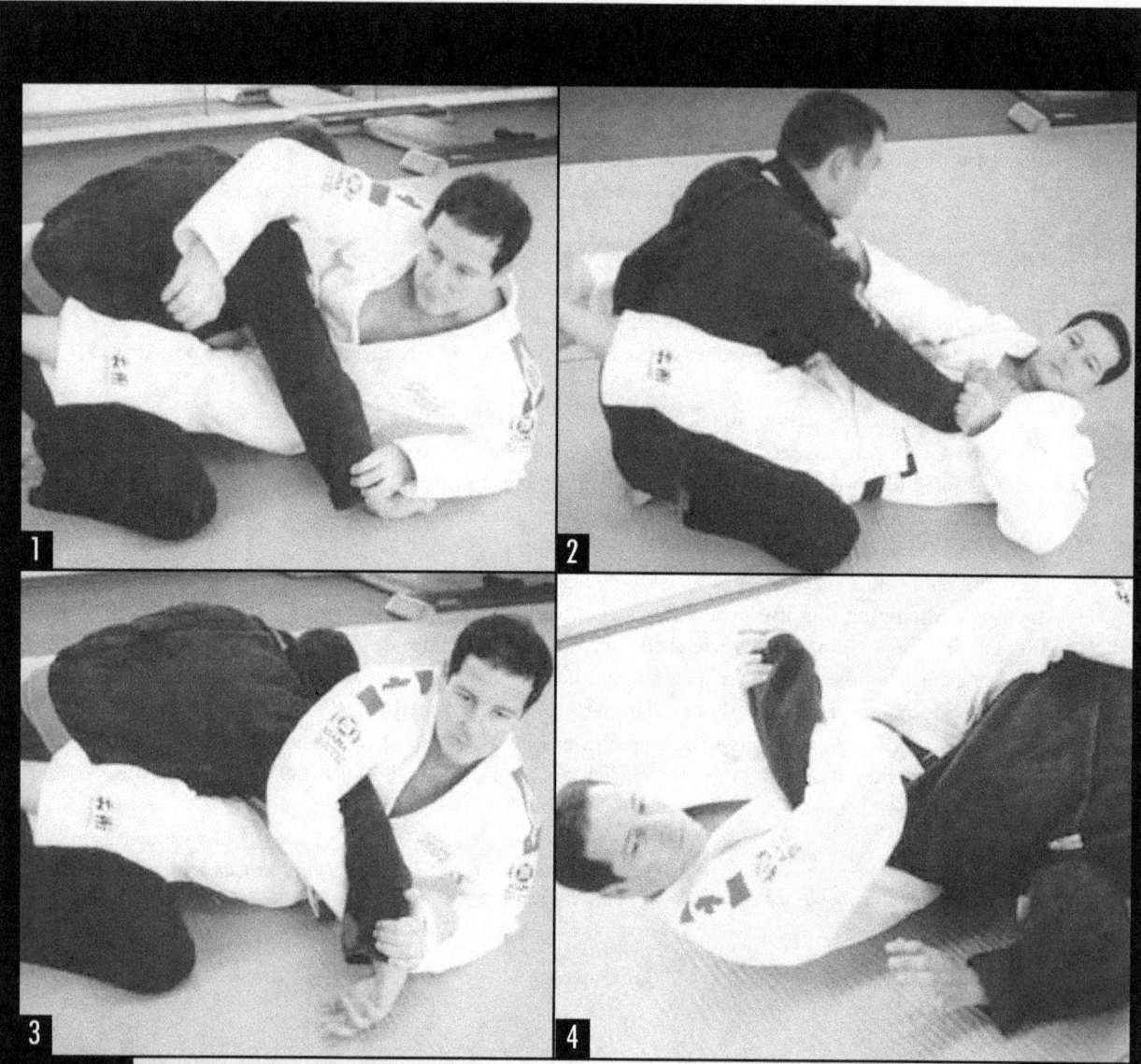

Closed-Guard Kimura

(1) In Brazil this sequence is often taught as one of the most basic attacks from the guard. You start with your opponent in the closed guard and a grip on his sleeve and lapel. (2) With your sleeve grip you pull your opponent's hand to the ground. At the same time you open your guard, escape your hips, sit up and reach over his triceps with the hand that had been on his lapel. (3) Reach your second hand over and through his arm and grab your own wrist. It is very important to have his arm, especially his upper arm, trapped tight against your chest. (4) Now, with his arm firmly trapped, keeping his hand well away from his body (so it will be harder to defend) escape your hips out to the side of his trapped arm. The act of escaping your hips is the most important part of this move. Scissors his body with your legs, keeping your calf firmly pressing down on his lower back—this keeps him from rolling. To apply the lock from here you do two things: first you move his elbow towards his head—this takes all the slack out of the system. The second and final touch is to try to bring his hand to the back of his head. Unless he is made of cooked spaghetti you now have him trapped in the Kimura lock.

Mastering the Kimura

The Kimura lock is one of the most important submission holds in jiu-jitsu. It is also found in many other grappling systems, where it might be called a hammer-lock, a chicken-wing, or ude-garami. Whatever the name, it is a powerful and versatile attack.

Marcus Soares and Stephan Kesting

Whenever you see grapplers competing, whether in Pride, the UFC, Abu Dhabi or the jiu-jitsu Mundials, you see the Kimura lock used to submit opponents and win matches! In Brazilian jiu-jitsu, the Kimura lock is named after Masahiko Kimura, who is widely regarded as the greatest judo player of all time. While on tour in Brazil in 1952, Kimura fought a famous challenge match with Helio Gracie. Helio first had to defeat Kato, a judoka in Kimura's entourage, to get the opportunity to fight Kimura himself. After choking Kato unconscious, Helio was permitted to face Kimura.

This match lasted 13 minutes and ended when Kimura caught Helio Gracie in an arm lock, causing Carlos Gracie to throw in the towel, signalling surrender. Kimura was most impressed that the much lighter Helio Gracie lasted as long as he did, and invited him to come teach in Japan. Almost 50 years later, the arm lock that defeated Helio is now known as the "Kimura lock" in Brazil, in homage to Kimura's great ability.

The Kimura lock is the favorite arm lock of Marcus Soares: once he locks it on, there is no escape. It is also the favourite arm lock of Marcus's teacher, Carlson Gracie, who won many vale tudo fights with this submission.

What makes the Kimura so effective is that you can apply it from closed guard, open guard, north-south position, or from the mount. You might be familiar with some of these moves already, but there are many fine points and details that are often overlooked.

There are many more variations for each of these positions, some of which you will find for yourself if you do some research and experimentation. There are also Kimura attacks from the side mount, half guard, half mount, turtle, standing and even from the back; it is a very versatile attack. We will discuss these, and many other submissions, in future issues of *Grappling* magazine.

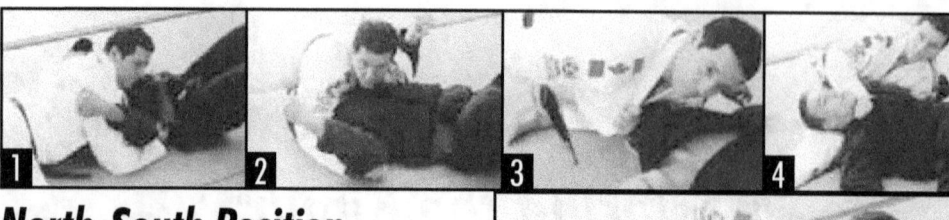

North-South Position Kimura Neck-Crank

(1) Start in the north-south position with one arm over your opponent's shoulder and one arm under his shoulder. Your bodyweight should initially be on the side of the under-hooking arm. (2) To set up the submission, start circling towards the over-hooked side, and trap his arm by encircling it with your own and gripping your own lapel. (3) This close-up shows you how exactly how to hold his arm and your own lapel. Your opponent is unlikely to suspect 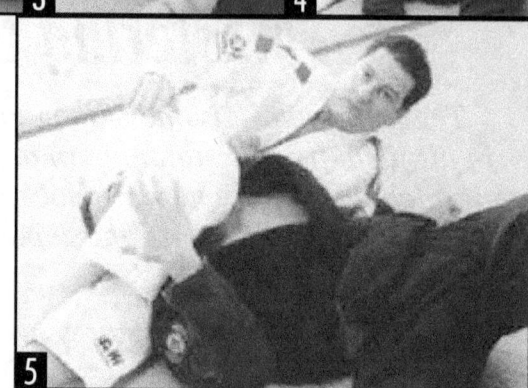 how close he is to a Kimura lock! (4) Now switch your base, bringing your thigh up under his head like a pillow. The next move will be to step your other leg up over his head and triangle your feet, trapping his head between your legs. (5) Now you lie back and pull on his arm, putting severe strain on his shoulder. If you don't believe that this is a Kimura lock try it on your training partner. When he taps, take a look at his arm: it should be bent into the exact same position as if you were applying a regular Kimura. At the same time as you are locking his arm, however, you can be neck-cranking and choking him by squeezing your legs together and pulling on his arm: a very bad position for your opponent.

Open Guard Kimura

(1) This time your opponent is standing in your open guard and trying to pass it. Start with a sleeve and lapel grip, with one foot pushing your opponent's hip and the other hooking behind his knee. Keep your opponent bent over to limit his ability to move or mount an offence. (2) If your opponent grips your knee then you know that he is probably going to try to push it down to the floor and pass your guard. Quickly switch your grips so that you are controlling the wrist of the hand on the knee and the lapel closest to that side. (3) Swing the 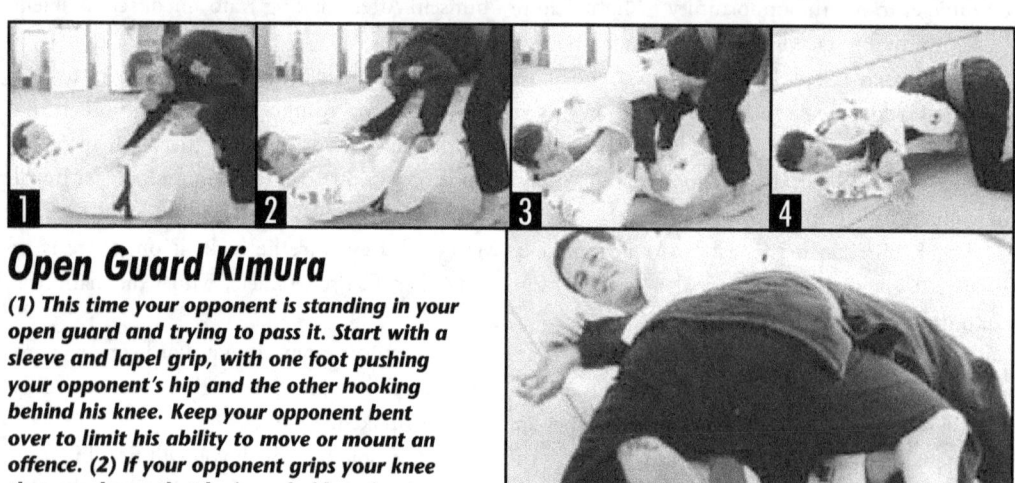 foot that was pushing his hip over his head and shoulder and insert that instep under his leg. Keep on pulling his wrist so that it almost comes close to the floor to prevent him from easily countering your attack. You might feel pretty awkward at this point but don't worry; you are very close to getting him to tap. (4) Now figure-four your arms to totally trap his arm. This limits the amount of movement in his arm and his ability to escape. (5) This photo clearly shows how your feet and legs are hooking both of his legs. Use a scissoring action to stretch his legs, completely off-balancing him. He is now in a position where it only takes a tiny movement of the arms and hips to apply the Kimura lock.

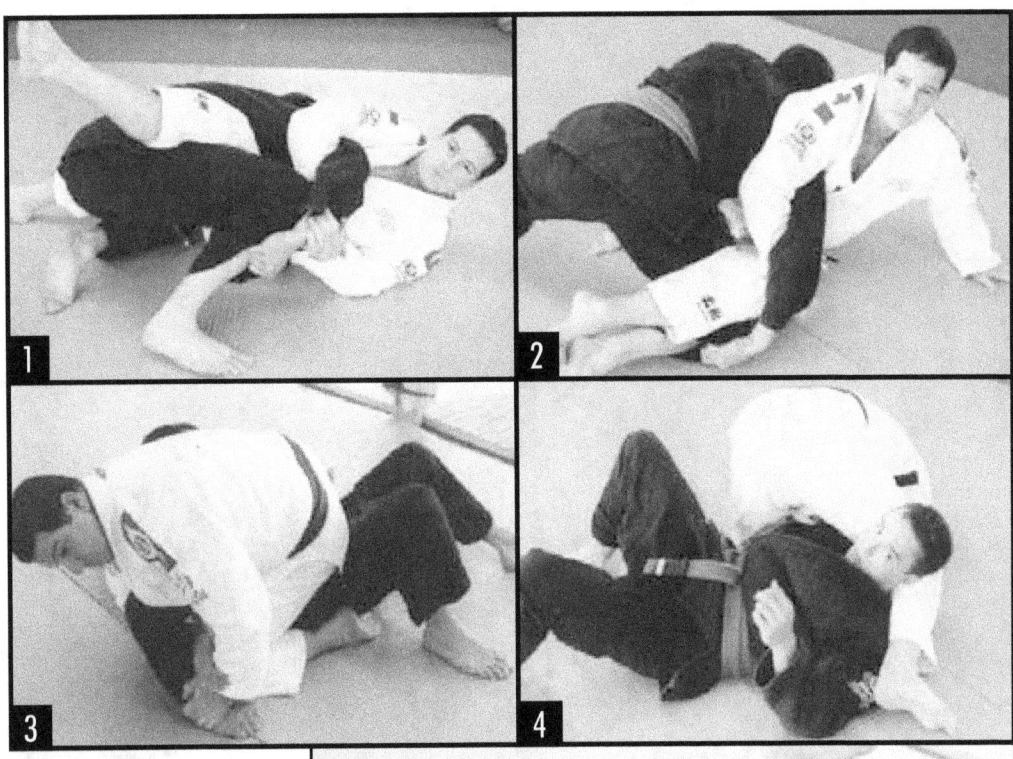

Mounted Kimura

(1) If your opponent is quick he may be able to counter your Kimura from the guard by posting his foot and grabbing his pants. You may be able to simply rip his grip free from his gi pants if you are stronger or he is sloppy, but the following is a more elegant solution to the problem. (2) Post your hand on the floor behind you, keeping his arm wrapped. You are now in a position to apply

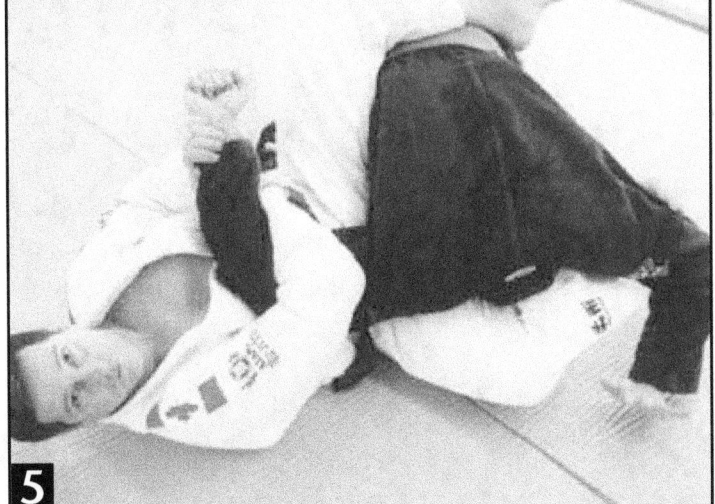

the hip-buck sweep by sitting up and twisting in the direction of the entangled arms. (3) You should now end up in the mount position. The mount is not a typical position from which to apply a Kimura, but here is a way to do it. (4) Keep the Kimura grip firmly on your opponent's arm. Now bring your near knee up into your opponent's armpit and post your head on the ground to base. Now you can step your other leg up and over his head. Hook his head with your calf—you may have to crank on his arm a little bit to lift his head off the ground. (5) Finally roll over your shoulder, ending up with your back on the ground, one leg over his body, another over his head, and his arm firmly locked in a Kimura.

BEST OF CFW ─── VOL. 1
GRAPPLING

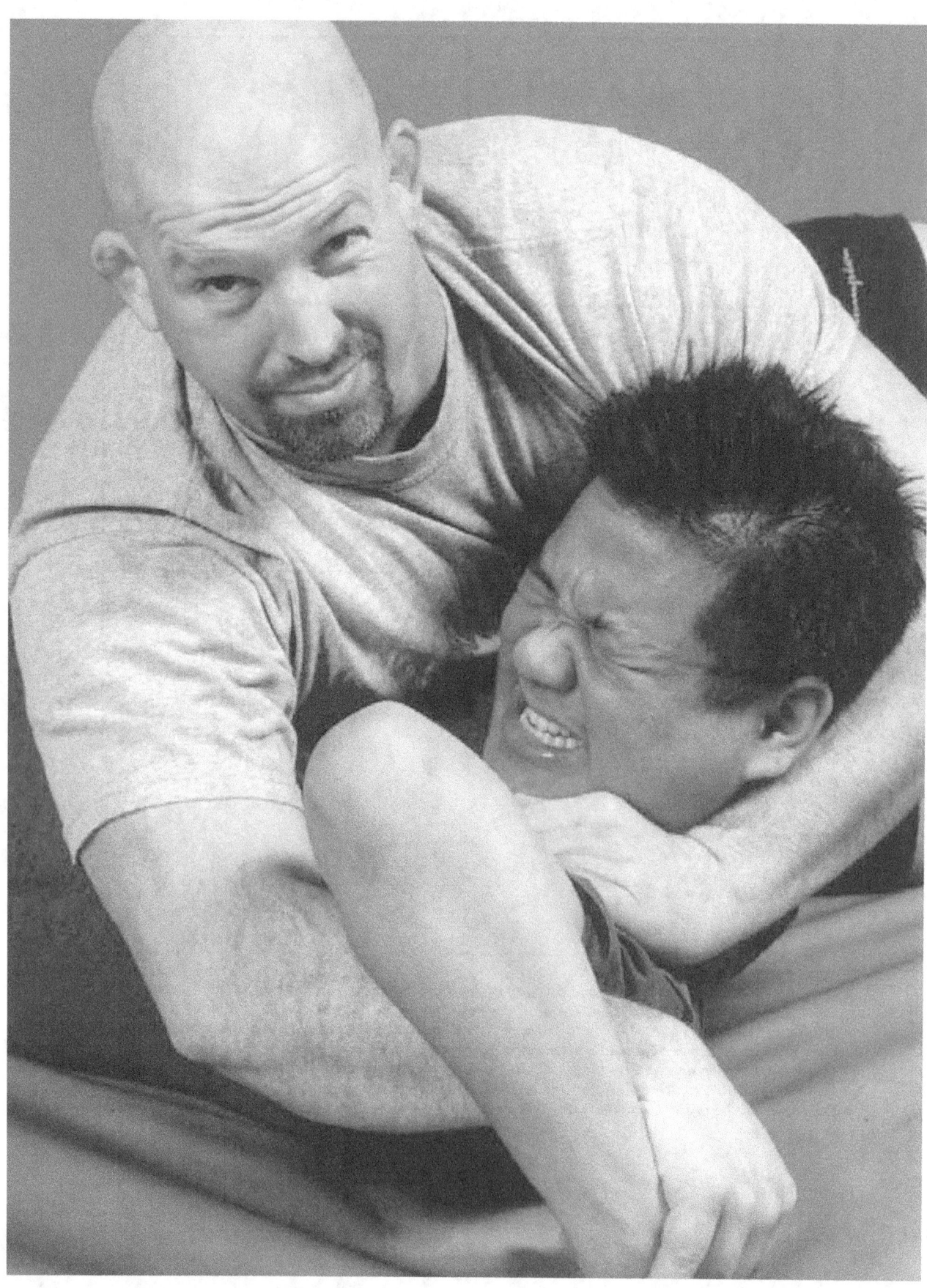

Catch Wrestling
America's Martial Art

Long before Olympic wrestling, Brazilian jiu-jitsu, and the UFC, Americans flocked to sold-out arenas to watch catch-as-catch-can wrestlers like "Farmer" Burns, Frank Gotch, and "Strangler" Lewis take on the world.

Matt Furey

Catch wrestling is not the first wrestling style that came to the United States, nor will it be the last. Catch wrestling is no different from any other progressive grappling art. Its practitioners were savvy enough to learn the best moves from many styles, then adapt and adopt what worked to their system. To truly understand the history of catch wrestling, never lose sight of the fact that America has always been a huge melting pot, attracting many cultures in search of freedom and prosperity. As each immigrant group ended their voyage here, they didn't just bring their earthly possessions, they also brought their heritage of sporting knowledge—which included wrestling skills.

It began when the first pilgrims arrived at Plymouth Rock—and most likely earlier than that. Not only did Native Americans practice many styles of wrestling, so did the British, Irish, French and other cultures who settled here. Later, the Japanese brought judo, jiu-jitsu, and karate; the Chinese kung-fu and Mongolian wrestling; the Koreans taekwondo and hapkido; the Filipinos kali; the Brazilians ground jiu-jitsu; and the Russians sombo. But there were also many other styles not so well-known.

The Irish, for example, are presumed to have brought collar-and-elbow wrestling to Vermont in the 1700s. By the mid-1800s a strange thing happened—an American style called "catch" wrestling suddenly appeared. It was very different from the jacket-based style of collar-and-elbow wrestling which was centered around throws. Our 16th president, Abe Lincoln, according to numerous accounts of the time, was quite accomplished at the art of "throwing" opponents in grappling matches.

By the end of the 1880's, though, during the early days of legendary American wrestler Martin "Farmer" Burns, the throwing-based style of catch-as-catch-can was, for the most part, outdated. Matches were not always won or lost by a throw. Burns, who was purported to have wrestled some 6000 matches in his career, won most of them by pinfall (forcing both of the opponent's shoulders to the ground) or by submission. Some of the contests, however, as noted in the book, *Lifework of Farmer Burns*, were still decided by a throw. How did America go from collar-and-elbow grappling,

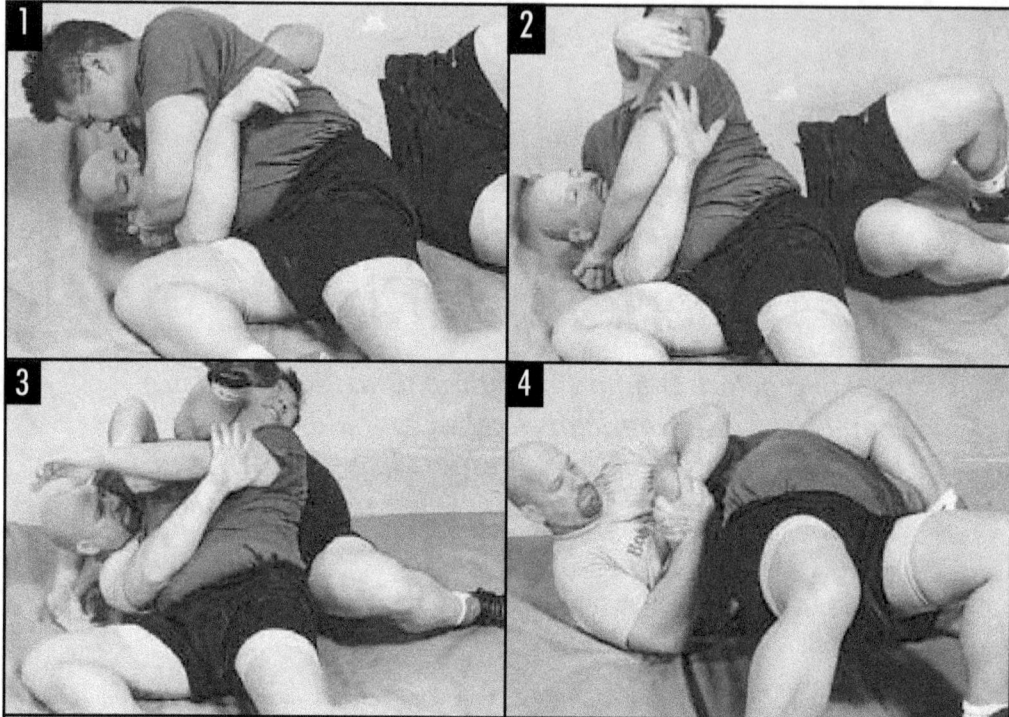

Cross-Side Submission
Trapped under his opponent (1), Matt Furey creates space by pressuring the nose (2), swinging the leg in front of the face (3), and applying a wrist lock while trapping the head (4).

a jacketed throwing art, to the bare-chest art of catch wrestling, replete with takedowns, throws, pinfalls and submissions?

American History Catch

You won't find the answer in any American history book. The most credible answer comes from someone who deeply understands both wrestling techniques and history. This man competed in the 1948 Olympics for his native Belgium in both freestyle and Greco-Roman. He turned pro in 1950, and for eight years (1950-58) trained at the famous Billy Riley Gym in Wigan, England (one of only two schools left in the world where the real professional style of catch wrestling was taught). This man, who would emigrate to the United States in 1961, became the greatest master of this brutal yet highly refined "lost" art of catch wrestling. This person is none other than Karl

Martin "Farmer" Burns

GRAPPLING

Gotch, the man who quickly became known in Japan as *kamisama* (god of wrestling) for his amazing knowledge and skills in the art of submission wrestling.

During Gotch's first trip to Japan, he won the people's hearts and souls with a display of wrestling ability never before seen. Not only could the 6'3", 250 pound Gotch throw with the grace, speed and finesse of a lightweight, but on the mat he was an unstoppable force. In workouts with Japan's top judo and jiu-jitsu men, he beat them so badly, even with a gi on, that they cried for mercy. Little did they know, that before emigrating to the U.S., Gotch had also gone into the judo halls of Europe. His techniques were so powerful that in his native Belgium, he earned his black belt in one day!

Karl Gotch with the great Kimura

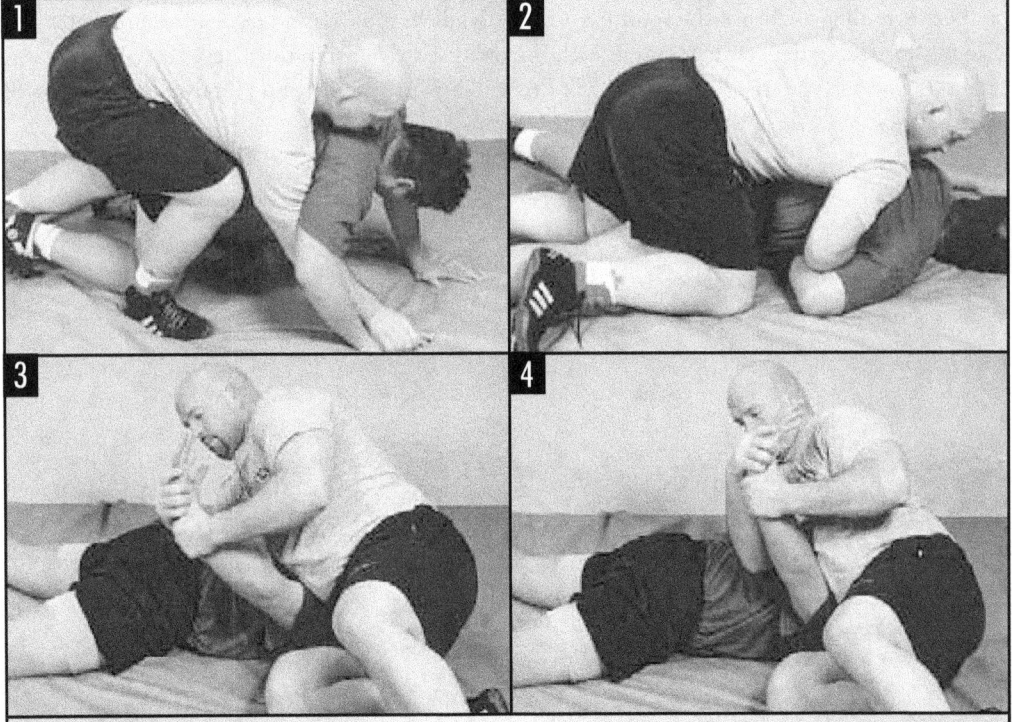

Back-Control Double Wrist-Lock
Controlling his opponent from the back (1), Matt Furey pulls the arm back (2), rolls to the side and extends the arm (3), and then applies a double wrist-lock for the submission (4).

Frank Gotch (lt.) shakes hands with George Hackenschmidt, "The Russian Lion," before their first bout in Chicago in 1908, before 30,000 fans.

Gotch's technique was so brutal that his wife once told a friend, "I was so glad when Karl quit going to judo and jiu-jitsu. It was so hard washing everyone else's blood from his gi every night."

I was living in San Jose, California when I first learned that 70-year-old Karl Gotch was in Florida. I immediately pulled-up stakes and moved my entire family to the Sunshine State to learn from this world treasure of wrestling knowledge. Along with everything else Gotch taught me about conditioning and catch wrestling, was a personal grasp of oral history not found in any book.

According to Gotch, all immigrants had brought their style of wrestling to the United States around the turn of the century. Not only had the Irish brought collar-and-elbow, but the Arabs brought their knowledge of leg wrestling, and the British, along with their boxing, brought three styles of wrestling—Cornish-Devonshire, Cumberland-Westmoreland and Lancashire Catch-As-Catch-Can. Taking the best methods of each imported style, along with whatever else made its way across the oceans, the Americans, with their keen ability to assimilate and innovate, quickly developed a wide-open style of wrestling—American Catch-As-Catch-Can.

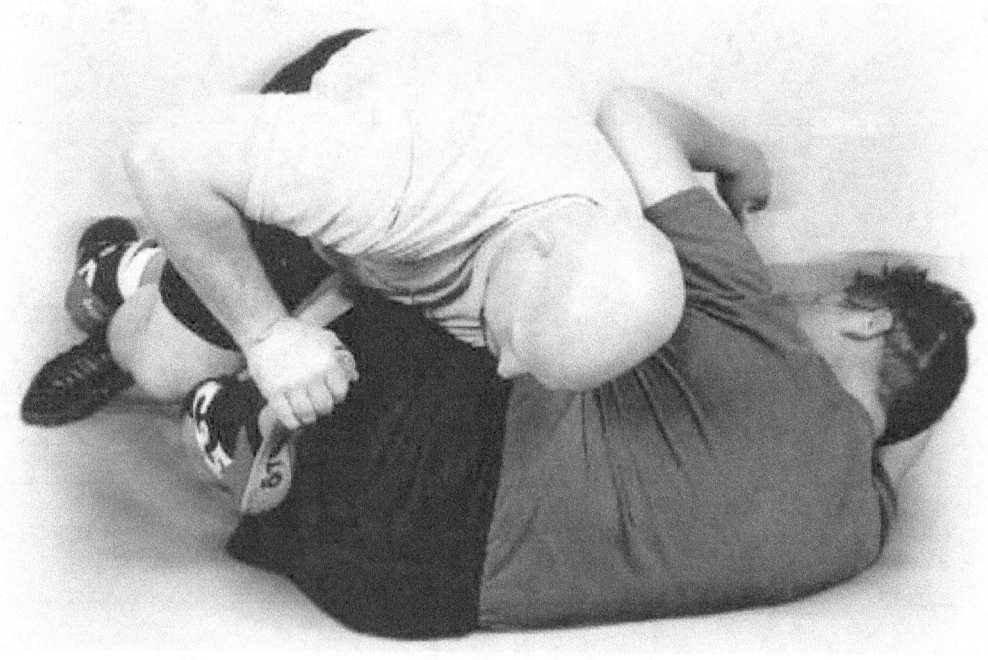

GRAPPLING

Farmer Burns

The foremost practitioners of the American style were Iowans Martin "Farmer" Burns and Frank Gotch. Burns, a wiry 165-pounder with a 20-inch neck, could take a six-foot hangman's drop and stay in the noose for three minutes while whistling Yankee Doodle Dandy. He used quickness, tenacity, endurance, and a devastating array of submissions to crush the biggest of foes. He regularly barnstormed through towns, taking on all-comers.

Burns was a mat shark with his skills. He often pretended be someone else, secured a match with the biggest and toughest man around, got others to hedge their bets, and then commenced to put on a show. In the best-out-of-three-falls matches, Burns knew exactly how to work the crowd. He would go through several minutes of "struggle" in the ring, making it appear that he was out-matched. Burns would keep the struggle going long enough to get his opponent somewhat tired, then he would make a mistake on purpose and lose the first fall. He then watched as the audience placed their bets again. When the size of the pot grew, he would destroy the opponent, quickly winning the next fall, but making it appear like "luck." More bets were placed. When the action began a third time, Burns snuffed his foe even faster than the second fall—then skated town with all the loot.

The same tactic was used by Burns' ace pupil, Frank Gotch, who traveled

Gotch's technique was so brutal that his wife once told a friend, "I was so glad when Karl quit going to judo and jiu-jitsu. It was so hard washing everyone else's blood from his gi every night."

the Pacific Northwest in the early 1900's, going as far as Alaska, where he wrestled under the name of Frank Kennedy. He took matches with railroad workers, fishermen and other rough-and-tumble characters, and returned home a short while later with $30,000—a fortune in those days.

Frank Gotch

As the story goes, before he developed his craft to its highest level, Gotch was a young and burly farmhand from Humboldt, Iowa, who had a reputation for being a tough wrestler, although completely untrained. He met "Farmer" Burns one evening in nearby Fort Dodge for a match. At the time, in terms of experience, when compared to Burns, Gotch had little wrestling knowledge. Yet, on the night of their match, the two fought to a draw. Burns immediately seized the opportunity to make Gotch his student, declaring that he would turn him into the world champion.

The story didn't make sense to me. If Burns was so good, how could he fight to a draw with a beginner? And if Gotch was so great, why would he want to be trained by someone he had just fought to a draw? Did Gotch somehow realize that Burns was much older but more knowledgeable? Or could the whole event have been another Burns' setup to make even more money? I suspect the latter. Otherwise there would be no reason for Gotch to entrust himself to Burns' care.

When I first began learning from Karl Gotch, I asked him, "Who was better, Frank Gotch or Farmer Burns?" Bear in mind I had heard that Burns was actually better and I wanted Karl's take on the matter. In reply, Karl said, "Gotch was better. He was much younger, much bigger, and stronger—and you must remember, the Farmer taught him everything he knew."

Some months later, however, Karl told me a different story. "I don't like to tell people this, but the truth is that even after Gotch won the world championship, Burns was better and could still lick him. I was told by those who knew, that one day in practice they had a go-behind contest. This is a contest to see who can get behind and take the other guy down the most times. Burns won the contest 7-3."

Frank Gotch became world champion in 1908, beating the Russian Lion, George Hackenschmidt, in front of 30,000 people in Chicago's Comiskey Park—the largest crowd to ever see a professional sporting event in America at the time. The question that everyone seems to ask, though, is how does catch wrestling compare to the more modern grappling arts of judo and jiu-jitsu?

Catch Wrestling vs. Jiu-Jitsu

Believe it or not, Farmer Burns addressed this very same matter in the final lesson of his 1914 mail-order course, *Lessons in Wrestling & Physical Culture*. Imagine that? The inherent rivalry between jiu-jitsu and wrestling is nothing new. Burns and Gotch, even in the early 1900s, did not simply slough off and ignore either of these fine arts. They looked into them and developed their style to make sure they could counter them. In many matches, Burns and Gotch defeated Japanese practitioners. When Gotch was world champion, he received an invitation to the White House from President Theodore Roosevelt, who was an avid student of boxing and judo. Gotch was pitted against one of the top Japanese judo men in a comparison of holds contest. Gotch was able to readily escape from the judo submissions while the same could not be said for the Japanese artist. We must remember this was back in the day when judo placed a heavy emphasis on submissions, including leg locks.

One of Burns' major claims to fame was the inability of any Japanese artist to choke him out. He said at least 1,000 people had tried, but their technique no effect on him. This may have had more to do with his freakish 20-inch neck than anything else—as he never demonstrated an actual technique that others can duplicate.

GRAPPLING

The Sport of Kings
By Drew Price

Wrestling, the eldest of all sports,
The essence of man's most primal instincts,
Its spirit permeates even the souls of the beasts.
An art of balance and timing,
A science of fulcrum and leverage,
Nowhere are all the elements of savagery and science
More harmonized than in the art of Catch.
Catch-as-Catch-Can Wrestling, the most complete style of wrestling,
The professional fighting style of the greatest grapplers of all-time.

 Ed Lewis
 George Hackenschmidt
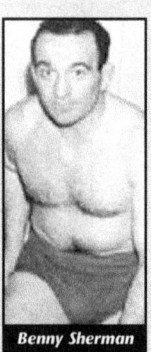 Benny Sherman

The Pro Method, a complex system
Of rides, reversals, takedowns, pins,
Laced with a knowledge of submission holds,
Referred to by the wrestler as "hooks",
Rendered the grapplers of old as nearly invincible.
No untrained one might compete against them,
For the amateur techniques paled in comparison to the pro.

 Bob Robbie
 Joe Robbie
 Ed Lewis and Karl Gotch

Today they speak of greatness,
They speak of grapplers in cross-trained styles
As being the best there have ever been.
"What's old is new, and what's new is old"
They know nothing of the greatness
Of the kings of men
Who ruled under the banner of pro-wrestling
In the early days of the last century.

While it can draw it roots from Pankration,
The king of Olympic sports,
Catch wrestling emerged from a blend
Of various European styles, namely Lancashire,
Whatever techniques worked were continually adapted
And refined until perfection was achieved.
Thus did American Catch-as-Catch-Can emerge
As the chosen sport of the peoples Of the Melting Pot.
Wrestling was the sport of the working men,
The builders of nations.

In the olden days the wrestlers traveled
On vaudeville acts or with circus companies
And took on all comers in winner take all matches.
Barnstorming, as it came to be called,
Was done for publicity as well as practice,
For wrestling was not as yet organized
And matches between true pros
Could be few and far between.

When the old-timers did meet
It was a spectacle worthy of Olympic greatness.
A "Shoot" was for "money, marbles, or chalk"—
It was a contest.
Each side bet money on their man,
Creating an incentive to win,
Often times the winner took all.

The rules were simple:
1. *Time limit*
2. *Best two out of three falls*
3. *A fall won by a three second pin, or by a submission.*
4. *Stranglehold barred*
5. *No biting, gouging, fish-hooking, or grabbing of the genitals.*
6. *No points kept.*
7. *If the mandatory number of falls not meet then bout ruled a draw.*

Thus we come to the Hierarchy of Catch,
The titles given here are the best example
Of the skill level attained by the wrestlers
Within their ranks.
On the bottom were the Journeymen,
Commonly employed in other circus
Or vaudeville acts, they knew little of wrestling
And often served the purpose
Of matching themselves against the pros
To draw interest from the crowd.

Next came the pros themselves.
The shooter, the one thoroughly versed
In all aspects of the pro method.
One capable of wrestling a legitimate match
And being able to back his claims.
They knew well all the tricks of the trade,
And knew well the "hooks"
Which made their art so deadly.

Higher still were the kings of the ring,
The absolute masters in the world
Of professional catch-as-catch-can,
These then were the Hookers.
These men were master shooters,
Only the best could develop
The lightning quick skills
Needed to enter these sacred ranks.
In these ranks mastery was complete,
Every facet of the game was perfected.
Submission was ever present
And inescapable by an opponent.

Upon the Bally the challenge was made,
The barker would cry:
"Who can stay just five minutes?
Who is man enough to try?"
A noble feat it was indeed,
To step upon the stage
And take the challenge.
Many a man valiantly tried,
But none might stand for long
Against the kings of men,
The masters of the ring.

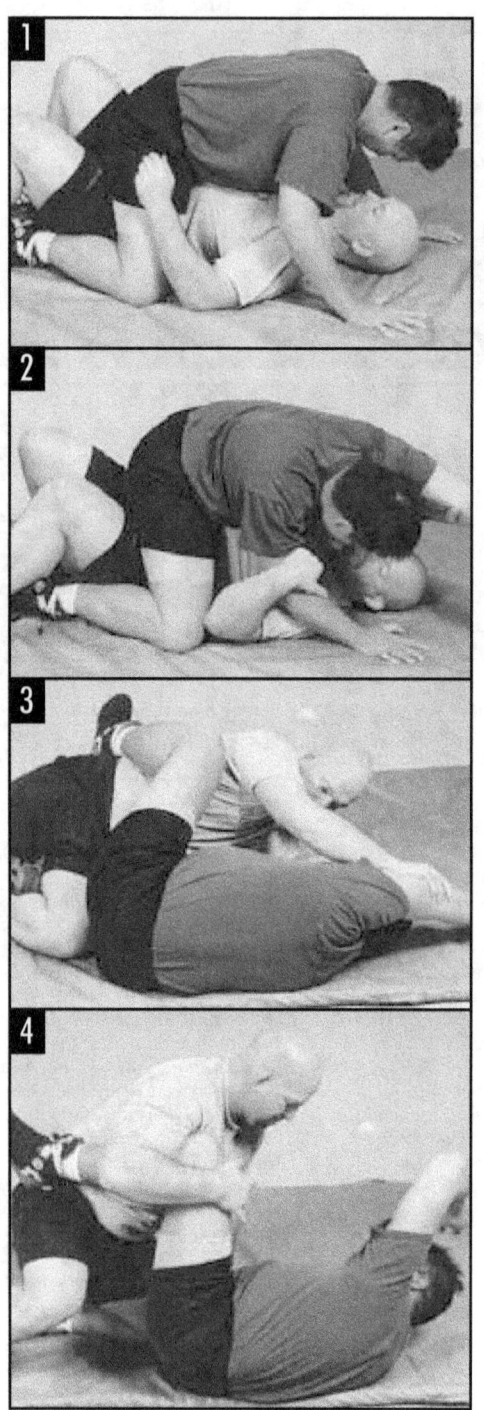

Matt Furey Competition and Training Profile

- Began training in wrestling at age 8.
- In 1981, was state-runner-up at 167 pounds in Iowa High School 3A State Championships.
- 1982-1984, member of three NCAA Champion teams at University of Iowa where he was coached by Dan Gable and J. Robinson.
- 1985, won NCAA II title at 167 pounds for Edinboro University of Pennsylvania, where he was coached by Mike DeAnna and Bruce Baumgartner.
- 1991, started training in various kung-fu styles.
- 1996, began learning Shuai-chiao kung fu (Chinese grappling) with Dr. Daniel Weng.
- 1997 won world title in Beijing, China, defeating Chinese and Mongolian national champion. Only American or foreigner to do so.
- Began tutelage under Karl Gotch in April 1999.
- Published "Combat Conditioning" in 2000, "Combat Abs" in 2001 and "No B.S. Fitness" in 2002.

Escape from the Mount
Trapped underneath his opponent's mount (1), Matt Furey traps the near arm and pushes on the far arm to unbalance his opponent (2). Rolling over while continuing to hold the arm extended (3), Furey then comes on top for the reversal (4).

GRAPPLING

Farmer Burns performing the dead-man's drop.

Frank Gotch, the Catch-As-Catch-Can Wrestling Champion of the World.

Karl Gotch, "The God of Wrestling."

Some years later, another catch wrestler, Adolph Ernst, who went by the name of Ad Santel, traveled to the Orient in hopes of making money from matches against Jigoro Kano's top judoka. Santel beat all but one of the high-ranking judoka he was matched-up against and, to Kano's dismay, declared himself World Judo Champion! All of this begs the question: If catch wrestling is so great, how did it become a lost art?

The Lost Art

Although some have tried to pin-point a specific reason, there are in fact, many. Some of the most common reasons given are that professional catch wrestling matches were too long for people to watch (one of the reasons given for the current demise of vale tudo), or that matches went from being real to fake. I personally believe the biggest of them is not that the matches went from real to show, but that those who knew the art didn't bother passing it on to anyone else. If it weren't for Karl Gotch, all we'd have about catch wrestling is highly suspect videos, teaching show holds masquerading as the real thing.

So when *was* pro wrestling real? It is generally believed that the world championship matches between Frank Gotch and George Hackenschmidt, held in Chicago in 1908 and 1911, were real. What is fuzzy about the matches though, are the claims made afterward. Right after losing the title to Gotch, Hackenschmidt praised the Iowan, saying he was too good, that he could do nothing with him, that he is the best. But upon his return to England, his story changed. "Gotch was a dirty wrestler," Hack was quoted as saying. "A cheater!" One source even has Hackenschmidt claiming that 200 butchers were ringside, ready to cut out his heart if he won.

The rematch was set for 1911. This time, however, instead of taking over two hours to whup the Russian Lion, Gotch went right out and won both falls in less than 30 minutes. Afterward,

Hackenschmidt said good things about Gotch in the U.S.—and changed it later to negatives in Europe. Gotch died young at age 39, while Hackenschmidt lived to see 90. To this day many people actually believe that Hackenschmidt was cheated, mostly because the Russian Lion had more than 50 years to say whatever he wanted, and there was no one alive who could challenge or dispute him.

Karl Gotch, who truly knows submission fighting, and the doings of pro wrestling, says there is no way that Hackenschmidt could have won. No matter how big or how strong, he maintains Hack didn't have the technique to keep up with Gotch because Hack was a Greco-Roman wrestler with limited submissions. Frank Gotch was a wide-open catch wrestler, who had a much greater diversity of abilities and training.

From Real to Fake

After the second Gotch vs. Hackenschmidt bout, it is said that professional catch wrestling remained real for a bit longer. Some claim that it was the overly long matches between Ed "Strangler" Lewis and Joe Stecher (one went for 9 hours) that killed it. Others simply say that the phony deal is an easier sell than the real thing and makes more money for the promoters. They'll say that when you pit two evenly-matched grapplers against one another, more often than not, they'll succeed in putting the audience to sleep. They'll also say that the purpose of pro wrestling is to make money; that if

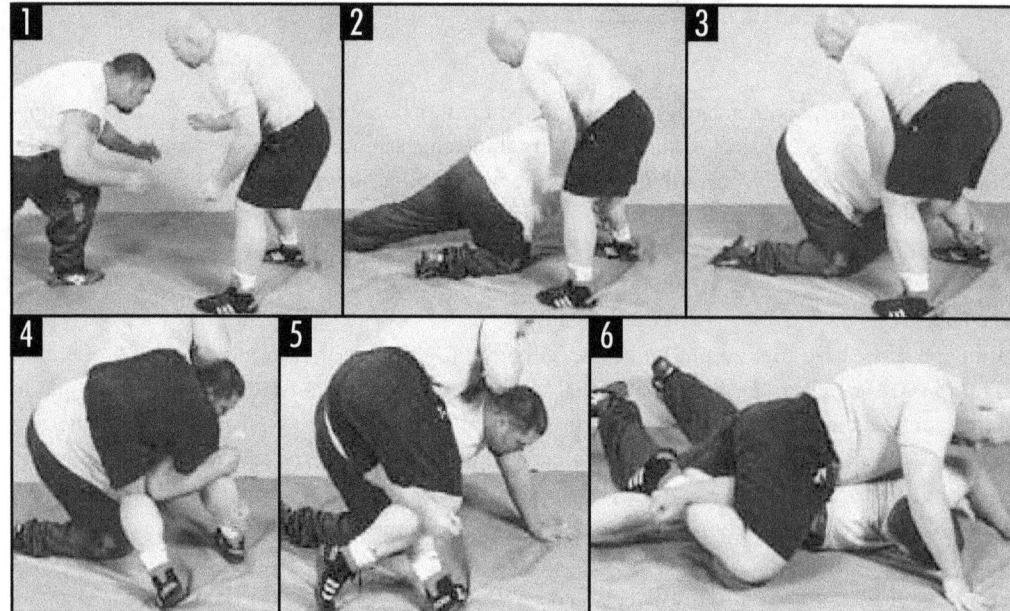

Single-Leg Takedown Counter
Matt Furey faces NHB star Mark "The Bear" Smith (1). Smith extends and shoots for the single-leg (2), then pulls presses forward to upset Furey's balance (3). Stepping to the side to reduce Smith's attack angle (4), Furey hooks the arm (5), then forces Smith to the ground and applies the finishing arm-lock (6).

you're not making money, it's a hobby, not a profession. They'll say that people won't pay for the real deal, but they will pay for the phony deal. And based on the fact that 20,000,000 Americans watch the WWF, ECW, WCW, and numerous other fake competitions each week on television, these statements appear true. In comparison, the Ultimate Fighting Championship, an event that nobly carries on the combat tradition of American catch wrestling, if not its exact techniques, is lucky to draw 100,000 viewers six times a year. Personally, I'd rather see one UFC than 100 WWF shows.

The Bottom Line

The bottom line for me is this: The only "truth" I can really know about professional catch wrestling is whether the techniques are as viable today as they were when "Farmer" Burns and Frank Gotch learned them. Moreover, are the catch techniques that Karl Gotch learned at the Billy Riley Gym in Wigan, England, as good, if not better, than what we're seeing being practiced today in other popular submission arts?

I sincerely believe that the techniques of traditional catch wrestling are, at the very least, equal if not more refined than today's most popular arts. Catch wrestling moves are not just "big guy" techniques that cannot be used by smaller, weaker practitioners. Most of the superstar catch wrestlers of yesteryear weighed less than 200 pounds. Farmer Burns was 165 and he regularly beat opponents twice his size. England's Billy Joyce (real name Bob Robinson), who along with brother Joe Robinson, taught Karl Gotch, were not big men. Ad Santel was not big. Benny Sherman weighed even less than Burns and, like Royler Gracie, would fight the devil himself.

Like any type of submission grappling, catch wrestling was built upon the foundation of many other wrestling arts which were then refined and incorporated into a comprehensive system of personal combat. While catch wrestling, at least the style taught by Karl Gotch, may have more elements of pain compliance than arts such as sombo, Brazilian jiu-jitsu, and judo, it is still based upon leverage and joint control. More than anything else, I believe the true legacy of catch wrestling is that we should never stop learning and never stop training.

BEST OF CFW — VOL. 1
GRAPPLING

John Donehue
On Top Down Under

Aussie John Donehue's tale is a classic example of how chance meetings can utterly transform a life, and lead someone in a direction they never thought they'd go.

Todd Hester

As a kickboxer and stand-up fighter with a desire go further in the martial arts, he traveled from his native Australia to the USA to train with legends such as Bill "Superfoot" Wallace and Benny Urquidez.

It was an almost casual comment from Superfoot that turned John's training and martial arts life upside down. "John, I want you meet a friend of mine named Gene LeBell. Gene has forgotten more about inflicting pain than you and I will ever know!"

With an endorsement like that from a champion like that, John was naturally very interested. Thus began a ten-year journey—an incredible transformation from a promising young kickboxer to one of the premier ground experts and mat instructors in the South Pacific.

But John Donehue is far from being done with his training, and he is actively on the mat with his students and still in contact with his teachers. Traveling the world to stay in touch with the world's top grapplers, and also to promote the sport of submission grappling and Brazilian jiu-jitsu, John Donehue is making sure that Down Under will stay on top.

Q: When did you start training martial arts?
A: I started boxing in Australia when I was about 15. Around that time Bruce Lee was very big, along with the *Kung-Fu* series on television. So I went out and found myself an instructor in that as well. At 17 I got a job working as a bouncer in different pubs and it was there that I met some guys who were ex-pro kickboxers and boxers. We would train in a garage together with hand wraps, a groin guard and mouthpiece only.

That was a great experience. We would start sparring stand-up, then if it got to a clinch situation we would go to the ground, and try whatever we could when we got there. Even though we really had no idea of what we were doing on the ground we probably had a better idea than most who never trained in that situation. It was a fun time though. We would train together during the week and try things out at the pub on weekends.

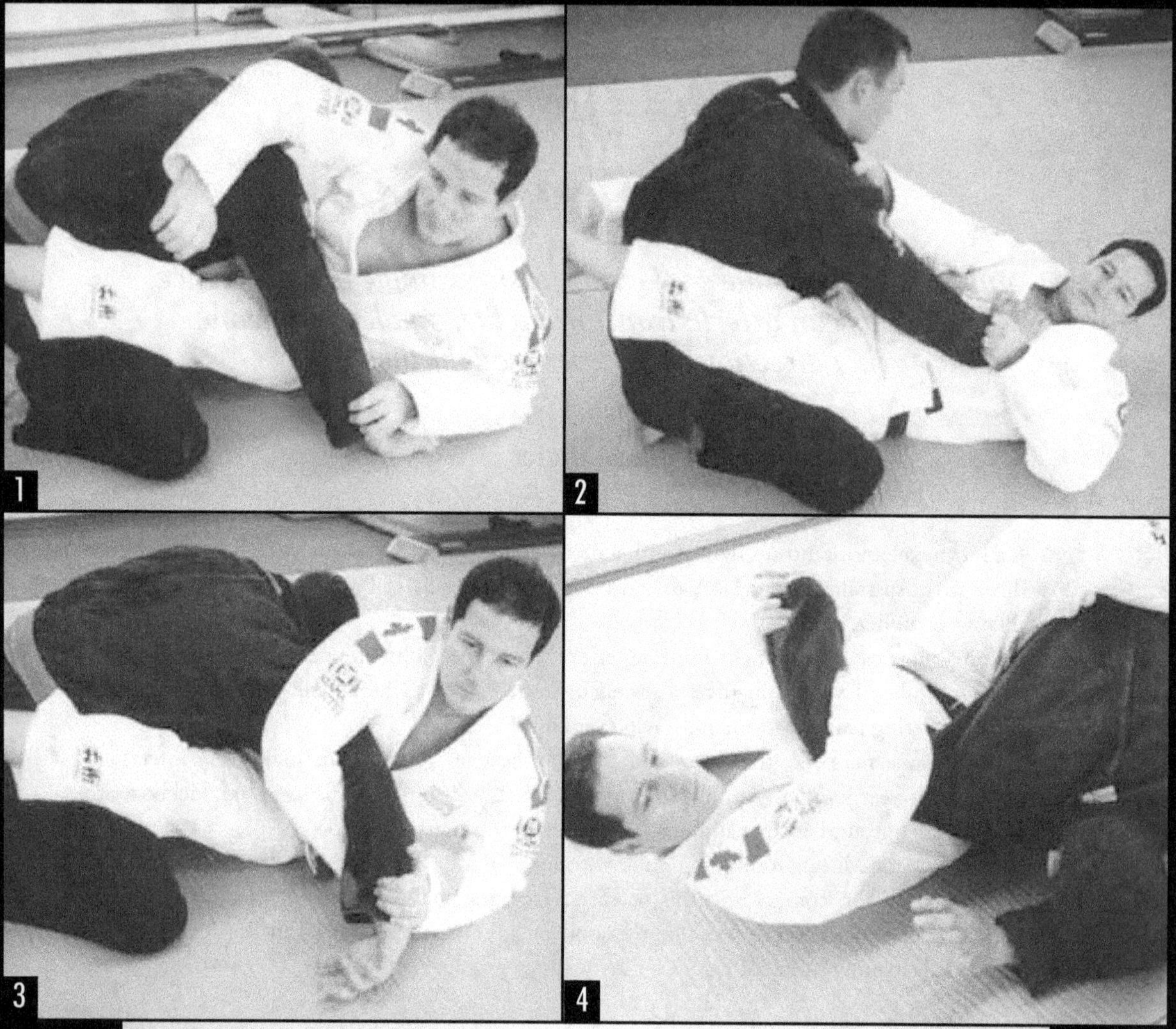

Closed-Guard Kimura

(1) In Brazil this sequence is often taught as one of the most basic attacks from the guard. You start with your opponent in the closed guard and a grip on his sleeve and lapel. (2) With your sleeve grip you pull your opponent's hand to the ground. At the same time you open your guard, escape your hips, sit up and reach over his triceps with the hand that had been on his lapel. (3) Reach your second hand over and through his arm and grab your own wrist. It is very important to have his arm, especially his upper arm, trapped tight against your chest. (4) Now, with his arm firmly trapped, keeping his hand well away from his body (so it will be harder to defend) escape your hips out to the side of his trapped arm. The act of escaping your hips is the most important part of this move. Scissors his body with your legs, keeping your calf firmly pressing down on his lower back—this keeps him from rolling. To apply the lock from here you do two things: first you move his elbow towards his head—this takes all the slack out of the system. The second and final touch is to try to bring his hand to the back of his head. Unless he is made of cooked spaghetti you now have him trapped in the Kimura lock.

Cross-Mount Neck Crank
Controlling his opponent from the side mount (1), John Donehue secures the arm and steps over the head (2), the pressures the neck with his leg for the submission (3)

Q: What brought you to the United States?
A: At around 22 or 23 I got the itch to pack up and travel overseas, which is pretty common for Australians. I was planning to go away for a year and work my way around the world. I stayed in Hong Kong for a while then went on to Los Angeles. I was lucky to have made friends with Bill "Superfoot" Wallace the previous year, by bringing him out to Australia for a seminar tour. He picked me up at the airport and had accommodations arranged for me. We would train together at the Jet Center when it was in Van Nuys just about every day. Training with people like Bill, Pete Cunningham and Benny Urquidez was amazing.

One night Bill took me to LA City College to meet this guy called Gene LeBell. Bill said this guy had forgotten more about inflicting pain than you or I would ever know. After my first training session in judo with Gene I was hooked. So that was the very beginning of my grappling training.

Q: What was the training like with Gene LeBell?
A: I was very lucky in those early days to have the opportunity to be invited to train at Gene's cabin on the weekends. It took some time but I was graded to black belt in judo under Gene, and also in his own private system a few years later. John Lewis and I got our black belts in Gene's system at the same time. John, of course, went on to a fabulous NHB fighting career and is now promoting the World Fighting Alliance in Las Vegas—a terrific event. In those early years there were really only a few of us that would go train with Gene on a regular basis: John Lewis, Silvio Pimenta, and myself. We are all still great friends.

We would get there around 6 pm and sometimes still be on the mat at 2 am or 3 am! Gene is fanatical, so if you wanted to train or ask questions he would stay up no problem. Not once did he say, "Okay, let's stop, I'm tired." *We* would have to say it, as we had the 2-hour drive home.

After training, we would sit and ask Gene about his experiences when he was young. It was very interesting because with the immense rise in popularity of no-holds-barred fighting over the last number of years, one could be excused for thinking it is all something relatively new. Not so. I would rank Gene as one of the true original NHB fighters—and one of the greatest. He is still extremely strong and very dangerous. Don't let the bad jokes fool you—he can bring it on.

Often Gene would tell us stories of when he would go into a town and he and a few other grapplers, or "hookers" as they were called then, would basically fight all comers in NHB fights. There was a bunch of them that would do these tours through the States. The money they made was barely enough to pay for their gas to the next town. They would fight the toughest guys in a town. Gene told us there were plenty of times when they were literally chased out of a town by drunken gangs who were pretty pissed that some guy in the ring had whipped the local tough guy.

Q: Those who have had the opportunity to grapple with Gene always say it is an unforgettable experience.
A: Gene feels like nobody else as far as I'm concerned. Everything he does is always painful and very dynamic. He has moves, locks, breaks, dislocations and controls for every part of the body. If I ever had a question, Gene could answer it. I'd be moving in a certain way and Gene would say, "Oh, stop, stop. Do it like this!" And a lot of the time you know he'd be looking at something and creating a solution there on the spot. So for sure, Gene was kind of scary to train with. Even though now he doesn't train as hard as he would like to because of his age and the number of injuries he has had, he is still amazing.

Q: What is Gene like on a personal level?
A: Gene and I are very close. He is also very close and important to my family. I always spoke to Gene about a lot of things

"I would rank Gene LeBell as one of the true original NHB fighters—and one of the greatest. He is still extremely strong and very dangerous. Don't let the bad jokes fool you—he can bring it on."

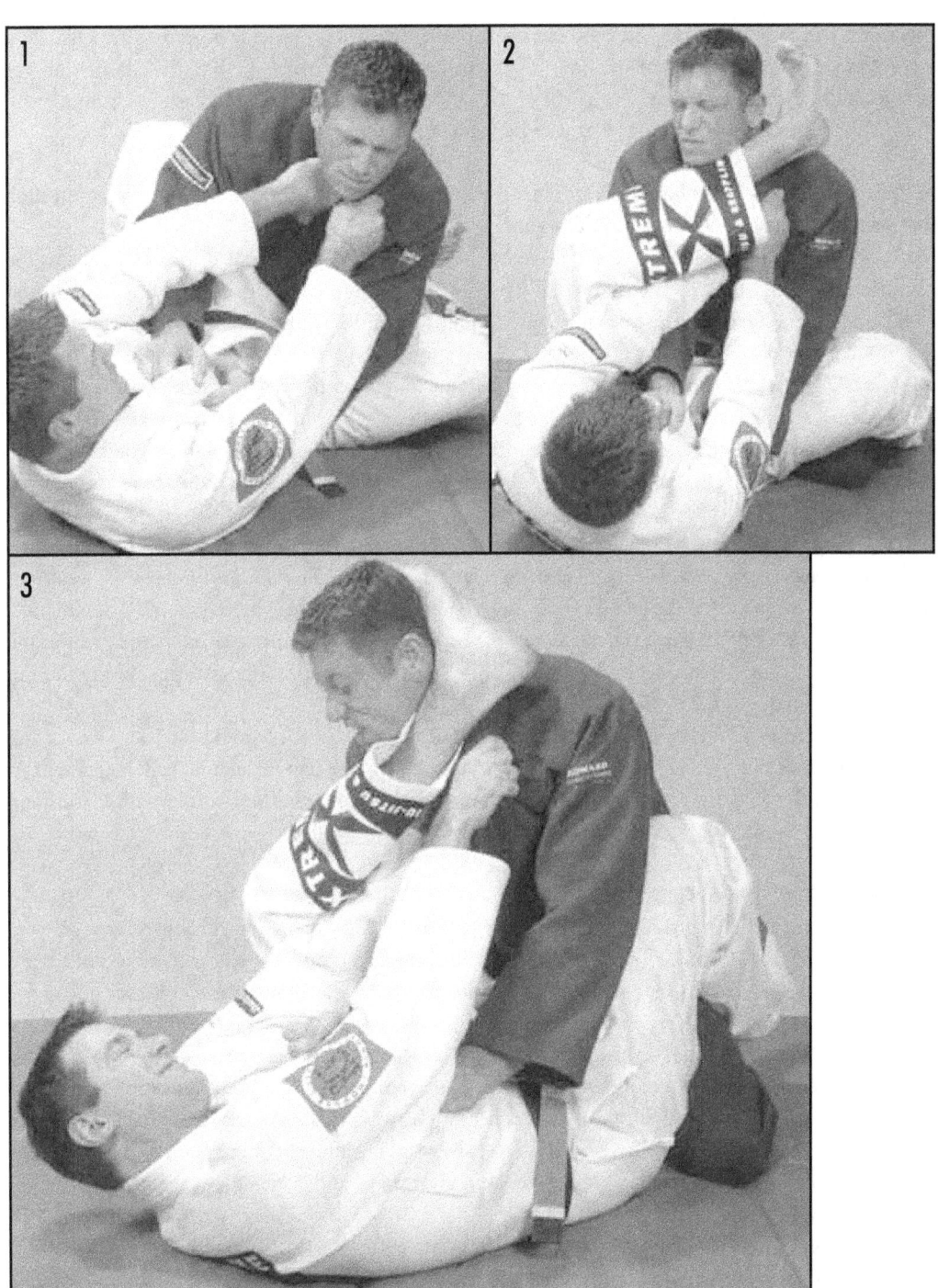

Open-Guard Leg Choke
Controlling both side of the collar from the open guard (1), John Donehue passes his leg over his arms, trapping the opponent's head (2), and extends the leg for the finishing choke (3).

besides martial arts. I was very lucky to see a side of Gene that not everyone gets to see. He is such a generous and warm person and I feel very lucky to be so close to someone like that. If anyone was my second father, in the States or anywhere else in the world, it is Gene. He has always been there for me, helping me out and doing whatever he could for me at any time.

Q: You also have a black belt in Brazilian jiu-jitsu from Rigan Machado. What is the connection between Gene, the Machado brothers, and you?
A: I had been training with Gene for two to three years, when Rigan and Carlos came up to the cabin one weekend to do some training. They had heard about Gene through Chuck Norris, Bob Wall, and others. That was the first time I met both of them. I obviously thought they were incredible at what they do.

It was right at this time that I was trying to train more and more with Gene, but he was very busy with his movie stunt work. So he suggested I go and train with Rigan and Carlos because it would give me more quality mat time and more experience. He thought it would be good if I got to wrestle with different guys and see a whole bunch of new stuff that Gene didn't have the time to work on with me.

So I ended up training with Carlos and Rigan in their Torrance academy through the week, then go up to Gene's cabin on the weekend and train with him. It was just the most incredible wealth of knowledge. The quality of the people I was lucky enough to work out with regularly was incredible. Both Rigan and Carlos are just phenomenal in their own right—incredible coaches and great at the way they move on the mat. So I really felt blessed to have such an extraordinary opportunity to train with the best in the world.

At this early stage, I really only had contact with Carlos and Rigan. I would see Jean Jacques and John sometimes but I think they were running a school in the San Fernando Valley area of LA. Occasionally I would see Roger too. But my contact and training was really only with Carlos and Rigan.

Q: What are their strong points?
A: Rigan's game has changed over the years. His pressure is really good and his movements are very powerful. His game is now definitely a big man's jiu-jitsu game, but he is still incredibly skilled and very technical. He uses his God-given strength and power well and puts them together effectively with his jiu-jitsu moves.

Carlos, on the other hand, is nowhere near as big as Rigan. But he is tremendously skilled, so his game is different. I love grappling with both of them because they are both fantastic. As I said, I haven't had as much contact with Jean-Jacques because he was usually at his own school across town. But his style is well proven. He is very aggressive, always going after the submission, which is a great quality that I admire in a grappler. He also keeps in great shape and is incredibly technical.

Q: How much different was their style from Gene's?
A: Many, if not all of the Brazilian jiu-jitsu techniques Gene taught, but in a different way. The Brazilian style of grappling is to me very snake-like. Very smooth, very flowing, and very technical. Gene is a lot more aggressive and dynamic. With Gene there was not really "do this to get to here to pass the guard to this or that position." He is more like "grab it and break it!" He doesn't care if it's your leg, neck, or arm.

That was the old catch-wrestling mentality. The catch-wrestling style that Gene teachers is a blend of freestyle-wrestling explosiveness, coupled with the most crippling of finishing holds. The Brazilian style, on the other hand, is a little slower paced—smooth, setting things up, and then submitting. The two styles are different, but compliment each other beautifully. That's why I feel so fortunate to have worked with both Gene and the Machados for so long.

Q: Do you think the Gracie family and Brazilian jiu-jitsu has opened people around the world to cross-training on the ground?

A: Definitely. I think martial artists are still in the dark ages when they say their art or one style has it all. That's okay to a point I guess, because loyalty is good and that's where they started and so on. But from a purely practical point of view, from the viewpoint of the complete martial artist, you have to open up your mind and cross-train. From my experience as a stand-up fighter, I now know that I would have been completely lost if someone had taken me to the ground and controlled me. As a pure stand-up fighter, I wouldn't have had an answer.

And people still say, despite all the evidence, "Well, I would just punch or kick him or hit him with our deadly simultaneous parry and strike." Well, I think we have seen enough now in the different NHB events to know that it just does not happen that often. And if it does, it is just a one-in-a-million chance that you are going to get that lucky punch or kick in. No art has all the answers. I don't believe BJJ has all the answers either. Nor does wrestling, or karate. But I think mixed together all the arts have something great to offer the complete martial artist.

Q: Didn't you also have the opportunity to spend time in L.A. with Bruce Lee's top student, Dan Inosanto?

A: Yes, that's right. Dan is the sort of guy—if you look at his history—who, if he sees the value in a style, takes that style seriously and studies it. He always tries to learn from the best. He works it into his own style's syllabus. He has an incredible training schedule that would stop a much younger and lesser man. He trains jiu-jitsu very seriously too. He trains regularly through the week. He does privates with Rigan or Roger Machado and has Jean Jacques teach at camps. Dan did privates with me every week and joined my class whenever he could. He trains with a personal trainer, does yoga, *plus* trains in all the different arts his academy teaches. He does everything because he obviously sees the value in cross-training.

Dan is a real quiet achiever and innovator in the martial arts world. He is definitely the epitome of the cross-trainer. I can't think of anyone who trains in more styles and trains more diligently in all those styles than Dan Inosanto. Also, Dan and his wife Paula were just wonderful to me over the years in L.A. They gave me so much help and support. It was such a pleasure and honour to learn and to teach at the famous Inosanto Academy and to work with Dan personally, too.

In addition to Dan, of course, and the pure BJJ guys, you have other world-class grapplers there such a Yuri Nakamura, Erik Paulson, and Larry Hartsell. Dan is a true martial artist who surrounds himself and develops top teachers. I can only hope some of his attitudes and personality rubbed of on me during the time I was able to spend with him.

Q: Do you think there is really such a thing as pure Brazilian jiu-jitsu?

A: Realistically, no. There may have been in the years gone by when, for example, Rickson Gracie was younger and BJJ was still basically confined to Brazil. Even in the early days, the famous Rolls Gracie trained wrestling and would compete in wrestling tournaments in Brazil. But now that it has

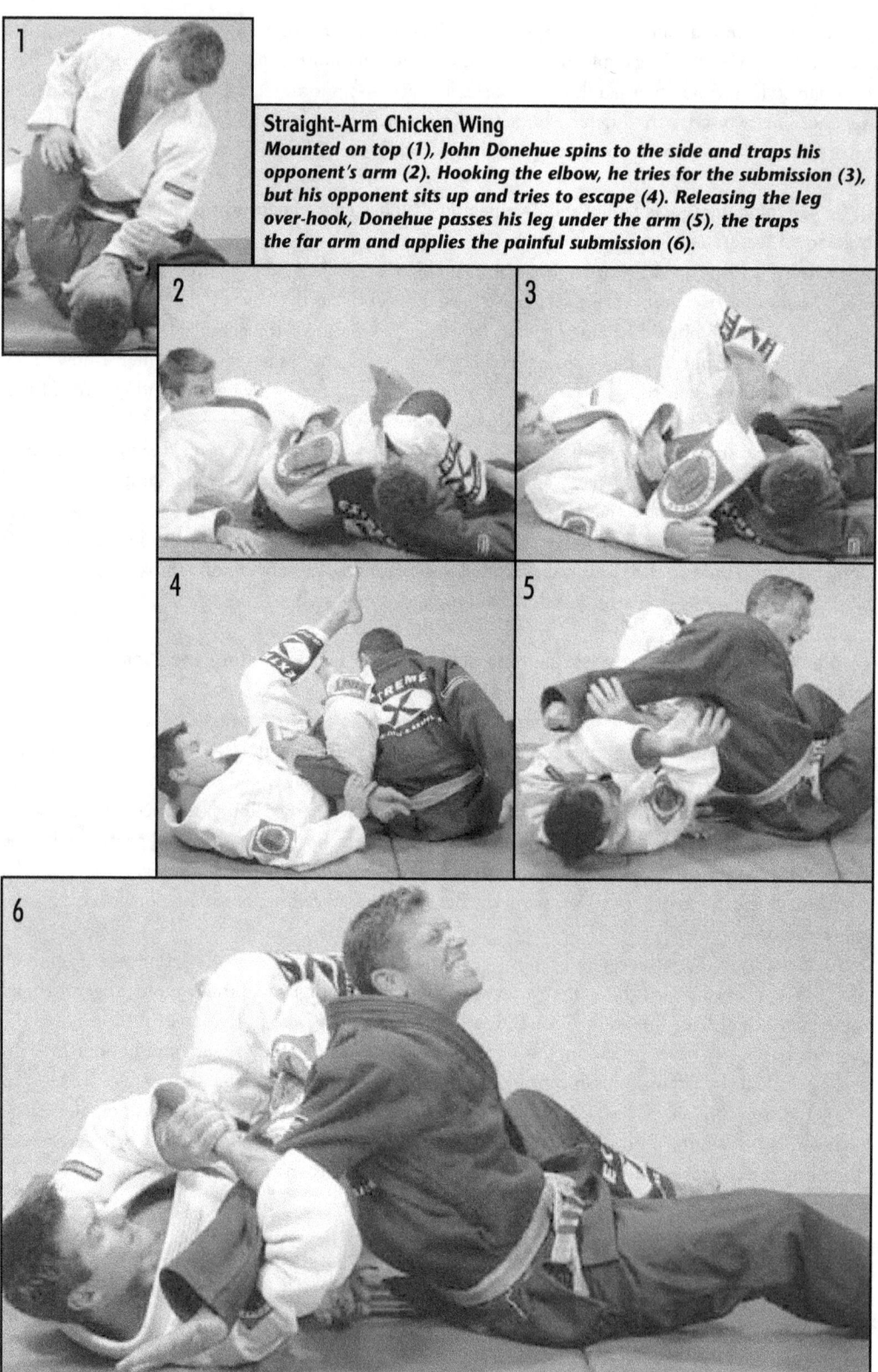

Straight-Arm Chicken Wing
Mounted on top (1), John Donehue spins to the side and traps his opponent's arm (2). Hooking the elbow, he tries for the submission (3), but his opponent sits up and tries to escape (4). Releasing the leg over-hook, Donehue passes his leg under the arm (5), the traps the far arm and applies the painful submission (6).

sort of exploded around the world and the BJJ fighters are training more with wrestlers and stand-up fighters, they are adding many new moves to their style. Jiu-jitsu is evolving, as it should. I don't think any mainstream martial art is pure anymore simply because if the art is worth it's salt and it sees something that is practical and is going to help, it should take it and incorporate it into their own system.

Q: What weaknesses do you see in BJJ?
A: Well, as I said, no one system has all the answers. There are weaknesses somewhere in every style. I think BJJ has weaknesses in the stand-up game. They are so focused on the ground that they have really neglected their stand-up. In the early days they were taking guys down who didn't know what was going on, guys who didn't have a wrestling background. Now they are fighting guys who they can't take down because they are wrestlers and that is their game—they do not want to be taken down and do not want to be on their backs.

On the other hand, I think that's a good thing because now you see the top Brazilian fighters cross-training with wrestlers to get a better understanding of how to defend against a takedown. And the wrestlers are doing the same, learning about the finishing holds, and what they have to watch out for. Because more than likely the wrestler will take you down, but they have to watch out for triangles and armlocks from the guard. The guard is a dangerous position for these guys, if they have no knowledge of it.

Q: You said you have benefited a lot from cross-training with wrestlers. In what ways do you think wrestling training has been helpful?
A: Well, once again, I was very fortunate to be able to train with a guy who is one of the finest wrestlers and coaches in the world, Rico Chiapparelli. I had been refereeing the Extreme Fighting events and then I met Rico at an event called The Contenders. Some of his guys were competing in it. We were introduced, exchanged numbers and started working out when we got back to L.A. He taught me 100 percent of the wrestling knowledge that I have, which is just a fraction of what he knows.

Training with Rico really opened my eyes to how bad I really was in the grappling stand-up game. Even though I have a black belt in judo, I would be lost without a gi if someone came in to double-leg me. I knew the rudimentary basics of sprawling and so on. But against a top guy who knows what he is doing, he *is* going to take me down and there is nothing I could do about it. So it really opened my eyes to the possibilities of where I need to be when standing up and it also gave my ground game a stronger base and balance and a lot of other things that jiu-jitsu didn't give me because they do certain things differently.

Rico and I trained together on almost a daily basis. He would teach me wrestling and I would teach him the submission side. Then we would try and put it together, figuring out what really worked without a gi and what didn't. Rico has had a lot of success with guys like Randy Couture, Dan Henderson, Frank Trigg and Vladimir Matyushenko because he could see the strengths and weaknesses in wrestling and in other styles and put everything together really well to build a fighter that would be pretty hard to beat in most situations. He is smart enough to cross-train, learn what the weaknesses and strengths were in jiu-jitsu, and also where his wrestlers could really get caught out.

He had his guys cross-train with boxers, kickboxers and BJJ stylists so they could get a broad knowledge of everything. Rico just seems to know what to do and not to do. He has helped me incredibly and is a good friend too. Because of contact with him I was able to work out with the guys on the RAW team and help them with submissions. It was refreshing to be around a group of guys who just wanted to train. They didn't care where you were from, what rank you were or anything. This I think is one of the downfalls of BJJ—all the politics of who you are and who you can or can't train with.

Q: How are the politics in Australia?
A: Unfortunately we have more than our fair share. As far as BJJ goes, we are still at the infancy stage of development, and that's as far as it will go as long as people try to control everything. There are not enough competitions and when the individuals from the different groups run them, unfortunately, they are called State or National titles but only their own group can enter or you are forced to join their organization just to compete. I don't think it's right. I wish it could be more like the States where in most of the tournaments that are run, every school comes to compete freely and openly. It only serves to help the sport grow. The people that suffer are the students. Win or lose you can always learn something from competition and it creates more contact between the schools and raises the standards. You can never get rid of all the politics. I understand this—but leave it out at competition time.

Knee-Bar Counter-Submission
John Donehue is trapped in a knee-bar by his opponent (1). Hooking the knee with his clasped hands, Donehue breaks the leg hook and relieves the pressure (2). Sitting-up to free his trapped leg (3), Donehue then falls back and pressures the ankle for the submission (4).

Side-Mount Choke
Controlling his opponent from the upright side-mount, John Donehue passes his opponent's collar to his far hand (1). Releasing the passing hand (2), Donehue clasps the back of the collar (3), and then pushes his opponent over and applies the finishing choke (4).

Q: So where do you go from here, John?

A: Well, I lived and trained in L.A. for ten years. It wasn't my intention to stay there that long but that's the way it happened. And it was an incredible experience. I have made a lot of life-long friends. Now I've returned to Australia with my family. I have set up a school here, Extreme Jiu-Jitsu & Grappling, and I'm trying to pass on to my own students the experiences I learned in L.A. We also started The Australian Jiu-Jitsu & Grappling Association, which organizes the South Pacific Abu Dhabi Trials along with other jiu-jitsu tournaments throughout the year, which are open to all competitors regardless of affiliation to overcome the political problems which could potentially ruin the growth of our sport. My objective is to build a really strong group so we can start competing on the world scene—in NHB events as well as BJJ and submission grappling events. This is already happening.

A few of the guys doing well include Larry Papadopoulos and Alex Cook who are both ranked number one in their weight divisions in Shooto, and Cris Brown, who beat Renzo Gracie in Abu Dhabi. He is also competing in jiu-jitsu now and wants to fight in NHB as well. He has wrestled freestyle in five Olympics and is also teaching the wrestling classes at my school.

I am also lucky to have an incredibly dedicated and talented group of students who through their own hard work have taken out the team title two years running in Australia's largest open tournament—The Australian Open Jiu-Jitsu Cup. We also had two of the four competitors who represented the South Pacific region at Abu Dhabi.

I also plan to come to the States every year, as I did this year along with some students. We trained at the Raw Center, the Machado's school, John Lewis' school in Las Vegas and with Gene Lebell so they can get a feel of what's out there. But my students are definitely my main focus for the future.

BEST OF CFW ——— VOL.1
GRAPPLING

The World Sambo Federation Hybrid Grappling System

Starting with the original techniques from Russian sambo, and adding modern techniques from Brazilian jiu-jitsu, judo, muay Thai, and wrestling, the World Sambo Federation has created a martial art that is everything to everyone!

Joe Schmidt

Dr. Darrin Pordash is the founder of the World Sambo Federation, a sambo world silver medalist, a 20-time tournament winner and a top student of Gokor Chivichyan. When Pordash isn't cracking bones on the mat as one of America's premier grapplers, he is busy cracking necks at his successful chiropractic clinic! Not only an accomplished sport grappler, Pordash has trained many world-class fighters who have competed in the UFC and Rage in the Cage, and in pankration, chute boxing, muay Thai, judo, sambo and Brazilian jiu-jitsu events. He often appears as a judge or director of NHB competitions and conducts sambo seminars all over the North America. Dr. Pordash founded the World Sambo Federation (WSF) in the mid-'90s, in an effort to provide top-notch submission instruction in an atmosphere also conducive to upholding traditional martial arts values of honor, moral growth, and spiritual development. A Christian organization, the WSF has since grown to 17 schools across the country with over 1,000 students. Just as important as grappling skill in the WSF is moral fiber. True to the founding principles, the organization only accepts students with exemplary character.

Q: Why did you organize the World Sambo Federation?
A: The WSF originated with the intent of combining the best fighting techniques from the most effective styles. Since the creation of the UFC, Pride, World Vale Tudo and various other no-holds barred tournaments, the world has been given the privilege of seeing one marital arts style pitted against another: wrestling vs. boxing,

175

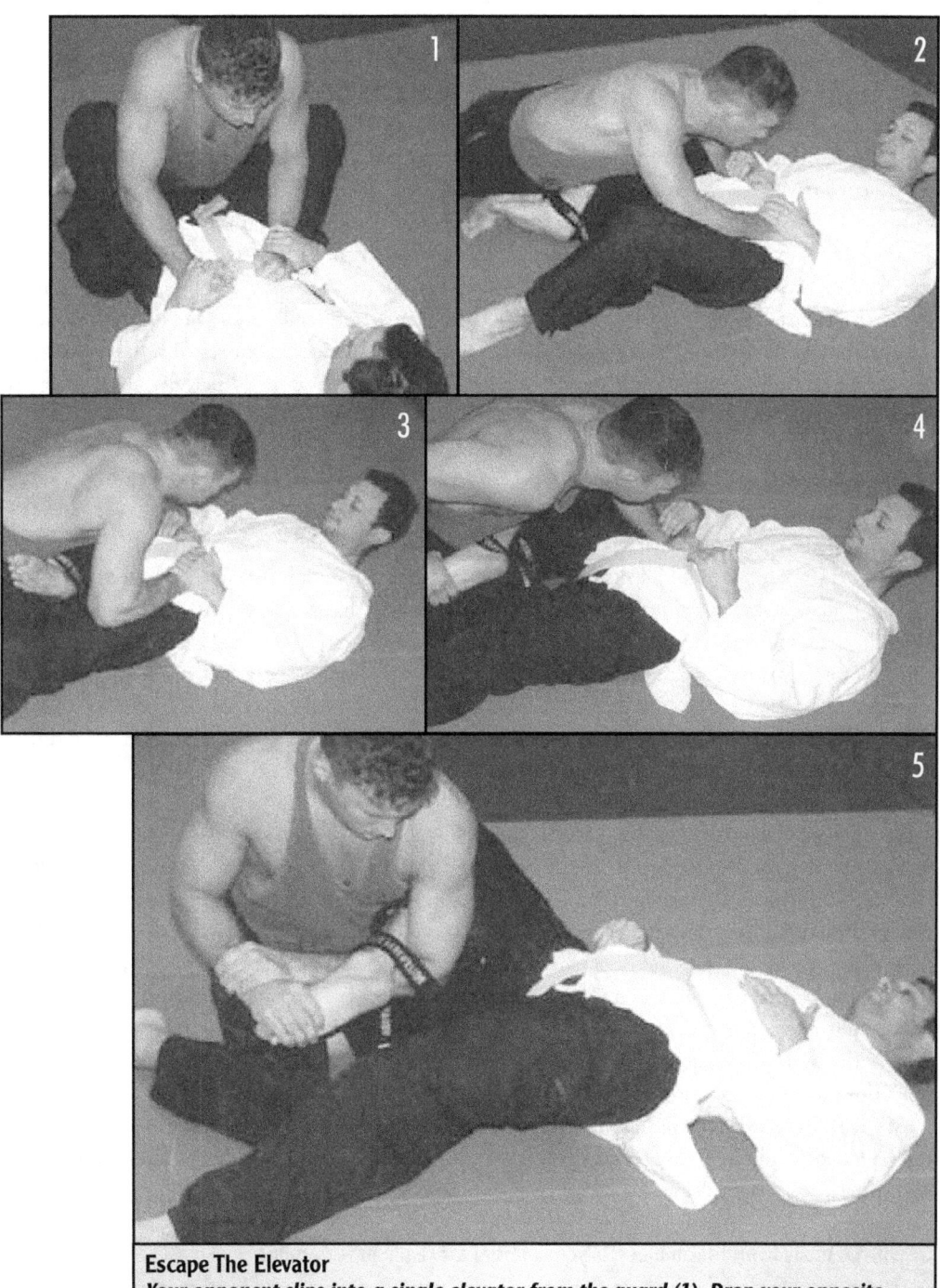

Escape The Elevator
Your opponent slips into a single elevator from the guard (1). Drop your opposite leg behind you (2). Bring the leg forward again but trap his foot in your hip (3). Grab your opponent's foot and stay tight (4). Under-hook his foot with your other hand and apply the foot lock (5).

sambo vs. jiu-jitsu, karate vs. kung-fu—we have seen it all. It's no secret that certain martial arts have proven more effective in the ring—the circle of truth. These arts are sambo, Brazilian jiu-jitsu, judo, wrestling, and muay Thai. Combat greats like Gokor Chivichyan, Royce Gracie, Rickson Gracie, Mark Kerr, Mark Coleman, Oleg Taktarov, Frank Shamrock, Bas Ruttan and others have taken the fighting world by storm and shown that technique is king of the ring.

We encourage great technique at the WSF. Since I am a doctor of chiropractic, I observe fighting from an analytical perspective. Our system is comprised of 400 techniques below black belt and another 2,000 over the black belt level. There are 10 belts, with 40 submissions per belt. There are six levels of black belt. Each level is comprised of techniques from the combined arts of sambo, Brazilian jiu-jitsu, judo, wrestling and muay Thai. There were literally thousands of techniques to choose from while devising our fighting system, so we only included the moves with the highest percentage of execution potential—or what we refer to as PEP. A PEP of 80 percent must be agreed upon among all the instructors before it is accepted into our system.

Q: Where do you acquire your techniques?
A: The resources used for our organization are vast and have entailed considerable expenses. Our chief instructor is Gokor Chivichyan, who is the greatest sambo fighter on the planet. He has won titles in NHB, sambo, judo, jiu-jitsu and other mixed-martial-arts tournaments. I have never met a more talented or skilled fighter in my 17 years of training. I have trained with Gokor for six years and other sambo instructors for 17 years. I also trained with members of the Gracie family and their students for 10 years, did judo for several years, wrestled for seven-and-a-half years, and did muay Thai for four years. I share my skills and training at no cost with the other instructors of our 17 schools across the nation. We also have an extensive video library that we use to study, test, and then implement techniques if the PEP is high enough.

Q: How do you obtain fresh, cutting-edge techniques?
A: Various students of mine have traveled extensively to train at great facilities like the Sambo 70 in Russia, the Kodokan in Japan and the Gracie Academy in Brazil. We get together to share and test new information throughout the year, especially at the World Sambo Federation Skills Camp, which takes place on the first weekend of January each year. We have recently decided to open our camp to the public. The camp is held at a 7,000 sq. ft. state-of-the-art facility in Evansville, Indiana. The entire floor is covered with Zebra judo mats and there is a regulation boxing ring and 10 banana bags at the back of the facility. We cover all aspects of grappling, NHB training, Thai boxing and sport throws during the camp.

We feel that our extensive training methods have contributed to the success of our fighters over the years. For example, I have trained such fighters as Jermaine Andre, Shawn White, Joe Schmidt, Tony Tucci, Joe Wright, Vince Fields, and Shawn Rose.

Q: With so many hybrid techniques, is your martial art really pure Sambo?
A: There are a few sambo organizations that don't approve of our hybridization of other arts with sambo techniques. They want sambo to stay pure. Let's analyze this for a moment. Sambo was originated by Russian military leader Vasili Oschepkov, Victor Spiridinov, and Russian judo player Anatoli Kharlampiev in the early 1900's. The intent was to create a self-defense system without weapons that would take the best techniques from 30 martial arts worldwide. The art was called

GRAPPLING

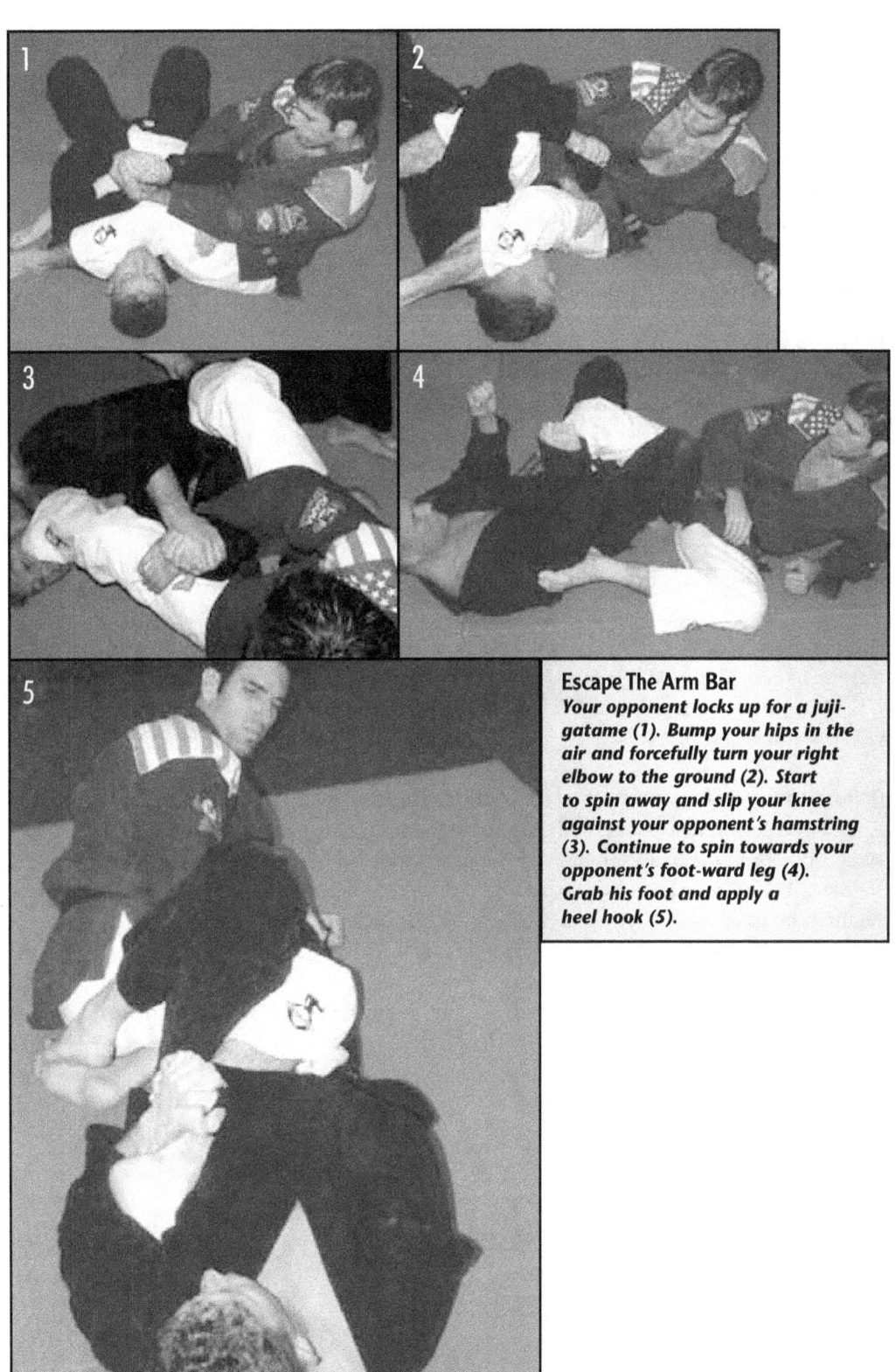

Escape The Arm Bar
Your opponent locks up for a juji-gatame (1). Bump your hips in the air and forcefully turn your right elbow to the ground (2). Start to spin away and slip your knee against your opponent's hamstring (3). Continue to spin towards your opponent's foot-ward leg (4). Grab his foot and apply a heel hook (5).

Sambo and was intended for the Russian military and police. They also used psychology principles and medical science to formulate their approach. So sambo's very beginning was as a hybrid system.

The WSF has reinvented the same approach in the 1990's. Our instructors have intensively studied the most effective fighting styles and enriched the eclectic art of Sambo through analytic hybridization. In the process of doing so, we realized that the most successful martial arts programs also have belt systems. Without the recognition of achievement, the average martial arts student will lose drive and quit training after six months. Realizing the difficulty of student retention, we established a belt system. The lack of such a system is the reason sambo was a dying art in the US in the 1980's. It is again a flourishing style of fighting both in our organization and Gokor's.

Q: How do you feel about Brazilian jiu-jitsu and the Gracies?
A: I feel nothing but respect. It is a great art with great fighters. Brazilian jiu-jitsu techniques are a large part of our system, especially the aspects of positioning. I found that all grappling styles have good techniques and average techniques. We extract the high PEP techniques only. For instance, I wouldn't look to Brazilian jiu-jitsu for throws, striking, or leg locks. We more or less teach throws from sambo, judo, and wrestling, with a few Brazilian jiu-jitsu takedowns. Our striking is 100 percent Thai boxing and our leg locks—over 150—are entirely sambo.

Q: When was the last time you were tapped-out?
A: Other than Gokor—and I've lost track of those—it was around seven years ago or so. I have traveled the country extensively the past five years and haven't tapped a single time. That is not to say there aren't guys who could beat me, I just haven't wrestled them yet. Gokor can tap me pretty quick if he wants, although he taps everyone. I've seen him tap Brazilian jiu-jitsu black belts in 10 seconds with one arm behind his back.

Q: How can someone become a part of the World Sambo Federation?
A: There are many events in the WSF that occur throughout the year, such as the Sambo Nationals every March and the Skills Camp every January—both held at the same facility in Evansville, Indiana. There are many seminars and grappling tournaments spread throughout the year. Additionally, all of our 400 techniques below black belt are on video and made available to each one of our instructors as well as to prospective new schools wanting to be chartered.

For more information on the World Sambo Federation, or to get information on being chartered into the organization, email Dr. Portash at **sombo@earthlink.net**.

BEST OF CFW — VOL. 1
GRAPPLING

The Essence of Brazilian Jiu-Jitsu

Brazilian jiu-jitsu is far more than the sum total of its individual components. It crosses all international boundaries with a mixture of myth, mysticism, heroes, and history.

Rigan Machado

Brazilian jiu-jitsu is many things to many people. For some it is the premier art of streetfighting self-defense, to others it is an "unbeatable" full-combat ring art, still others love it for its sportive and fitness aspects. While it does contain many undeniable fighting, sportive, and fitness elements, it is far more than the sum total of it's individual elements.

Based on the fighting precepts of the samurai, Japan's ancient ultimate warrior class, and tempered with the relaxed and casual temperament of Brazil's unique cultural and ethnic mix, Brazilian jiu-jitsu is an art that has gained worldwide acceptance as a style that anyone can do, for any reason, regardless of age, sex, size, or race. The essence of Brazilian jiu-jitsu transcends political boundaries, economic circumstances, or accidental place of birth.

I have often pondered the fact that in Brazilian jiu-jitsu, while you're on the mat, everyone is truly equal. The family tree or the family fortune does not determine a student's standing in the academy. Rather it is based upon hard work, practice habits, mental determination, and moral strength. So many times I have seen millionaire white belts turn to poverty-stricken black belts for advice, support, and technical assistance. Wealth in jiu-jitsu is determined by what is in your heart, not by what you have in your wallet.

More than anything else, I believe that the bare essence of Brazilian jiu-jitsu is that you are what you do. This simple fact is what has made it so popular around the world. While it is true that the mat can be the ultimate proving ground, it is also true that it is the ultimate crucible that allows those who practice the art to truly know and understand each other. The best friends I have ever made are those who I have learned from, trained with, and taught during the course of my Brazilian jiu-jitsu career.

Just as the spiritual and moral aspects of jiu-jitsu can be broken down into the basic elements of human interaction, the technical aspects of jiu-jitsu can also be broken into easy-to-understand principles. A two-year blue belt probably knows 80 percent of what a black belt knows. What makes the difference between the two is the timing and feel that only comes from spending hours and hours "rolling" on the mat. Understanding these physical basics is as indispensable to understanding the essence of Brazilian jiu-jitsu as is an understanding of its moral, philosophical, and historical foundations.

GRAPPLING

Standing Guard Pass Ankle-Lock
Facing an opponent using the open guard, Rigan Machado controls the knees (1). He steps to the side while still controlling the knee (2), grabs the foot while putting his knee on the stomach (3), then reaches back and applies the finishing ankle lock (4).

"Control the situation rather than letting the situation control you. You must adapt the details, but keep the big picture the same. Use all the same tools, just in different ways."

Gi or No Gi

One of the most basic elements in jiu-jitsu is the difference between training with the gi and without the gi. The difference is that with the gi, the submission game is much more technical. When you wear the gi, you have many more chances to catch your opponent. You have a chance to use the gi to your advantage. You have a much better control for your opening moves. You can tighten up different points on your opponents body which set him up for the move to follow. A proper submission, whether it is an arm lock, knee bar, or whatever, is all a result of a proper opening and that is where the gi is most helpful. When you don't have the gi, you have to use a lot of speed and strength. It is not so much a technical match as it is a physical match—many of the techniques are either limited or completely eliminated. The number of chokes you can attempt are greatly reduced; arm locks are harder to get, because you lose so much leverage that you have to get much tighter to your opponent. So there are negatives to not having a gi. However, depending on your strategy, there are also potential advantages to both.

GRAPPLING

I believe today that it is very important to train both with and without a gi. The way I train is the way I like to teach. I have trained with the gi most of my life. But I like sometimes to challenge myself by adapting the techniques I learned with the gi to grappling without the gi. In this way, I keep myself from getting too comfortable with one way of training—because then you stop learning.

No Holds Barred
It is very true that most no-holds-barred fighters training without the gi. But in my academy, for example, I have 200 students, but maybe only 10 percent of them want to go into professional fighting. The rest, 90 percent, want to learn jiu-jitsu for fun, for fitness, for self-defense, or to compete in sport tournaments. That's why the sport rules were invented—it's a way to give the students goals for their training. Tournaments are something to shoot that aren't as violent or intense as professional fighting. And the gi is better for tournaments because it creates more options for the students who are competing in them.

Grips
One of the main differences between using the gi or not, is the type of grips you use. With the gi, sometimes you can do a lot of different set-ups in order to expose your opponent to a submission. You can keep a comfortable distance from your opponent, stay loose, and still grab the lapel, or the material around the elbow, or even the gi at the hip or the knee, and still control him. But with no gi, the game is much different, you can't control your opponent from a distance and still set him up

Over-The-Top Guard Pass With Ankle-Lock
Rigan Machado rests sold base in his opponent's open guard (1). Placing his hands on the floor to keep from getting swept, he leans forward (2). He slides forward (3), until he turns his opponent over (4), then secures the leg and applies the finishing ankle lock (5).

> *"You have to train the sportive methods, but then always keep adapting them and yourself to be able to use them in real situations. You can't lose sight of that or you lose sight of jiu-jitsu itself."*

for a finishing hold. Because a grip that would work with a gi, will be quickly broken with one. There is no lapel to grab, for example, and if you try to hold the neck, the opponent just has to turn his head a little and you slip off. So instead of grabbing for specific points on the body, you have to think about controlling entire regions of the body. For example, instead of controlling the lapel from a distance, you have to get close and control his entire upper body by circling your arms around his body, or by trapping his arm under your arm.

But in either situation, you have to think like a grappler. You have to change your approaches to a move, but you should still be trying to hit the move. In other words, don't let the fact that you have or don't have a gi throw you off your grappling strategy—don't let it take you out of your game. Control the situation rather than letting the situation control you. You must adapt the details, but keep the big picture the same. Use all the same tools, just in different ways.

Chokes

While many people think that it is easier to apply chokes with the gi, it actually depends more on the situation. For example, to do the basic rear naked choke, or the back choke, is much easier without the gi, because your arms get real slippery in a match because of the sweat and you can slide your arm in much easier and get deeper penetration with less effort. When you have the gi it is sometimes more difficult because the material adds a lot of friction and the arm won't slide in as easily. The gi actually stops the back choke many times. With the gi, when you have the back, I think the collar choke is a much better technique to use. So you have to

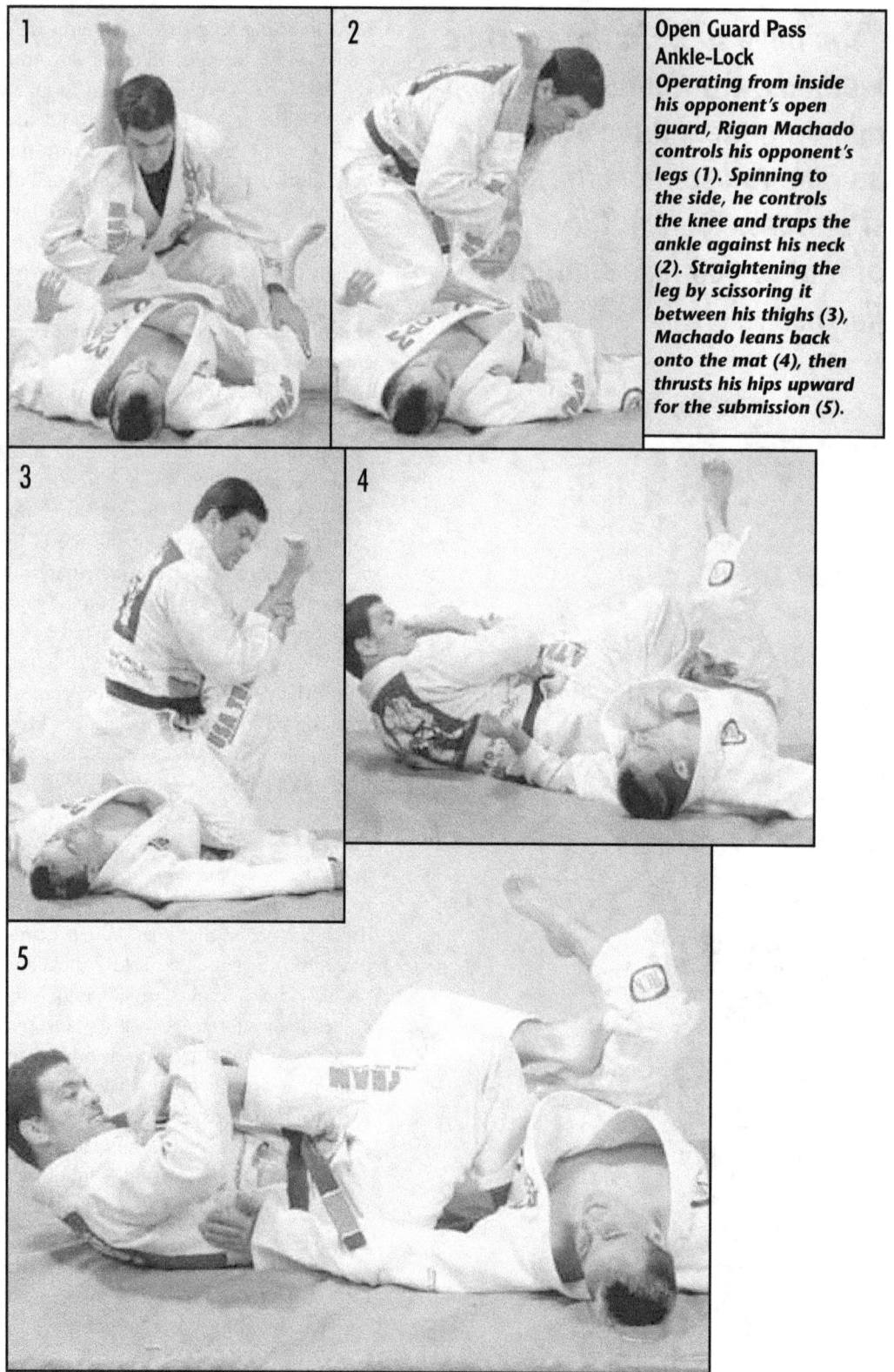

Open Guard Pass Ankle-Lock

Operating from inside his opponent's open guard, Rigan Machado controls his opponent's legs (1). Spinning to the side, he controls the knee and traps the ankle against his neck (2). Straightening the leg by scissoring it between his thighs (3), Machado leans back onto the mat (4), then thrusts his hips upward for the submission (5).

adapt your entry while keeping the ultimate goal the same—to give your opponent a little nap. It's just with the gi, there are more options.

Techniques

There are more techniques with the gi, because there are more options for each move. For example, with I'm practicing take-downs, you have a chance to try a judo throw, to use the gi to block when someone tries to sweep you, or to open someone up for you to sweep them. But when you take away the gi, you pretty much take away all the judo throws—or at the very least they are severely limited. It's much easier for you to slip in, go low, and shoot for the legs with a Freestyle wrestling technique than it is to try a judo hip throw. So right there you're eliminated the option of the judo throw.

But this is a very relative thing, and it goes both ways depending on what art you've been practicing. When you put a wrestler in a gi, for example, they can easily get lost because they have no idea what to do when someone grabs them by the clothes instead of the body. So a jiu-jitsu man can use that to his advantage. The guard is another example where I use the gi to keep him close to me. Without the gi, a wrestler will have a lot more room to operate. But with the gi I can control him by controlling the gi with my arms, without having to clinch. I can keep him from going to the side more effectively, or in the mount I can keep him from escaping from the bottom. There is much less chance to slip away.

So when I train with the gi, I practice those types of moves that would be to my advantage, and then training without the gi I also focus on those things that will help me the most. However, the key thing to remember is that the angles are always the same. The only thing that changes is the grip—the way you control your opponent for the entry. But everything else is the same.

Leg Locks

I am often asked why Brazilian jiu-jitsu is weak on leg locks. That is a good question. For a long time you didn't see a lot of leg locks because of the rules. In the tournaments in Brazil, 10 or 20 years ago, those things were not allowed. Now, though, they are legal and you see a lot more knee bars, heel hooks, and foot locks. The heel hook, though, which puts so much pressure on the knee and the hip, and can cause very serious damage, is the one that jiu-jitsu schools in general, I think, don't like to see in day-to-day training. No one wants to get their ligaments torn up and their knee destroyed. A lot of people just do jiu-jitsu for fun or self-defense, so I think not letting students use that move is a way of protecting them and keeping the training safe. That's the big advantage of jiu-jitsu, after all, over other martial arts—you can train really, really hard and not get hurt. So I think that jiu-jitsu teachers want to preserve that concept.

But little-by-little you see more different types of leg locks added to the jiu-jitsu arsenal. Jiu-jitsu has four different belt levels: blue, purple, brown, and black. People at the brown and the black belt level are those that have started to use more leg techniques. And that is spreading to the lower belts now.

Self Defense

The real purpose of grappling, in the Brazilian jiu-jitsu way, is to be able to apply the moves in a real situation. So you have to use moves that can cause damage. But you don't have to damage other students to practice them. So even non-leg-lock moves, such as neck cranks, are not things that I like to see students use on each other. If I see someone doing excessively dangerous moves to other students then I will tell them to stop. If they continue, then I will ask them to leave the school before anyone gets hurt.

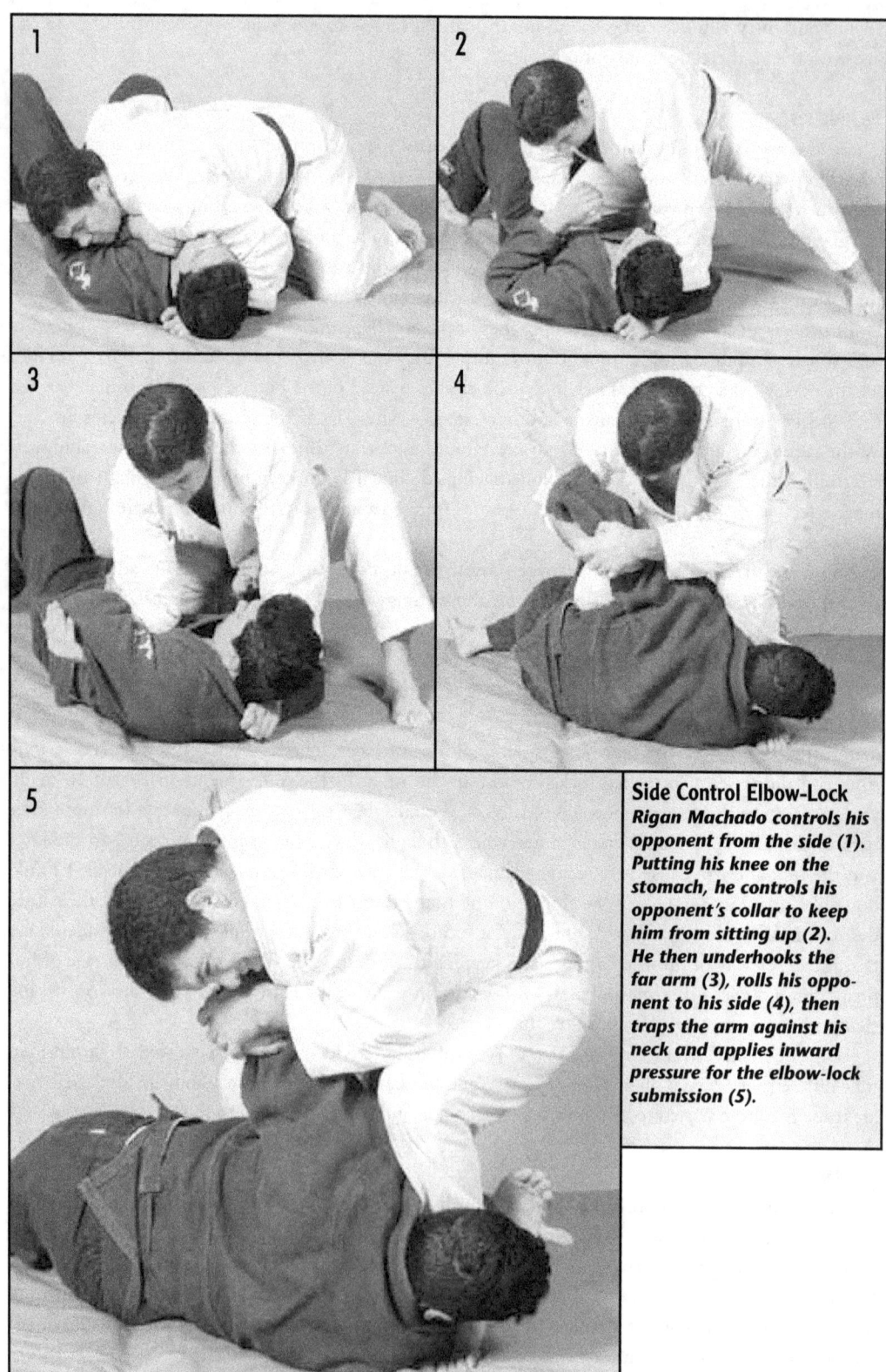

Side Control Elbow-Lock
Rigan Machado controls his opponent from the side (1). Putting his knee on the stomach, he controls his opponent's collar to keep him from sitting up (2). He then underhooks the far arm (3), rolls his opponent to his side (4), then traps the arm against his neck and applies inward pressure for the elbow-lock submission (5).

Training Philosophy?

You can train a martial art, or a martial sport, such as jiu-jitsu, which is both, for sportive uses. But while you're doing this you always have to think about reality. You have to train the sportive methods, but then always keep adapting them and yourself to be able to use them in real situations. You can't lose sight of that or you lose sight of jiu-jitsu itself. That is the base idea of Brazilian jiu-jitsu—practice for sport, but be able to apply it for real.

The Future of Brazilian Jiu-Jitsu

One of the criticisms I hear about the art of jiu-jitsu is that it is not as dominating as it used to be in no-holds-barred fighting. When the UFC first started and my cousin Royce was winning it very easily against men who greatly outweighed him, jiu-jitsu was basically an unknown art. No one know how to counter the guard, the mount, or the side control. People were literally walking into submissions. Instead of keeping the art hidden though, to maintain that technical advantage, my entire family began to travel the world to spread the art.

My brothers Carlos, Roger, and Jean Jacques all have students on nearly every continent. My cousins Royler, Rickson, Royce, and Relson are constantly on the go teaching from Europe to Japan, and from Australia to Russia. If anyone is responsible for the world catching up to Brazilian jiu-jitsu,

it is those who actually created Brazilian jiu-jitsu itself! This is not an art that we ever tried to hide—it is just the opposite. So the fact that so many people now understand the guard, the mount, and all the other positions is not a sign that we failed, but rather that we succeeded.

I believe that Brazilian jiu-jitsu grows a little every day. When a new way to escape the triangle is found, it quickly spreads from school to school, around the world. New methods of passing the guard or new arm locks are known by all with a month or two. This constant sharing of knowledge creates a camaraderie that binds us all together and makes us feel as one. I only see a bright future of jiu-jitsu around the world. In ten years time you will see one hundred times as many students all over the globe. All members of the jiu-jitsu family—regardless of what their last name is—will keep learning and growing and sharing together because we love the art. That is our ultimate strength.

> "If anyone is responsible for the world catching up to Brazilian jiu-jitsu, it is those who actually created Brazilian jiu-jitsu itself! This is not an art that we ever tried to hide—it is just the opposite. So the fact that so many people now understand the guard, the mount, and all the other positions is not a sign that we failed, but rather that we succeeded."

Rigan Machado's new book, The Essence of Brazilian Jiu-Jitsu, *is now available from Unique Publications.*

GRAPPLING

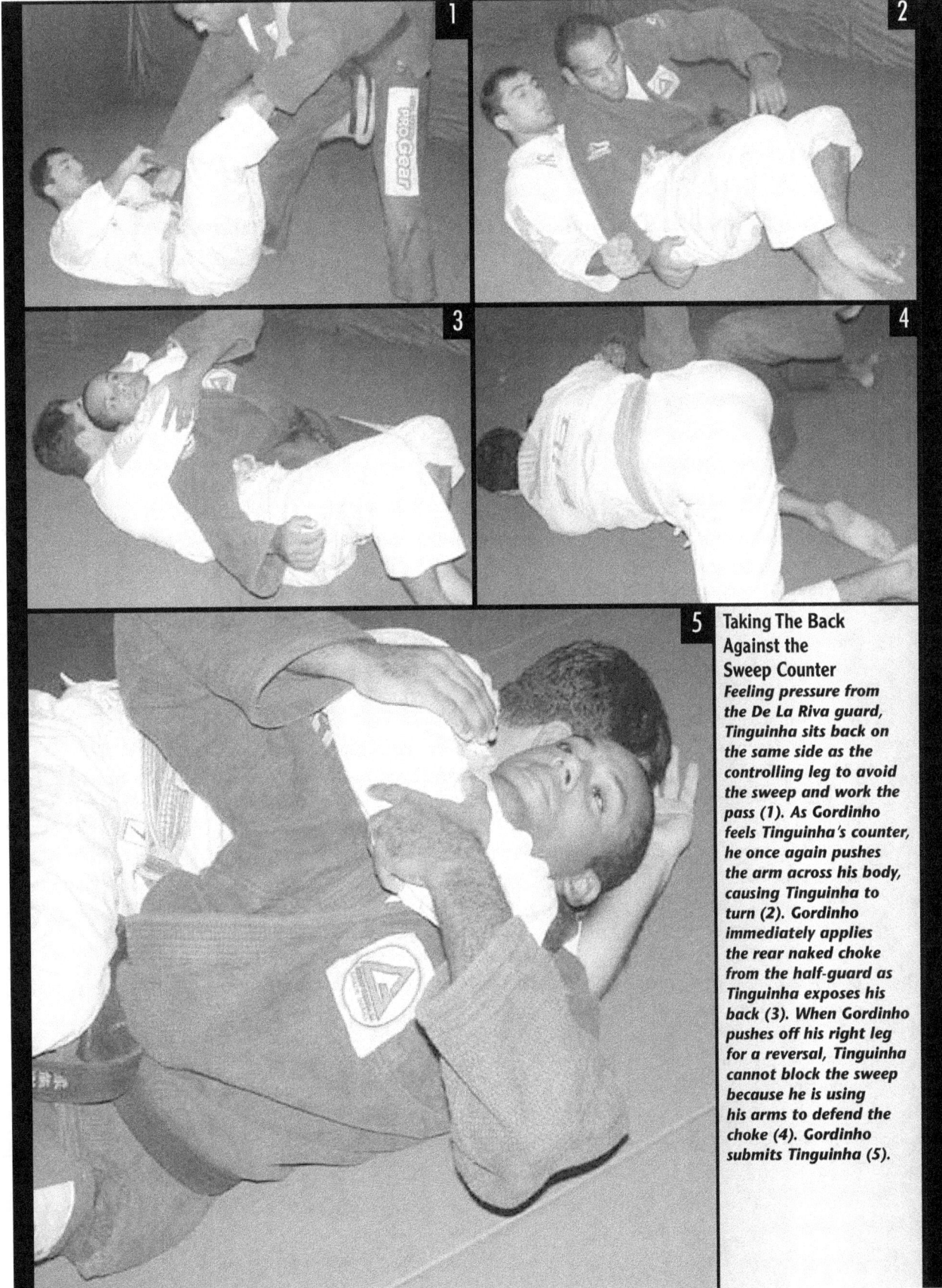

Taking The Back Against the Sweep Counter

Feeling pressure from the De La Riva guard, Tinguinha sits back on the same side as the controlling leg to avoid the sweep and work the pass (1). As Gordinho feels Tinguinha's counter, he once again pushes the arm across his body, causing Tinguinha to turn (2). Gordinho immediately applies the rear naked choke from the half-guard as Tinguinha exposes his back (3). When Gordinho pushes off his right leg for a reversal, Tinguinha cannot block the sweep because he is using his arms to defend the choke (4). Gordinho submits Tinguinha (5).

Secrets of the De La Riva Guard

Ricardo De La Riva created the technique bearing his name in the early days of jiu-jitsu, and used its signature grapevine leg-trap to beat many opponents. Due to the efforts of Rafael Correia, the De La Riva guard has seen a recent revival on the competition circuit.

Kid Peligro

Gracie Barra black belt Rafael "Gordinho" Correia is no stranger to competition. Gordinho grew up in the shadow of his legendary brother, "Gordo" Correia, a man known in Brazil as the King of the Half-Guard. A four-time world and Brazilian jiu-jitsu champion himself, Gordinho is known for using his famous brother's half-guard techniques as well as his own crafty guard moves, sweeps, and submissions. Being the younger sibling of a legend, Gordinho assimilated his brother's understanding of the half-guard position and used it quite competently.

But Gordinho wanted to make his own mark on the Brazilian jiu-jitsu landscape and decided to study and develop a classic technique- the De La Riva guard. Ricardo De La Riva is still very much alive and teaching in Florida, a long distance from Gordinho's home in the Barra district of Rio de Janeiro. But the miles between them didn't stop Gordinho from doing his own research into a technique that he greatly admires and updating it for modern competition.

"I was looking to further refine a position to complement my guard game," Gordinho says, "and add to the arsenal that I already have from the half-guard. Being that I train at Gracie Barra, and we are well-known for our guard play, it was easy to refine the movements. All I had to do was to ask the brain trust at the Gracie Barra Academy and they did the rest. Carlos Gracie Jr., Marcio Feitosa, Roleta Magalhaes, my brother Gordo, Helio Soneca, Soca Carneiro, Mauricio Tinguinha and all the others came and pitched-in and helped."

In updating a position that everyone is familiar with, Gordinho had to take into account what the guard was meant to do to, and then adapt it to modern techniques. "Originally, everyone's favorite thing to do from the De La Riva guard was to sweep," Gordinho explains. "But as the position became a staple of competition, it became harder and harder to execute successfully. So that caused us to add a few twists to an old classic."

According to Gordinho, the key to the De La Riva guard is to keep pressure on the leg that performs the grapevine, while using the foot to hook the opponent's hip. He emphasizes that it is very important to be alert and maintain that pressure, otherwise you leave yourself open to a knee-bar. You also need to grip and control the opponent's ankle that you have the grapevine on, in order to create an imbalance while at the same time cross-controlling your opponent's arm.

When mastered, Gordinho insists that this odd combination of grips will cause major instability to your opponent's base and open up a wealth of possibilities. Nowadays, Gordinho's preferred application of the De La Riva guard is to take the back and submit the opponent with a rear choke; however, the De La Riva guard offers many other possibilities as well.

As Gordinho points out, "In the first series I show how you can take the back when the opponent is either on his knees or standing up and trying to pass. The secret of the success for these two

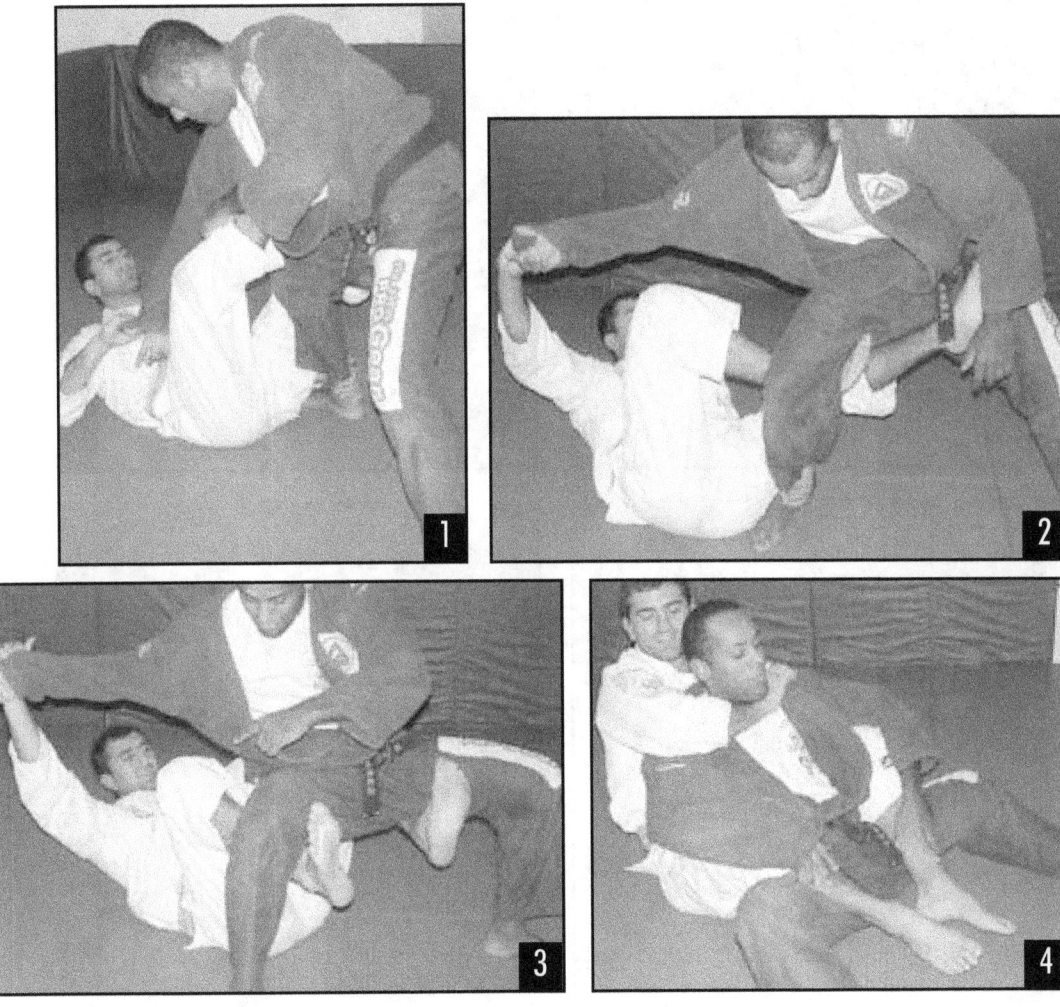

Taking The Back Against A Standing Guard Pass
Gordinho's opponent, Tinguinha, attempts a standing pass against the De La Riva guard (1). Gordinho stretches his left leg while pulling his opponent's right arm across his body. As Tinguinha loses his balance and falls forward, Gordinho slides around to control the back, using his right leg as an additional hook (2). Gordinho grips and pulls on Tinguinha's belt and arm, while at the same time stretching his legs and causing the opponent to fall back (3). With the back position achieved, the hooks in place, and the collar choke ready, Gordinho is now ready for the submission (4).

moves is to completely cross the opponent after you cause then to lose their balance and bracing themselves to withstand the attempted sweep. As they are bracing themselves and concentrating on maintaining their balance, you slip to the back."

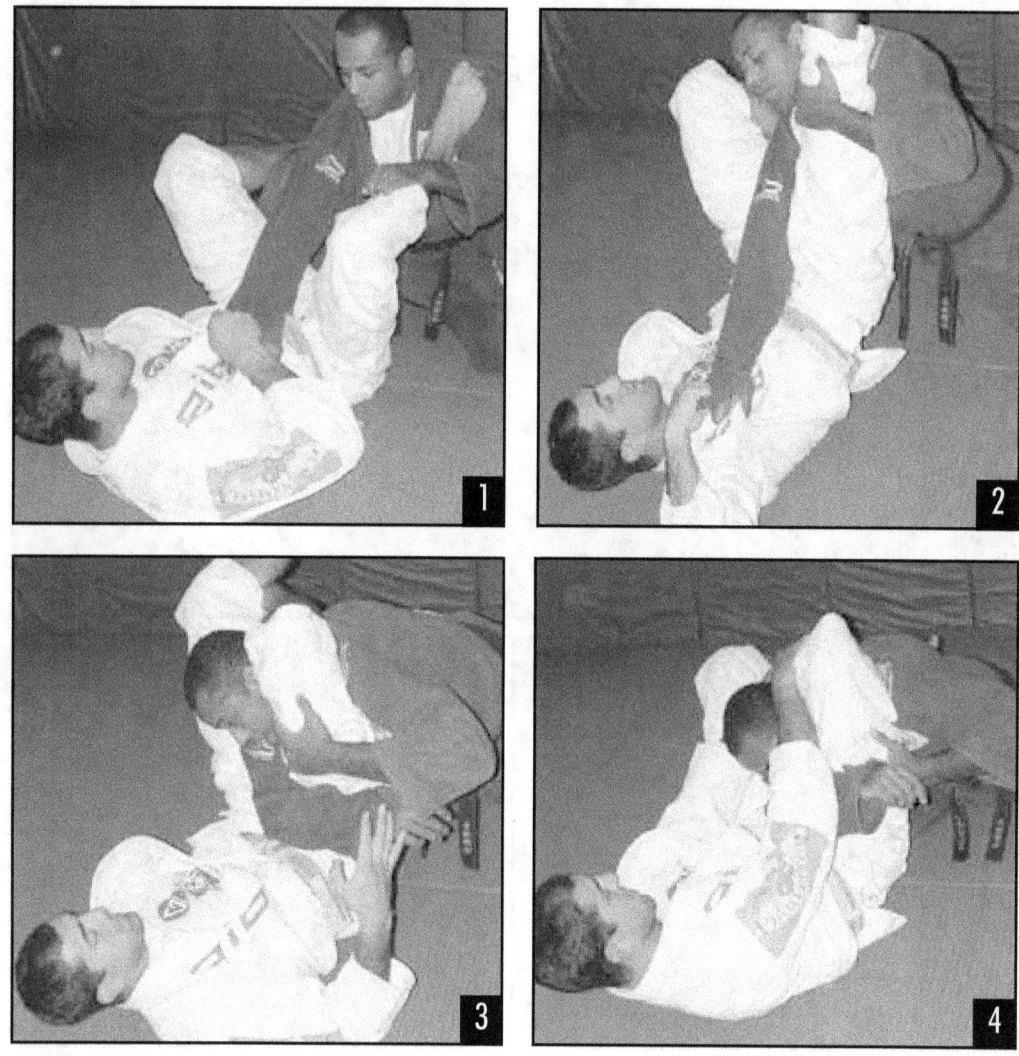

Triangle Choke From The De La Riva Guard
Working from the De La Riva guard, Gordinho releases his left hook then applies pressure with his right foot on Tinguinha's shoulder while pulling the arm (1). As Tinguinha falls forward, Gordinho puts his left foot on Tinguinha's right hip. Gordinho then uses that to lift his own hip and stretch his right leg while putting his weight on Tinguinha's left shoulder (2). Gordinho then closes his legs around Tinguinha's arm and head and pulls Tinguinha's arm across his body to add pressure to the choke (3). Gordinho then pulls Tinguinha's head towards him and the pressure from the triangle causes the submission (4).

Taking The Back From An Attempted Sweep
Gordinho is in the classic De La Riva guard, with his the left leg in a grapevine around training partner's Tinguinha's right leg, and holding cross control of his arm (1). Reverse angle detail of the grapevine and Gordinho's left hand gripping the right ankle for extra control (2). Gordinho uses his right leg to push Tinguinha's knee while at the same time pulling the right arm across his body to cause Tinguinha to lose his balance. Additionally Gordinho pulls the right ankle while stretching his left leg to add leverage to the attempted sweep (3). As Tinguinha braces his arms to avoid the sweep, Gordinho slips around and controls the back (4).

The De La Riva is not just for defense, it's also a great platform for submissions. "My favorite submission is the *omoplata*," Gordinho explains. "By using the same principles and a little different hip motion, I can get the shoulder lock. Of course, I am not opposed to doing a triangle as well."

Like any other technique in jiu-jitsu, practice makes perfect. "My suggestion for jiu-jitsu practitioners," Gordinho further explains, "is to practice these techniques and then experiment with the position. If you do that then new options will open up. It happens just about every day at Gracie Barra and there is no reason why it shouldn't happen at other schools as well. Practice until you have the mechanics of these five options down. Once you understand the basic principles of the De La Riva guard, then the sky is the limit."

GRAPPLING

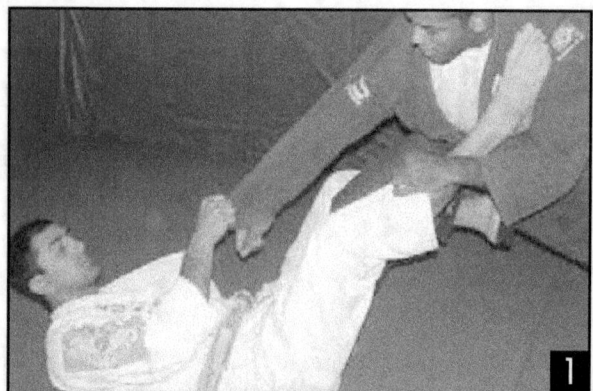

Omoplata (shoulder lock) From The De La Riva Guard

Gordinho has Tinguinha in the De La Riva guard (1). Using the same motion as for the sweep, he takes the back and causes Tinguinha to lose his balance. This time, however, Gordinho uses his right leg and causes Tinguinha to bend forward (2). Gordinho then uses his left leg to lock Mauricio's right arm in the classic omoplata shoulder lock (3). Gordinho then sits up while pushing his hips forward, to apply the pressure on Tinguinha's shoulder for the submission (4).

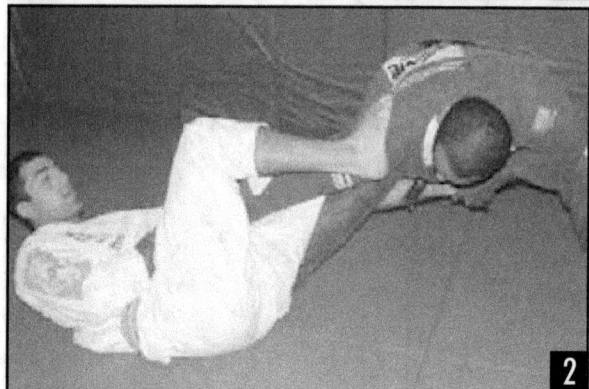

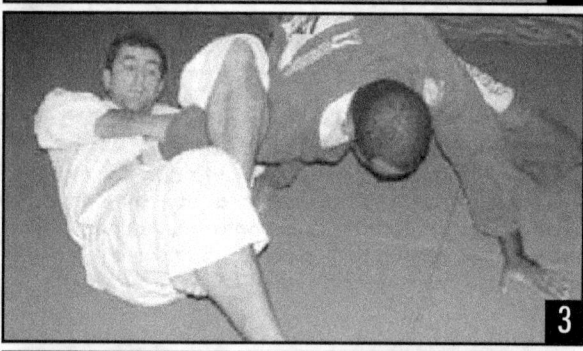

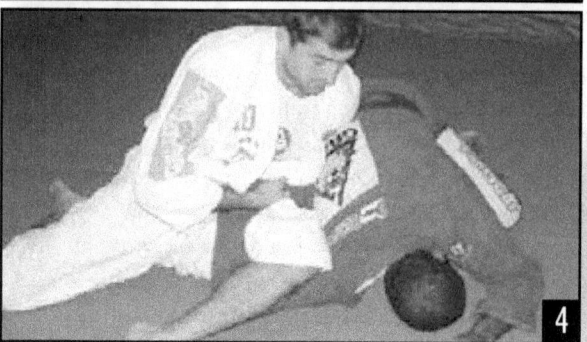

GRAPPLING

"It's always great to see the elite athletes doing well in competition; but it's more rewarding for me to see someone come into my school overweight and with no self-confidence—then a year later they are an athlete, brimming with confidence and making huge gains in their personal lives."

John Will
Where There's a Will, There's a Way

There is a man whose name is synonymous with excellence in martial arts throughout Australia and the South Pacific. His life story is a cross between Raiders of the Lost Ark, Bloodsport and the Croc Hunter.

Jeremy Ta'kody

He was the first Australian to be awarded a Brazilian jiu-jitsu (BJJ) black belt, and was one of the original "Dirty Dozen," the first 12 non-Brazilian black belts in the world. He has been a catalyst of destiny for countless people, inspiring and motivating thousands to make changes in their lives. He has helped guide many through the troubled waters of life, and through his blood sweat and tears laid a pathway for others to excel and improve far beyond their expected ability. He has braved the jungles of Indonesia; wrestled half-naked in the ghettos of India; fought tooth and nail while training in Thailand and Brazil; confronted machine-gun wielding customs officers for confiscating artifacts; and risked life and limb by wading waist-deep through shark and crocodile infested waters.

He possesses rare qualities of passion, analysis, and communication, and those who know him marvel at his ability to shape circumstance and coincidence in such a way that his life can hardly be called luck. He is a father, a husband, a mentor, a coach, and a friend. He has passion and purpose, loyalty and honor, and above all radiates an indefinable quality that can only be called the spirit of adventure. His name is John Will—and there is no one quite like him in the entire world.

Q: You have influenced thousands of martial artists both in Australia and abroad, and seem to have a natural affinity for teaching and instilling exceptional analytical thinking in people from beginners, to the highest grade instructors. How did you discover your love of martial arts, and what enabled you to develop the mindset that has taken you so far?
A: My interest in the martial arts began before I was a teenager. Schoolyard scraps and such motivated me to read all I could about self-defense; and later as a teenager, I took up wrestling, Goju Kai Karate and TKD before heading of to Asia for more full-time training. I guess reading books by such authors as Gilbey, Smith, and Draeger, really fired my imagination—eventually I just had to go and find out for myself what it was all about. Nowadays, we all live in a "big picture" world. Information is abundant and easy to access. But it wasn't like that when I began training in the martial arts. Luckily for me, my father instilled in me the habit of big-picture thinking, and so from the

Duck-Under to Inside Back Control
John Will faces his opponent (1). Controlling his wrist (2), he raises the arm and ducks under that armpit (3), pivots on his inside foot towards his opponent (4), and establishes inside back control (5).

very outset I saw the various styles I was studying as only pieces of the puzzle and not the whole solution. That was a healthy way for me to begin. I have never been stuck or blinkered in my approach to training. In fact, I think I have a pathological need to stay at the cutting edge—otherwise I would probably become bored and lose interest.

Q: How did you meet the Machado brothers?
A: I met the Machados on a visit to the States in the late '80s. In fact, I met Rigan Machado at Rorion Gracie's house, while doing an interview on Brazilian jiu-jitsu. I mentioned to Rigan that I was heading to Brazil to do some training and he told me that he was going down himself in a few days time, and that I was welcome to join him. I did, and that was the beginning of my training in BJJ. I had a great time down there, especially training with Jean Jacques Machado, who at that time was running a huge school with some of the top competitors in the country under his guidance. It was fantastic!

Q: Which other grappling instructors have you trained with?
A: Other Brazilian jiu-jitsu instructors whom I was introduced to by Rigan Machado include Crolin Gracie, Rilion Gracie, Renzo Gracie, Carlos Gracie Junior, Rickson Gracie, Jorge Periera and of course, Rigan's other brothers, Jean Jacques, Roger, Carlos and John. Apart from training with these

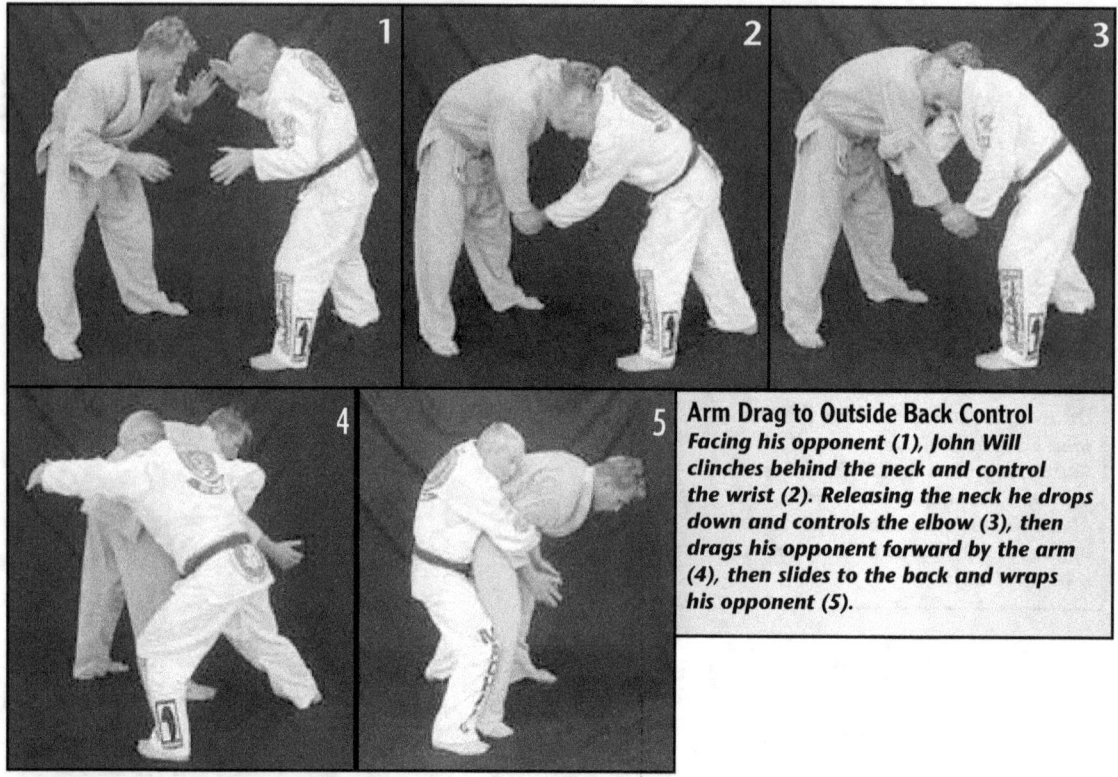

Arm Drag to Outside Back Control
Facing his opponent (1), John Will clinches behind the neck and control the wrist (2). Releasing the neck he drops down and controls the elbow (3), then drags his opponent forward by the arm (4), then slides to the back and wraps his opponent (5).

BJJ instructors, I have spent time with Gene LeBell in Los Angeles as well as other coaches in the northern part of India.

Q: How do you maintain your interest after all this time?
A: Training has to be challenging. Once it's no longer challenging, it's time to look for a taller mountain! I am lucky in that I have great friends who are also great martial artists; and I think to a degree we all keep each other motivated with new ideas and training methods. Richard Norton for example, turned-up at my place the other day with one of those Swiss Balls; he's just finished reading and learning everything he can about them and immediately starts formulating ways of relating those ideas to martial arts training. It's that kind of cross-discipline thinking that keeps things alive and moving forward for me. Richard and I feel safe trying new things, thinking outside of the boundaries, and exploring new possibilities together; it is important for martial artists to surround themselves with a people they can do this with.

Q: Apart from your work in Australia, do you still go overseas on a regular basis?
A: Yes. A couple of times per year. I conduct a seminar circuit that includes schools in New Zealand and the States several times per year. Besides that, I have many good friends that live outside of Australia and it is important to me that I catch-up and spend time with them as regularly as is possible.

Q: Who do you spend time training with in the States?
A: I spend as much time as I can with both Jean Jacques and Rigan Machado; as they are my Brazilian jiu-jitsu instructors as well as being good friends of mine. I also try to get in some kickboxing with Pete Cunningham; a great coach and still the very best in his field. If Richard Norton and I can hook up, we always will spend time together on then mat or in the ring. He is the best training partner one could ever hope for—creative, extremely talented, and always hungry to improve and innovate. I also love spending time with other Machado black belts that I came up through the ranks with; particularly Dave Meyer, one of my best friends and a lifetime training partner. I look forward to the opportunity to get together with people like these; to solve a few problems and get each other up to speed on what's going on around the place. I love those brainstorming sessions; they are loads of fun!

Q: What led you to grappling in the pits of India? What were the rules? How do the Indian wrestling systems differ from BJJ?
A: I have been to India several times, researching and training in several of the indigenous combative systems there, including their style of wrestling. There are a couple of forms, but their main system is similar to Olympic wrestling as far as objectives and methodology goes. The main difference is that there are no mats, so it's all done in an earth-filled pit. Great fun and a real cultural experience! Very different from BJJ though, it's not a submission style; rather a pinning and takedown system. The Indians, though very poor and underprivileged by Western standards, train extremely hard and are some of the most well-conditioned athletes I have ever seen.

There are also some rare and very hard-to-find styles there, that have an ancient heritage—like Vajramushti. This is a submission wrestling system, similar in make-up to Brazilian vale tudo. There is one major difference, though, and that is the Vajramushti combatants each wear a knuckle-duster strapped to their right hands to aid in destructive striking power. A dangerous system, to say the least. It is really practiced only by one main family—the Jyesthimullas—in the state of Gujarat. India is home to some amazing fighting arts, many of which date back many, many centuries.

Q: You were the first Westerner to compete and win gold in the Silat World Championships, held in Jakarta, Indonesia. Can you describe your training and explain how you managed to be accepted into such a closed society?
A: That was a while ago—back in 1982. My training in the seven years leading up to that event and the earning of my black belt in Bakti Negara pentjak silat was an interesting time. Training was tough, with a lot of emphasis put on practicality. Elbows, knees, head-butts, and thigh kicks were all basics, and we trained hard in those type of techniques. Long-range kicking and hand work came second. There was also a fair amount of weaponry, which I had to be dragged kicking and screaming to learn, I wasn't all that interested in that part of it. I did the work though, and now am glad of the experience. Silat was a good foundation for me because it gave me a great overview—hands feet, elbows, knees, grappling and weaponry. Jack of all trades, you might say.

Q: Why don't you teach Silat anymore?
A: Well, I have moved on from being a rough generalist, and more toward a specialist at what I do. Things are different now, people are just getting better at everything. All aspects of training are

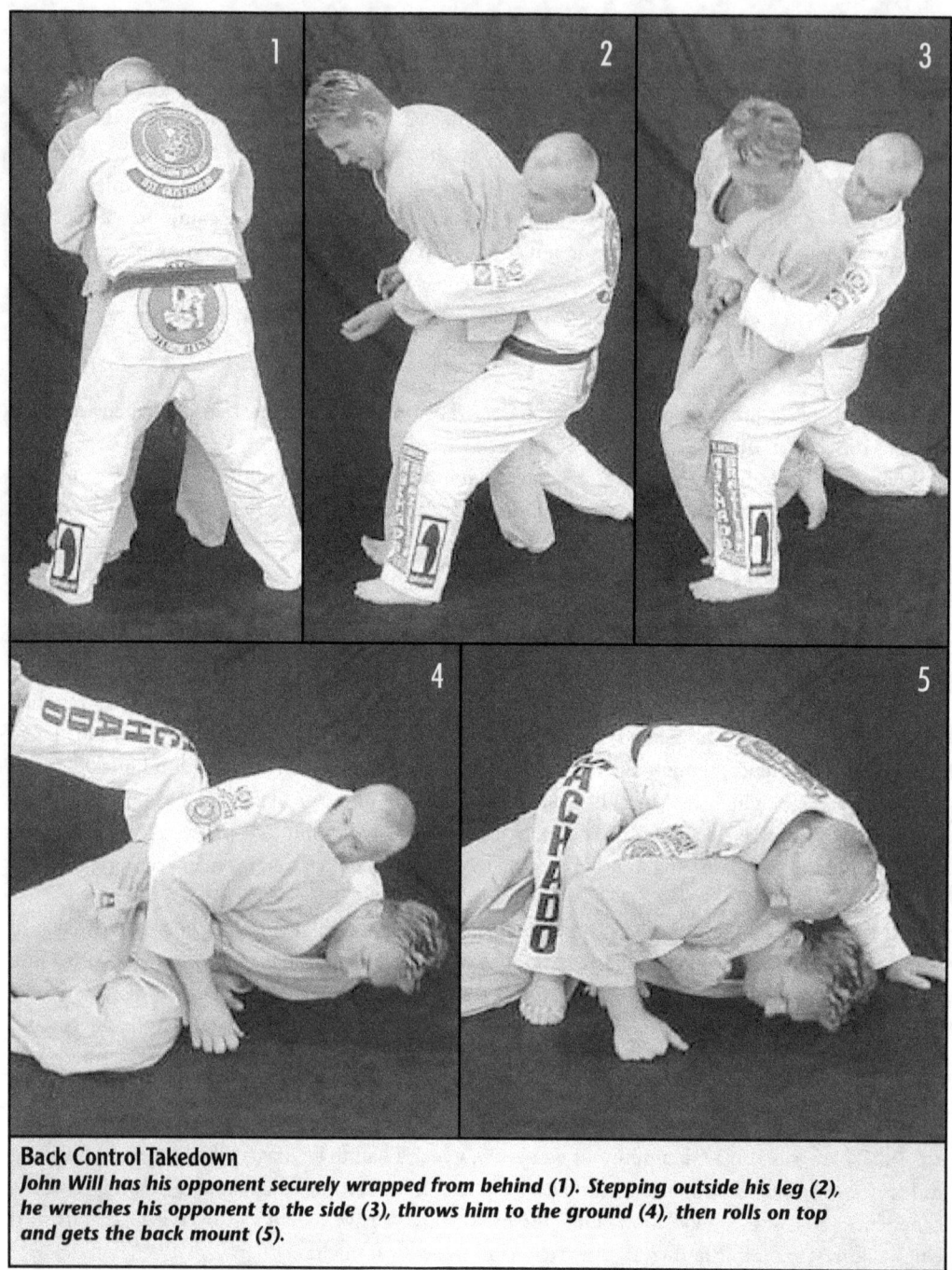

Back Control Takedown
John Will has his opponent securely wrapped from behind (1). Stepping outside his leg (2), he wrenches his opponent to the side (3), throws him to the ground (4), then rolls on top and gets the back mount (5).

improving and evolving on almost a daily basis. That's what I am interested in now. I studied quite a few styles of Silat back in those days; and all of those instructors have helped make me who I am right now. I owe a debt of gratitude to each and every one of them.

Q: Does martial art practice enable practitioners to develop powers of the mind? Have you ever witnessed things through your travels that defy logical and rational explanation?

A: I have to say that I am skeptical. I don't wish to hurt anyone's feelings but that is just the way I am. I hope to be proved wrong, but I believe in leverage, mechanics, tactics and smart training not "The Force." I have seen strange things in the early days of my travelling but I have to say that I was more impressionable then. But hope springs eternal, huh?

Q: Your three books on Brazilian jiu-jitsu are martial arts bestsellers. Can you briefly describe each, why you wrote them, and how people can obtain a copy?

A: The three I've written so far are *Brazilian Jiu-Jitsu Fundamentals*, *Brazilian Jiu-Jitsu Guard*, and *Advanced Brazilian Jiu-Jitsu Attacks and Escapes*. They have sold very well and I have had tremendously good feedback on all of them. People can easily purchase them over the Internet through my Web site www.bjj.com.au.

Q: Elvis Sinosic is one of your purple belts. Though he lost to Tito Ortiz in UFC 32, he scored a decisive victory over Jeremy Horn in UFC 31. How does he compare to your other fighters in Australia? What is their standard compared to fighters around the world?

A: Elvis is a great competitor, but he has many training partners in Australia such as brown belt Anthony Perosh and my other purple belts who are also of an extremely high standard. Their BJJ training, coupled with good stand-up skills, makes for an excellent environment in which the less-experienced fighters can learn and improve. I would like to think that the Australian fighters are comparable to others at an elite level in other countries. The biggest difference is that we don't have the huge population that other countries have; so perhaps where other schools might have 10 or 15 purple belts, three browns and two black belts on the mat in any one training session, we might only see four or five purples, one brown and one black belt. Part of it is a numbers game—the more people on the mat the richer the training environment and the more interesting things get! But numbers are improving at home; our Machado BJJ tournament is drawing well over 100 competitors now. These numbers may seem small to the American audience, but remember there are more people living in Los Angeles than in all of Australia!

Q: How do you feel about students competing in mixed-martial-arts events? Is it encouraged or are most training for self-defense, or sport jiu-jitsu style tournaments?

A: Most of the training I offer is for the average person. The average person doesn't want to compete in the UFC or go on to become a professional MMA fighter. I don't mind my students competing, but I do not go out of my way to the exclusion and detriment of the average student and cater to that type of training. I want to give the average person the chance to become an extraordinary person—these are the people that really need martial arts training. Good quality martial arts training can make a huge difference in the ordinary person's life; these are the changes that matter to me! It's always great to see the elite athletes doing well in competition; but it's more rewarding for me to see someone come into my school overweight and with no self-confidence—then a year later they are an athlete, brimming with confidence and making huge gains in their personal lives. That's what it's really all about!

> **North-South Collar Choke**
> *Controlling his opponent with the knee on the stomach (1), John Will reaches down and grabs the back of the collar with his outside hand (2). Inserting his inside hand into the front of the lapel (3), he spins to the north-south position and applies the finishing choke (4).*

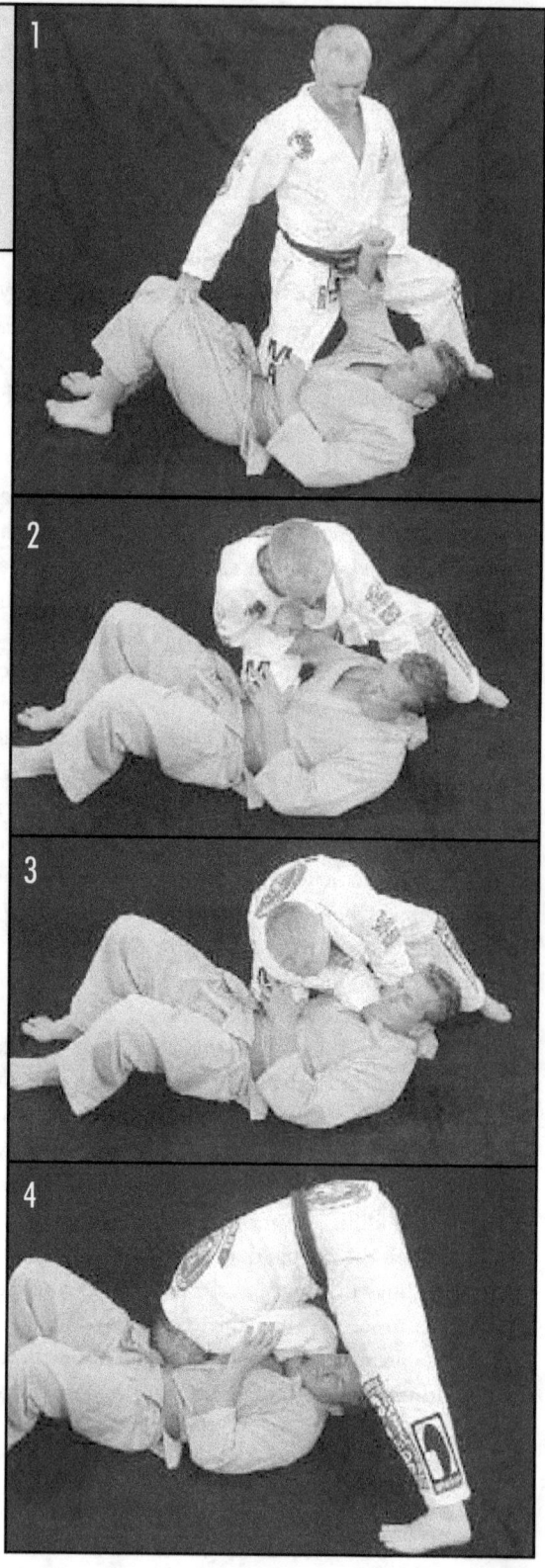

Q: Can you describe the structure of your school?

A: Everyone who starts training at my school begins in the Introductory class. They stay in there, learning the basics for three months, then move up into the Novice class. After more time there, they move to the Intermediate class and finally to the Advanced class. Most of my classes are one hour in length—if the workout is structured and scientific, that's plenty! The progression is important; we have to work with people at a level that allows for maximum improvement without scaring them away. We have to challenge them, not destroy them. Some people come in with lots of baggage that we are unaware of; rape victims, victims of violence, et cetera—the last thing they need is a bashing on the mat. We have to reach out to these people and ease them into the more challenging aspects of training. They are the real people we are dealing with—we have a responsibility to take care of them.

Q: What is the syllabus for white belt to blue belt? How long does it take students to reach the different belt levels?

A: Our syllabus encompasses a well-rounded cross-section of controls, positions, escapes, and finishes. We do not encourage people to specialize too early. The Machados always encouraged me to be well-rounded, especially in my formative years of training; I try to do the same with my students. The goal is for the blue

BEST OF CFW — VOL. 1
GRAPPLING

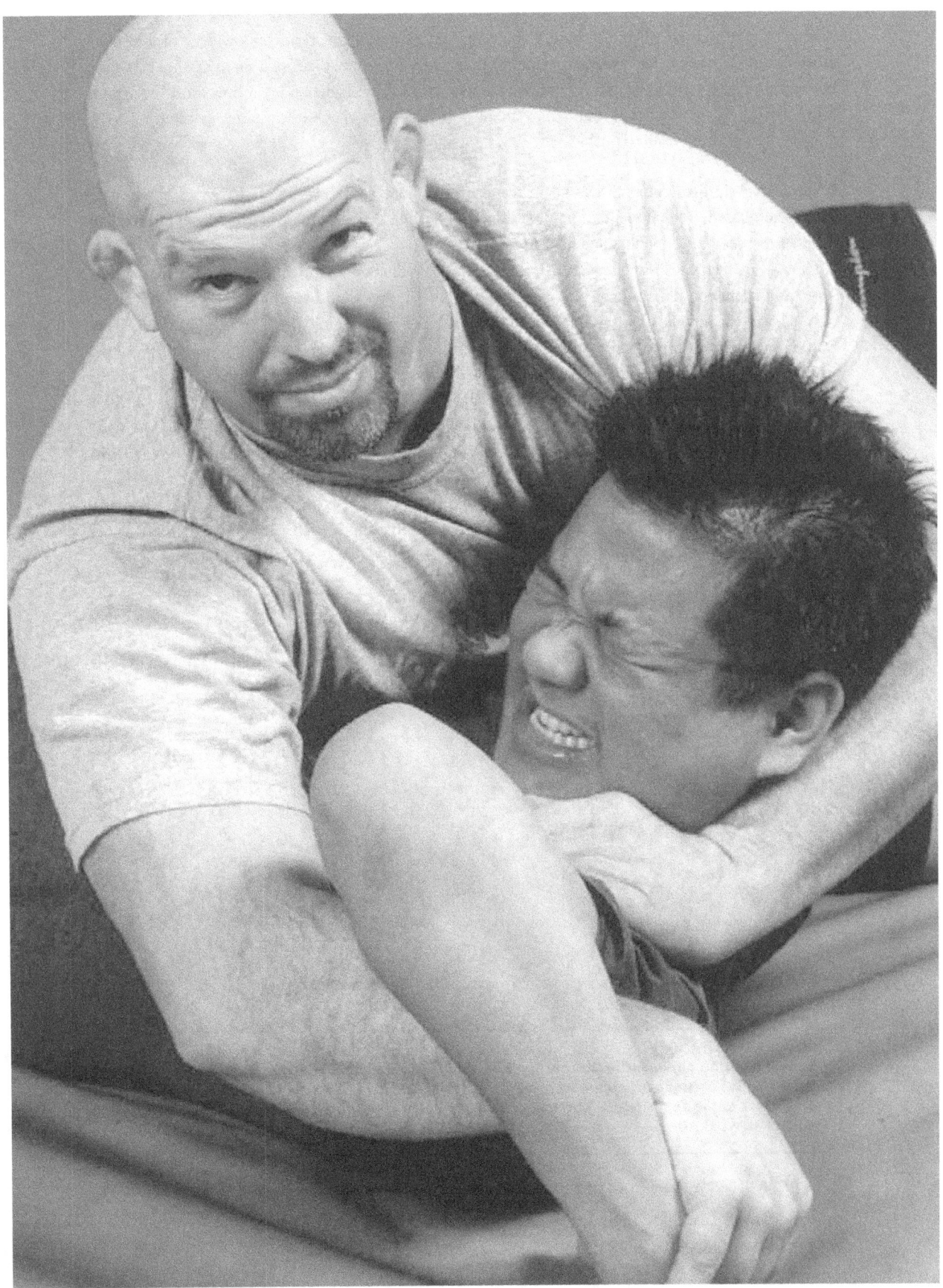

belt to be very well-rounded and have a thorough practical and theoretical knowledge of a healthy cross-section of basics. The average person who trains twice a week can expect to attain their blue belt within one to two years. After that, it becomes hard to say; it depends on how hard they train, how many times a week they train, how many injuries they get while training, et cetera. Maybe another two to three years to purple belt.

Q: High-level jiu-jitsu competitions seem to becoming more and more points-based as opposed to submission-based. Do you feel that point systems will inevitably cause the watering down of Brazilian jiu-jitsu into judo-style pinning and holding?
A: To a degree what you say is true. BJJ competition has changed a lot in the last 10 years; there is more and more emphasis put on the winning by points rather than by submission. The Machados have always encouraged their students to win by submission. I think that it is important to keep training with this in mind—after all, the basic premise has always been to win the fight. Otherwise, why not just take up college wrestling and at least be better at the takedown aspect? If you look at the history of Olympic wrestling and where the emphasis has changed over the years, it then becomes easy to imagine that the same could well happen to BJJ.

As to solutions, I suppose there are an endless amount of ideas—each would have to be tried and tested. A few submission-only tournaments might be worth a try. Ten minutes rounds for example—no points and only submission wins. No submission, then both fighters are out. There are problems to work out, but the action would be guaranteed. Another idea might be the first-to-fif-

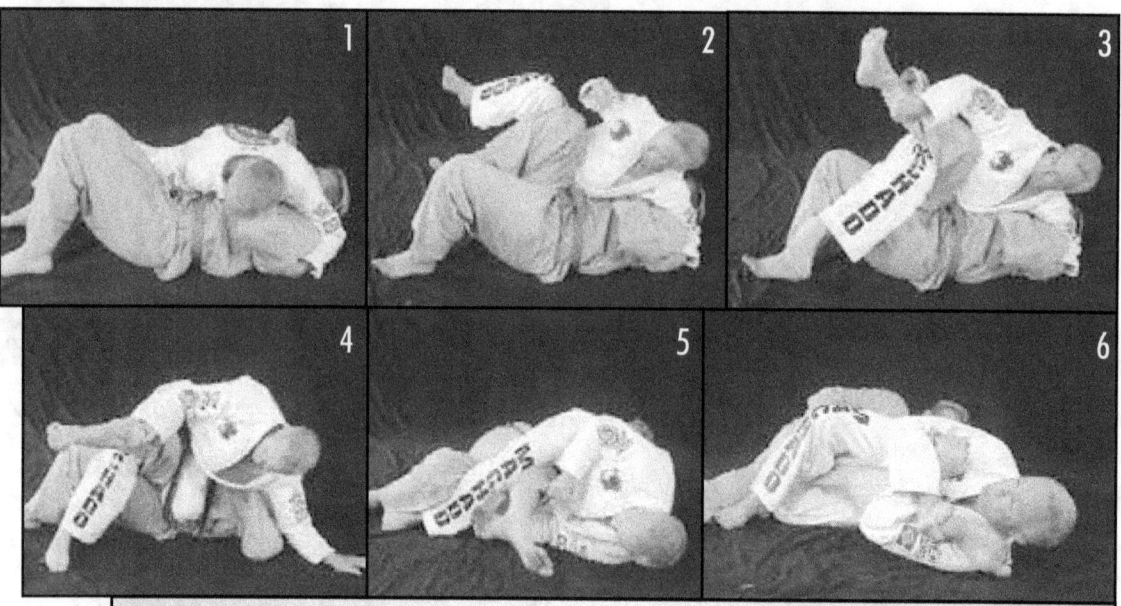

Side Control Knee-Bar
John Will holds his opponent securely in the side mount (1). Raising his leg to take the mount (2), he slides his leg between his opponent's leg (3). Putting his outside knee on his opponent's stomach (4), he slides to the opposite side and traps the leg (5). He then straightens it and applies the finishing knee-bar (6).

teen-points wins, but with a time limit to do so. We have to find ways of encouraging submissions and making it more interesting for spectators; particularly if we want to attract television and therefore sponsors.

Q: Extreme sports such a skateboarding, motorcross, and skysurfing are drawing big name sponsors. What is the future of sport jiu-jitsu? Will sponsorship grow for it as it has for other extreme sports?
A: Sport jiu-jitsu is growing all the time. It's a great way for people to test themselves in a competitive arena, where the opponent isn't going to care too much about you—unlike the mat environment in the school! For competition to grow, there has to be less emphasis on politics and more and win-win for BJJ! This is difficult as there is a lot of political intrigue going on in BJJ circles. I think that sponsorship can play an important part in the growth of Brazilian jiu-jitsu competition. People spend a lot of time and money travelling to compete in tournaments, so it would be nice for them to go home with something for their efforts. I've seen BJJ tournaments where if you didn't belong to the right school, then you didn't even walk away with the competitors T-shirts you were supposed to get. That kind of BS has to stop! What can *we* offer the sponsors? That is the question we should be asking.

Most people who run tournaments are continually asking sponsors for things—I think it's important to go to a potential sponsor and tell them what we can do to increase their business. It has to be a win-win situation for both tournament promoter and sponsor alike. Also, I believe in loyalty to a sponsor. It's important not to dump someone who has been looking after you just because someone comes along with a better offer. After all, isn't loyalty one of the traits of martial arts we are trying to teach our students? Before instructors can change people for the better, they themselves have to behave with honesty, loyalty, and integrity—we can't conveniently put aside these qualities just to make a few dollars or build ourselves a bit bigger following. As instructors we must lead by example—a cliche, I know—but also a truth!

Jeremy Ta'kody is the editorial director of Blitz, *Australia's leading martial arts magazine. He can be contacted via email at* **jeremy@blitzmag.com.au**

GRAPPLING
BEST OF CFW — VOL. 1

GRAPPLING

Leka Vieira
A Fist in a Velvet Glove

The first woman black belt world champion in Brazilian jiu-jitsu, Leka Vieira is on a mission to open doors and spread the art of jiu-jitsu to women in America.

Jose Fraguas

Breaking barriers and paving the way for a new generation is something only a few special individuals ever have a chance to do in any human endeavor. Courage, passion, dedication and will power are the basic qualities these pioneers have. Once the road is marked and the door opened, it is far easier for those who come behind to follow. Leka Vieira, a young Brazilian jiu-jitsu black belt is one of these modern-day trailblazers. Originally from Rio de Janeiro, she found herself in the United States with a mission—to introduce Brazilian jiu-jitsu to American women. Last March, for the first time in history, she took an American jiu-jitsu women's team to the Pan-American Brazilian Jiu-Jitsu Championships in Florida. Thirteen women comprised that group, but Vieira feels that it is just the beginning of a revolution in the sport. She strongly feels that the best is yet to come for American women in Brazilian jiu-jitsu.

Q: How long you have been practicing Brazilian jiu-jitsu?
A: Since I was 16. So that makes 10 years of continuous training.

Q: Have you ever practiced other styles?
A: I have always trained in Brazilian jiu-jitsu. When I came to America I started to train judo with Sensei Mojica and Sensei Carrera .I train consistently at their place and I'm currently a brown belt under them. Judo has helped me very much in my jiu-jitsu. I think is a great complement because judo focuses on throwing and unbalancing your opponent while standing. It's a different approach than jiu-jitsu and it has enriched my overall skill in the grappling arts.

Q: Who were your instructors in Brazil?
A: My first teacher was Aloisio Silva. After that I had the opportunity to train with Royler Gracie and Vinicius Aieta from the Gracie Academy in Rio de Janeiro. They are great teachers and their knowledge of the art is truly awesome.

Q: How did you begin your training?
A: When I started Brazilian jiu-jitsu, in three months of training I lost 18 pounds. That was something very shocking to me in my early days. I still have the pictures and sometimes when I look at them I can't believe it. My memories of my beginnings in the art are mainly of that. I believe that when you do something you really want to do, you use your will power to keep your physical focus. It is only with inner dedication that your skills will reach a higher level and you will improve. I'm doing something that I love, and if you do something that you love, you'll always have a good time.

Q: Has your approach to jiu-jitsu changed over the years?
A: Definitely! I started at a very young age and jiu-jitsu is definitely an art where you have to use your mind to progress. As I became older and more experienced—fighting in many tournaments—my level of understanding has deepened. I had the opportunity to train with many different partners and that helped me a lot too.

Q: How do you see the role of women in jiu-jitsu? Do you think events like the UFC should include women's fights?
A: Women are breaking barriers every day and they have started to fight NHB events—although not as much as many of us would like. I hope the people in charge of NHB and vale tudo—such as UFC or Pride—will give us a chance to show what we are capable of. As a fighter, I don't think it matters if you are a man or woman. It's just a matter of public perception and proper marketing.

Q: Do you think Americans are closing the technical gap with Brazilians?
A: Yes I do. In America we have many good jiu-jitsu academies whose have good black belt instructors. I can give you a lot of examples of Americans fighters who have won major tournaments such as the World Championships and the Pan-American Championships. Look at Erica Montoya, the first American woman to became world champion, or B.J. Benn, Ricco

GRAPPLING

Guard Pass to Side Control
Leka Vieira is trapped in her opponent's guard (1). Gathering her legs underneath her, she stands up in base (2), places her knee against the base of the opponent's spine (3), and then lowers herself, breaking the closed guard (4). Pressing down on her opponent's leg she jumps outside the opened guard (5), then slides up to side control (6).

Rodriguez, Garth Taylor, Gazzy Taylor, and many others. They are all examples of American champions who have competed successfully against Brazilian fighters. I think this is good for the sport.

Q: Do you still have more to learn?
A: For sure! To become a black belt is not the end of your training, it is just the beginning. When I got my black belt I said, "Now I'm ready to learn the good stuff!" It's only when you reach that level that you see the art from a different perspective. You are mature enough to really start growing as a jiu-jitsu practitioner.

Q: Do you change and modify your teaching depending on the student?
A: I do, but my overall method is the same and very consistent. What I do is to modify the drills and tactical approach depending if I'm training and teaching beginners or advanced students.

Q: What are the major changes in the art since you started?
A: The biggest is the increase of women doing Brazilian jiu-jitsu. When I started, it was very unusual to see women in tournaments. But today when you go to a competition, you can see a lot of women competing at a very high technical level. In the last Pan-American Games I took a team of 13 women. Five or six years ago this wouldn't have been possible. I consider myself very lucky because I got the chance to train with Royler Gracie and Vinicius Aieta during my days in Rio de Janeiro. Here in United States I'm training with the Machado brothers, who have incredible knowledge and experience in the art. So I'm very happy for the opportunities I've had.

Q: What advice would you give to a woman who wants to train Brazilian jiu-jitsu?
A: When a woman starts to look for a place to train, they should immediately find out if the instructor is a real black belt who can assist and help them to achieve their goals while training safely. I always like to say that if you get sick and need a doctor, do you go to look for a medical student or for a real doctor to take care of you? Don't put yourself in the wrong hands. It is important to use what we learn not only as a method of self-defense but also as a way to live a healthier life. If you

decide to compete, do it to have fun. Keep your body in harmony with your mind and spirit. The rewards are out there for you.

Q: What keeps you motivated?
A: To know that every single day I'm learning something new and that I'm evolving as a fighter and a person .I'm very open-minded so I'm always prepared to learn. That's how I approach my training and my life.

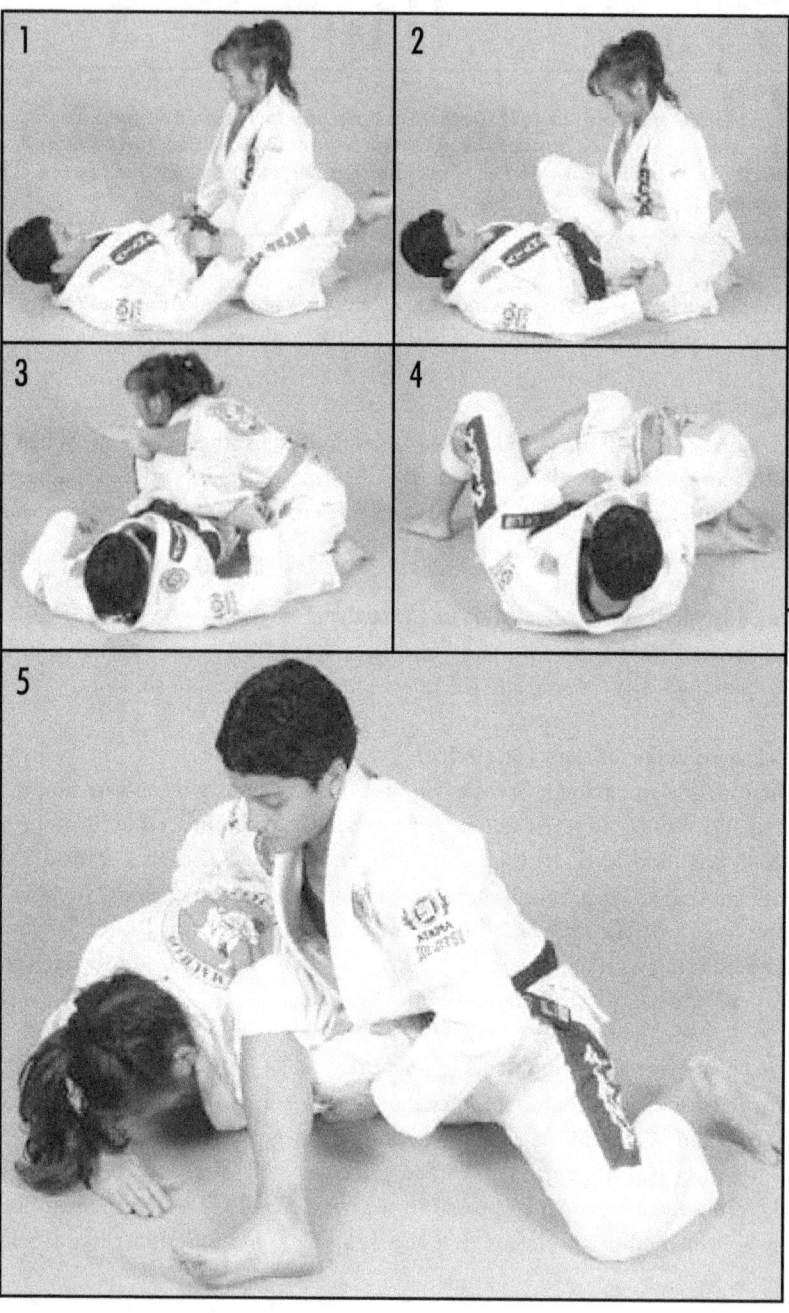

Closed Guard Shoulder-Lock
Leka Vieira traps her opponent in the closed guard (1). She releases the guard and places his feet on her opponent's hips (2). Pushing off with her far leg, she spins out and hooks her opponent's arm with her leg (3). Keeping the arm trapped, she pressures the shoulder (4), then sits up and applies the finishing lock (5).

GRAPPLING

Q: Are you a spiritual person?

A: Yes, I am. For instance, before my fights, I like to read a Bible passage that makes me feel strong and confident. Its meaning is very strong and touches me deeply.

Q: Have you ever considered learning any striking arts such karate or taekwondo?

A: I never have, because Brazilian jiu-jitsu makes me feel confident and could help me in case I need to use it for self-defense. Martial arts like taekwondo or karate use punches and kicks; but how could a thin and small woman like me use kicks and punches against a big guy? A big man will always have the advantage because he is stronger than me. In jiu-jitsu, due to the leverage in the art, you don't need to be a big person to take care of any situation. When men attack a woman they don't use punches or kicks, they always try to grab her—this situation is perfect for a woman trained in jiu-jitsu. The major problem for a woman is not to be caught by surprise. But you can be feminine on the outside and very tough on the inside—like a fist in a velvet glove. I feel very confident because the more aggressively an attacker tries to grab me, the better I can use my jiu-jitsu. Jiu-jitsu is the art of leverage and if you know how to use leverage properly, you'll be just fine.

Q: What is your personal philosophy of training?

A: My philosophical basis has always been to train as hard as I can, but never forget that woman do not need to compete on a professional level against men or do technical comparisons with them. I want my space and in order to get it I also need to respect their space. From the mental point of view, I have a few principles that I have made a part of my personal philosophy—dedication, discipline, determination, focus, willpower, and self-belief. Those are always with me and I repeat them constantly in my mind. Regardless of how much you train, you have to remember that there is always room for growth.

Q: What's your favorite jiu-jitsu memory?

A: The memory that will stay with me forever is my first year as a black belt when I became the first woman black belt world champion.

Q: How do you approach cross-training?

A: I treat my judo and running training as supplementary exercises to help my Brazilian jiu-jitsu. If you want to be a champion

Spider Guard Triangle Choke
Leka Vieira controls he opponent from the guard (1). Grabbing her opponent's sleeves to control the arms (2), she releases her legs and places her feet in classic spider guard position—one on the shoulder and one on the arm (3). Pulling her opponent's far arm inside her legs (4), she pulls her forward and locks in the triangle (5), and finishes by simultaneously pulling her opponent's head downward for the finishing choke (6).

or just a good player, keep your focus in your art and don't let other training activities distract you from your goal.

Q: What will make the sport grow?
A: I believe that in order to improve the art and take it to the next level, everyone should get together and make a global union, following lead of the CBJJ (Jiu-Jitsu Confederation of Brazil) and the IBJJF(International Brazilian Jiu-Jitsu Federation). They are the most important organizations in the world and are under Master Carlos Gracie Jr. I'm very thankful to him because due to his dedication and hard work we have the biggest tournament in the world with fighters from all over the globe coming to compete in Brazil each July. Because of him I can say that I'm the women's World and Pan-American champion. He has opened a lot of doors for women in jiu-jitsu. I'm with him all the way.

Q: What are your plans for the future?
A: As a fighter, it's to become Pan-American champion and World champion in 2002. As a teacher, to keep working hard to spread the art of Brazilian jiu-jitsu in America among women. I'm the only woman black belt in America so not only is that my wish and my goal, it is also my responsibility.

I would like to thank the Machado brothers, all my students, and my sponsor Atama Kimonos for all their help and support. I would like to invite all the women already training, to compete in our Brazilian jiu-jitsu tournaments. Practitioners of other martial arts are particularly welcome to come and train with the women's jiu-jitsu team. We are there to enjoy and share the art we love. Everybody is welcome.

For more information on Leka Vieira visit www.machadojj/leka.com. *She can also be contacted for classes and seminars by emailing* lekavieira@yahoo.com

Basic Spider-Guard Sweep

Tinguinha has Marcio Feitosa in his open spider-guard (1). In a sudden move, Tinguinha releases the pressure on his right leg while pushing with his left, causing Feitosa to lose his balance (2). As Feitosa continues to lose his balance, Tinguinha uses his right leg in a sweeping motion to pull Feitosa's left knee, while maintaining pressure with his left leg (3). Tinguinha completes the sweep by going on top while keeping pressure on with his left leg and pulling Feitosa's left arm with his right arm (4). Tinguinha finishes the move with the traditional knee on the stomach (5).

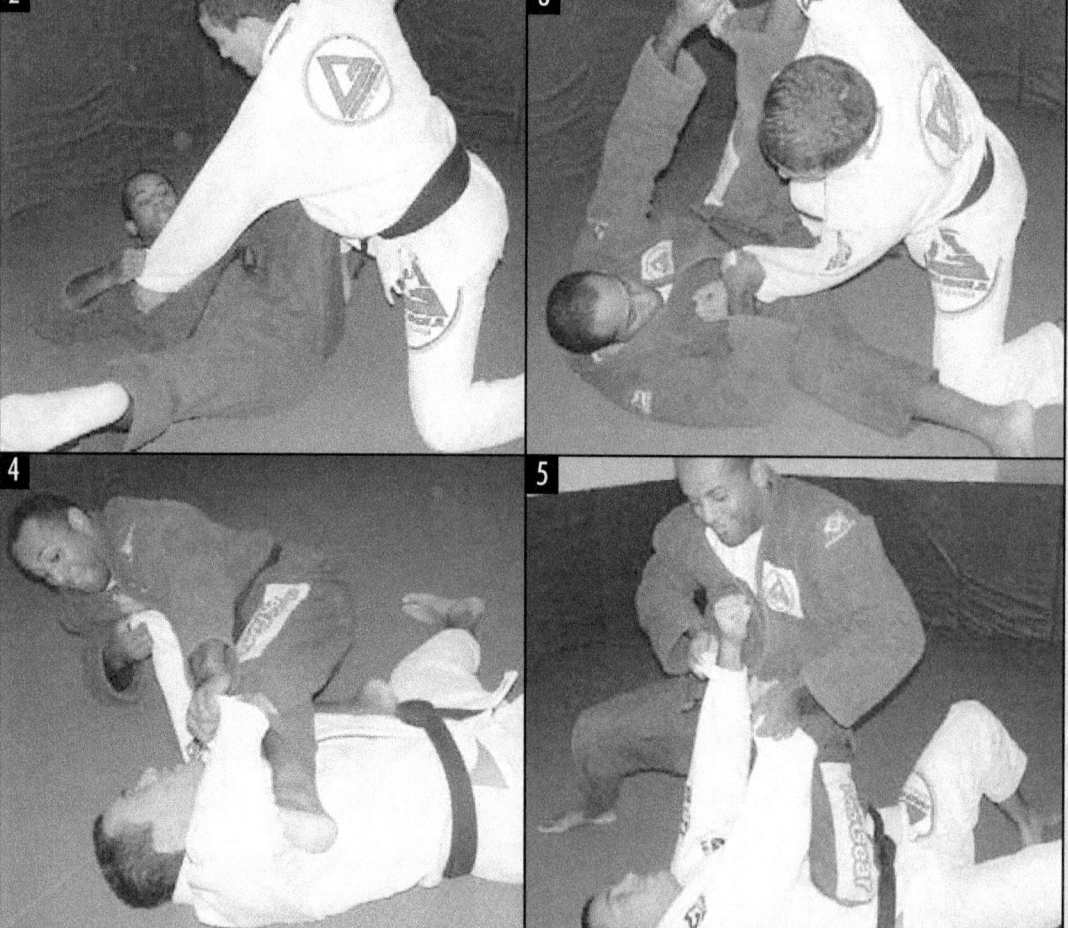

Advanced Spider-Guard Sweeps

Evolved from the traditional open guard, the spider guard is a deadly variant which enables those who master it to snare their opponent and draw them into an inescapable web.

Kid Peligro

The open guard is like an old friend. Sometimes we rely on it so much that we overlook its strengths and powers. Recently, because of the pressures of competition, a new series of options have been developed for the open guard. In *Grappling* magazine's endless search to share the latest and greatest technical moves, we decided to go to the source of some of the world's most wicked sweeps—the powerhouse Gracie Barra team. The search led straight to Gracie Barra black belt Mauricio "Tinguinha" (pronounced Chin-geen-ia) Mariano. Tinguinha has been practicing Brazilian jiu-jitsu for 14 years and was awarded his black belt in 1996 by Carlos Gracie Jr. Tinguinha is well known for his creative guard sweeps, and he has used them effectively on his way to winning a Brazilian national title, a Brazilian national team title, and a closetfull of other trophies.

Mauricio "Tinguinha" Mariano

Closed-Guard Basics

The closed guard was the original master position of Brazilian jiu-jitsu. From there it enabled practitioners to dazzle their opponents with a variety of chokes, arm locks and sweeps. The strength of the closed guard is the fact that you control your opponent's distance and balance. By moving your hips from side to side and applying pressure with a well-placed foot on the hip, you can induce a lot of confusion and mayhem. Additionally, you can use your legs to push and pull your opponent thereby breaking their posture.

Breaking The Closed Guard

But human beings are crafty—especially Brazilian jiu-jitsu fighters—and they started to devise many different ways to break the closed-guard lock. They soon found that by using good posture and placing a knee on the base of the spine, you could force open the guard. Other methods of breaking and then passing the closed guard were developed and soon another option had to be added by the fighter on the bottom—that is when the traditional open-guard gained prominence.

Open-Guard Basics

The open guard added a great deal of flexibility to the bottom position. By holding onto one sleeve, and putting one foot on the opponent's hip and the other on the bicep, bottom fighters could avoid having the closed-guard broken open and gain better control an opponent. While the open guard was not as useful for collar chokes because of the distance between the fighters, it opened the way for more triangle chokes, arm bars, and sweeps. By using the legs in conjunction with hips and arms, an offensive-minded fighter could cause a lot of headaches to their opponent. However, when new, effective counters were developed to the open guard, fighters again looked for an option. That option was the spider guard.

Spider-Guard Cross Sweep
Tinguinha has already released the pressure on his right leg while pushing with his left (1). Continuing the motion, Tinguinha changes the right-hand grip from Marcio Feitosa's left sleeve to the right leg, and rotates his body toward him while applying extra pressure with his left leg on the biceps and lifting the right knee with his right arm (2). Tinguinha's circular motion causes Feitosa to be swept (3). He secures the sweep by landing next to his opponent (4).

GRAPPLING

The Advanced Spider Guard

Simply by changing the placement of the foot, from the hip to the biceps, and by holding both sleeves instead of one, the open guard became the spider guard—it has been making life miserable for those in the top position every since. By shifting pressure from one leg to the other while pulling on the sleeve, opponent's quickly lose balance and base. The spider guard generally involves controlling both of an opponent's sleeves while applying pressure to their biceps with both your legs. As you shift pressure from one leg to the other and pull on the opposite sleeve, you create an unbalanced force which destroys their base. By combining this motion with other grips and leg rotations, you can add a variety of options for attacks and sweeps.

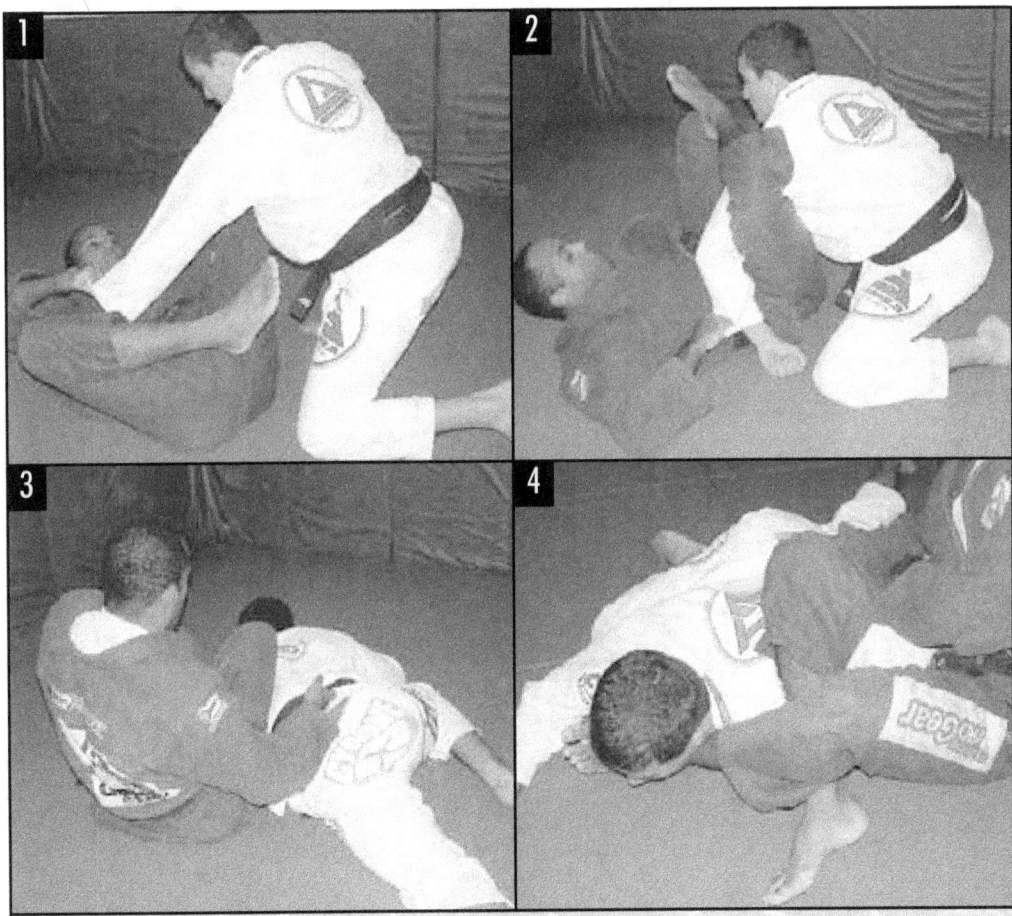

Spider-Guard Shoulder Lock
From the spider guard, Tinguinha releases the pressure on his right leg while pulling on Marcio Feitosa's left sleeve (1). Tinguinha hooks his right leg on Feitosa's arm, starting the traditional omoplata (shoulder) lock(2). Tinguinha switches his right hand grip to Feitosa's belt while applying pressure on his shoulder by extending his body and his right leg (3). The opposite angle shows the omoplata lock as Tinguinha applies pressure with his hip, while adding a variation in which Tinguinha places his left foot in front of Feitosa's face to add pressure to the shoulder (4).

Spider Guard Sweeps

Mauricio "Tinguinha" Mariano prefers spider guard techniques as a sure way to score points or induce a submission. "The first technique is a basic spider guard sweep," say Tinguinha. "At Gracie Barra, we are always experimenting and improving on what is already available. In this variation, the scissors motion of the lower leg was added because a lot of grapplers were starting to base-up on the opposite knee. Then after they got used to that sweep, they started to avoid the scissors and another variation was needed. By adding a rotation we introduced a different twist and a sense of confusion."

Once the opponents are worried about spider-guard sweeps, you open up a lot of possibilities. In this case, a good option is the *omoplata* or shoulder lock. "The shoulder lock is very natural from

High-Guard Sweep
Tinguinha changes from the spider guard to a high closed-guard. He grabs Marcio Feitosa's left sleeve with his left hand and hooks the left leg with his right arm (1). Tinguinha attempts an omoplata sweep by kicking his right heel towards the ground while holding Feitosa's left sleeve and left leg. Most of the time, this motion will sweep the opponent forward. In order to avoid being swept, Feitosa needs to posture up by raising his head and pushing his hips forward (2). As he senses the defense by Feitosa, Tinguinha goes for the next sweep by doing a reverse summersault while still controlling the left arm and leg (3). Tinguinha secures the sweep by lifting Marcio's left leg (4).

here," says Tinguinha, "because you already have the foot near your opponent's open arm. Rodrigo 'Minotauro' Nogueira has been using the omoplata from a similar position in his NHB victories in Pride—so the position works for gi, no-gi, and no-holds-barred.

Tinguinha likes to add the high closed-guard as another option for sweeps. He states: "Sometimes the opponent is so worried about the sweeps that he steps in to counter the pressure on the biceps, then I switch to the high closed-guard attacks. This one is my favorites because it adds several options. You can have an omoplata submission, but if that doesn't work you can go to a forward sweep from the same attack. If that also fails the summersault will for sure cause your opponent to go over, and then it is two points!"

A Spiderweb Of Deceit
Whatever the move, the main principle behind the spider guard is to keep the opponent guessing and to be unpredictable. The many options and potential movements from the spider guard are inherently difficult to time and to predict. For those reasons, the spider guard will most likely be drawing victims into its web for a long time to come!

Mauricio "Tinguinha" Mariano teaches in Fullerton, CA, and can be contacted by email at tinguinha@yahoo.com *or by calling (714) 579-3348.*

GRAPPLING

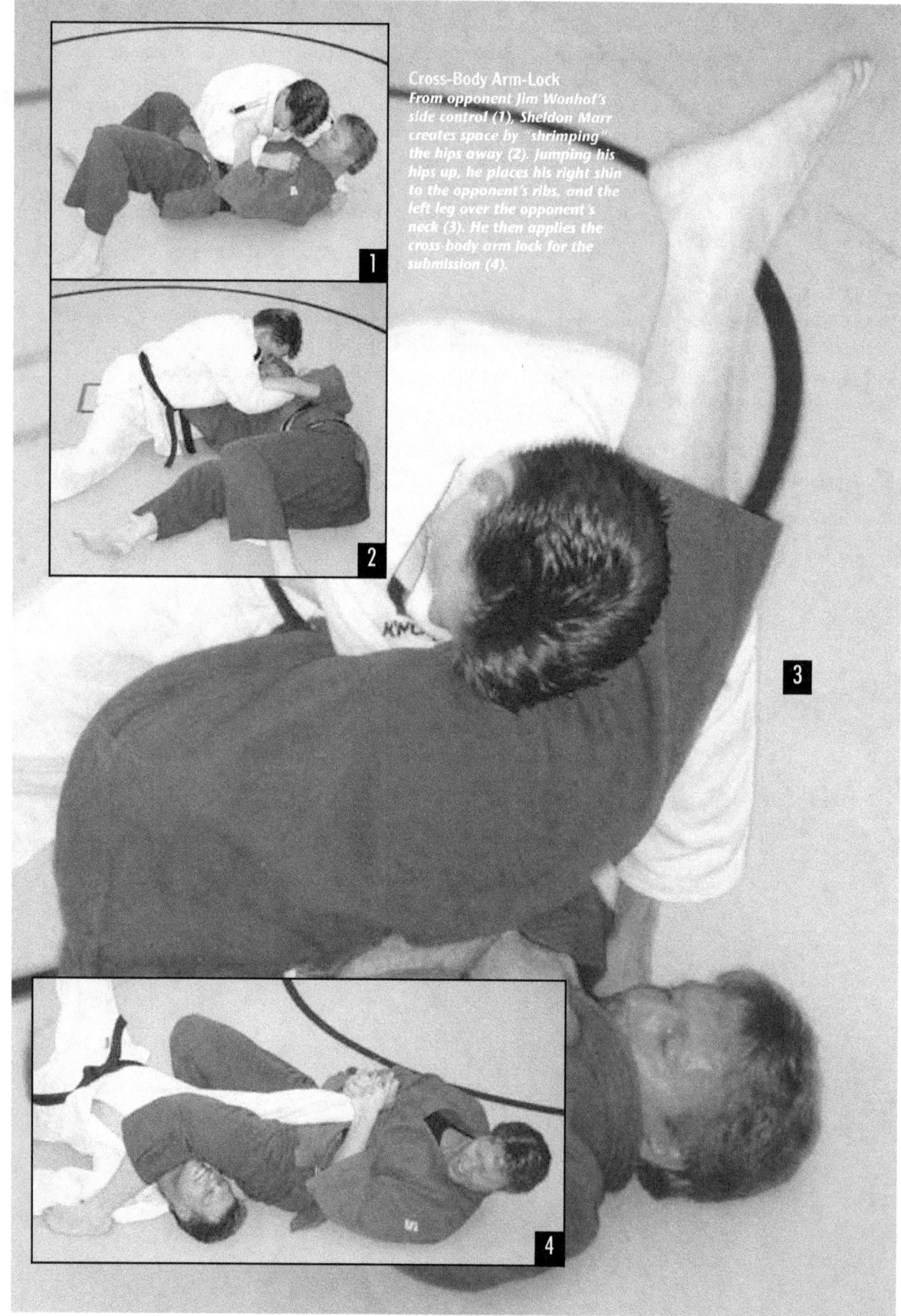

Cross-Body Arm-Lock
From opponent Jim Wonhof's side control (1), Sheldon Marr creates space by "shrimping" the hips away (2). Jumping his hips up, he places his right shin to the opponent's ribs, and the left leg over the opponent's neck (3). He then applies the cross-body arm lock for the submission (4).

Sheldon Marr
Life on the Edge

Sheldon Marr's Grappler's Edge Academy of Denver, Colorado, is acclaimed as one of the top grappling teams in America— and they have the credentials to back it up.

Beau Clark

With six U.S. national team titles in jiu-jitsu and submission grappling, the Grappler's Edge team is definitely on a roll. Although he insists on giving recognition to his fighters, the lion's share of the credit for the team's long-term success has to go to founder and chief instructor Sheldon Marr. Having coached his students to national and international titles in jujitsu, submission grappling, judo, wrestling, pankration, and mixed martial arts (MMA), Marr has earned a reputation as one of the most tenacious and committed grappling instructors in America.

Marr has been involved in the martial arts for over 37 years, and is a former judo and wrestling champion. Marr started training in judo at age 5 (in 1964), under his father, well-known judo instructor Wally Marr. By age 17 he was a national judo champion and a California State wrestling champion. But in wrestling practice in 1976, while throwing his opponent with *uchi mata* (a judo throw), he hit his head and broke his neck. But Marr was to prove that you can't keep a good grappler down.

In 1980, against doctor's orders, Marr returned to judo competition and picked up right where he had left off. In fact, his comeback attempt was so successful that in 1982 he was selected to the U.S. Olympic Judo training squad, and moved from California to the U.S. Olympic Training Center (OTC) in Colorado Springs, Colorado. Unfortunately, making the Olympic Team was not to be. In 1984, the U.S. Olympic Committee banned Marr from further competition due to complications of his prior neck injury. He was forced to retire once more—this time for good.

Coach Sheldon Marr with son Nick Marr, winner of the 2001 Dave Schultz Memorial Cup.

Grappler's Edge instructors (L-R) Mike Nuss, Bert Griggs, Jim Bacon and Sheldon Marr.

Sheldon Marr's Coaching Awards

1998
Instructor of the Year by Jujitsu America

1998
World Martial Arts Hall of Fame

1998
International Black Belt Hall of Fame

1998–1999
Martial Arts Masters, Pioneers, and Legends Hall of Fame

2000–2001
U.S. Martial Arts Hall of Fame

1999–2001
USA Federation of Pankration Athlima

Grappler's Edge at the 2001 U.S. National Submission Grappling Championships. Back row (L-R) Mike Nuss, Steve Stobaugh, Craig Pumphrey, Sheldon Marr. Front row (L-R) Eric Koble, Nick Marr, James Dinette.

GRAPPLING

Grappler's Edge at the 2001 U.S. National Jujitsu Championships. Back row (L-R) Nick Marr, Tom Coffman James Maurer, Steve Stobaugh, Eric Koble. Front row (L-R) Jim Wonhof, Sheldon Marr, Scott Marshall.

"That's when I decided to become a coach," says Marr. "I really didn't have much of a choice if I wanted to stay in grappling." After leaving the OTC, he moved to the Denver area and started coaching wrestling at Cherry Creek High School. From 1985 to 1991, his teams dominated the Colorado State Wrestling Championships (placing 4th in 1988, 3rd in 1986 and 1987, 2nd in 1989 and 1990, and winning the team title in 1991). Some of his students even went on to become collegiate All-Americans and NCAA champions! In 1992, Marr took the position of Defensive Tactics Instructor with the Denver Sheriff Department, and in 1995 he opened the Grappler's Edge Academy.

Not surprisingly, Marr met with immediate success as the Grappler's Edge team won national team champions in 1996, 1997, 1998, 1999, 2000 and 2001, establishing him as one of America's most respected grappling instructors. Along with fellow Coaches Keith Hackney and Mark Schultz, Marr also coached Team USA to a world team title at the 2000 World Pankration Championships in Lamia, Greece. In 2002, Hackney and Marr will again be the U.S. coaches at the world championships. Marr credits his success in both competition and coaching to his own great instructors, including Wally Marr, Wally Jay, Willy Cahill, and Charlie Lee.

Grappler's Edge National Champions
(Jujitsu, Submission Grappling, Pankration)

Scott Marshall—2001, 2000, 1999, 1998; *Jim Wonhof*—2001, 2000, 1999; *Nick Marr*—2001, 2000; *Eric Koble*—2001; *Steve Stobaugh*—2001; *Craig Pumphrey*—2001; *John Taylor*—2000, 1999; *Greg McGraime*—2000, 1997; *Frankie Sanchez*—2000; *Mike Farmer*—1999; *Jim Bacon*—1998, 1997; *Larry Parker*—1998, 1997; *Casey Hopkins*—1998; *Barry Weldon*—1997; *David Wolf*—1997; *Bert Griggs*—1996.

Grappler's Edge has also produced an additional 50 national medallists to date.

Q: What distinguishes Grappler's Edge from other grappling academies?
A: We've been at this for quite some time, so I think we have a more experienced staff than most schools. I started training in judo about 37 years ago, and wrestling about 27 years ago. I've been teaching and coaching both sports for over 20 years. My assistant instructors have similar backgrounds as well. Bert Griggs and Jim Bacon are both former national judo and jujitsu champions, and Mike Nuss is a former collegiate All-American wrestler. So we have about 120 years of experience between us, and that's a lot more than most schools can say.

Q: What grappling system do you teach?
A: We actually combine the arts of jujitsu, judo, wrestling and sombo into one system, then throw in a little kickboxing to round it out. We're not a traditional martial arts school in a lot of aspects. We don't teach judo in one class, and jujitsu in another, et cetera. It really doesn't matter to us if a technique originated in Japan, Russia, Brazil, or wherever. If it's an effective technique that people are using in competition, we want to know about it so we can at least know how to defend against it.

Q: Do you teach Brazilian jiu-jitsu?
A: I don't have any formal training in BJJ. So no, we don't teach BJJ. However, I think our system has been influenced by BJJ to some extent, as our students compete against BJJ practitioners quite a bit. Also, we've had some students come to us that have had BJJ training. But again, it's not my expertise and I don't pretend that it is, and I think our focus is different. We spend a lot more time working on takedowns and throws than most BJJ schools. At least half of our practice is up on our feet working takedowns. We like to say that we'd rather throw you than know you.

Q: Has Grappler's Edge competed against Brazilian jiu-jitsu?
A: We've competed in BJJ competitions on a regional level, such as the annual SLAM, and RAGE events, for the last five years, and so far we've won every tournament we've went to. But, of course, you don't see the Machado brothers showing up to these tournaments, so that might be quite a different story!

Q: How do you think you'd fare against the Machado Competition Team?
A: Honestly, it would be pretty hard to beat the Machados at their own game—they're great at what they do. We had Carlos Machado teach a seminar at our school a year or two ago, and he was awesome, so I have a lot of respect for those guys. Actually, Jean-Jacques Machado keeps sending us information on his tournaments, and we're planning on going out there one of these days. It's just hard to raise the money to send a full team out to California on short notice. But we really do hope to go out there some time and test ourselves.

Q: You seem to bring a lot of big names to teach at your school.
A: Yes, Carlos Machado came out as I mentioned. We've had UFC veterans Ken Shamrock and Keith Hackney out a few times, as well as Olympic wrestling champions Mark Schultz and Kevin Jackson. We've also had Olympic judo coach Ed Liddie, 18-time national judo champion Leo White here, and kickboxing legend Maurice Smith.

I'm lucky because they're all good friends of mine, and they're all willing to help. I probably wouldn't be able to afford any of them, otherwise. But they're all great people as well as great instructors, so I'm happy to bring them in when I can. I think a lot of martial arts instructors don't bring in

GRAPPLING

the big names because they don't want to admit to their students that there's someone out there that might know more than they do. I think that's ridiculous! I may have been a pretty good judo competitor at one time, but Ed Liddie and Leo White are two of the best in the world. I was also a pretty good wrestler, but Mark Schultz and Kevin Jackson are two of the best in the history of the sport. So I'm more than happy to expose my students to the very best!

Q: You opened your school in 1995, and you won the AAU National Jujitsu Team Title in 1996. How did you put together a championship team so quickly?
A: I was a high school wrestling coach from 1985 to 1991. By 1995, a lot of the kids I coached were getting out of college. So they joined my school and became the nucleus of the Grappler's Edge

Counter-Takedown Knee-Bar
1) As Jim Wonhof attacks Sheldon Marr with a single leg takedown, Marr places his right foot behind Wonhof's right knee (not shown). Marr then pulls downward on Wonhof's neck with his right hand, grasping behind his left ankle with the left hand (2). Marr then continues to roll over his left shoulder (3), and submits Wonhof with a knee bar (4).

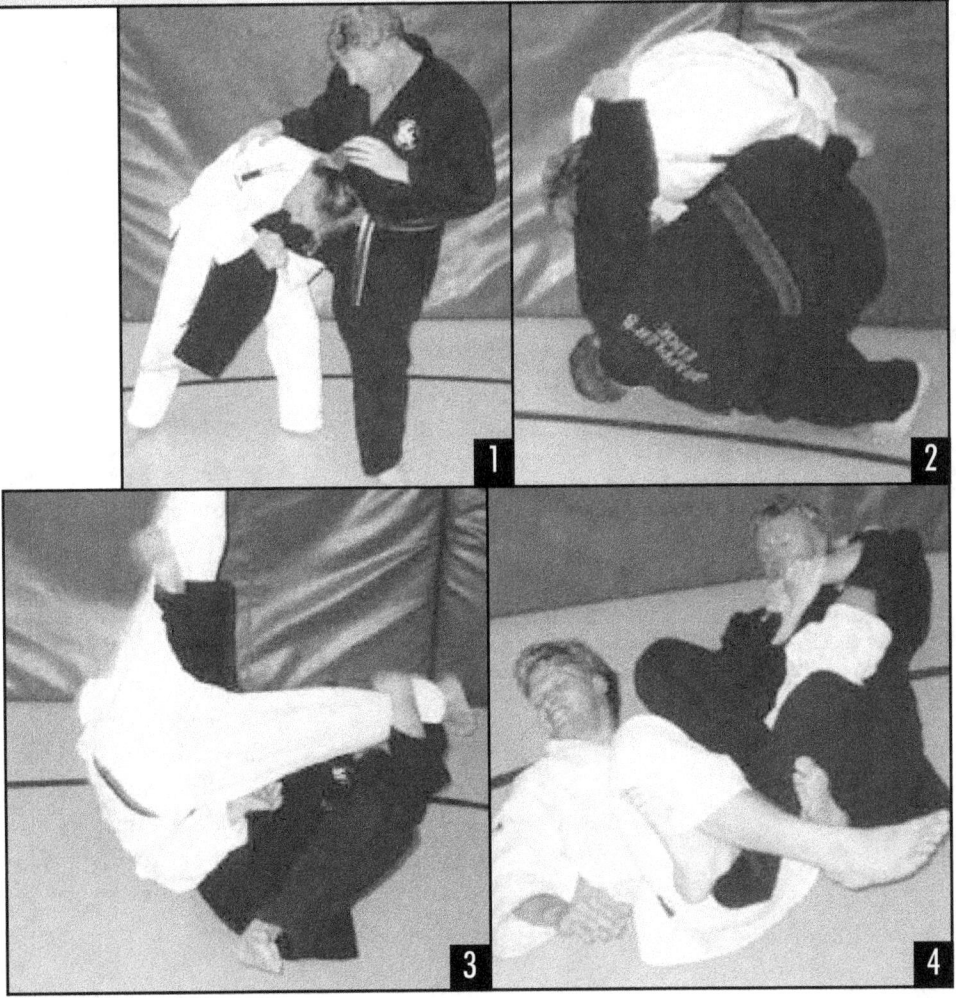

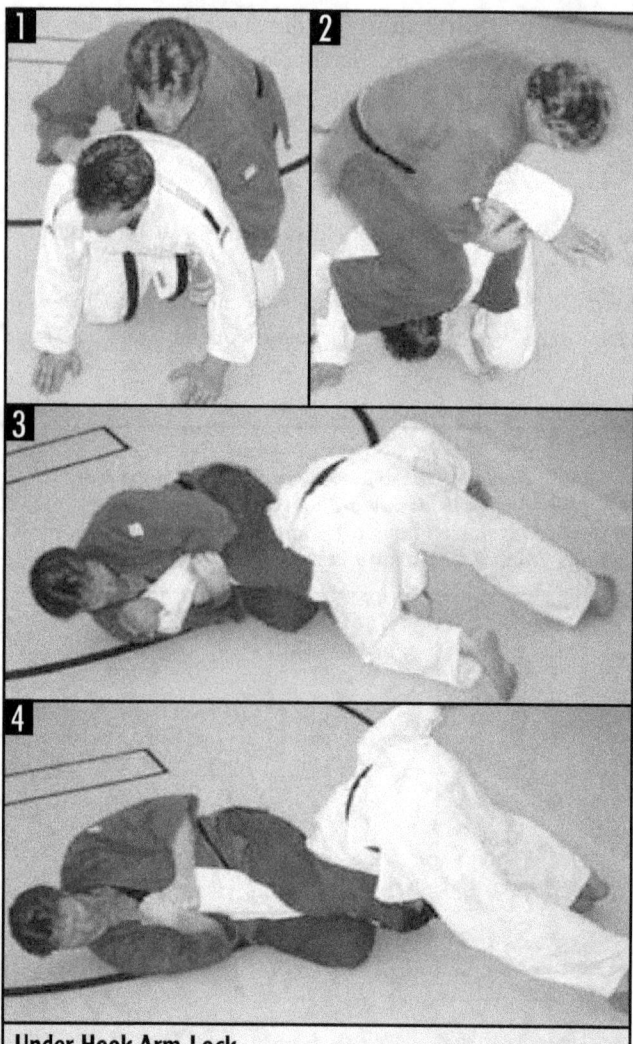

Under-Hook Arm-Lock
Sheldon Marr hooks opponent Jim Wonhof's left leg with his left leg, and under-hooks his left arm with his left arm (1). He then places his right shin (and all his bodyweight) on the back of Wonhof's neck (2). As Wonhof collapses to the ground, Marr falls to his right side and secures the left arm (3). He then secures the wrist, presses his hips forward, and applies the arm-lock submission (4).

team. My assistant instructor, former national judo champion Bert Griggs, won the gold medal in the heavyweight division at that tournament, and all my wrestlers won silver and bronze medals—all in the black belt division. That was enough for us to win our first team title, and the following year we won gold medals in five of the seven weight classes.

Q: Do your students compete in MMA events?
A: We've had a few students compete in the MMA events in the past, including UFC and Pride, and we've been to Tokyo, Kiev, Abu Dhabi, and more. But most of our students really aren't that interested in these events, so that's really not what we train for as a team. We're sticking to the amateur jujitsu, submission grappling, and pankration events right now, and I think we're pretty good at what we do.

Q: What's happening with the pankration movement? Are you still involved?
A: Well, to tell you the truth, it's slowed down a lot since the International Olympic Committee stated there will be no new sports in 2004. The Greek Ministry of Sports wants to re-introduce pankration to the 2004 games in Athens as their national sport, just as Tokyo did with judo in 1964,

and Seoul did with taekwondo in 1988. But the IOC is saying there are too many sports in the Olympics already.

Well, I agree that there are too many sports in the Olympics already, but pankration is not new—it was in the Olympics for over 1,000 years! What they should do is eliminate some of the ones that nobody watches or cares about and get rid of all the team sports—then there wouldn't be too many. I think the Olympics should be about who the best athletes are, not about who the best teams are.

If they did have it, I think we would do well. The U.S. men's team won the team competition at the 2000 World Pankration Championships held in Lamia, Greece, and we also won more individual medals than any other country. So Team USA was off to a great start. But now that we probably won't be a medal sport in 2004, I think the participation is leveling off in this country. That's really a shame too, because whether pankration will be in the Olympics or not, it is still a great sport that martial artists from all backgrounds can compete in on a regional, national, or international level.

Q: What's an average practice like at Grappler's Edge?
A: We start out by jogging around the mat for about 5 or 10 minutes, then we'll do our balance drills—which include shrimp-crawls, drags, duck-walks, shots, rolls, cartwheels, round-offs, head-kips, and bear-crawls— for another 5 or 10 minutes, and then we'll stretch for about 15 minutes. After that we'll usually do takedown drills for about 15 minutes. After that comes the technique session, in which we either teach new techniques or drill old ones for about 45 minutes. This usually includes 15 minutes of takedowns, 15 minutes of ground fighting and 15 minutes of striking. This varies, of course, when preparing for competitions. Then we take a quick water break, and come back for 30 or 40 minutes of *randori*—sparring or rolling. Then finally, we'll end the workout with 5 or 10 minutes of conditioning drills. Our practice sessions last 2 hours, but sometimes we'll go over a little.

Q: Realistically evaluate your team.
A: I'd say we're the best team in the Midwest—I think we've proven that. I think the Machados are probably the best team on the West Coast, when they're at full strength, and on the East Coast, Renzo Gracie's team is awesome. But then you've also got all the professional MMA teams as well, like the Lion's Den, the RAW Team, the Miletich Camp, et cetera—they're all great. So to answer your question honestly, we're probably not the best overall team in the country—but we are striving to be one of the best.

For information on Sheldon Marr's seminars or video training series call (303)433-EDGE or email **info@grapplers-edge.com**

BEST OF CFW — VOL. 1
GRAPPLING

GRAPPLING

Marvin Eastman
No Justice, No Peace

I'm called "The Beastman" because of my aggressiveness in the ring. But whether facing a King of the Cage opponent or the battles of everyday life, I have high standards of justice.

Marvin Eastman with Loren Franck

People should be rewarded for following the rules and penalized when they don't. That philosophy comes in handy for me, a seven-year Nevada corrections officer. Yet justice is even more important to me as a mixed martial artist. Like many in the sport, I began fighting at an early age. Greco-Roman wrestling caught my eye when I was seven. At that age, I didn't know how complex the sport was, but I loved it—so much that I wrestled throughout high school, winning the 191-pound California state championship in 1987. If I learned justice anywhere, it was on my high school wrestling team.

Pro Football Experience
In 1989, I left Merced, California, where I was born and raised, and accepted a University of Nevada at Las Vegas football scholarship. After starring as the school's running back for two years, I signed with the Calgary Stampeders, one of the hottest teams in the Canadian Football League. While in the CFL, I was soberly reminded that actions have consequences. The better-playing team wins. In other words, no justice, no peace. After two years with the Stampeders, I returned to UNLV and earned my bachelor's degree in criminal justice. While in Calgary and in college, I considered an NFL career—and even trained with the Raiders—but I wasn't selected until midseason, when I was offered a position on the practice roster. I didn't want to play football anymore, so I passed on the Raiders' offer and finished my degree. Besides, I had started wrestling again—just working out and mixing it up—and I was hooked.

Decision To Fight
When the Ultimate Fighting Championships began in the early 1990s, I was more excited than anyone. During my post–high school wrestling years, I wanted to learn boxing, karate or some other stand-up fighting art. But while growing up, I heard of street fighters knocking out so-called karate experts. They just punched them in the face, which immediately ended the fight. So, as you can imagine, I wasn't very excited about traditional karate. I needed a fighting art that really worked. As

I continued searching for such an art, a friend told me about muay Thai leg kicks and elbow strikes. I was also fascinated by the Brazilian jiu-jitsu of the UFC. Both experiences prompted me to find a school that taught full-contact fighting. In 1995, I visited a Brazilian jiu-jitsu school in Las Vegas but walked out when the instructor wanted $100 per session. It was allegedly one of Royson Gracie's schools, but it merely taught his style.

So I visited a muay Thai school, where the instructor taught me to leg kick. I was sold when he showed me how devastating those techniques are. I also learned muay Thai elbow strikes, which are absolutely awesome. After months of hard training, I began competing in muay Thai and eventually distinguished myself with an 8-1 fight record. There was only one problem: I couldn't make money at it. While seeking something better, I met Terry Trebilcock, the driving force behind King of the Cage. He was scouting additional fighters and had little trouble recruiting me. Since then, I've expanded beyond the KOTC to wherever the best opportunities are. Grappling is the ultimate challenge for me in many ways, but I have no regrets. My determination and hard work paid off.

Marvin Eastman battling Vernon "Tiger" White.

"I began competing in muay Thai and eventually distinguished myself with an 8-1 fight record. There was only one problem: I couldn't make money at it."

GRAPPLING

A Striking Advantage

A black belt in muay Thai, I often apply the art's most effective techniques in my grappling matches. I fight to win. And by using muay Thai thigh kicks, I establish dominance by chopping down my opponent's legs, one limb at a time. Opponents can't move after you destroy their legs. Even the toughest fighters will be neutralized and at your mercy. After an opponent absorbs one of my leg kicks, he'll concentrate on defending his knees and inner thighs. While doing so, however, his head is vulnerable. I use punches to set up most of my leg kicks. Some of my grappling opponents try leg kicks of their own, but they usually can't turn their kicks over and strike the soft part of my thigh with their shin. This hard-on-soft contact makes the kicks extremely effective. If legs kicks don't do the job, I supplement them with muay Thai elbow strikes, either alone or in combinations. My favorites land right on top of my opponent's head. Other elbow strikes travel diagonally and smash his face or temples.

Reverse elbow strikes are also effective, but they're difficult because you must set them up. Some fighters don't use them because you turn your back on your opponent during execution. That's not a problem for me, though. I lure my opponent toward me or sucker him with a feint, so he's not worrying about where I'm facing. When he reacts, I sidestep and blast him with the back of my elbow. Now that's my kind of justice. Muay Thai reverse elbow strikes are much more effective than spinning backfists, which grapplers seldom use because of the distance required. Spinning backfists are easy to counter too. Just step in and elbow strike your opponent's extended arm. Do it right and you'll break his elbow. Many fighters pull away from an incoming spinning backfist, but that actually makes it more effective. To close the distance and smother the strike, simply step toward him as

Marvin Eastman defends a shoot from Marc Laimon.

the backfist approaches. But reverse elbow strikes? They're totally safe—except for your opponents.

Strong As Steel

Because my grappling incorporates muay Thai, I'm often asked about shin conditioning. My advice? Don't hit your shins with rolling pads. Your lower legs are too sensitive for that—at least initially. Some martial arts movies portray such a practice, but in real life, your shins are best conditioned by kicking a heavy bag. Shin conditioning doesn't happen overnight, either. It's a slow process. First, bruise your shins by kicking the bag. Then allow them to heal. After several weeks of conditioning, they'll become calcified and eventually callused. After many months, they'll be hard as sledgehammers—and just as deadly. By relentless shin kicking, a fighter can destroy one leather bag a month.

Some leg-kicking grapplers numb their shins with novocaine. Sure, such injections prepare your shins for severe punishment, but the bones become brittle. My boxing coach, Skip Kelp, is helping refine my entire game by assimilating muay Thai into my grappling. Many muay Thai techniques don't apply to boxing and vice versa, but both arts are crucial for successful submission fighting. That's why I work so hard on my stand-up fighting. Although Kelp is a veteran boxing coach, he also knows mixed martial arts and helps me tremendously with my pad and bag work. He's upgrading my boxing skills too, such as the way I turn my hands over, and he's helping me move more quickly in the ring.

Eastman felled by a low blow.

No Justice

My search for justice climaxed on April 29, 2001, when I battled Vernon White for his KOTC title near Sacramento, California. It was clearly my most controversial fight. As our match began, he switched to southpaw. I remained conventional. We both punched several times, and then he tried an inside leg kick, which I checked with my knee. He punched again, but I pinned him against the cage and tried to jump-knee his face. Shortly afterward, back in the middle of the cage, he again changed from a conventional stance to southpaw, and while my legs were open, he kicked me in the groin. My metal muay Thai cup protected my front, but the kick went up between my legs. White claimed it was a glancing blow, but it was a solid kick. I was fouled—and everyone knew it. And though I was in agony, my coach told me to take pain. Reminding me I had trained too hard to give up, he sent me back into the cage. And I went. Throwing in the towel because of a low blow isn't my idea of justice.

After a 20-minute rest and running on pure adrenaline, I re-entered the cage. I wanted that title. But when your opponent fouls, even if only once during the fight, the damage is done. Instead of focusing on my tactics, I thought he would foul me again. I've seen other fighters get cut for the first

Eastman landing on Tiger White.

time, and they're attention was diverted for the rest of the fight. They could think only about their cut. I had a similar experience against White. In round two, he tried a knee strike, but his foot again smashed upward between my legs. It was such an obvious foul that fans booed. I'm a warrior, which means I fight to the end. I could have quit, and everyone would have understood, but I took the pain and went the distance. My reward? Incredibly, White won by decision. I didn't win a single round.

No Peace

Where's the justice? Every fighter deserves respect. Unfortunately, I gave White too much of it, and I've since learned my lesson. Now I warn opponents, "Fight me and I'll whip you." That's self-confidence, not disrespect. My opponents and I socialize together after we fight, but we're adversaries in the cage. Many people want to see a Marvin Eastman-Vernon White rematch. I'm certainly willing, but he had the opportunity and declined. If we fight each other again, I don't want judges deciding the outcome. I'll put White to sleep and end the controversy. To improve my fighting, I'm reviewing my recent bouts.

When I battled Quentin Jackson in June 2000, I was relentless. That style works for me. In my last few bouts, I held back, which doesn't help me win. I should have stared my opponents down and shouted, "You don't belong in the ring with me." I should have destroyed them, but I hesitated. So I'm resuming my old style, which is like Mike Tyson's. Most of his fights are finished before they begin because he scares his opponents to death. And from now on, I'll be like Tyson. I'll intimidate my opponents. I'll bust 'em up and knock 'em out. Every fighter needs this confidence. And every fighter needs justice in order to find peace.

GRAPPLING

Gerson Sanginitto
Generation Xcellent

The responsibility for teaching updated Brazilian jiu-jitsu techniques has fallen to a generation of new, dynamic black belt instructors who work the "trenches" every day, spreading the art to beginners and experts alike.

Jose Fraguas

When the art of Brazilian jiu-jitsu took the world in early '90s, the two most significant families to spread the art and serve as a source of worldwide knowledge were the Gracies and the Machados. A decade after Royce Gracie won the first UFC, however, a second generation of capable instructors has taken on the responsibility of sharing and updating the technical aspects of the art. Many things have changed in Brazilian jiu-jitsu, due to the highly charged competition atmosphere, and new technical developments have made some of the techniques used as recently as 10 years ago obsolete!

Gerson Sanginitto is one of the second generation of Brazilian jiu-jitsu instructors, and has been teaching in the United States for over five years. His knowledge of the grappling arts is not just limited to the coveted rank of *faixa preta* (black belt) in Brazilian jiu-jitsu, but also holds a black belt in Japanese judo. This is a combination that many top Brazilian fighters and instructors consider exceptional, due to the different emphasis the two arts put onto throwing techniques (judo) and ground techniques (Brazilian jiu-jitsu).

A direct student of the president of the Brazilian Jiu-Jitsu Federation, Carlos Gracie Jr., Sanginitto has shared many hours of training with some of the top-names of jiu-jitsu, including both Rigan Machado and Renzo Gracie. In many ways, it is safe to say that the future of the Brazilian art is in the hands of this new generation of young teachers who still have the passion and drive to teach a first-day white belt with the same motivation they have when they impart knowledge to a class full of brown belts.

Q: How long have you been practicing martial arts?
A: I started in 1973 and I haven't stopped since. I haven't specifically trained in any other styles than grappling. I started judo first, and then began jiu-jitsu in 1984. As far as other martial arts systems like kung-fu, taekwondo, and karate, I never trained steadily, although through friends I have been exposed to them. My teacher is Carlos Gracie Jr. but there are also many people who have taught me

a lot about jiu-jitsu. These include Paulo Cesar Mulatinho, Rigan Machado, Renzo Gracie and Antonio Rodrigues.

Q: Have you ever had to use jiu-jitsu in a real fight?
A: Back in the '80s, in my early 20's, a friend of mine invited me to go to Ipanema to visit a karate academy and learn some of their moves. At first, we were only exchanging techniques in a friendly manner. But when it came to free training, things changed a little. I started to train with one of the instructors. He surprised me and came after me and really wanted to beat me up. I was thinking that this was going to be just an easy practice of the punches and kick I had just learned. But instead, the guy came at me right away and surprised me and gave me a fat lip. After his punch I went after him to tap him out. I was not trying to punch him back, but I was enraged and wanted to prove that my technique was more effective than his. So I went for a double leg, took him down, mounted him, and then all of a sudden changed my mind and started to punch the guy in the face! I kept going until my friends finally made me stop. I guess that was my first vale tudo and the end of my karate training!

Passing the Half-Guard on the Inside
Gerson Sanginitto is trapped in his opponent's half-guard (1). He secures the collar and the sleeve (2), then extends the arm upward and pressures the neck downward to create space (3). Sliding his knee between his opponent's legs (4), he brings his entire leg out of the half-guard (5), then sits-out and controls his opponent from and upright cross-side position (6).

GRAPPLING

Q: Were you a natural at jiu-jitsu?
A: I don't know if I would say it that strongly, but I did learn the movements very easily. I remember that when I got my blue belt, I became an instructor for beginners because I always had a certain skill for teaching. It was probably because I always liked to teach, and I truly enjoy doing it. I guess the main reason why I was fast at learning jiu-jitsu was because of my judo training. I really think that my previous training in judo helped me a lot in my jiu-jitsu evolution. I was very comfortable with the idea of grabbing an opponent and grappling them on the ground. My transition to jiu-jitsu was very smooth and easy. Of course, there were aspects that were more difficult to absorb, but the idea of the grappling game was already in my body.

Q: Do you like vale tudo events such as UFC and Pride?
A: It's great exposure for jiu-jtsu fighters and for jiu-jitsu itself—these events demonstrate the effectiveness of Brazilian jiu-jitsu. Groundwork was something that nobody knew before the UFC. Royce Gracie opened doors for a lot of people because he showed martial artists from other styles how much it helped to have a knowledge of grappling. In general, I believe that all mixed martial arts events are positive. They bring publicity to all the martial arts and they help the sport of grappling to be recognized and to grow. When it comes to the athletes themselves, they acquire the added bonus of personal recognition and a little extra income. Fighters who participate in these events have to be extremely dedicated professionals. It is a job that requires hard training and full concentration. Besides building inner strength, the athletes learn different styles so they can understand and defend themselves against all attacks. So I feel MMA helps the technical aspects of all martial arts to improve.

Q: Do you think that jiu-jitsu in America has caught up with jiu-jitsu in Brazil?
A: American students are definitely improving, but they are not quite there yet. Jiu-jitsu has been a mainstream martial art in Brazil since the early '80s and has been practiced since the early '20s. Also, the number of practitioners is a lot higher and the number of competitions is incredible—there are events every weekend. However, now there are many top Brazilian instructors living in the U.S. and they have American students who have a natural ability for the art. I'd say that pretty soon the Americans are going to get even with Brazil. But for now, Brazil is still number one.

Q: Do you feel that you have more to learn?
A: Definitely! A big part of jiu-jitsu is learning something every day—especially since jiu-jitsu is a growing and evolving art. It is in constant development. This is true not only in techniques, but also in regard to new strategies and tactics to use against different opponents. Skillful and creative fighters are always creating new positions and improving the game. So, we are always learning and implementing our knowledge with each other. As a practitioner and as a instructor, my schedules are different. As a practitioner, I use more time to building my physical conditioning, while as an instructor I have to dedicate time to planning out the best strategy for teaching a class. It is important that my students fully understand the principles of the art and consequently keep improving their game, endurance, and confidence. That takes planning on my part.

Q: What are the major changes in jiu-jitsu since you began training?
A: Brazilian jiu-jitsu has evolved a lot since the early '80s. Initially, BJJ was made up of just the Gracie family and their friends. Nowadays, the media has shown the world how great this martial art is. It started as a small community, but it has now become one of the greatest martial arts in the

world. All this has happened without breaking or changing its principles, which proves its strength and effectiveness. A few years ago, the art of jiu-jitsu was more aggressive than it is today. The rules have changed a lot, so all practitioners, including myself, had to adjust our game accordingly. My game had to become extremely strategic and aggressive, since now a single mistake can be lethal. The level of the game is so high that any little mistake can cause you to lose a match. In the old days, for instance, there was a huge difference between a purple belt and a brown belt. Nowadays, you see purple belts giving a real hard time to both brown and black belts! The purple belt may lose in the end, but they give the top guys a run for their money. I think this is good for the art and the sport, because it means the technical level is going up.

Q: Who would you like to personally train with?
A: I would like to train with Rickson Gracie—or at least get on the mat with him just to feel his technique. Carlos Gracie Jr, took us to his academy a few times, but I have never trained with him personally. Everyone is a little different in

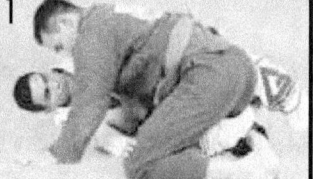
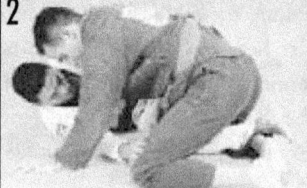

Half-Guard Throw Reversal
Trapped on the bottom, Gerson Sanginitto holds his opponent in the half-guard (1). Bringing his right leg inside to create space (2), he slides his hips to the side (3), and then switches legs and puts his left leg inside his opponent's fight knee (4). Underhooking his opponent's left leg (5), Sanginitto the raises his opponent into the air, destroying his base (6), throws him to the opposite side of the underhook (7), then rolls into a cross-side position of control (8).

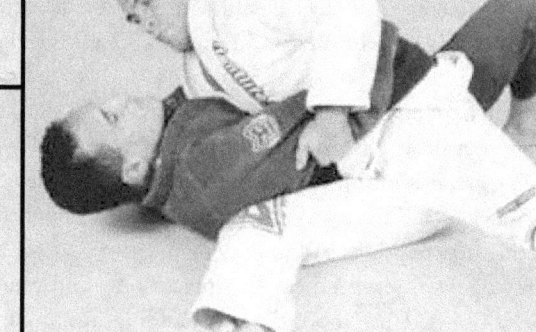

GRAPPLING

jiu-jitsu, so it is good to train with all the top people. The strength of jiu-jitsu is in its differences. A person should find the style that best fits their aptitude and their desire. It is very important for students to find a place where they feel comfortable. Only in the right environment, can the right learning and improvement occur. Even now, my passion for the art and for teaching is what keeps me going. It brings me great fulfillment to see my students successfully applying a technique that I taught.

Q: Do you think it is necessary to fight on the street in order to try out jiu-jitsu self-defense techniques?
A: Not really, because nowadays a fighter can have specific training in his own academy and also test his skills in no-holds-barred events. However, if someone has fought a lot in the streets, this person does learn what they are capable of and might have an advantage over a person that does not have such experience. These real situations teach you how to effectively deal with the adrenaline rush, which can work in your favor or against you.

Passing the Half-Guard on the Outside
Trapped in his opponent's half-guard, Gerson Sanginitto places his hand on his opponent's right biceps (1). He extends his body to create space (2), the drop down and controls both legs with a tight arm-grip (3). Sliding his leg out from between his opponent's legs (4), Sanginitto then slides to the side (5), and establishes a strong position of control from the cross-mount (6).

"The media has shown the world how great this martial art is. It started as a small community, but it has now become one of the greatest martial arts in the world. All this has happened without breaking or changing its principles, which proves its strength and effectiveness."

Q: What's your opinion about mixing styles?
A: I think it is good to know more than one style. The goal of an athlete should be to become a complete fighter. However, a person should specialize in one style and enhance his skill with some training in other styles. Brazilian jiu-jitsu requires great dedication and steady training. I don't believe that a student should jump from art to art, because in the end they won't achieve full proficiency in any style.

Q: Has Brazilian jiu-jitsu been of personal benefit to you?
A: It brings me great joy and has brought me many new friends. I feel like I'm a part of a big family. It brings discipline, confidence, and attitude. Also, the challenge of competition helps to keep me fresh and excited about the sport. A successful competitor in Brazilian jiu-jitsu has discipline, dedication, persistence, and passion for what they do. Natural ability is the start, and these qualities will keep you in the game. But you have to work hard. I guess these qualities are common not only in Brazilian jiu-jitsu, but in any serious competitor from any legitimate sport. It takes these qualities to become a good competitor.

Q: Is supplementary training important?
A: After grappling students have committed themselves to BJJ, they can complement their skills with other types of training. In particular, cardiovascular conditioning is crucial for the jiu-jitsu athlete. Weight training and stretching are also effective tools that with greatly help a fighter. But I

always stress the fact that nothing replaces time on the mat. Technique is your main thing everyone needs to develop and that only comes from mat time. Hours spent pumping iron won't improve your jiu-jitsu if your technique is not good. Focus on technique first and then later move to supplementary aspects to enhance your technical skills.

Q: What are your plans for the future?
A: I want to keep teaching for as long as I can. Also, since I'm a film student, I'm working on the production of several Brazilian jiu-jitsu training tapes. "Gordo's Half-Guard" tape series is on sale right now. It covers all of his best attacks, passes, and sweeps. It's a great opportunity to learn more about this specific topic, since it is so important to improving anyone's game. Gordo is the master of these techniques. He started to develop the half-guard game in the late '80s because he injured his left knee and wasn't able to play his full guard. So he adjusted his half guard and converted a defensive game into a very aggressive and effective offensive attack. Today it is part of the full spectrum of Brazilian jiu-jitsu, especially in tournaments. Every blue belt knows it well, because it is a necessity now. Gordo always emphasizes in his classes that if you want to be successful in this game, you have to put yourself in a situation of risk. The secret is to make your opponent think that you are going to be hunted, but then at the last minute become the hunter yourself. Determination, confidence, and of course, a lot of training makes the half-guard game possible.

I'll be releasing new videos of other black belts and of many major tournaments. Right now, I have Pan American 2002, Antonio "Nino" Schembri, and Roberto "Roleta" Guimaraes. Check out www.brazilianjiu-jitsutapes.com. I want to make it a place where people can find any tape they want.

GRAPPLING

BEST OF CFW — VOL. 1

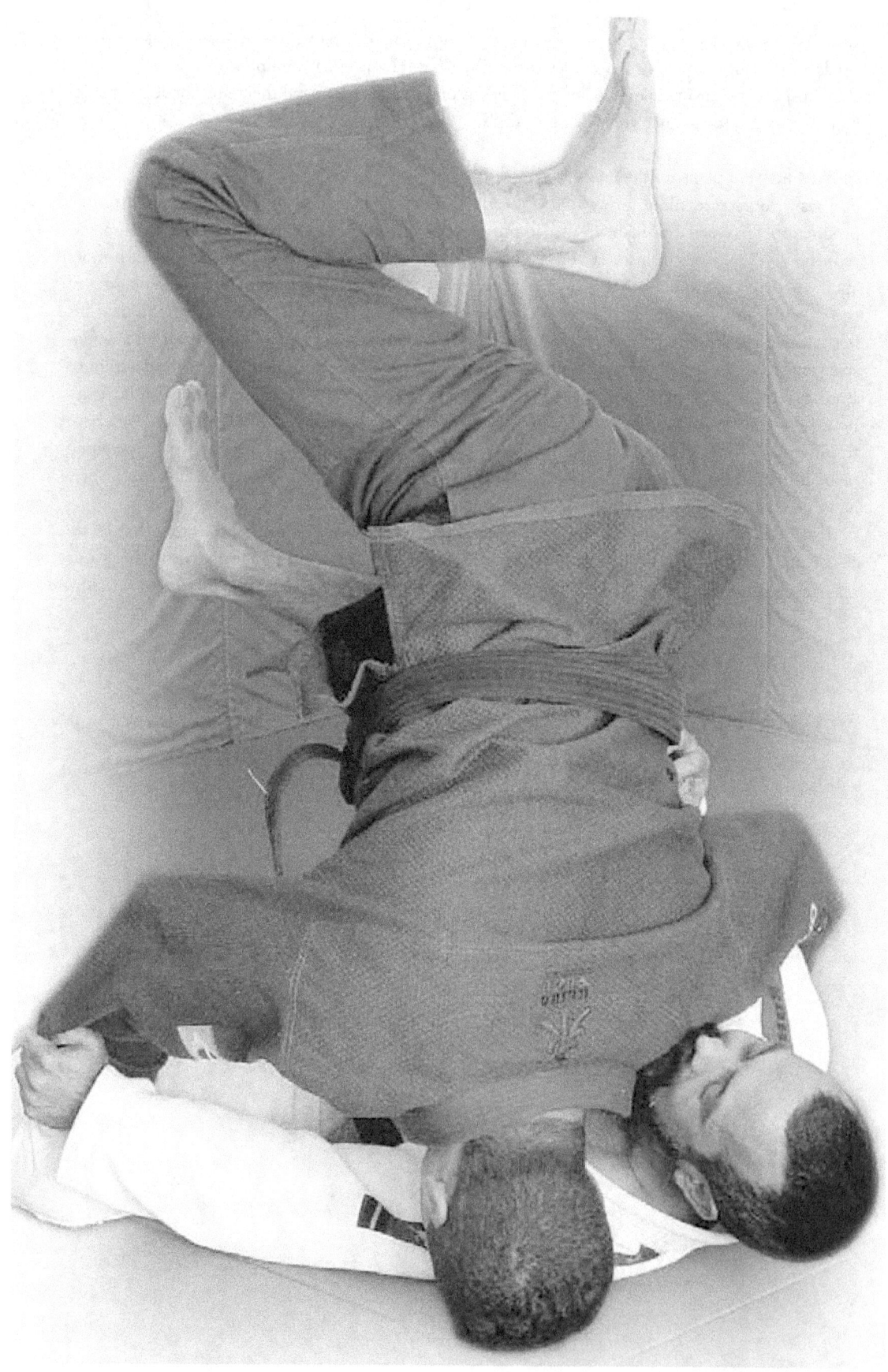

GRAPPLING

Leozinho Vieira's Extreme Jiu-Jitsu
The Star Guard Pass

Kid Peligro

Leozinho Vieira is one of Brazilian jiu-jitsu's brightest young stars, having won the world title twice and the national individual and team title countless times. The winner of the 2000 International Pro-Ams, and more recently the 2002 Pan American title, Leozinho is equally adept at grappling with and without the gi, as he showed in his epic battle against Mark Kerr at the 2000 ADCC World Submission Wrestling Tournament. Vieira's most striking characteristic is his flashy style. Leozinho has used his incredible natural ability to develop a wide array of cutting-edge techniques. A product of the Alliance Team, this student of Romero "Jacare" Cavalcanti has been shocking the Brazilian jiu-jitsu establishment since his debut as a brown belt in the Nationals in 1998, when he used his eclectic, original, and effective techniques on his way to the title.

Leozinho explains that he has learned a lot from watching children train Brazilian jiu-jitsu. He was the chief instructor for the children's class at the Master Academy, and was fascinated by the fact that children were always exploring new territories and were not bound by conventional techniques and limitations. With that in mind, Vieira began his quest for new ways to solve old problems. One of his favorite techniques is his "star" guard passes. Leo states that the star pass is extremely effective against any opponent, especially strong ones. As he says: "The strong opponent likes to keep you away with his legs, and it is almost impossible to close the gap to pass the guard in the conventional way. With the star guard pass, you don't fight with the legs but avoid them altogether. This is the true way of jiu-jitsu—not to fight power with power but to find an intelligent way to avoid the problem."

Leozinho was the recent winner of the Ground Impact event in Tokyo Japan. Ground Impact is a professional Brazilian jiu-jitsu show in which Leo fought and defeated Japan's Yuki Nakai in the main event. Leo used the star guard pass against Nakai to the thrill and delight of the Japanese spectators, who were not used to seeing his acrobatic style of the sport.

Leozinho continues: "The star guard pass is perfect against the butterfly guard. You can fool the opponent into thinking that you are going to try to smash him by pressing his back to the mat, and then spring to his side with a quick burst of speed and grace."

Vieira also likes the star pass against the spider guard: "The spider guard is a favorite of competitors and can be a very difficult guard to overcome. If the opponent has good quick legs, and shifts the pressure from one leg to the other, it makes it hard to attempt anything. By using the star pass, you can quickly avoid the pressure and end up with the three points for the pass."

Another great usage for the star pass is against the traditional open guard. Leo uses it because it allows him to get to the side without having to deal with the opponent's attacks such as the triangle and arm bars.

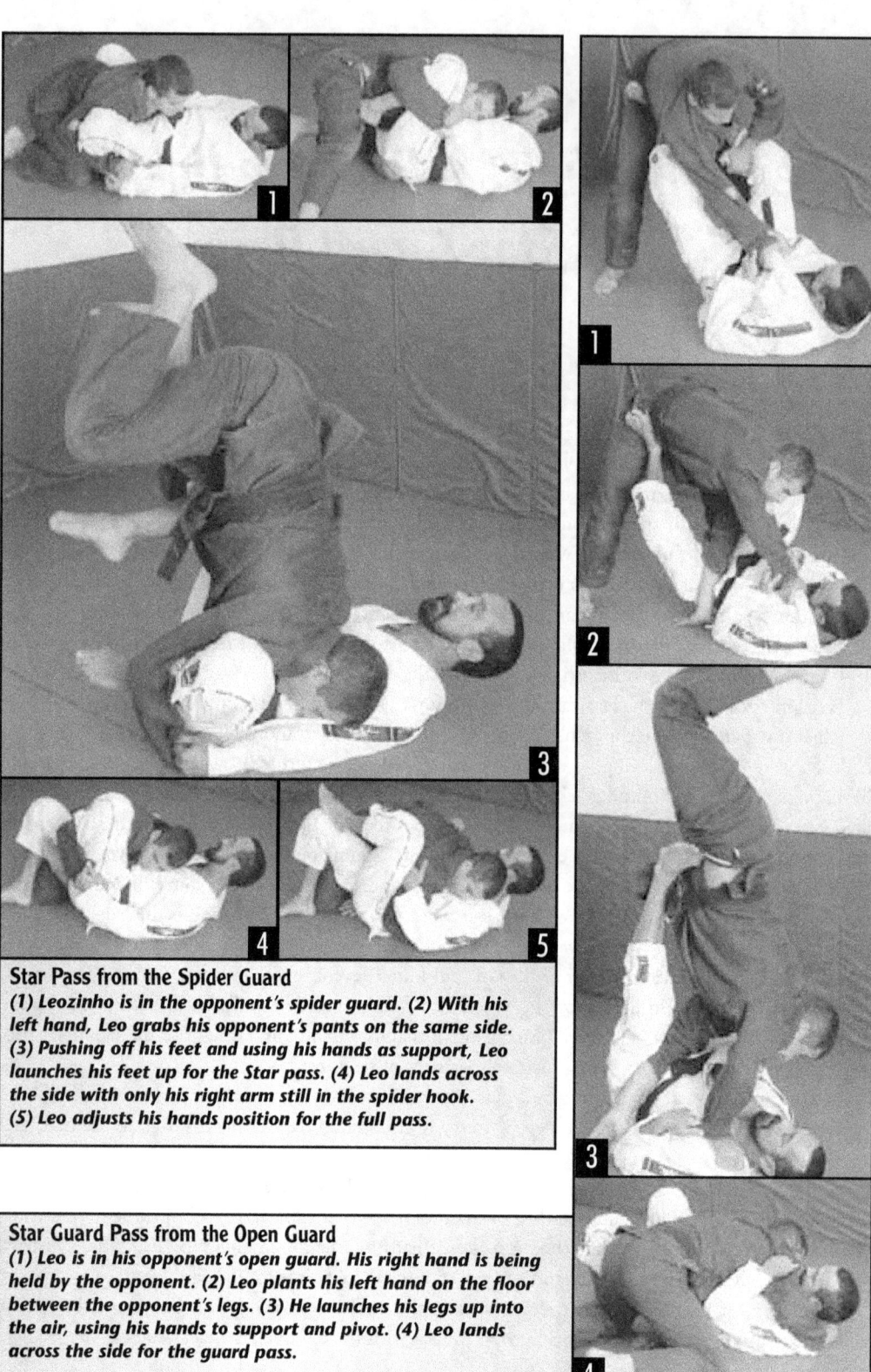

Star Pass from the Spider Guard
(1) Leozinho is in the opponent's spider guard. (2) With his left hand, Leo grabs his opponent's pants on the same side. (3) Pushing off his feet and using his hands as support, Leo launches his feet up for the Star pass. (4) Leo lands across the side with only his right arm still in the spider hook. (5) Leo adjusts his hands position for the full pass.

Star Guard Pass from the Open Guard
(1) Leo is in his opponent's open guard. His right hand is being held by the opponent. (2) Leo plants his left hand on the floor between the opponent's legs. (3) He launches his legs up into the air, using his hands to support and pivot. (4) Leo lands across the side for the guard pass.

GRAPPLING

Star Guard Pass to the Back
(1) Leo is attempting to pass his opponent's sitting guard. Leo uses his right hand to grab onto the opponent's collar. (2) Leo plants his left leg on the mat between the opponent's legs. (3) Using the hands for base Leo, launches his legs up (4), aAnd lands on his opponent's back.

Star Guard Pass from the Butterfly Guard—Variation
This variation of the star guard pass from the butterfly guard is one of Leo's favorites. (1) Leo is in his opponent's butterfly guard. (2) Using his left hand, he grabs onto the opponent's left knee. (3) Pushing off his feet, he turns the opponent onto his side while using his left shoulder to trap the legs. (4) Leo throws his legs up into the air (5), and lands with the guard passed.

Being that Vieira is a showman in addition to being a great competitor, he developed this move as a way to quickly finish fights. He states: 'If you can shock the opponent and quickly take his back right from the guard pass, you can end the fight with a submission. Normally after you pass the guard and go directly to the back, the opponent is so stunned that you can sink the choke in."

BEST OF CFW — VOL. 1
GRAPPLING

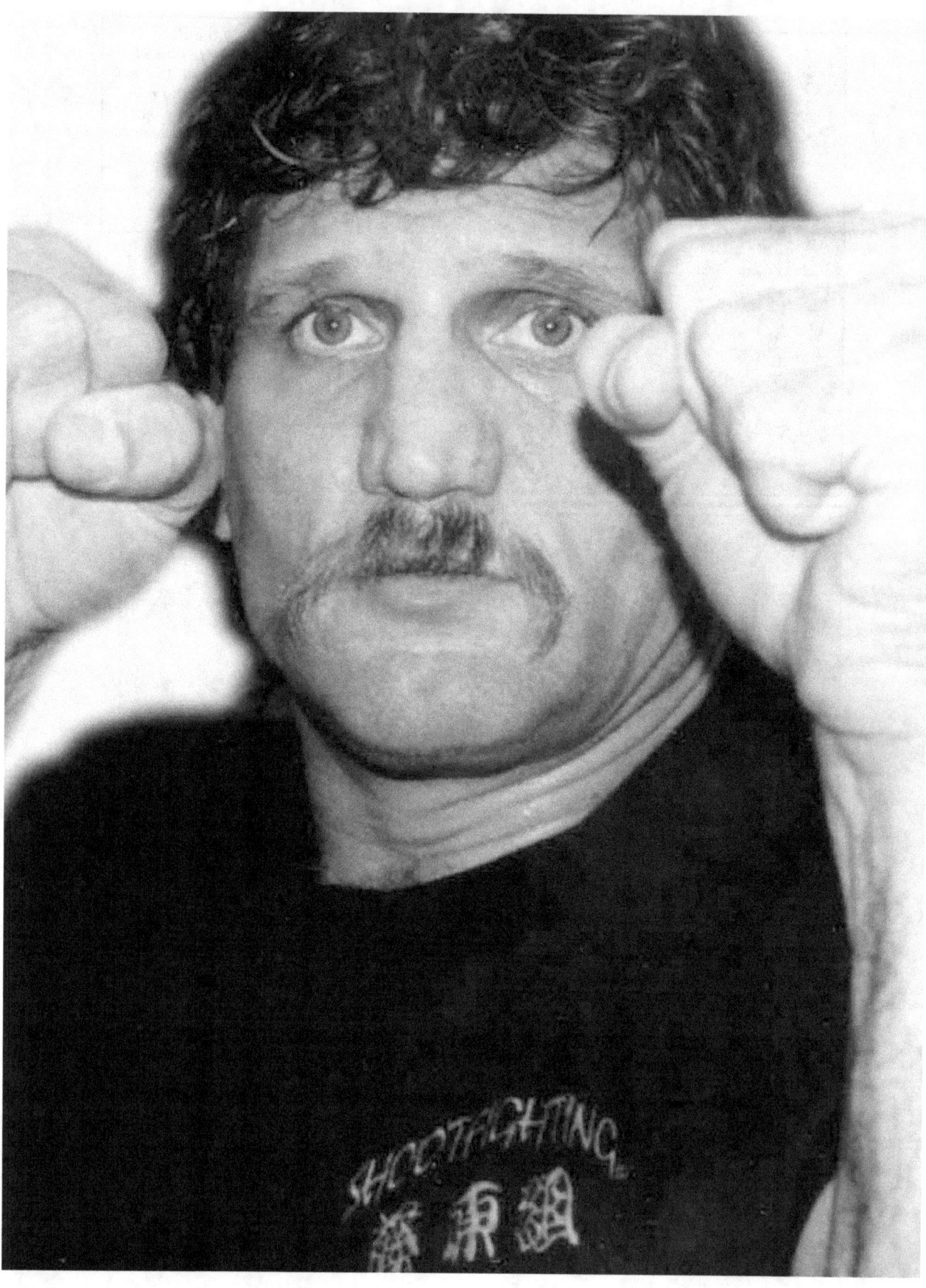

GRAPPLING

Bart Vale
Behind the Vale

Florida shootfighting and mixed martial arts pioneer Bart Vale speaks out about his career, no-holds-barred fighting, and the evolution and future of mixed martial arts.

Martin Bartlett, Story and photos

When most of today's top martial artists were deciding what to wear to the Junior High dance, Bart Vale was deciding if he should stay in Japan and compete before thousands of rabid fans or go back to the States and continue his training. Bart chose to do both. He went on to win numerous titles in mixed martial arts before it was even *called* mixed martial arts. In the early '90s he started his shootfighting schools in Miami, Florida. There are now numerous schools all over the world teaching the style of fighting he brought back from Japan and formally dubbed "shootfighting."

When you hear Bart Vale talk you get the feeling that martial arts is his life and all he lives for. That is not a far-fetched statement for a man who has competed in everything from tough-man competitions to kickboxing shows to no-holds-barred cage fights. Entering his school, you get the feeling that you just walked into a sauna. Even in the scorching Miami heat, the fighters who train at Vale's school go outside to cool off in the blazing sun.

Still very large and intimidating, standing 6' 4" and weighing 250 pounds, Vale is no longer an active mixed martial arts competitor—but his legacy lives on through his students. Although he has earned a 7th degree black belt in Chinese kenpo, Vale now spends all his time training fighters in the art of shootfighting.

Q: How did you get started in martial arts?
A: In the early '70s I was introduced to the martial arts by a buddy of my stepbrother. He encouraged me and told me to go to Tracy's Martial Arts School, which is the school we are sitting in right now. I originally came to it and then ended up buying it years later.

Q: What took you to Japan?
A: In the early '80s, I was raising funds for the Jerry Lewis Telethon. I collected so much money that they gave me a 30-second spot on TV. I was going to go down there and show some kicking and punching. So I got up on stage and I did my thirty-second demo. Well, there was a Japanese man in

GRAPPLING

> *"Of course, I'm thinking to myself that I'm gonna smoke this kid, and for the first few seconds I did very well. came over with some nice roundhouse kicks to the head and then he shot in on me, took me down to the ground and slapped-on a heel hook and really cranked my leg. I started yelling and screaming, and Sammy was just laughing."*

the audience named Masami Soronaka, or "Sammy" as I now call him. After the demonstration he came over to me and said, "I've never seen an American your size kick as high and as fast as you do. Would you like to compete in Japan?"

Well, at the time all I knew was kickboxing, so that's what I assumed he meant. So I said I would. He told me to go over to Tampa and work out with some of the Japanese fighters. So I went over there and got into the ring and the guy I faced was much smaller than me. Now we weren't wearing gloves or anything and Sammy said, " Not so hard. Not trying to kill each other. Just wanna see what you guys can do and how you work." Of course, I'm thinking to myself that I'm gonna smoke this kid, and for the first few seconds I did very well. I came over with some nice roundhouse kicks to the head and then he shot in on me, took me down to the ground and slapped-on a heel hook and really cranked my leg. I stated yelling and screaming, and Sammy was just laughing. He said, "Oh, I forgot to tell. It is almost like kickboxing." He then explained submission fighting to me and started showing me the techniques right there. I immediately said that I've got to learn this stuff, this is incredible. He said, " OK. You come with me to Japan, I train you." So I started going to Japan and training in this style.

Q: After a few years of training, you started to compete in an organization called the UWF, right?
A: Yes. We had Shamrock in there at the time; he was going by "Wayne," I think. Funaki and Suzuki were there, as were Norman Smiley and Mark Star. But most of these guys came in after the new UWF, because in the late '80s the original UWF split up. One

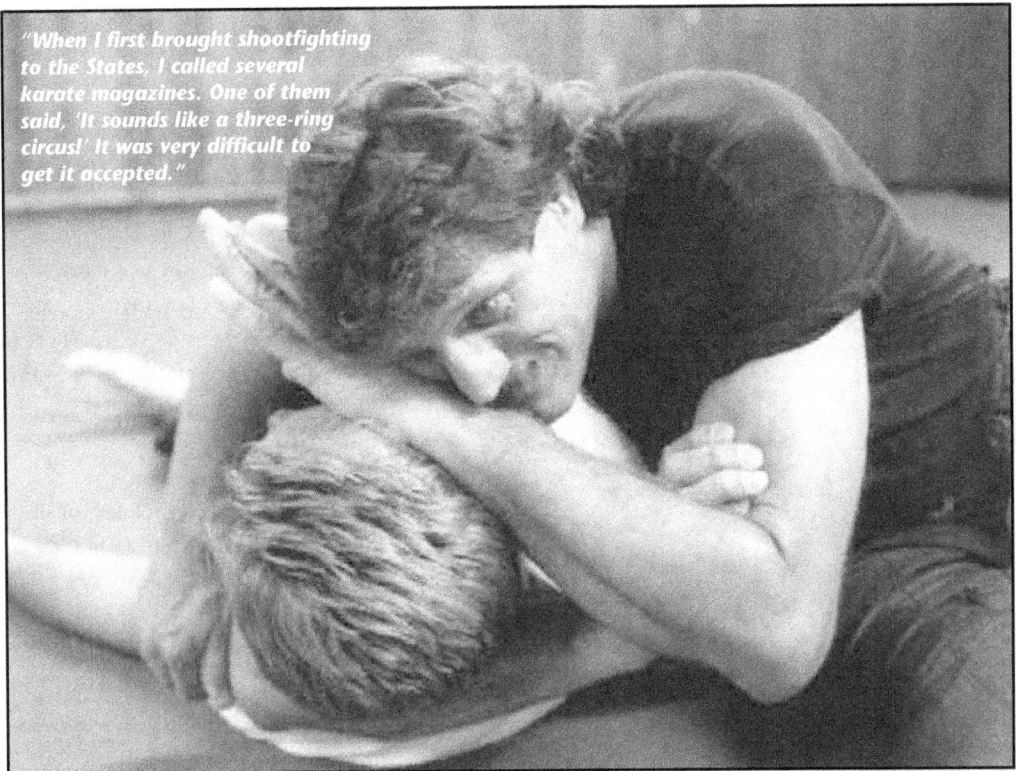

"When I first brought shootfighting to the States, I called several karate magazines. One of them said, 'It sounds like a three-ring circus!' It was very difficult to get it accepted."

night they all decided to go different ways. Akira Maeda, who was UWF Rings, decided to get all the foreigners from Holland, Russia, and different countries. Takada, who went with Yamasaki, took all the Japanese fighters who were in the original UWF group. And then Fujiwari, who was also called the UWF Spirit, took all of the American guys—and I was at the top of that list. In fact, I was in charge of all the Americans who came over to Japan. In fact, before Ken Shamrock was ever allowed to go to Japan, Soronaka asked me if we should bring him. So I was the person that gave Ken his start—this was right after he got into a fight with the Nasty Boys and got injured. He was supposed to come down that weekend to Florida to work out with me, but he couldn't make it. So I said to Soronaka, "Lets just bring him over to Japan, I'll see if he's good enough when we get there." Well, he was phenomenal—just an excellent grappler. His stand-up was weak, but that was because it was new to him. The problem at that time was that fighters were either strikers or grapplers—there was no such thing as a well-rounded fighter. So we started combining them. Shootfighting was the original style that started combining both stand-up fighting and total body submission.

Q: What was it like competing in Japan as a foreigner?
A: It was awesome! First of all they treated me very nicely. I was very surprised by this because I've gone to a lot of different countries to compete in kickboxing and toughman competitions and for the most part I was treated like a outsider. Japan was the first country that ever made me feel like an equal. They weren't yelling at me to go back to America or throwing stuff at me in the ring. In most of my fights in Puerto Rico, I had to fight the audience—I couldn't get out to the ring to fight my opponent! I went down to Ecuador to fight and I was fighting just to get into the ring. Later, when I went to Russia to

Mount Reversal Arm Lock
Trapped on the bottom, Bart Vale covers up (1). When his opponent tries to punch, Vale bridges his hips upward, throwing his opponent over his head (2). Trapping the arm to prevent his opponent from reestablishing top position (3), Vale rolls to the side, traps the arm between his head and shoulder, and then applies a finishing elbow lock (4).

compete, they were basically on the same level as the Japanese and showed me a lot of respect.

Q: After the UWF split up, you went with Fujiwara and the PWFG and became the first non-Japanese shoot-fighting champion. What was that like?
A: That was awesome! I was the first foreigner ever to beat the Japanese at their own game. In fact Kinishki, who's the big Hawaiian sumo guy out there in Japan, weighs something like 650 pounds. After I beat Fujiwara for the title he called me up yelling and screaming, because he wanted to be the first foreigner to beat the Japanese. But unfortunately for him it was me.

Q: You also had the infamous knockout of Ken Shamrock in '92. Could you tell us a little about that?
A: That was an exciting fight for me. Ken was a good grappler and was extremely strong. I knew realistically if I was to beat Ken, it would have to from stand-up rather than ground grappling. I was convinced that he could handle me on the ground better than I could handle him. I had planned to do more striking, but Ken controlled me more than I anticipated and took me down several times. But when we got up from one of the breaks, Ken came at me like a kickboxer, which was my backyard. He came at me throwing wild punches, and when he did I backed up for a second. The I came back in and caught him with a straight strike to the head, which dazed him. From that point on, I followed with two or three shin strikes to the head, which knocked him out. But realistically, if he hadn't come at me like a kickboxer the result might have been different. He basically walked right into what I wanted to do.

Q: In 1995 you fought in the States in the World Combat Championships, where you destroyed a tough, young fighter named Mike Bitonio. In that same tournament, you were scheduled to fight Renzo Gracie, but couldn't continue after your grueling first match. Do you wish you could have fought him?
A: I really wanted the opportunity to fight him. The whole event was geared for a fight between Renzo and I. It really surprised me that they didn't put us together in the first round. Instead, they put Bitonio against me

GRAPPLING

and Renzo against Ben Spikers. Now I had figured out my game plan. Since it was a no-rules fight I was going to use a headbutt. In a ground situation, when somebody is controlling your arms, sometimes the only thing you have is the top of your head. That's what I planned—I was going to save that for Gracie. But unfortunately, Bitonio grabbed my hair and started pulling it. And that's when I hit him with the headbutt and put 55 stitches in his face. But that was meant for Gracie.

Q: Many people were looking forward to seeing you fight Renzo.
A: Yeah, so was I. I just can't see how a 150-pound guy can beat someone who weighs 250. I can understand it if the 250-pounder has no fighting experience. But you have two experienced people, and one is 250 and one is 150, I can't see it happening. I bench pressed 600 pounds at the time—so a 150 pounds meant nothing to me. I could do that with one arm. Not to take anything away from Gracie, he's good at what he does, but so am I.

Q: You also fought in the now fabled Extreme Fighting Championship where you squared off against Murakami Kazunari, who has since went on to become a pro wrestling star in Japan. Although you ended-up losing that fight, it appeared early on that you had a solid arm-bar on him. Were you surprised he didn't tap?
A: I was real surprised. But when I look back at that chicken wing, I can now see that I was a little bit above the elbow instead of below it. Basically, that was the only way he was able to withstand that hold, because I wasn't really on the joint. It was close though. I know it was painful to him, but I couldn't slide it high enough to tap him. My game plan didn't work out quite the way I wanted it to.

Q: He was known as a judo player; did it surprise you when he started striking?
A: I was quite aware that anything could happen. Because that happened in a fight down here in the States, when I fought a guy named Mark Star, who was a very good wrestler. He dislocated my jaw with an elbow strike. Again, it was me thinking that he was a wrestler and wouldn't throw any strikes. So that's how I got hurt.

Q: Why didn't you enter the UFC or Pancrase?
A: Pancrase was Funaki's company. Because I was on Fujiwara's team, they didn't want anything to do with me. I know there was a lot of animosity between me and the Japanese fighters because Fujiwara treated me better then he treated them. Then the Japanese cut Fujiwara off and left him and the UWF and started Pancrase. Over in Japan something that disloyal doesn't usually happen—but Funaki and Suzuki did it anyway. And I know they would never have let me fight Pancrase because I was with Fujiwara. I started with him and these guys came in three or fours years after me, so I wasn't going to leave him.

As far as the UFC goes, they offered me fights a couple of times. The problem with the UFC was that you only got paid decent money if you won the whole thing. Now that would have been fine for me 20 years ago. When I did all those toughman competitions I used to pay 50 bucks to win 100. But those days were long gone for me when the UFC came around. I want to get paid no matter what. The UFC wouldn't do that; they only paid you if you won. I wasn't interested in that.

Q: Tell me your thoughts on Mark Coleman.
A: Awesome grappler. I think he can be real dangerous when he gets everything together. I've watched a few of his fights where he put his opponent away really quick. I noticed in some of his

fights that it looked like he got tired much sooner than he should have. Somebody then told me that he only trains for a five-minute match, because that's as long as anybody can stay with him. In a lot of his fights that works, but as the fight goes on and they stay longer with him, he does get tired.

Q: How about Benny Urquidez?
A: Benny is awesome! I've had the opportunity to meet him several times and I had the opportunity to watch some of his fights—not only in the U.S., but also in Japan. Awesome fighter—I can't say anything else—he's just awesome.

Q: Have you seen Gokar Chivichian compete?
A: Oh yeah. An excellent, excellent grappler. But he needs to gear a little more of his fighting style to deal with stand-up fighting.

Q: Bob Wall?
A: Bob Wall has been a movie idol of mine for years. He is an extremely talented martial artist, somebody that I highly respect, and a person I have the honor of being friends with. I just love to hear his stories about Bruce Lee and Chuck Norris.

Q: Gene LeBell?
A: You just went one step above Bob Wall. Gene LeBell has mythical qualities. When I started in martial arts, that name was already one of the big ones in the martial arts world. He became a friend of mine, and I am in proud to be in his organization. Knowing him is a dream come true to me.

Q: Karl Gotch?
A: I trained with him for several years. A little story about Karl Gotch. A guy I knew named Jerry Flynn was working at a nightclub at that time. He kept running into this young wannabe bad-ass that kept running his mouth. Well, Jerry said to him jokingly, "I know this 65-year-old man who would tear you up." The kid was very cocky and said he would kill any old man. So Jerry went to Karl and told him, and Karl told Jerry to bring him over. Now this was a 65-year-old man against a young, strong kid. So Karl got hold of him, got him on the ground, and twisted him every way but the right way. And while he's doing this, Karl is explaining to those of us watching what he's doing and what he's going to do next. The kid just couldn't stop him. Karl is just that good. Simply the best. He is impossible to describe. He would take on all-comers of any style. Simply incredible.

Q: How about a current fighter like Dan Bobish?
A: Dan and I first met when we took him out to the fields to run sprints. He had to do eight sprints and run around the field six times, which was over a mile. Then we took him back to the dojo and stared to workout with pads. So I had him go the first minute just throwing single hands. Then the second minute he had to throw combinations with his hands—left, right, step left, step right, repeat. Then the next minute we were going with double combinations and so forth, going through the entire workout. And the next thing he did was roundhouse kicks on a Thai pad.

Now let me tell you, I weigh roughly 250, give or take, and Bobish was throwing these roundhouse kicks with pads, moving me like I was nothing. He just slammed into the pads, and across the ring I went. He had a real good pivot motion in his hips so he could use all of his 330 pounds. He worked out a few minutes like that and then we put him up against the wall and we got like ten guys in the studio to go up against him and try to move him against the wall, take him down, or move him. Well, he went all the way through ten guys. And then he had a one-minute rest and did it again. Now I don't know if you saw his fight against Eric Pele, but he went into the second round and Pele was sucking wind and Bobish was standing there like it was nothing. I mean Bobish was in great condition at that time. Then he just went back to King of the Cage in Reno and did it again against Mike Kyle.

Back Choke Neck Crank
Bart Vale is trapped on the bottom position, with his opponent controlling his back (1). Throwing his hips upward, Vale causes his opponent to lose his leg grip and to slide forward and to the side, exposing his head (2). Reaching upward with both hands, Vale grasps his opponent securely behind the head and pulls downward for the neck crank submission (3).

I've already talked to the Japanese about him getting in Pride. They've already put him in a magazine called *Gong*, a very popular fighting magazine. He's being announced in Japan as the first fighter from the Bart Vale organization to compete in Pride. Unfortunately, I don't know which Pride they are talking about, but I'm looking for Bobish to start setting some records there because he's very well-conditioned and very dedicated.

Q: What was it about shootfighting that made you want to bring it back to the States and devote your life to it?

A: In most fighting systems there always seemed to be something missing. Jiu-jitsu or judo just addressed the grappling part of fighting, and kickboxing and kenpo just addressed the stand-up part. What shootfighting did was to address both the stand-up and the ground fighting and the transitions between. And when I looked at I realized that the martial arts world is missing a lot if they don't have these two things combined. When I first brought it to the States, I called several karate magazines. One of them said, "It sounds like a three-ring circus!" It was very difficult to get it accepted. But I never gave up. I just kept going.

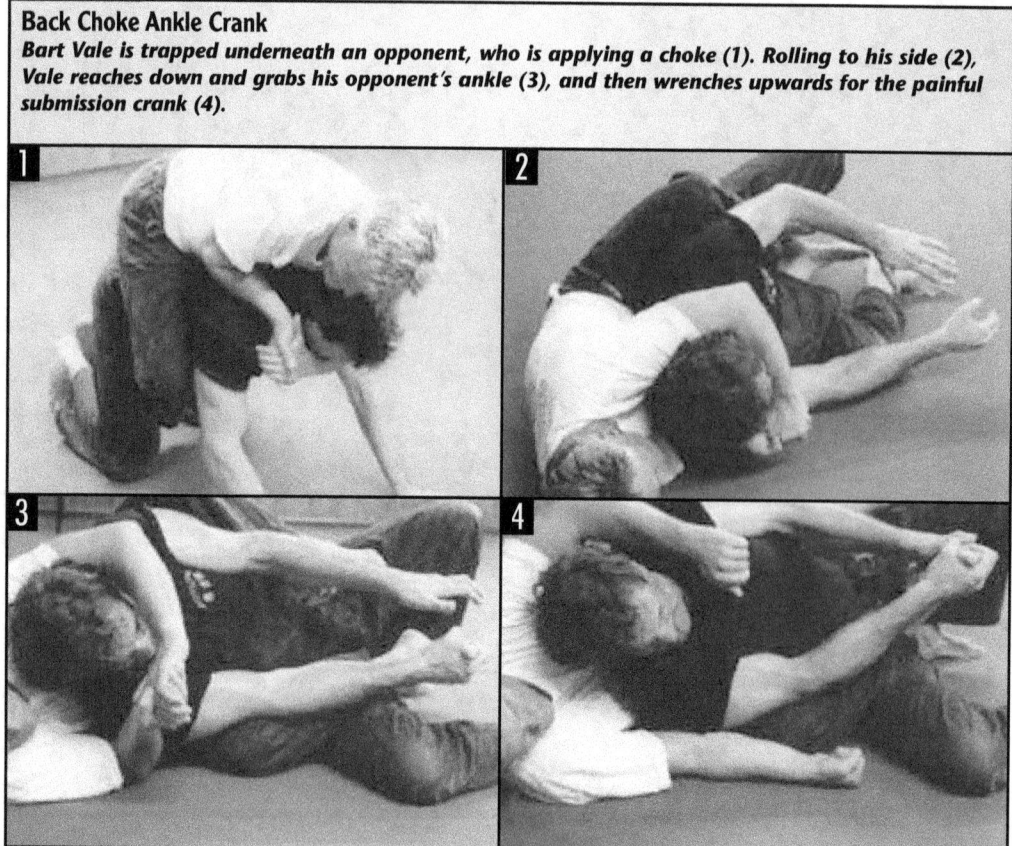

Back Choke Ankle Crank
Bart Vale is trapped underneath an opponent, who is applying a choke (1). Rolling to his side (2), Vale reaches down and grabs his opponent's ankle (3), and then wrenches upwards for the painful submission crank (4).

GRAPPLING

Q: What makes shootfighting rules different from UFC or Pride rules?

A: One thing that made shootfighting different than the early UFC was that it incorporated rules that allowed you to do techniques instead of just brawl. For instance, if you had an opponent in a choke, and he couldn't escape, he had the option to grab the rope. The referee would then break the fighters and start them standing up again. So you got a second chance to try again rather than just give up. I think that's more of a Japanese thing. They hate to see anybody give up—it's death before dishonor and if you can grab the rope you're a hero. Of course, as the UFC went on they incorporated more and more rules. One of our rules is no striking on the ground at all. Down on the ground you do your grappling, and one the feet you do kickboxing, elbow strikes, knee strikes, and takedowns. You also can't hold onto the ropes to avoid a takedown. The UFC is starting to gear more towards what shootfighting has been all along.

For more information on how to get involved in the ISFA, to book a Bart Vale seminar, or to locate a shootfighting school in your area, call Bart Vale at 305-266-1601, write to him at 6469 SW 8th Street, Miami, FL 33144, or e-mail www.isfa@2shoot.com.

Bart Vale and his two sons.

"Now this was a 65-year-old man against a young, strong kid. So Karl got hold of him, got him on the ground, and twisted him every way but the right way. And while he's doing this, Karl is explaining to those of us watching what he's doing and what he's going to do next. The kid just couldn't stop him."

GRAPPLING

Terrere with the throw.

2002 Brazilian Jiu-Jitsu Pan American Tournament

With the ADCC tournament cancelled, the 8th edition of the Pan Ams promised to be the best ever as Brazilian jiu-jitsu stars flocked to Kissimmee, Florida, for the annual choke-a-thon.

Kid Peligro, Photos by Paul Thatcher

With over 800 competitors from around the world, this two-day event is undoubtedly the biggest gathering of BJJ practitioners on American soil. Traditionally, the Pan-Ams is where the bright, new stars of the sport shine. Over the years, Saulo Ribeiro, "Nino" Schembri and "Margarida" Pontes announced their arrival as major players on the world BJJ scene by taking top honors in the tournament. Unfortunately, Margarida was absent because of a recent motorcycle accident—but he was just about the only big star who was. This year, without the ADCC World Submission Tournament to take away some of the stars (both events traditionally occur during the same month), the Pan-Ams drew the top names in the sport, making it even more difficult for newcomers to succeed. However, the mere presence of the elite stars does not guarantee them a title, and to prove this point there were some big surprises.

Day One
The first day opened in the Kissimmee Center with six competition areas hosting some of the best matches seen in this event in quite a while. One of the biggest advances this year was in the woman's category. This division seems to be growing by leaps and bounds both in numbers and in technical skill. With veterans such as "Leka" Vieira, "Luka" Dias and D.C. Maxwell leading the way, a host of new female fighters are beginning to make their mark on the sport. This year, the winners included 16-year-old sensation Kyra Gracie, who closed-out her division with teammate Shanon Logan. In the black belt competition, Leka Vieira took the gold in the advanced division.

In the men's blue belt division, notables such as ADCC champion Jeff Monson competed and did well. Monson managed to take the masters super heavy, showing that he can fight even with a gi. Of course having the Brazilian Top Team's Ricardo Liborio as a full time BJJ instructor doesn't hurt! Still in the blue belt division, super fighter Asa Fuller took his weight class and absolute division by winning seven matches, while teammate "Chewy" won his weight division in the seniors. In the purple belt category, Gracie Barra's Joe D'Arce closed out his division with teammate Braulio Estima.

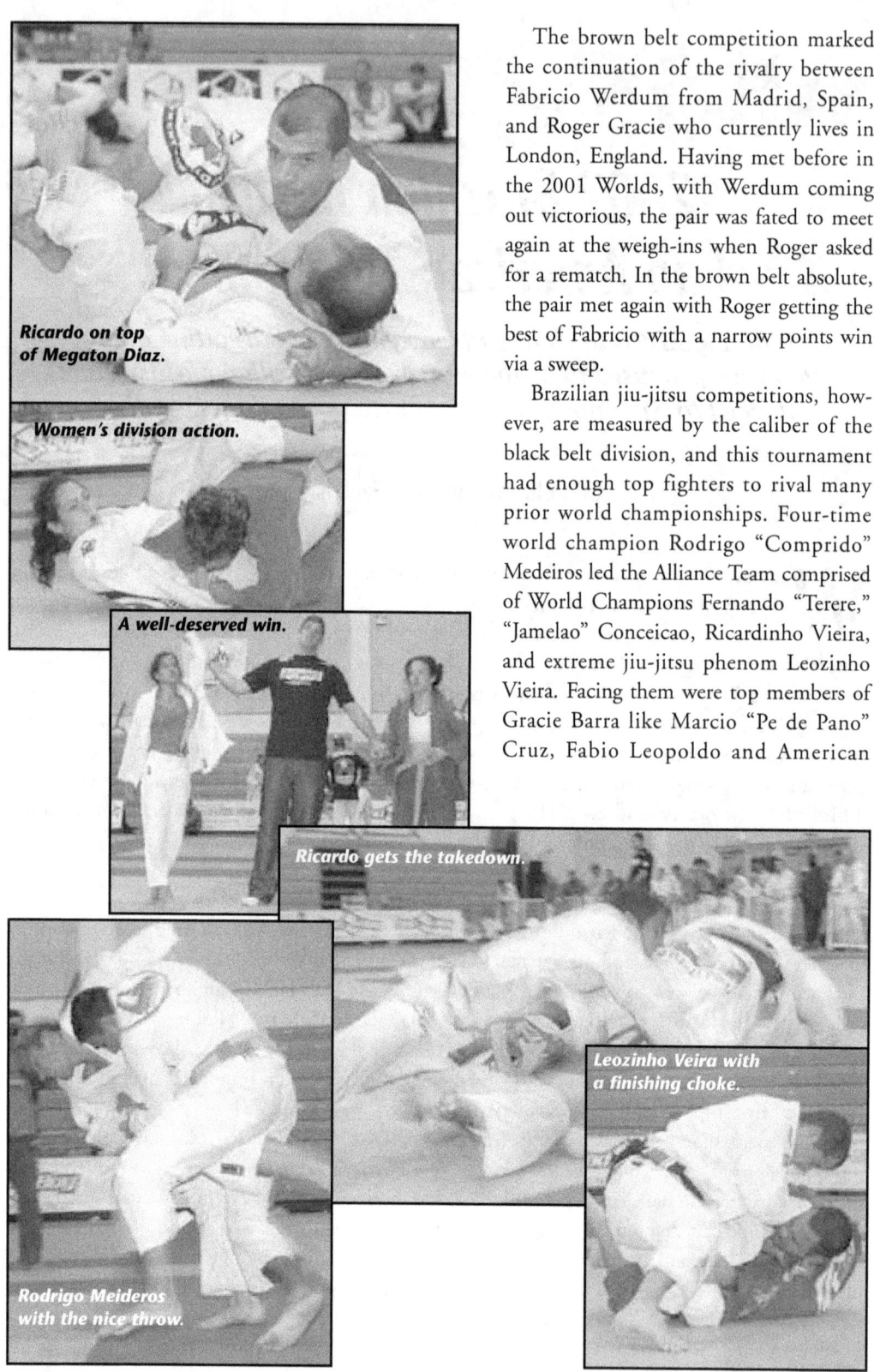

Ricardo on top of Megaton Diaz.

Women's division action.

A well-deserved win.

Ricardo gets the takedown.

Rodrigo Meideros with the nice throw.

Leozinho Veira with a finishing choke.

The brown belt competition marked the continuation of the rivalry between Fabricio Werdum from Madrid, Spain, and Roger Gracie who currently lives in London, England. Having met before in the 2001 Worlds, with Werdum coming out victorious, the pair was fated to meet again at the weigh-ins when Roger asked for a rematch. In the brown belt absolute, the pair met again with Roger getting the best of Fabricio with a narrow points win via a sweep.

Brazilian jiu-jitsu competitions, however, are measured by the caliber of the black belt division, and this tournament had enough top fighters to rival many prior world championships. Four-time world champion Rodrigo "Comprido" Medeiros led the Alliance Team comprised of World Champions Fernando "Terere," "Jamelao" Conceicao, Ricardinho Vieira, and extreme jiu-jitsu phenom Leozinho Vieira. Facing them were top members of Gracie Barra like Marcio "Pe de Pano" Cruz, Fabio Leopoldo and American

GRAPPLING

Jameola looking for the takedown.

Surprise! Jacare (R) with Paul Thatcher and Leo.

Ricardo on top.

Rodgiro Meideros looking for the takedown.

The Viera brothers looking tough.

Alberto Crane, while Gracie Humaita replied with "Xande" Ribeiro, "Megaton" Dias, Fredson Alves and "Wizard" Batatinha. The end result was an event to remember and some big surprises.

Ricardinho Vieira showed why he is the current world champion by taking the super feather title over "Megaton" Diaz. Ricardinho proved to everyone that his incredible guard game is getting better and better. Phenom Leozinho Vieira decided to come out of his semi-forced retirement in the Pan-Ams and showed that he hasn't missed a step. The young gun had stayed away from competition last year in order to pursue his teaching goals. Having settled that, Leo showcased the same incredible and plastic Mr. Fantastic style that has made him one of the best and most exciting fighters to watch in any tournament. Vieira took the title with two submissions in the two matches; including the finals where he debuted his new "Brabo" choke—a wicked collar choke of his own creation.

In the light division there was big controversy in the finals between Daniel Correa and Carlos "Portugues." At one point, Portugues started a takedown attempt and Correa reversed it and ended up on top. In a strange call, referee Leo Vieira gave an advantage to Correa rather than the takedown points. Correa and his teammates argued with Vieira for the rest of the match. It was to no avail, however, and Carlos took the title.

Surprise number one occurred in the medium weight category, where Delson "Pe de Chumbo," a relative newcomer to the black belt division, defeated world champion "Terere" on his way to the title. Terere was the heavy favorite, having won the Brazilian title in his weight division and then doubling-up in the absolutes by defeating the ever-dangerous Marcio "Pe de Pano" Cruz in the finals. With a style very similar to Terere's (constant movement and playing with the opponent's mind), Delson had shown flashes of brilliance in that same event—but at the brown belt level, As the two faced each other in the semifinal, Delson beat Terere at his own game, having out psyched him out early in the match.

"Xande" Ribeiro started this year big, with a win in the medium heavy, sharing the title with friend "Jamelao" Conceicao. Xande used his incredible half-guard game to disconcert his opponents while at the same time confirming that his overall game is one of the strongest in the world right now. Xande, who is currently residing in the U.S., has taken to training wrestling with local high school and college coaches. Since then, he as won two major events—one at the Arnold Classic and the other at Grapplers Quest—announcing to the world that he is going to be a force equal to or better than brother Saulo. Gracie Barra's Fabio Leopoldo then closed out the heavy with teammate Muchiatti. Leopoldo has been steadily coming into his own of late, and this time he reached peak form at just the right time.

Then it was time for surprise number two as "Café" Dantas defeated four-time world champion "Comprido" Medeiros in the finals of the super-heavy. Café opened up with a takedown but Comprido matched those points by a sweep—only to fall into Café's game again and lose via points. These two have a history of tension leading back to lower belt times, and this result will only serve to intensify that rivalry.

Marcio "Pe de Pano" Cruz cannot be called a newcomer or a rising star as he has been wining tournaments since his blue belt days; but by winning both the super-heavy and the absolute, he sent a message to the other top submission fighters that he means business. Cruz, who possess a guard that has been called similar to of Roberto "Roleta," but more dangerous, used his devilish guard to submit Alex "Negao" with a triangle choke—then he did it again in the absolute! Against the Alliance's Eduardo Telles, Cruz quickly pulled guard, from where he applied a Kimura lock for the submission. Cruz then closed-out the absolute with teammate Fabio Leopoldo, insuring a Gracie Barra sweep.

Some of the tournaments top guns.

Tough action.

Team Results
1. Gracie Barra
2. Alliance Team Jacare
3. Cia. Paulista

GRAPPLING

Terrere pulls guard.

Jeff Monson, on top, won big.

Rodrigo Meideros controlling the top.

In the final team standings, powerhouse Gracie Barra took the top spot. But Romero "Jacare" Cavalcante continued to prove that he is one of the top, if not *the* top coach and teacher in the U.S., as his Alliance team finished high in yet another major tournament and claimed the Pan Am silver medal.

Conclusion

It will be interesting to attend the Mudials in July and see if the Pan-Ams keep their reputation as the predictor of the world champions. Comprido will be looking for revenge and to continue his string of consecutive world titles. Xande Ribeiro will be in top shape—as will brother Saulo—who has been on a mission to return to the winner's podium after last years setback against Margarida. If healthy, Margarida will want to show the world that his world title wins in 2002 were no fluke. Of course, Pe de Pano will have something to say about that. The Vieira brothers will also be in the thick of things. In another hot contest, Ricardinho will be ready to face the wrath of five-time world champion Robinho Moura, whom he beat for the title last year. Only after the Mudials, will these questions be answered.

Black Belt Division

Super Feather
Ricardinho Vieira defeats "Megaton" Dias.

Feather
Leozinho Vieira, won the division with 2 submissions.

Light
Carlos Eduardo de Souza beats Daniel Correa.

Medium
"Pe de Chumbo" defeats Fernandinho "Terere" in the semis and wins the title.

Medium-Heavy
Alexandre "Xande" Ribeiro wins, closing the division with teammate "Jamelao" Conceicao.

Heavy
Fabio Leopoldo closes out the division with Gustavo Muchiatti, also from Gracie Barra.

Super Heavy
"Café" Dantas defeats "Comprido" Medeiros by points in the final.

Over
"Pe de Pano" Cruz submits Alex "Negao" Paz from the Brazilian Top Team.

Absolute
Marcio "Pe de Pano" Cruz closes out the division with Gracie Barra teammate Fabio Leopoldo.

BEST OF CFW — VOL. 1
GRAPPLING

Bob Schirmer
Chicago's Trainer Of Champions

Loren Franck

Instructors teach mixed martial arts for various reasons. Some couldn't last 10 seconds in the ring, but they train world titleholders. Other teachers are former champions who stay active in the sport by nurturing future champions. Chicago's Bob Schirmer? He's in a class by himself. Now 46 and still a top-notch grappler, he dedicates his life to teaching mixed martial arts. Shonie Carter and Brian Gassaway, two of grappling's greatest, are Schirmer students—and his pride and joy. He's also one of the Windy City's most revered law enforcement trainers. And his ability to transform troubled youth into exceptional martial artists is legendary. Perhaps Schirmer loves teaching because he craved formal fight training while growing up. Though a master of several combat arts, he learned most of his fighting skills by experience. Or maybe Schirmer's four years of boxing and wrestling in the U.S. Marine Corps motivated him to train future fighters. Either way, the man is impressive. And his school, the All-American Academy, is quickly becoming a Midwest Mecca for mixed martial artists. *Grappling* caught up with Schirmer shortly before his July trip to Beijing, where he coached a 10-member U.S. grappling team to victory over China's most formidable submission fighters.

Q: What fighting art did you first learn?
A: My dad taught me to box when I was young. A highly skilled amateur boxer, he sparred with Tony Zale, Billy Con and other leading fighters of his day. I loved boxing as soon as I put the gloves on. When I was seven, the park near my house sponsored a wrestling program, which was my first experience on the mat. I had a real knack for the sport, and when my first year of competition ended, I won the Chicago city wrestling championships. You had to weigh at least 65 pounds to enter, but I was too skinny. So I put locks in my pocket, silver dollars in my mouth and made weight.

Q: What turned you on about wrestling?
A: You must be fast and strong to succeed in wrestling. Besides, it's great exercise, and it really keeps you in shape. Wrestling is also extremely competitive. It brings out your best athletic skills. As in chess, you analyze opponents, take advantage of their weaknesses, and capitalize on your strengths. Wrestling has helped me play baseball, football and other sports too.

Q: What's your experience in no-holds-barred and ultimate fighting?
A: I go way back with NHB and the UFC. In fact, I competed in the first Illinois NHB fights, defeating 245-pound Ed Konecky in one minute and 15 seconds. I fought frequently in the sport's

early days but wasn't allowed to compete at UFC 5, which is when huge guys began competing. At 5'7" and 165 pounds, I was deemed too small, too old, and the UFC was having trouble insuring me. So I took my talent elsewhere.

Q: Do you hold any titles?
A: I was a Bangkok Brawl champion, the interservice taekwondo champ, and I won the Chicago Challenge no-holds-barred championships.

Q: What were your toughest pro fights?
A: There were two, both against Carlson Gracie Jr. The first, in 1996, was called a draw. But Carlson received the win on dubious points, which made everyone wonder why there was overtime if he was winning on points. That same year, as part of Team USA, I was preparing to compete in the World Shidokan Championships. I planned to fight there again in 1997, and promoter Eddie Yashimura said I was in.

Q: What went wrong?
A: Several days before the '97 Shidokan, Carlson's agent approached me. "Would you like to fight Carlson on a jiu-jitsu card?" he asked. "Sure," I said. "But let me call Eddie and make sure it's OK." It was only a week before the '97 Shidokan, and I didn't want to hang Eddie out to dry. He approved our fight, but after it was arranged, I was told, "No heel hooks and no wrist locks." In other words, my hands were tied. My second match with Carlson was NHB, and though it had no submission, the promoter awarded me the trophy. In writing, he admitted I clearly won the fight.

Escaping The Guillotine
(1) Bob is caught in a tight guillotine but all is not lost. (2) Bob lays his arm over George Spacek's shoulder to release some pressure. (3) Bob turns toward the hand and pulls down on the base of the thumb. (4) Bob steps behind George, taking him off balance and drops him to his back. (5) Bob posts the arm away from George's body. (6) Bob goes for the arm lock.

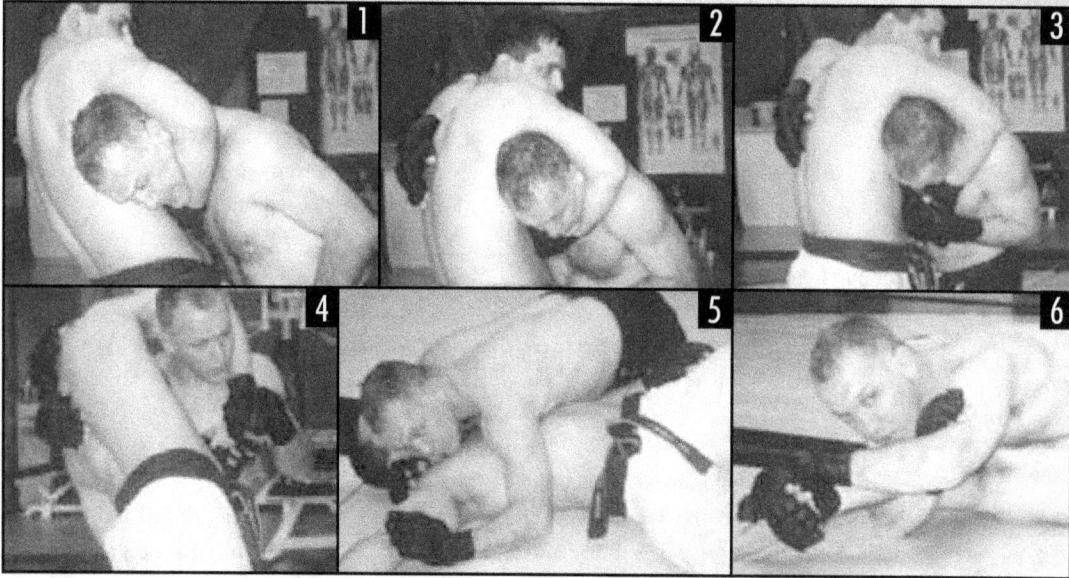

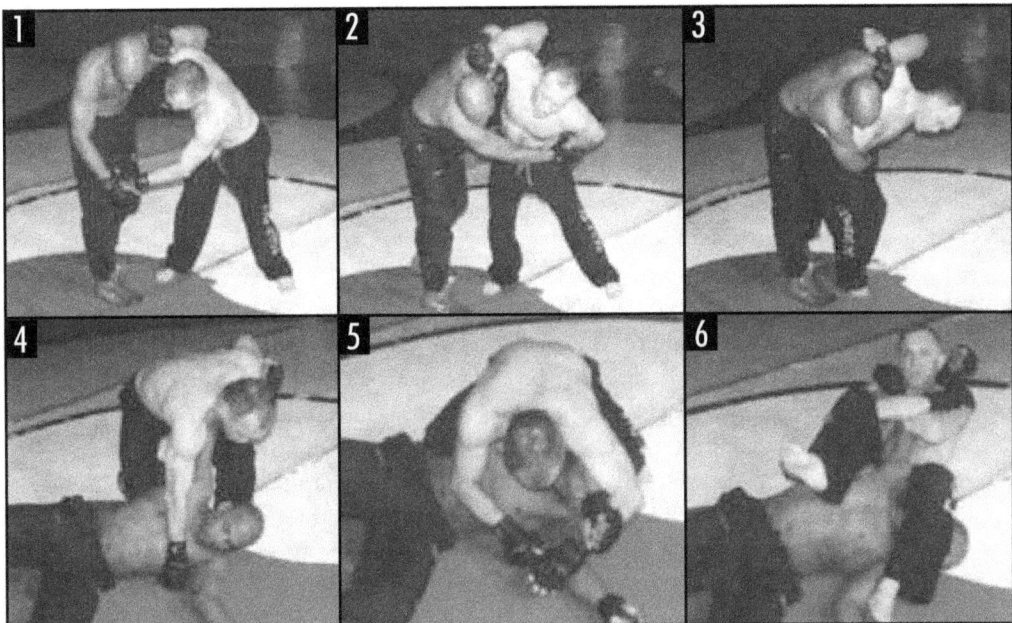

Underhook to Arm Bar

(1) Shonie Carter has a wizzer and Bob has an underhook. This very common position is all about leverage—whoever has inside head control is in control. (2) Shonie grabs hand control so Bob pulls his hand toward his back which turns Shonie's hip making his weight transfer to one leg. (3) Bob back steps and pops his hips—never step inward, back stepping reduces the chance of him countering. (4) Bob maintains hand control as Shonie hits the ground—this makes Shonie extend his arm. (5) Bob drops his weight on the extended arm with Shonie's elbow locked high on Bob's chest. (6) Bob drops back into a tight arm bar. Bob never grabs the hand but hugs the arm, placing the radial bones of both his arms on Shonie's wrist, causing great pain and reducing the possibility of a counter.

Carlson conceded the match to me afterward. In the books, it went down as a draw, but he clearly lost. In the first 20 minutes, neither of us scored much, so we fought 10 minutes overtime. Carlson's side hoped he'd tap me, but he never came close. We both agreed beforehand that if there was no submission, the bout would be a draw.

Q: Are you a versatile fighter?

A: Definitely. I've grappled in Abu Dhabi, kickboxed in Ireland and wrestled for the Marine Corps. I've fought throughout the world—in far too many places to count. My fight record is like Shonie's. He's fought dozens of "smokers" in Chicago bars—the kind where you show up on Tuesday or Thursday nights and fight four times. I've coached Shonie when he's had six smokers a night. He doesn't do them anymore, and neither do I, but we've both fought in many of them.

Q: Do you and Shonie always get along?

A: Does anyone? When Shonie first came to my school, he was a tough guy. But he tapped-out like crazy. He had been looking for schools and had defeated everybody he fought. Then he came to my school—and he stayed. He even lived in my dojo for two years. Shonie and I are close to each other.

Sure, I get mad at him when he does stupid things, but we get over it. He's training at my school at least four days a week.

Q: You said you were a U.S. Marine.
A: Yep, from 1974–1978. I boxed at Camp Pendleton, probably the largest Marine base in Southern California. And, of course, I boxed in smokers. My fights usually lasted two rounds, and I knocked every opponent out unless he didn't enter the ring. I was undefeated.

Q: Were boxing and wrestling your official jobs in the Marine Corps?
A: Not initially. In Coronado, California, I attended "raider package" training, which is a school for elite Marines who seek and destroy special targets and liberate POW camps. After I defeated the Navy champ in a Coronado smoker, his coach, who was there, wanted me to join the Navy wrestling team. But as a Marine, I couldn't wrestle for the Navy. So, after completing raider package training, I was sent to Quantico, Virginia, where I began to wrestle "officially" for the Corps. After Quantico, I went to Hawaii, where I was captain of the Marine Corps taekwondo team. My Marine Corps job changed to battalion recon (MOS 0321) in Hawaii after serving on the Marine wrestling team.

Q: What were your toughest Marine Corps fights?
A: The 12 guys I fought in 1978 while attending Recondo school in Hawaii. We fought each other one-on-one, and victory came by executing throws and killing blows. We wore GI boots and jungle pants—no martial arts uniforms. Our ring was a bear pit. I always won, which meant I fought the entire squad.

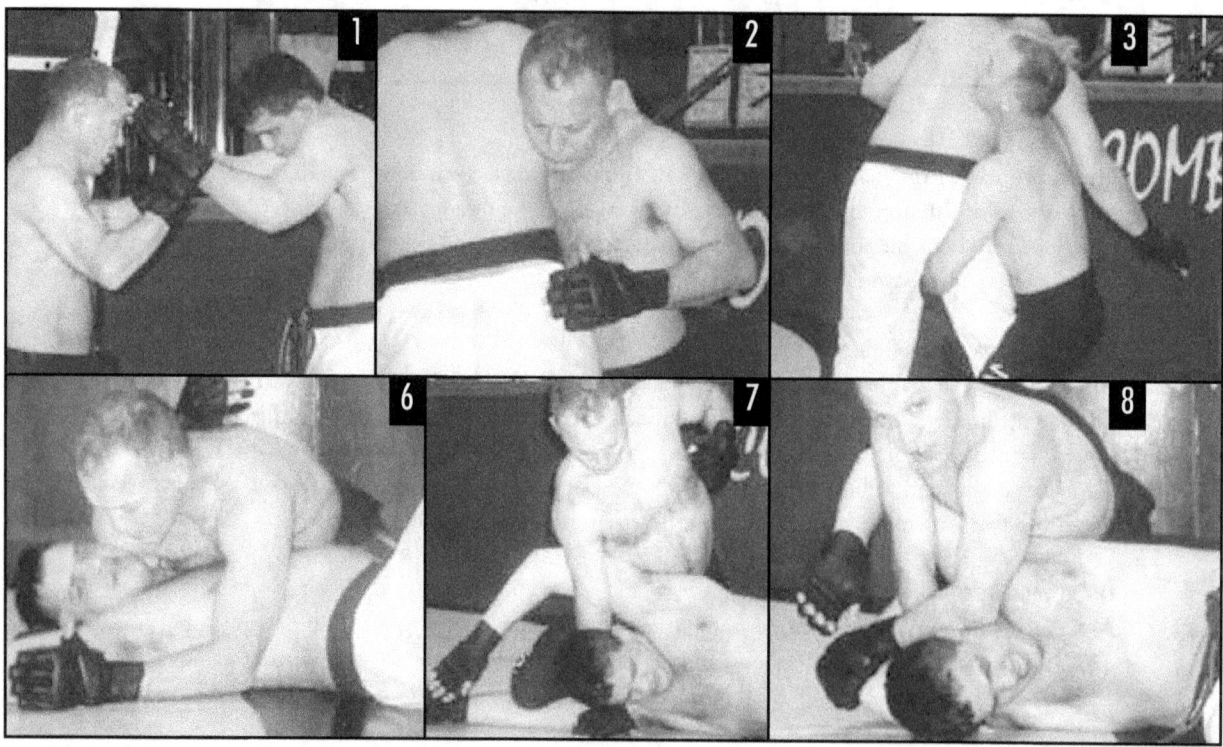

GRAPPLING

Q: Do you still fight?
A: Oh, I'll never stop. I recently battled Wander Braga in the World Jiu-Jitsu Championships. Now that was a war! He submitted me in the last 30 seconds of our 10-minute match. It was close all the way. He didn't clean up some old man. I was ahead 2-0 when Braga caught me with an arm bar. He's one of the best grapplers out there. No one wants to lose, but you learn from it and move on.

Q: After your Marine Corps discharge, you founded combat-do, your own fighting system. Why?
A: As a teenager, I studied boxing, judo, taekwondo, wrestling and other fighting arts. I started my own system because some guys boxed, others wrestled, but few did both. While I was in high school, one of my science teachers told me, "It's all physics, Bobby. It's all physics." So I started to analyze the relationship between physics and fighting. Ed Parker, founder of American kenpo karate, had broken new ground on the subject, and Bruce Lee had perfected his own scientific applications of the martial arts. After studying Newton's laws of motion, I pondered how to combine muscle groups to increase strength. I wondered, "How can I use fulcrums and levers—simple machines that use minimal force to lift maximal weight—to optimize my fighting?"

Q: What are some important scientific concepts of combat-do?
A: One is the water principle. You can't hold water with your bare hands. There's no tension, no handle. And in grappling, if there's no handle—that is, if you're not telegraphing motion—opponents won't know where you're going. Watch Shonie, Brian or my other

Duck Under to a Weave Series
(1) Bob and George square off. George has his elbows up which leaves an opening for a duck under throw. (2) Bob doesn't lift the arm but ducks down keeping his back straight. He gets his body tight to George to avoid getting thrown with a makikomi. (3) Bob is perpendicular to George—his back is straight and his legs are wide based as he lifts with his legs and hips. (4) Bob maintains a good back arch to achieve height and control. (5) Bob drops George onto his back and gets a strong side mount. (6) Bob Keeps George's arm posted up and his own elbow in George's side so he can't get his arm back to center. (7) Bob weaves his arm in an over and under position, extends his arm to get good leverage and bangs away. (8) Bob drops his punching arm on George's head, pressing his elbow into the jaw while lifting up on the lower arm. (9) Bob steps over George's head and posts the belly with his free hand so George can't turn. (10) Bob locks his leg with his hand and falls back into an armpit arm bar.

Underhook to a Heel hook

(1) Shonie Carter has a wizzer while Bob gets his head on the inside and extends his hand on Shonie's head. (2) Bob back steps with his left leg using his right leg as a pivot—this move forces Shonie to step up bringing his leg into Bob's reach. (3) Bob grabs the heel while pulling in and pushing out with the underhook. This gets Shonie's weight back making him fall easily. (4) Bob follows the fall and brings his knees tightly to the sides of Shonies's leg while maintaining hold of the heel. (5) Bob falls to his back hooking the heel. Caution: At this point arching the back and bringing your hips forward will lock the heel bit can cause a tear in your partner's knee.

guys fight and you'll see what I mean. Shonie fights loose, often getting into a submissions but getting right out.

Q: By using the water principle?
A: Applying a four-part principle, which can help you escape all submissions. First, using your chin as a wedge, make sure you can breathe. The thumb turns the hand. If you grab the base of your opponent's thumb and apply a fulcrum and lever on one of his fingers, you can turn his thumb outward. This will turn his hand outward and release the choke. The second step is to center. Combine your muscle groups to maximize your strength. Let's say your opponent applies an arm bar. Come to center and pop up over so your arm is at your chest rather than extended. If an opponent applies a knee bar, ankle rake or heel hook, bring your body to the extended part, not vice versa.

Q: And the third step?
A: Extend him. If he's strong and ties you up, you must extend him using fulcrums and levers, which can be enhanced by body position. The longer the lever (your body), the more weight you can lift to execute takedowns and to escape submissions. The fourth step is to feel the path of least resistance. After extending your opponent, he won't be at center anymore, so a path opens. You can feel his path by using the water principle. If you're tense, however, you won't feel it. Follow the path of least resistance and you'll usually escape.

Q: Why are combat-do takedowns so effective?
A: Combat-do doesn't just adapt a few takedowns from other fighting arts. We have our own entire takedown system. For instance, I love the left hand. In NHB, you can blind opponents to set-ups and shin kicks by effectively using your left hand. Combat-do fighters use their hands to set up their kicks and use their kicks to set up their elbows, which in turn set up throws. Also, you can use elbow or head control to take opponents off center, after which you can apply simple takedowns. One is the "bus driver," a head and elbow movement that resembles turning a bus. Rotating an imaginary steering wheel, position your opponent's weight on one of his feet. Take that foot from under him, then take him down with a reap, single or double-leg takedown, or an ankle pick. A bow-and-arrow technique can also shift his weight to one foot. Simply extend one arm while releasing the other. This also sets him up for reaps, sweeps and throws.

Q: Combat-do is all about options, isn't it?
A: It virtually gives you unlimited options. And keeping your options open is crucial when you're in the ring. If one technique doesn't work, try another. Follow the center centrifugal force. Your opponent will counter, but when he does, he opens himself to attack.

Q: Is combat-do the ultimate grappling art?
A: I think so. Combat-do isn't based on opinion. It's rooted in scientific principles that circumvent and thereby weaken your opponent's ability to fight. Opposite and opposing force plays a major role in this process. Accordingly, we use four types of pressure: 1) focus, 2) diffuse, 3) focus-impact and 4) diffused-impact. To succeed in grappling, you must know what to do and when to do it. That comes from training. My students practice Thai boxing, kickboxing and san chao, which is Chinese kickboxing. We also wrestle and throw. In fact, at the All-American Academy, we're like the judo guys—we'd rather throw ya than know ya!

"Oh yeah. I love to throw. In one NHB fight, I threw a 240-pounder belly to back. He was huge but went up and over effortlessly. In another fight, I easily threw a 265-pounder. Again, it's all science."

Wander Braga and Bob Schirmer at the World Jiu-Jitsu Championships.

Q: So you've relied on throws during your career?
A: Oh yeah. I love to throw. In one NHB fight, I threw a 240-pounder belly to back. He was huge but went up and over effortlessly. In another fight, I easily threw a 265-pounder. Again, it's all science. Newton's first law says that energy travels straight until acted upon by another force. Therefore, I tell my fighters, "If force comes at you, let it travel the way it wants at a vector of 30 (15 either side)." That prevents your opponent from digging in off one foot. He's already committed to a movement. And if he pulls on you, go with that force, because you can reap, apply an ankle pick or execute a duck-under. Let his force dictate. Let him supply your takedowns and submissions.

Q: Do combat-do throws mainly set up submissions?
A: All of our throws can result in submissions. But we have fun with throws too. For example, for three years our school had a Chicago TV program that featured local grappling matches, and my guys fought in many of them. These hams were determined to make the show's highlights, so they executed their best tosses for the "throw of the week" segment. Shonie and I were often featured in the highlights. So were Brian Gassaway, Rolando Higueros and George Spacek. Effortlessly lofting a big burley opponent over your shoulder is a glorious feeling.

Q: Why did you name your school the All-American Academy?
A: Because I'm an ALL-American grappler. I'm not teaching Brazilian jiu-jitsu, Oriental martial arts or anything else that stems from foreign soil. In my early days, I trained in judo and taekwondo, so I've learned from Asian martial artists. But my art is American—and so is my school.

GRAPPLING

Q: Why train mixed martial artists for a living? Why not an easier career?
A: An easier career? Before I taught combat-do full-time, I was a cop in Oak Park, which is on Chicago's West Side. From 1984 to 1993, I worked undercover burglaries and robberies—high-publicity cases. If there was a burglary pattern along the Washington Corridor, the department sent me on it. I'd find the guy, make the pinch and go to my next case. Or there might be a robbery pattern, so I'd be a decoy, find the robber and arrest him. I went undercover in many ways: as a cable TV guy, a painter or a moke in a Toyota. I'm small and attract little attention. I made scores of dangerous arrests and received over 50 commendations. I've been attacked with knives three times on the job. I was never cut, though, because I used elbow control.

Q: What about your upcoming trip to China?
A: I'll be taking a U.S. grappling team to Beijing this summer. As coach, I'm already making my fighters concentrate on san chao. Don Rodriguez and I took a team to China in 1998, and the trip was very rewarding, so I'm eager to return. To successfully coach, you need at least two months with team members to understand their moves, strengths and weaknesses. So, for the Beijing trip this summer, I plan to train with the team ahead of time. I have some tricks up my sleeve to help us win.

Q: Any you can reveal?
A: Many san shaou fighters keep their hands down and rely on fast kicks, especially fast low side kicks. However, you can trap low side kicks by becoming a vehicle of impact. When your opponent nudges you, go with the movement, lock in on it and control him. When he aims a turning kick or a roundhouse at you, use the bent-line principle. Watch his hip and shoulder creases. Then position yourself inside, bend the line of force and avoid impact. Your opponent will be off balance, so take him down with an inner sweep, a "tree top" or with another throw. Nothing would please me more than to beat the Chinese at their own game. And when we do, all of our hard training will have paid off.

Bob Schirmer is available for exhibitions and seminars. Contact him at the All-American Academy, *2138 S. 61st Court, Cicero, IL 60804; (708) 222-8100, or visit* www.combat-do.com.

GRAPPLING

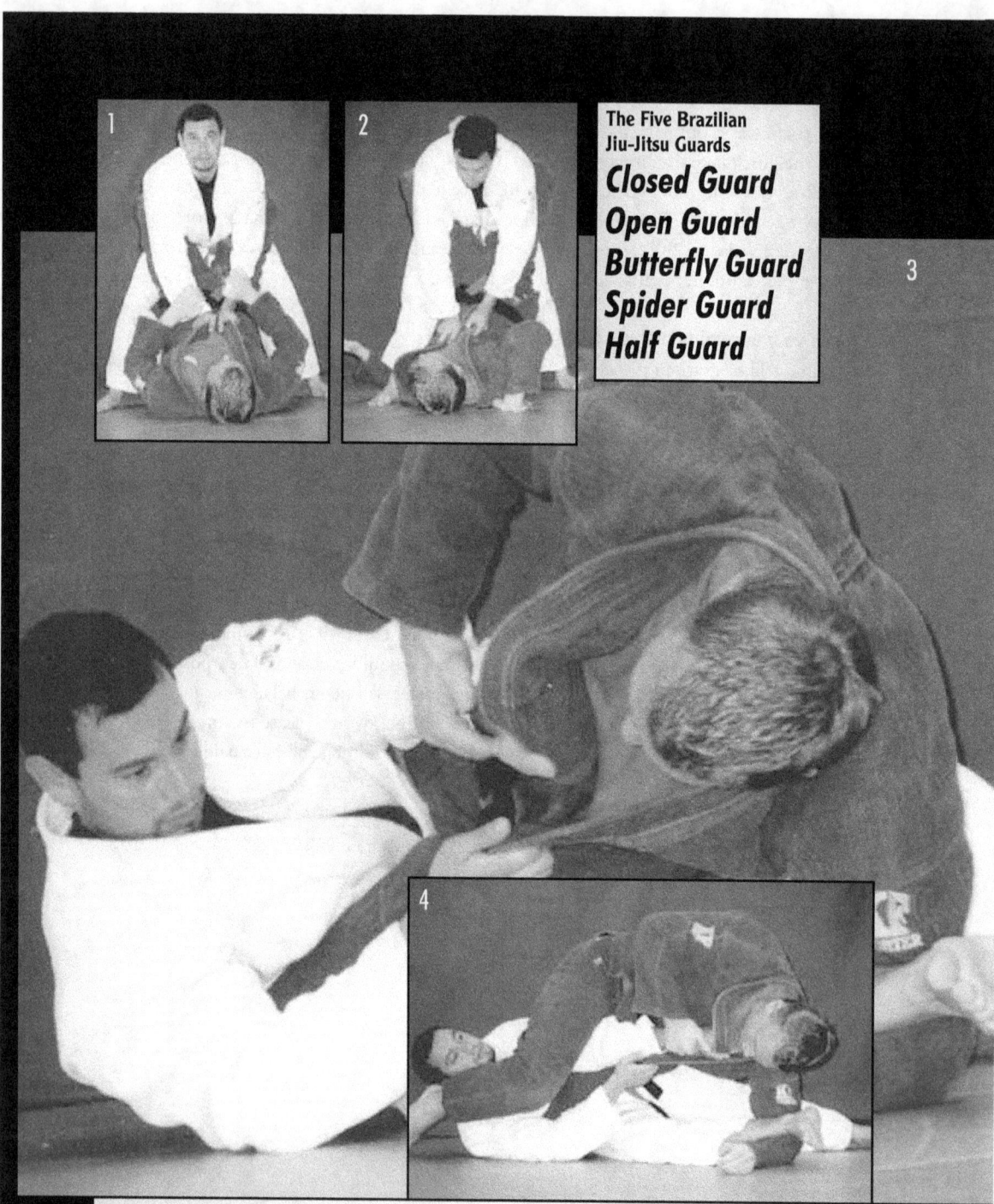

The Five Brazilian Jiu-Jitsu Guards

Closed Guard
Open Guard
Butterfly Guard
Spider Guard
Half Guard

Closed-Guard Sweep
The opponent stands up as the defender holds him in the closed guard with his legs locked around the waist (1). The defender places his right hand on the floor, palm down and fingers pointing inward, while hooking his left arm around the attackers ankle (2). Scissoring his leg together, the defender pushes off with his right hand and pulls inward with his left arm, upsetting the attackers balance and throwing him to the floor (3). Continuing to roll over on top, the defender traps the arm between his legs and applies pressure on the elbow for the submission lock (4).

The Big Four Basic Sweeps From the Guard

The guard is what separates Brazilian jiu-jitsu from all other grappling arts. Knowing how to use your guard and sweep someone is a must to be considered a well-rounded grappler.

Jerry Laurita

When you look at all the different grappling arts, they all have many techniques and principles in common. They all share various takedowns, throws, and pins. This is true of collegiate or freestyle wrestling, Olympic or Greco-Roman wrestling, or the various types of Asian grappling arts such as judo or Mongolian wrestling. One of the main principles, however, that sets Brazilian jiu-jitsu (BJJ) apart from these numerous other grappling arts, is the use of the guard to fight from the back and to attack an opponent from a position that is deemed to be very inferior.

When Royce Gracie first introduced BJJ to the world in the very first Ultimate Fighting Championship (UFC), no one had ever thought that an art which practiced fighting on the ground with your back on the floor would ever be able to defeat punchers and kickers. How wrong they were. This was the ultimate demonstration of what a martial art was supposed to be—using techniques to defeat bigger and stronger opponents. In large part, the use of the guard was what helped Brazilian jiu-jitsu to gain a reputation and to attract so many faithful followers.

Executing a sweep from your back, and then turning it into a triangle choke or an arm bar almost seems like magic. Who can forget Royce Gracie's classic victory over Dan Severn in the UFC where, after being abused for nearly 15 minutes by a man 100 pounds heavier, Gracie fought Severn off using the Brazilian guard and then upset his balance with a sweep and finished him with a triangle choke.

One of my favorite things to do—even more than submitting someone—is to sweep someone over from the guard. Knowing that I can sweep someone when they are standing over me, thinking they are in control, and then go on the attack at anytime and make them submit is just awesome to me. In practical terms, it can also save your butt when you are wrestling against bigger and stronger opponents who are trying to muscle you.

The Brazilian guard game is extremely sophisticated and you never really see how involved it is from watching no-holds-barred fights. That is because in an NHB match, the first or second sweep option usually works and there is no need to go into the more advanced techniques. In U.S. BJJ tournaments you will sometimes see advanced techniques from visiting Brazilian experts, but the level of

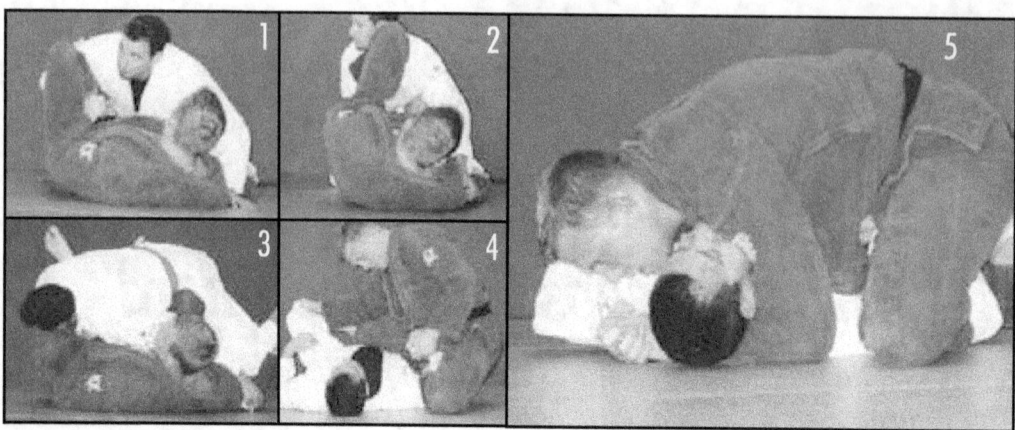

Open-Guard Sweep to Biceps Lock

The defender has his legs around the attackers waist but without locking his ankles together. Grabbing the opponent's right wrist, the defender inserts his left leg between the biceps and forearm while grabbing the ankle with his right hand (1). Keeping his wrist grip tight, the defender brings his knee up to the attackers face (2). With the arm trapped, the attacker is unable to keep his balance as the defender rolls him to the side and over his body (3). Coming to an upright position, the attacker keeps the arm trapped between his leg and his body (4), and then leans forward and traps the head while applying submission pressure to the trapped biceps with his leg (5).

Butterfly-Guard Sweep

The defender, sitting up with his feet on the attackers legs, faces him in the classic butterfly guard (1). Pulling the attacker forward, the defender inserts his legs inside his opponent's thighs, pulls his head forward, and grabs the belt (2). Clinching him tightly around the body, with his forward arm between the attacker's arms (3), the defender falls back and corkscrews to the right, while kicking his legs up to throw his opponent's body into the air (4). Rolling to the top, the defender establishes a strong mount position (5).

competition in the U.S. is nowhere near the level that it is in Brazil, so again the most advanced techniques are not needed.

In the U.S., most practitioners only need to be concerned with the basics—one can spend a lifetime trying to perfect them and still fall short! There are five different types of guards that are most practiced in the U.S.: the closed guard, the open guard, the butterfly guard, the spider guard and the half guard. While there are numerous sweeps and permutations from each guard position, there are several basic sweeps which are important for everyone to know. The half-guard is an entire religion in and of itself, and deserves an article all its own.

As an American practitioner who learned and trained the art of BJJ here in the States, I feel there are some basic sweep techniques which work very well for us non-world champion weekend warrior types, and which can be perfected in a relatively short time. Therefore, I would like to go over basic sweeps from the closed, open, and butterfly guards.

If you have ever been to a Brazilian jiu-jitsu tournament you will find everyone uses one of these guard sweeps depending on their body type and personal preference. What is even more amazing is that they all work. In order to successfully sweep someone you need to be able to transition into a position where you can upset your opponent's balance while maintaining control and not letting him pass your guard.

By learning how to sweep from the guard, it will make your guard a more powerful weapon when you grapple. It will also make your attacks more effective because your opponent will be so concerned with having to defend your sweeps he will become vulnerable to your attacks.

I also believe that by having a good guard and knowing how to sweep from the guard, you will become a more, well rounded grappler. Again, start with the beginning students to practice these techniques, before you move on and try them on the more advanced guys. Like always, in training, be patient with yourself and your training partner and don't be afraid to ask questions—and also to answer them. Learning the basics is a lifelong process—so have fun with it and enjoy yourself on the mat!

Phoenix-based Brazilian jiu-jitsu instructor Jerry Laurita can be contacted by email at <u>lauritabjj@aol.com</u> or by phone at 623-582-3153. For information on classes or seminars visit his website at <u>www.arizonablackbelt.com</u>.

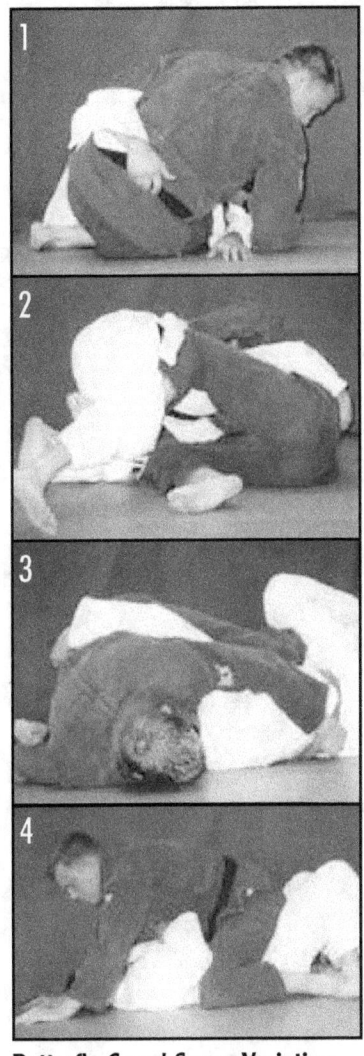

Butterfly-Guard Sweep Variation
After pulling the attacker into his body from the butterfly guard position, the defender turns over onto his right thigh and traps his opponent's left elbow with his right arm (1). With the arm trapped, he continues to roll to the right, lifting his opponents upwards with the leg which is inserted inside the right knee (2). Continuing to roll, the defender grabs the attacker's belt with his right hand (3), and then ends up in a strong mounted position (4).

GRAPPLING

"An option when the opponent turns to all fours," says Leozihno, "is to go to his back. I like this position a lot; I started using it in competition many years ago as a brown belt. I used it in the Brazilian nationals against two opponents with good success and I am still using it today. I recently fought in a professional BJJ match against Yuki Nakai in Japan and used it against him as well. The secret of this move is to cinch the grip on the opponent's chest very tightly and use the momentum of your legs going over your head to pull the opponent's body over with you. It is a very cool move."

Cross-Side Attack Against All-Fours
The opponent is on all-fours with Leozihno on his back (1). Leozihno grabs the right foot with his right hand, and the right knee with his left hand (2). He then pushes forward with his chest as he pulls the opponent's leg and foot with his arms (3). He then gets across the side (4).

Leozinho Viera's Extreme Jiu-Jitsu Taking The Back

Leo Vieira is one of the most dynamic and creative fighters in Brazilian jiu-jitsu. In this extreme series, he explains the ins and outs of defeating an opponent who has solid base on all-fours.

Kid Peligro, Story and Photos

Multiple-time world and national Brazilian jiu-jitsu champion Leoziho Viera rocketed to submission grappling stardom during his sensational match in the Absolute division of the 2000 ADCC World Submission Wrestling Championships. Despite being 90 pounds lighter than opponent Mark "The Specimen" Kerr, Leozinho was not scored upon or taken down by Kerr during the entire 10-minute match, and only lost due to a minus point penalty. Kerr, in an interview with *Grappling* Magazine, stated that Leozinho had taxed him beyond his normal range.

Leozinho recently competed in Japan in the inaugural Ground Impact, in a professional Brazilian jiu-jitsu match. He fought the feature match against Japanese legend Yuki Nakai and won by submission using his tremendous array of creative, cutting-edge moves. He most recently competed in the Jean Jacques Machado 2002 California State Open winning the lightweight division using his incredible arsenal of extreme, totally original moves.

Leozinho developed most of his eclectic arsenal by watching and playing with the kids at the Alliance Academy in Rio, where he taught the childrens classes for years. According to Leozinho, "Kids are not bound by normal limitations; they only know what is fun for them. They do crazy things that no adult would ever try. I take that same attitude and try to not be bound by convention or structure."

In this series, Leozinho demonstrates his favorite ways to fight when his opponent is on all-fours. This happens frequently when you have nearly passed their guard and they turn over.

"It is very common for opponents to turn to all fours as you attempt to pass their guard," say Leozinho. "Because the opponent turns to all-fours, you do not get the three points for passing the guard. I use this move to secure the points by taking them across to the side position. The secret of this move is to grab the leg and foot and just hold them. This way, you takeaway any option for your opponent to brace to that side. From there, you begin to push off with your feet and use your chest to pressure your opponent over. You then pull on his leg to complete the pass. When done correctly, it cannot be stopped."

"Sometimes when I try to use the Rock and Roll," Leozinho says, "the opponent tries to resist too much and I switch to the Rock and Spring. Sometimes I use it because I have used the Rock and Roll too much and want to vary it to keep them guessing. This is a very good position that will surprise even the most experienced opponent."

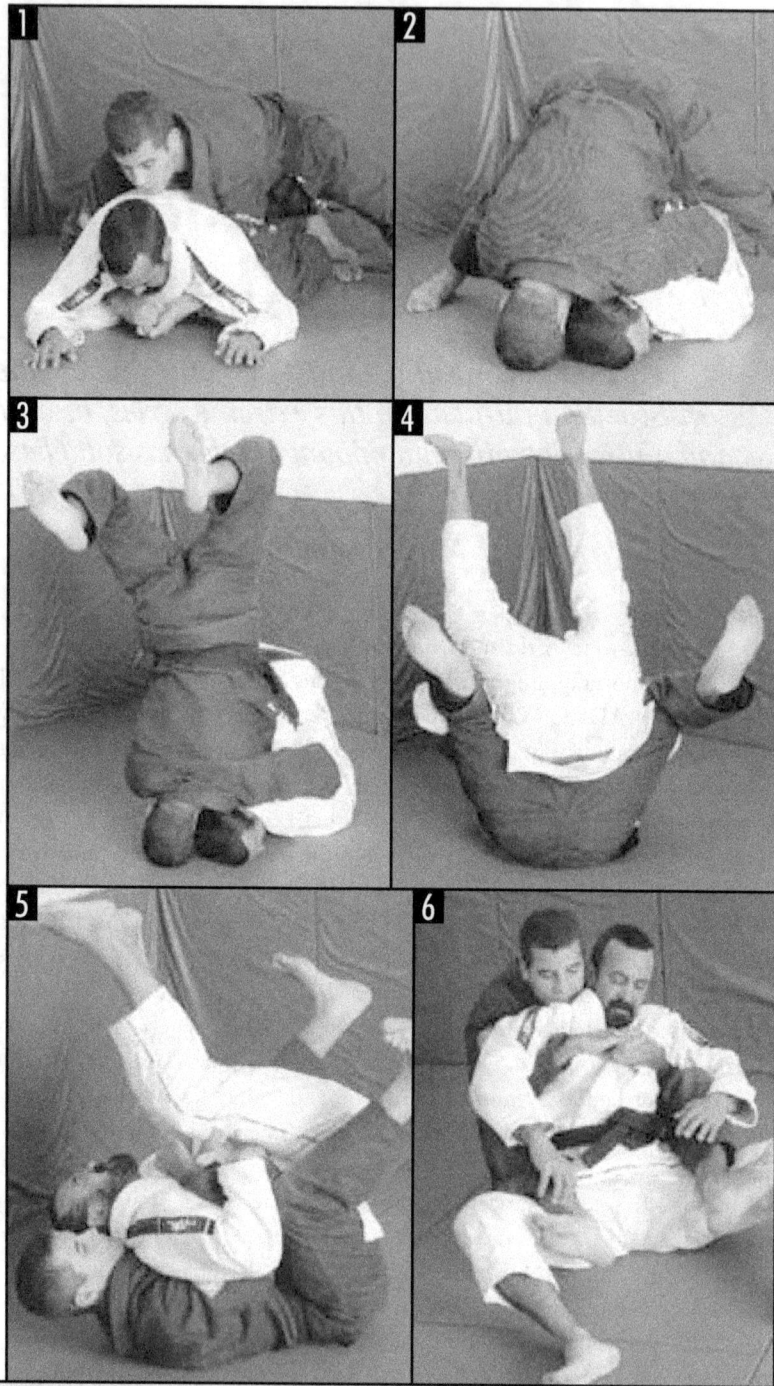

Rock and Roll—Taking The Back Against All-Fours
Leozihno grabs both hands together under the opponent's armpits and cinches the grip around the opponents chest (1). He then puts his head to one side of the opponent while opening his legs (2). Pushing of his feet he throws his legs over the head (3), and uses that momentum to pull his opponent over with him (4). Side view of the previous motion (5). Leo completes the move by putting the hooks in and taking the back (6).

GRAPPLING

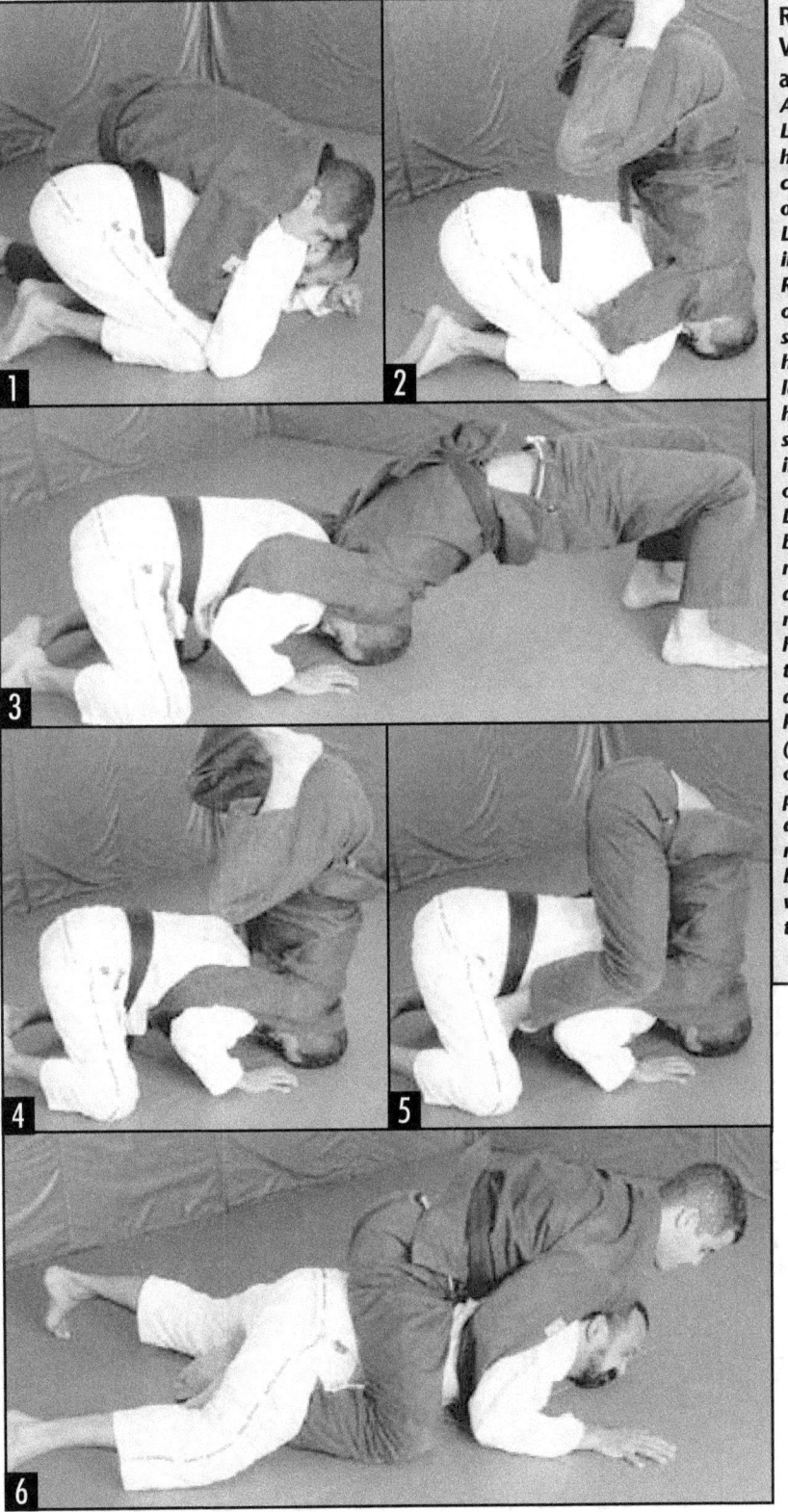

Rock and Spring— Variation of the Rock and Roll

As in the Rock and Roll, Leozihno grabs both hands together and cinches the grip on the opponents chest (1). Leozinho continues similar to the Rock and Roll by placing his head on the ground and springing his legs over his head (2). As he lands with his feet, he has opened up some space to put the hooks in by opening the opponent's elbows (3). Leozinho then springs back over, adding even more pressure on the armpit and opening more space to put the hooks in by stretching the opponent's body and separating his knees from the elbows (4). As he comes back over the top, Leozinho places his hooks in (5) and stretches the opponent flat on the ground by applying pressure with his hips against the back (6).

"This is another good variation of taking the back," says Leozinho. "In this case the opponent is blocking one of my hands from coming in and grabbing the other. I developed this position while playing with my brother and with the kids in class. Kids love to roll over and do summersaults, and I have incorporated some of their moves into my jiu-jitsu."

Back Roll Choke

Leozihno's opponent is on all-fours and Leozinho is on his left side. This time rather than grabbing both hands under the armpits, Leozinho places his left hand under the neck. He then grabs his right wrist while his right hand grabs the opponent's left wrist with his right hand-right arm under the opponent's right armpit (1). Continuing on the opponent's side Leozihno leans forward and applies pressure on the shoulder (2). He then rolls over the shoulder and pulls the opponent over with him (3). The opponent has to follow as the pressure on his neck is too much. Notice that Leozinho leaves his left leg on the ground as he rolls over, making it easy to put that hook in (4). Leozinho is still holding the opponent's left wrist and uses his left leg to apply the hook while attacking the neck with his right hand. The opponent has to use his right hand to defend the choke, leaving Leozihno free to insert the right hook (5).

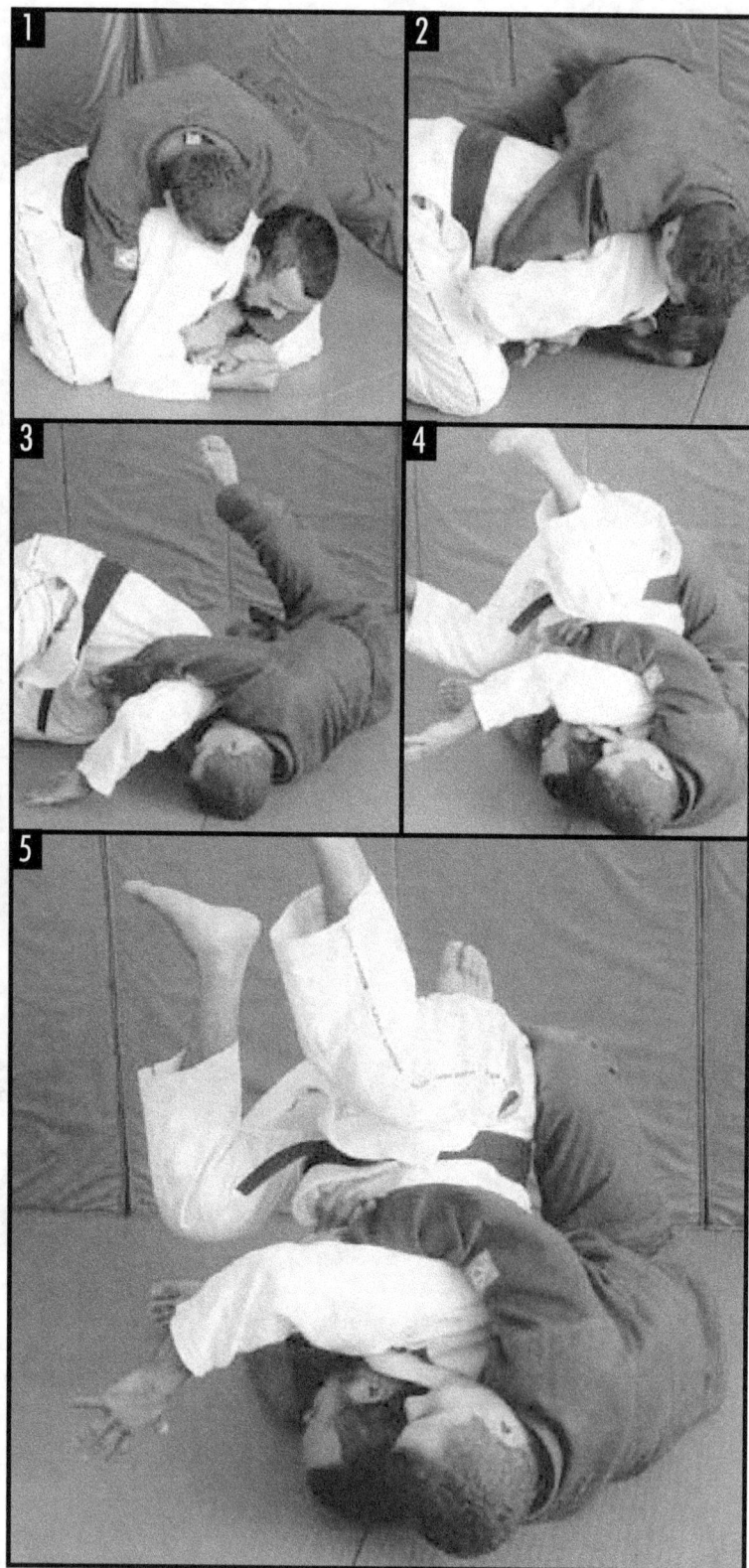

GRAPPLING

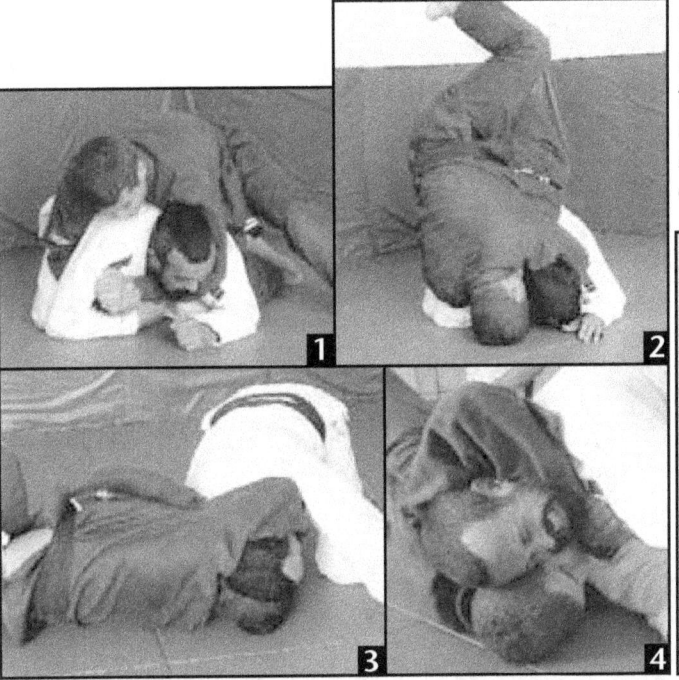

"I will use this option when I am behind on points and time is running out and I need to finish a fight quickly," says Leozinho. "This will work on even the toughest necks."

Back Roll Quick Choke— Variation of Back Roll Choke
Leozinho starts out much the same as in the Back Roll Choke except that instead of grabbing the opponent's wrist, he grabs his left hand with his right and chinches it around the neck (1). Leo summersaults over the right shoulder (2). This time, instead of pulling the opponent over with him, Leozinho just tightens the grip around the neck and blocks the opponent's right shoulder (3). Detail of the choke (4).

"This is another of my 'kid' positions. I came across this one with some of the kids again. They love to gang up and jump on your back and try to choke you. Since I block their hooks, they just stand there and try to pry them open. I borrowed that and made it into the Owl Attack."

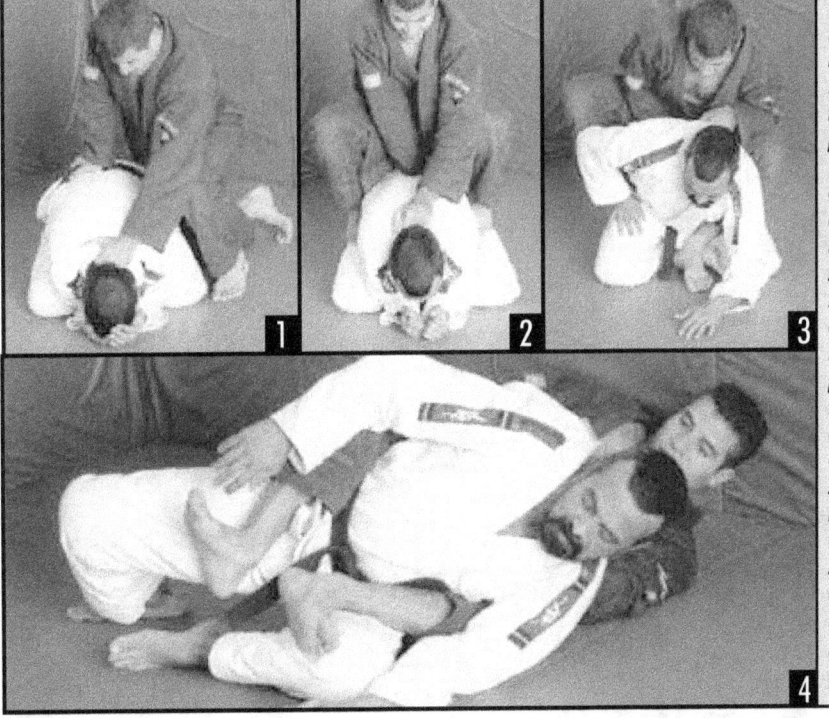

The Owl Attack
Leozinho's opponent is on all-fours. Leozinho holds the belt and collar and pushes down (1). While still holding onto the belt and collar, Leozinho uses the hands to spring up and put both feet on the opponent's legs (2). Leozinho then pushes off his feet and lifts the opponent's torso, opening up enough space to put in one hook. Leozinho then falls to that same side (3). As they are rolling over, Leozinho places his other foot into correct position (4).

BEST OF CFW — VOL.1
GRAPPLING

The 7 Methods of Low-Kick Defense

The low leg kick is one of the most effective weapons used to take grapplers out of their game in mixed martial arts. If you want to be successful, you have to learn to defeat it.

Erik Paulson, *Grappling Magazine* Technical Advisor

The low kick is commonly referred to as the cannon, the dynamite, or the baseball bat. This refers to the devastating effect that is felt when it lands. The advantage of using this kick over high kicks is that it cannot be easily trapped and used as a throwing lever, it can be quickly "reloaded" to keep grapplers from following it in and gaining inside takedown position, and it is thrown at the head level of a grappler shooting in for a single or double-leg takedown. Just the threat of a low leg kick has many times turned the tide in a fight and kept otherwise fearless takedown artists at bay, leaving them open for hand strikes and eventual knockouts.

Leg kicks are common to many striking systems and so are widely employed. You can find very effective low leg kick techniques in martial arts from countries such as Thailand (muay Thai), Burma (bando), France (savate), and Japan (kyokushinkai karate). All of these martial arts have extremely useable and functional methods of low kick delivery for use in sport fighting and self-defense. Many other combination styles and systems have also adapted and added this technique to their arsenal.

The strategic objective of low leg kicks is to punish your adversary every time they either step into your kicking range or come inside and then back away from you. A good low leg-kicker will never allow his opponent to get into kicking range without making him pay for every inch of real estate gained. After a while the arms will drop, the eyes will look downward, and the fighter on the receiving end will not be thinking about delivering punishment, but rather trying to keep absorbing it.

Targets for the low leg kick depend on the rules you're fighting under, but some of the favorite traditional targets include the knee (primarily for self-defense) the outside thigh (a specialty of kickboxers) and the inside thigh (muay Thai's favorite target). It is also used by some of the more advanced grapplers in mixed martial arts events to create an opening to enter for a low freestyle takedown attempt, or to step in and clinch high after delivering the kick in order to execute a Greco-Roman or judo throw.

Savate-Muay Thai Crosstraining (STX)

In the hybrid kickboxing method that I teach—Savate-Muay Thai Crosstraining (STX) I utilize multiple methods, principles, and techniques from many different fighting arts in order to best deal with the low leg kick:

1. **Savate**—mobility, instant return, perpetual motion.
2. **Muay Thai**—power tools, blocking system, timing.
3. **Shooto**—striking versus grappling, catching and attacks.
4. **Jun Fan/JKD**—interception, broken rhythm, halfbeat.
5. **Filipino Kali**—destruction and angularity.
6. **Indonesian Silat**—crashing and entering.
7. **Western Boxing**—timing, good hands, power punching, head cover and movement.

The 7 Low-Kick Defense Methods

By utilizing the most effective bits and pieces from each of these arts, I have extracted seven different methods and strategies for low kick defense:

1. **Check or shield**—block the kick, retain posture, or fire back.
2. **Ride**—absorb power for instant return —punch, knee kick or shoot.
3. **Evade**—not get hit, frustrate your opponent, and take advantage of his being off-balance.
4. **Intercept or jam**—stuff your opponent or stun him, thereby not allowing him to get off a full power kick.
5. **Destruction**—injure the tool so the opponent won't attack or will think twice before using it again.
6. **Crash or Shoot**—come in hard as soon as the opponent is off balance from a committed blow.
7. **Catch**—pick up a kick and return a punch or knee, and then shoot-in or go straight to submission.

Which Method Is Best?

There is no real "best" way to counter a low leg kick. Everything is subjective and comes about as a result of analyzing what you opponent likes to do, and then using the method that best fits your capabilities and strong points. What you will do in a fight will depend on your game, your opponent's game, and what you are trying to achieve. Obviously, victory is the primary goal, but there are many different methods that lead to victory that need to be considered. These intermediary steps can include striking, staying on the feet, takedowns, ground and pound, or quick-kill flash submissions. The best method to achieve your particular goal depends on how good you get at each particular method and how skillful your opponent is at defending them.

Remember, mentally understanding these methods and the theoretical principles behind them does NOT necessarily mean that you can recognize and apply them quickly. Even if you get to the point that you CAN recognize and apply them, it doesn't mean that your body has the physical ability to successfully execute them. Even if you can physically do them, it does not mean that you can pull them off successfully under pressure from a skilled opponent's attack.

Some people have this ability, but they are few and far between. I remember when I was training with Rickson Gracie several years ago and happened to show him several Shooto leg locks. I'm sure some of them were things he had never seen before because they were not common in Brazilian Jiu-Jitsu at the time. The next day, however, when I came to the academy, Rickson sparred with the entire

GRAPPLING

1. Check or shield

2. Ride

3. Evade

4. Intercept or jam

5. Destruction

6. Crash or shoot

class and submitted everyone using the same leg locks I has shared with him—and then he submitted me! If you happen to be Rickson Gracie more power to you, but the last time I checked there was still only one of him. So for the rest of us mere mortals, we need to apply concerted training principles in order to develop our skills.

Technique, Repetition, Isolation, Go (TRIG)

The best way I have found to train various fighting principle, including leg kick defenses, is by the TRIG concept. What makes TRIG so powerful is that is makes you focus on one principle until you get it right. Part of the reason I developed TRIG was because I have a very short attention span and tend to not focus on one thing for very long. But utilizing TRIG you're training different ways, but within the same concept.

1. Technique—take one technique at a time and really focus on it. Consider what you do best, what you are trying to achieve and then realistically implement a method that fits you. For example, if you can't kick above your waist, then devising a low leg kick defense that entails a reverse, spinning head kick is not being realistic. Focus on techniques that you CAN do.

2. Repetition—put it into high repetitions and repeat it until it is second nature. If you want to practice beating a low leg kick by catching it, then work on that method every day for an hour. Do it over and over. There is no substitute for repetition.

3. Isolation—isolate it into a drill. It is impossible to spar continuously without getting hurt or without getting burned-out. So get some pads, work out movements with a training partner, and then develop drills that will simulate whatever method of leg kick defense you choose to practice. Football players in the NFL don't play a full-on game every day—they don't even scrimmage every day. By far, most of their training involves drills. That goes for every other major sport as well. Mixed martial arts should be no different.

4. Go—put it into practice until it becomes engrained into your muscle memory and becomes an automated response under pressure. The key here is "under pressure." When you do spar instill a sense of urgency in the person you are sparring with. For example, walk into your gym and say, "Who here thinks they can kick me in the leg and get away with it?" Or practice leg kicks with a friendly dinner bet on who can land the most.

Conclusion

The various low leg-kick defense methods are very diverse, and I like to practice them all when I'm sparring. This variety keeps me from getting bored, develops my timing and control, and keeps my opponent constantly guessing and off-guard to my next technique. You never want to be predictable as a fighter. Of course, you don't need to master the entire list of defenses to be successful in defending the low leg-kick; you only need to get good at two or three of them in order to be flexible enough to deal with different ring situations and also different opponents. Remember—train hard, train smart!

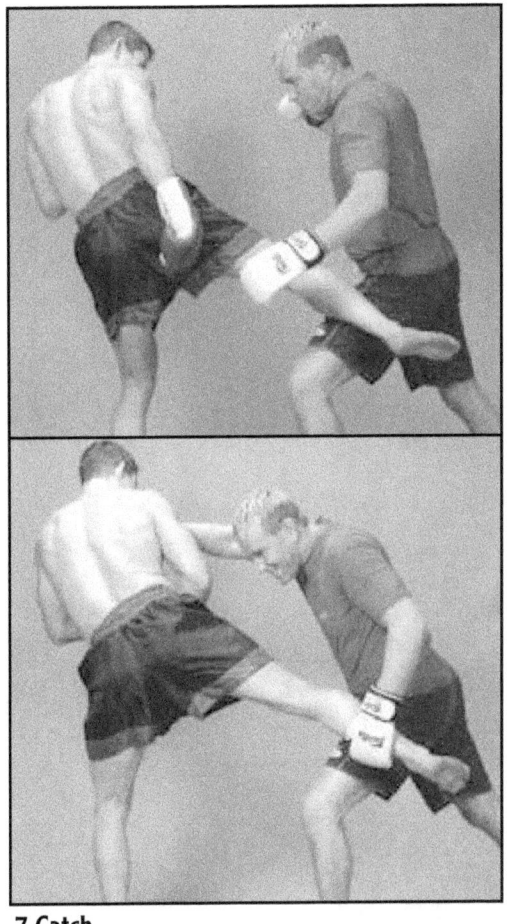

7. Catch

The 2002 Erik Paulson Combat Submission Wrestling (CSW) stand-up seminar tapes, which includes low leg-kick defenses, are available through www.erikpaulson.com *or by calling Erik Paulson at (310) 785-5805.*